Sex, Work and Sex Work

Sex is often seen as the antithesis of what organizations are about – control, instrumental rationality and the suppression of instinct and emotion in the service of production. *Sex, Work and Sex Work* argues not only that sexuality pervades every aspect of organizations, but also that organization pervades every aspect of our sexuality. This two-way conceptualization lends the book its two-part structure. The first part considers the ways in which organizational behaviour is shaped by sexuality, for example in a gendered industrial dispute; sexual harassment; studies of professionals who work with sex offenders and in the organized practice of sadomasochism. The second part of the book explores how sex is organized for commercial purposes, and considers sex work as an industry which can be analysed like any other.

Key features of the book include: organizing as sexual activity; connecting desire, the erotic, the abject and organization; the 'hidden' penetration of organization processes by sexuality; the 'dark side' of sex and organization and the importance of transgression; the double effect of discursive and material placing; organizing sexuality within prostitution, and prostitution as a highly complex and varied industry.

Sex, Work and Sex Work draws heavily on the work of Bataille, Foucault and Deleuze and Guattari, yet is grounded in extensive fieldwork involving managers, professionals, flight attendants, professionals who work with sex offenders and sex workers. It is an innovative and groundbreaking study written for professionals and researchers in business and management, gender and sexuality studies.

* * *

Joanna Brewis is Lecturer in Management at the University of Essex. **Stephen Linstead** is Associate Director and Research Professor of Management at Sunderland Business School, University of Sunderland. He is co-editor of *Understanding Management*, *Management: A Critical Text* and *The Aesthetics of Organization*.

Sex, Work and Sex Work

Eroticizing organization

**Joanna Brewis and
Stephen Linstead**

Routledge
Taylor & Francis Group
LONDON AND NEW YORK

First published 2000
by Routledge
2 Park Square, Milton Park, Abingdon, Oxon OX14 4RN

Simultaneously published in the USA and Canada
by Routledge
711 Third Avenue, New York, NY 10017

Routledge is an imprint of the Taylor & Francis Group, an informa business

© 2000 Joanna Brewis and Stephen Linstead

Typeset in Baskerville by Taylor & Francis Books Ltd

British Library Cataloguing in Publication Data
A catalogue record for this book is available from the British Library

Library of Congress Cataloging in Publication Data
Brewis, Joanna
Sex, work and sex work: eroticizing organization / Joanna Brewis and
Stephen Linstead.
p. cm.
Includes bibliographical references and index.
1. Prostitution. 2. Sex. 3. Sex in the workplace. 4. Organizational behavior.
5. Sex role.
I. Linstead, Stephen II. Title.

HQ117 .B73 2000
306.7–dc21

99–059923

ISBN 0–415–20756–8 (hbk)
ISBN 0–415–20757–6 (pbk)

ISBN - 978 0 4152 0757 7 (pbk)

For Barbara and Chris

Contents

Acknowledgements

As usual with any project of this kind, to individually thank everyone who has helped with or influenced this book in any way would be to instantly double its length. We hope therefore that a general but sincere vote of thanks to the relevant massed hordes will suffice! However, there are some people whom we do need to single out, given the significance of their contributions. First, we must thank Stuart Hay, now at Pearson, who had great faith in this project from the start and was unfailingly enthusiastic and supportive in its development. He is also a very amusing e-mail correspondent! Likewise, Michelle Gallagher of Routledge, who took over responsibility for the book from Stuart, has been very patient and sympathetic with us, especially in dealing with the numerous requests for last minute extensions. Thanks to Michelle too – we hope it was all worth it! We also need to mention John Sinclair, of Napier University, and Chris Grey, of the University of Cambridge. John and Jo collaborated on the original sadomasochism project, which resulted in several conference papers during 1996 and 1997. Many thanks to him for allowing us to ground our argument in chapter 5 (Sadomasochism and organization) in some of his ideas, as well as for being so much fun to work with. Chris worked with Jo on the original re-eroticization project, which was published as a journal paper in *Gender, Work and Organization* in 1995. Thanks are therefore due to him, again for permission to use some of his ideas as a basis for our discussion in chapter 6 (Re-eroticizing the organization), and for being an excellent all-round collaborator in the first instance.

Moving on, Gibson Burrell of the University of Warwick proved to be a very incisive and attentive reader, and we are extremely grateful to Annette Richards for undertaking the onerous task of producing our index, and doing it so well. Jo's erstwhile colleagues in the Department of Business and Management at the University of Portsmouth Business School also deserve thanks for their support in making her sabbatical (and therefore an awful lot of work on this book) possible, as do her current colleagues in the Department of Accounting, Finance and Management at the University of Essex for allowing her the time and space to make crucial final revisions to the manuscript. The Department of Management at the University of Wollongong granted Steve a short sabbatical which allowed critical early research to be done on this project; Sunderland

Business School supplied resources for indexing; and Nick Linstead ate far too much junk food as a result of Dad working on yet another redraft. We would also like to give very heartfelt thanks to all the respondents who gave up their time to talk to us and whose experiences have provided so much useful and interesting material for this book. Finally, we realize that our long-suffering partners, Chris Potter and Barbara Britton, have had an awful lot to put up with during the production of this book ... so a special thank you to them for all the late nights, working weekends, missed evenings out, failures to cook, clean or wash up, snappishness and stress!

The usual acknowledgements are also due to the following:

Plenum Publishing Corporation for use of material from an earlier version of chapter 1 which appeared as Linstead, S.A. (1997) 'Abjection and organization: men, violence and management', *Human Relations* 50, 10: 1115–45.

Blackwell Publishers Ltd for use of material from an earlier version of chapter 2 which appeared as Linstead, S.A. (1995) 'Averting the gaze: power and gender on the perfumed picket line', *Gender, Work and Organization* 2, 4: 192–206.

Blackwell Publishers Ltd for use of material from an earlier version of chapter 6 which appeared as Brewis, J. and Grey, C. (1994) 'Re-eroticizing the organization: an exegesis and critique', *Gender, Work and Organization* 1, 2: 67–82.

Blackwell Publishers Ltd for use of material from an earlier version of chapter 8 which appeared as Brewis, J. and Linstead, S. (2000) ' "The worst thing is the screwing" (1): consumption and the management of identity in sex work', *Gender, Work and Organization*, 7, 2: 84–97.

Blackwell Publishers Ltd for use of material from an earlier version of chapter 9 which appeared as Brewis, J. and Linstead, S. (2000) "The worst thing is the screwing' (2): context and career in sex work', *Gender, Work and Organization* 7, 3.

Sage Publications Ltd for use of material from an earlier version of chapter 11 which appeared as Brewis, J. and Linstead, S. (1998) 'Time after time: the temporal organization of red-collar work', *Time and Society* 7, 2: 223–48.

Jo Brewis and Steve Linstead
Colchester and Sunderland
October 1999

Introduction

Reading sex into organization, reading organization into sex

Sexuality has traditionally been seen to be the very antithesis of what organizations are about – which tends to be constructed as control, instrumental rationality and the suppression of instinct and emotion. Sex and work, it is argued from this perspective, don't mix. However, more recent arguments have suggested that this is in fact a denial of the obvious – that sexuality pervades every aspect of organizations, but that this is not conventionally acknowledged. In this book we explore this claim in detail by analysing the interconnections between sex and work in two different ways: the first looks at the channelling of sexuality in organizations, exploring how work may be seen as sexually organized; the second at how sexuality is commercially commodified, and how sex work itself becomes organized. Thus we read sex into organization in the first part of the book, and organization into sex in the second part of the book.

Sex work here functions not only as the focus of the second part of the book, but as the crucial *brisure* between sexuality and organization. This is because we find sex work subject to a double rejection – the first in the discursive construction of 'normal' sexuality by virtue of its being commercialized and organized, and hence inauthentic; the second in the discursive construction of organizing because it is sexual, and hence illegitimate. Sex work therefore captures and constitutes an example of a category of both psychological and social being which is an important element in our understanding of the processes of desire – the abject.

Considering the abject involves paying attention to several aspects of desire which re-eroticization theory (Burrell 1992a), as one response to the idea that work is always and already sexualized, neglects. Re-eroticization theory, as Burrell constructs it in 'The organization of pleasure', suggests that the removal of oppressive structures will allow the full emergence of *eros* in all its creativity and relational process to make organizations more passionate, human and exciting places to be. Perhaps less idealistically, Gherardi (1995) argues for the recognition that all work is sexualized to a degree, and accordingly ought to be considered to be a form of sex work, as people trade on their sexuality in negotiating their path through organizations. Both of these approaches suggest that desire is commodified in modern organizations but neither addresses fully the connections between organizing processes and desiring processes. The construction of desire, which in most approaches to organization at least remains implicitly Freudian, is not directly assessed, and neither is the connection between the light and the dark sides of desire – the inescapable connection between death and the erotic.[1]

In the first part of the book, then, we trace the ways in which sex and organization can be seen to be interwoven through a reconsideration of our core concepts – organization, economy and work, desire, abjection, sexuality, the erotic and eroticization. Thus we suggest that, in order to understand organization, it is imperative to understand sexuality – that organizing is always and already a sexual activity. We argue our case by discussing male managers' experiences of physical, psychological and sexual violence and the ways in which this impacts upon their managing; the resistant deployment of sexuality in a gendered industrial dispute; the discursive construction of sexual harassment and its implications for 'real' male and female subjects; the working lives of professionals who represent, counsel, support and treat sex offenders; and the insights that the disorganizing but at the same time highly organized sexual practice of sadomasochism might afford into organizing *per se*. Moreover, having traced the penetration of organizational processes by sexuality in ways that often go unrecognized, this part of the book concludes with a critical examination of re-eroticization theory in an attempt to establish the precise extent to which the modern organization can be eroticized. Indeed, although with Hearn *et al.* (1989) we are concerned to outline and analyse 'the sexuality of organization', our conclusion here is that this sexuality tends either to be colonized as part of attempts to enhance the bottom line in a highly competitive and complex global market, or fundamentally disrupts the organizational effort to generate utility, to create surplus, to engage in useful activity. This assertion proceeds directly from our redrawing of the boundaries between sex and death, from our reconceptualization of desire as energy, flow and flux.

In part I, then, we look at some of the important dimensions of sexuality present in organization, and their consequences for organizational theory. The second part of our enquiry reverses this process as we look at dimensions of organizing present in one form of sexual activity, namely prostitution, and again consider the consequences of this for sexualizing theories of organization. The challenges which are presented for organization theory by prostitution – primarily to incorporate the theorization of the body, the subject, desire, agency, partial and multiple identity, signification and simulation, power and interest – are matched by corresponding empirical complexities. These range from the micro-analyses of conversation in individual encounters, through the processes of construction of the assemblage of the encounter, the identification of localized occupational features, the processes of subjectification which shape the types of sexual encounter possible, and the global features which encompass both the domination and trafficking of female prostitutes in particular, and their economic and social liberation. However, despite the large number of studies which have been conducted of sex work and sex workers over the last 150 years in the West, the double effect of discursive and material placing which organizes and structures prostitution has not yet been addressed within any single study, and we take this as our focus in this part of the book.

To further expand on our argument, it is useful to start with the common and mythologized description of prostitution as the 'oldest profession', perhaps reflecting enduring discursive constructions regarding the persistence of male sexual libido in particular, amongst other considerations.[2] As Kempadoo (1998a: 3) puts it, prostitutes 'service vast sections of the worlds' [*sic*] male populations and render what many consider vital to the well-being of manhood … However, discourses positioning sexuality as an epistemological or power/knowledge project have existed in multiple forms throughout history and across cultures (Foucault 1979, 1986a, 1990; Laqueur 1990; Brewis 1996).[3] Consequently, the way that sex work is understood varies according to the particular historical moment and the cultural milieu in which it is located. Our central tenet of the double effect of placing on prostitution therefore consists, first, of what follows from discursive positioning, in that the definitions of prostitution applied by investigators, prostitutes and clients (as well as others involved in the industry, such as representatives of law enforcement agencies) will be partially governed by the prevailing, and often conflicting, discourses on sexuality of one particular time and place. Generally speaking, the relative dominance of particular discourses, combined with existing tensions and patterns of (dis)agreement with more marginalized discourses, shape and situate prostitution in locally and temporally idiosyncratic ways. By identifying varying discursive formations, and accepting that they inevitably have particular power/knowledge effects (Foucault 1980), we can as a consequence begin to understand how some of the meanings attached to sex work, and the experiences that prostitutes have of the work that they do, become possible, and also how they might be oppressive for some and liberating for others with only minor modifications to their content. Moreover, attitudes to prostitution are a useful indicator of historical changes in wider social attitudes (Giddens 1991, 1992; Hawkes 1996), as well as of cross-cultural difference – and it is also relevant here that prostitutes' activities complement the 'sex work' which takes place or fails to take place in others' 'conventional' sexual relationships (Duncombe and Marsden 1996). As Brewis and Grey (1994) and Hawkes (1996) observe, the widely promoted concept of 'lifestyle sex' continues to raise anxieties about sex for those of us in the West, though now in the form of worries about sexual performance, strength and frequency of orgasm, variety and type of sexual activities, rather than through moral or physiological concerns. Sex work in its broadest sense is therefore something in which all couples need to engage, given that 'The sexual … faces an implicit challenge to live up to the promises made on its behalf' (Simon 1996: 134). Duncombe and Marsden (1996) indicate how difficult this may be in practice, even without the media pressure on sexual lifestyles, as part of the challenge of keeping a long-term relationship alive. Indeed, some couples opt for celibacy (or, more correctly, chastity) when their efforts in this regard fail (also see Giddens 1992). Sex workers respond to this performative need, to reassure others that they can have technically competent sexual encounters, even some simulated affection, yet they also offer more than this and in the process they subvert the activities of the public 'anxiety-makers'. Indeed, for many of their clients, they allow and enable life to go on. As London sex worker Rachel Collins suggests:

> It is not so feas[i]ble in the [AIDS] era for us to sleep around to gain sexual knowledge, but sexual compat[i]bility is one of the most important aspects of any long[-]term relationship. This ha[s] given rise to the growth in educ[a]tional program[me]s and videos and I bel[ie]ve an increase in the use of male [and] female prostitutes by men and women who now look at this service as a commodity instead of something seedy.
>
> (Collins 1997)

Nonetheless, many prostitutes pay the price for this in a struggle to maintain their own sense of self-worth, given the ways in which prevailing discourses position their profession and construct them as individuals.

Placing, moreover, also refers to the specific and material effects of locality which influence the precise forms of prostitution which are able to emerge and interact in any one locale and therefore impact significantly on prostitutes' experience and interpretation of their work. Consequently, theories or frameworks produced by the study of individual prostitutes or particular areas within prostitution inevitably reflect local and intimate knowledges, and are thus 'localized' themselves. There may also be tensions between these local knowledges and global messages, media presentations and forms of social relations varying from the idealized 'hooker makes good' image of Garry Marshall's *Pretty Woman* (1990) to the much less glamorous reality of organized sex tourism. Prostitution, we argue, is therefore difficult to characterize with any finality because it is both problematic, caught in an anxious tension of the global and the local in a geometry of difference, and polymorphic.

Thailand serves as an especially useful exemplar of this tension. Here, paradoxically, while sex tourism is a mainstay of the Thai economy, prostitution remains illegal. The political economy of the industry is accordingly complicated by a wide range of working conditions – including prostitutes being chained to beds, contracted to bars, or plying their trade in expensive apartments. But the successful reintegration of many women back into rural society after exiting prostitution in urban areas depends upon their having 'earned the respect of their community through supporting parents and younger siblings' (Van Esterik 1995: 252; Cook 1998). Prostitution, then, though not necessarily a desirable profession, is not always a source of shame and dishonour – much depends on the local situation, how the occupation is socially interpreted, why individuals take it up and the scope sex workers have for developing and sustaining their own ethical system (Pongpaichit 1982; Hantrakul 1988; Pettman 1996; Montgomery 1998; Stivens 1998). However, the influence of global commercialism (Robinson 1993: 246; Kempadoo 1998a) and the recreational needs of the military–industrial complex (Enloe 1990, 1993; Pettman 1996: 201–3) on the fragile rural economies have wide-ranging effects at all levels which still need to be understood (Bishop and Robinson 1998).

Importantly, because placing has until now not been afforded the attention it deserves in the study of sex work, we have many rich accounts of prostitution in cities and towns from Brazil to Bangkok, and a number of illuminating larger-scale surveys, but the space of articulation between the two is only sparsely inhabited. In the second part of the book, then, we argue that variations across time and place which affect the organization of sex work should not be underestimated as they are both a condition and a consequence of the emergence of sexuality more broadly. Overall, our approach throws a different light on investigations which tend to make powerful and vividly illustrated arguments based on a small section of the sex work community, whether taking pro- or anti-sex positions. We argue, accordingly, that prostitution is a widely varied and textured occupation, while also suggesting that future efforts should attempt to redress the common failing in some of the most important studies of this work to date – that is to say, an insufficient recognition of the degree to which their conclusions depend on culturally specific local data. These studies have therefore, however tentatively, presented a prematurely universalized argument, without taking into account the complex and perplexing dynamics of how the local and the global intersect and interact in the formation of contemporary sexualities and sexual subjectivities. In contrast, we present prostitution as a highly varied profession, as shaped and structured by the double effect of discursive and material placing. We also argue that in certain significant respects it closely resembles more 'mainstream' industries, yet it is also unlike these industries in others. Moreover, its commodification of sexual desire places it at the margins of 'normal' sexuality. This double rejection makes prostitution abject, but also allows us to examine the ways in which sexuality is organized within the profession and therefore to further consider the interweavings of sex and work.

Outline of the book

Having outlined our general argument, and explained the way in which the book is structured, we will now discuss the key themes and content of each chapter in more detail. Chapter 1 looks at abjection in the process of organization through male experiences of violence and the construction of masculinity. This chapter introduces themes of male anxiety and repulsion and the ways in which extra-organizational relationships and psychological processes can affect management styles. It is built on the case of one manager and his father, examining how masculine violence can cast its shadow over the career of a victim. Other examples illustrate that, even where it is not pathological, violence is part of masculinity and requires the anxious male subject to take up a position in relation to it – whether at work or in terms of their sexuality. We also argue that violent behaviour in organizations has long-lasting effects which can make it difficult for managers who have suffered to manage positively and for growth.

Chapter 2 moves to consider the relationships between discursively formed masculinity oriented around male anxiety, as explored in chapter 1, and gendered dimensions of industrial relations, where the abject may symbolically align with an oppositional object. We develop the theme of power and look further at how gendered effects work their way into normalized organizational relations on a collective scale. In looking at the case of a strike by Cathay Pacific airline flight attendants, we use primary data gleaned from contact with the airline as well as secondary data from published accounts of the strike, television footage and press releases. The analysis reveals how anxious the position of the apparently powerful male can be – and how it can be subverted. Female flight attendants used all the sexualized tricks which the company had helped them to hone in order to win over the public in opposition to the company. Yet, although morally defeated, management found themselves prey to a forbidden desire. In the face of this display of seduction and rhizomatic power, they were simultaneously attracted, threatened, repulsed and yet engaged by the mirroring of the phallus.

In chapter 3, we extend our consideration of the exploitative potential of sexuality raised in the previous chapter by engaging with the body of knowledge around workplace sexual harassment. Here we suggest that the discourse which structures and constitutes harassment as 'bad', 'power-tainted' sex-without-desire, which has specific and highly problematic consequences for female members of organizations, may actually produce consequences counter to those which its proponents espouse – specifically, that its power effects may actually contribute to the conditions of (re)production of sexual harassment itself. Our key point here concerns the social regulation of the abject – the ways in which 'normality' seeks to contain and drive out those aspects of itself which it cannot abide, such as harassment, but which always return to haunt its boundaries.

Chapter 4 also deals with the ways in which the abject is constructed and (incompletely) cast out by normalizing processes in organizations and the wider society. This chapter, based on a small scale qualitative interview study with British professionals who work with sex offenders, starts from the premise that the modern Western discourse of sexuality constitutes us as believing in the proper inviolacy of that sexuality. Our understanding of sexual offences therefore conflates the offence and the offender and relegates both to the abject. However, the processes which construct sexual offenders and their offences in this way involve professionals who support, counsel or represent these individuals. How, then, do these professionals deal with the tensions of working within the space of the abject? Our analysis suggests that those interviewed for this chapter have most difficulty when confronting the nature of the offenders' crimes – that is, they subscribe to the prevailing construction of sexual offences as peculiarly awful – although they also profess no small measure of sympathy for the individuals whom they encounter. Dealing with these offenders as damaged individuals, and therefore dividing the 'criminal' from the 'crime', to some extent seems to mitigate the need for emotional labour, because this strategy rejects the actual offence but reconstructs its perpetrator as capable of rehabilitation.

The penultimate chapter in this first part of the book, chapter 5, brings together the microprocesses of abjection, as initially explored in chapters 1 and 2, and the mesoprocesses of inclusion and exclusion, introduced in chapters 3 and 4, in a discussion of sadomasochism (S/M). Drawing on secondary data from academic studies and published accounts by practitioners of sado-masochism, we present S/M as a disorganizing set of practices revealing the socially grounded nature of self, being, the body, desire and pleasure. That is to say, it resists discursive constructions of sexuality because it is predicated upon a disparity of power and the infliction of pain, which nevertheless may be dialectical and reversible. S/M also calls into question the Cartesian dualism of reason and the passions, the cerebral and the physical. However, it is at the same time highly organized, so as to enable its practitioners to engage with dangerous desires and to move beyond accustomed limits, without experiencing self-annihilation. Trust and reciprocity are therefore crucial considerations here, given that the unattenuated indulgence of such desires may propel human beings past the limits of mind and body. Accordingly, S/M may have important lessons to teach us about modern organizing, in terms of the dialectic of organizational power, the potentialities of intimacy at work and the bureaucratic exclusion of the erotic from the public realm, to which we also attend.

Chapter 6, in concluding the first part, takes a critical look at the idea that modern organizations need to become less repressive in a sexual sense, so as to liberate more generally creative forces within them. Here we set out the main lines of argument typical of re-eroticization theory, and identify some of its key weaknesses, but note that the failure of critics of this approach to move beyond it positively has been a result of them omitting to confront the understanding of desire upon which both the theory and the critique rest. Moreover, it is on the basis of our reworking of desire in this chapter that discussion across the book explores the contours of its processes, and its psychological and social construction, explicitly addressing some of the aspects which both re-eroticization theory and its critics have so far left unexplored, and leading to a reconsideration of the erotics of organization in our conclusion.

In chapter 7, the first in the second part of the book, we present a theoretical argument which focuses on the ways in which prevailing discursive constructions of sexuality, and therefore prevailing understandings of sex work, are underpinned by implicit or explicit ontologies of human desire. In suggesting that these ontologies are mainly Freudian, we draw upon the work of Foucault on discourse and Deleuze and Guattari on desire and argue both for an increased focus on the work of the former and a movement towards developing analysis based on the work of the latter in understanding and representing desire as something profligate and experimental, something which does not have an endpoint and which cannot be satisfied. This chapter therefore points up some of the often unacknowledged tensions which animate sex work research; theorizes the significance of the placing process for understanding prostitution in all its various forms; and suggests some theoretical and methodological ways forward for research in the field.

Chapter 8 extends our exploration of the ways in which prostitution is interpreted and understood by suggesting that the development of late modernity has been characterized by a transition from production to consumption as the basis for identity. Those sites where production (work) and consumption (leisure) intersect are therefore of particular interest to the theorist of contemporary self-identity – including the sex industry, where the body (or its parts) is commodified and made available for hire, perhaps (but not always) requiring the prostitute to work to preserve a sense of self which is separate from that involved in the client transaction. Prostitutes may therefore have to employ various methods to sustain the mask/s which make supporting oneself through the sale of sex possible at the same time as establishing control over the client encounter and ensuring that the client leaves with a feeling of satisfaction rather than one of guilt. It is these masks which are our focus here in exploring the construction of prostitutes' identities, but we also attend to the problems inherent in analysis which assumes that such masks are universally deployed across sex work, by all sex workers, with all clients.

The analysis in chapter 8 therefore concentrates on the interactional features of identity construction; chapter 9, on the other hand, deals with the contextual features which shape this construction. Identities, as we have already implied, are negotiated in a discursive context where attitudes towards sexuality (as well as to work, leisure, etc.) may delimit or enable the possibilities that sex workers have for establishing and developing themselves as subjects. In this chapter we look at this wider context and extend our consideration of prostitutes' work from the client encounter to the career. Here we examine three pivotal discursive fields in order to identify the variations within each field, and the consequent variety of opportunities, choices and constraints that emerge for individual prostitutes, depending on the discourse/s through which they identify themselves. This discussion combines themes raised in chapters 7 and 8 in that it focuses on the ways in which discourses underpin and inform the work and non-work lives of prostitutes, and also highlights the variation that is evident in the ways in which prostitutes understand and experience the work that they do.

Chapter 10 moves from a consideration of discursive placing to discuss the other dimension in what we identify as placing's double effect. In this chapter we review the material effects of location on the activities of prostitutes working in different areas of the industry and in different countries. Where the prostitute is 'placed' in terms of legislative climate, market segment, labour market and mutual support networks provides a highly specific local context for the organization of sex work in any one setting. We also suggest that these four key dimensions of place may well be related to each other in specific and important ways, mediated by six cross-dimensional influences – cultural context, legal ideology, gender relations, race and ethnicity, migration and trafficking, and organized crime.

In chapters 7 to 10, then, we examine sex work in the context of historical time, first, as it gives rise to particular discursive formations and specific material effects in various locales, and second, as a broader social construct in our discussion of career. In chapter 11, we turn our attention to the interactional and relational aspects of time by considering how prostitutes and clients experience it in and around the encounter. Any differences between worker and client as regards the significance of time are not necessarily rigid and invariable, as some analyses which attempt to link time and gender have argued. Workers (who are female in the main) may experience their encounters with clients as (masculine) time which needs to be controlled and rationalized or, alternatively, as emotional and connected (feminine) time. Equally, clients (who are male in the main) may approach the encounter looking for affectionate and intimate (feminine) time or determined to script the interaction in a mechanistic (masculine) way – to avoid being arrested, for example. Time in the encounter is therefore not pure – it may be complex, contaminated, even reversible. Moreover, the ways in which worker and client live out and think about time points again to the socially constituted nature of self-identity, as discussed in chapters 8 and 9 in particular, and across the book more generally. It also underlines the complexity of our identity work: that it might focus on some dimensions of our identities in one geographical and temporal space, and on others elsewhere. This labour is neither without conflict nor without contest.

Methods and approach

How, then, do we go about this exploration of the sexuality of organization on the one hand and the organization of sexuality on the other? Our methodology, broadly speaking, is threefold. First, we draw on literature, and thus on theoretical frameworks and concepts, from a range of different disciplines including organization studies, human resource management, sociology, psychology, anthropology, philosophy, feminism, history, geography, economics, politics, social policy, legal studies, criminology, cultural studies and medicine. This of course is entirely in keeping with our interdisciplinary insistence that the organization be analysed through the lens of sexuality, and sexuality through the lens of organization.

Second, we employ a wide range of secondary data to illuminate, substantiate and develop our theoretical arguments. This is taken from published academic research (and was collected using ethnographic methods such as interviews, conversations and observation in the main), novels, films, documentary histories, the Internet, newspaper articles, television programmes and participants' autobiographical accounts of their activities. The majority of the data relied on are qualitative, chosen because of their detailed depiction of the work and non-work lives of those members of society in whom we are most interested.

Third, we also refer to data from our own fieldwork, which included semistructured interviews with a British manager and members of his family (chapter 1), with representatives of Cathay Pacific (chapter 2), with three British professionals who work with sex offenders (chapter 4) and with female prostitutes working in a variety of locations such as the street, massage parlours and private premises in Port Kembla, Sydney and Wollongong, all locations in New South

Wales (chapters 7–11). This technique was selected in the first instance to yield richly descriptive data, which can be explored in depth for nuances, patterns and attitudinal clues in a way that quantitative data cannot, giving a feel for the beliefs or experiences under examination and allowing both researcher and reader some purchase on what it is like to inhabit the lifeworlds of our respondents. Moreover, semi-structured interviewing permits flexibility such that what is discussed is dictated by the respondent more than it is by the interviewer. This is crucial since researchers cannot necessarily predict what others see as important (Rubin and Rubin 1995), and, as Sanger (1996: 15) argues: 'Over-structured approaches to unfamiliar settings fall foul of the language, customs and behaviours implicit in them.' It is also true to say that the often controversial nature of the subject matter of our primary research – violence, industrial action, sexual crime, prostitution – to some extent required that the interviews be characterized by a level of informality in order to allow development and discussion of relevant issues. Again this is easier to achieve in the more open and relaxed context of a semi-structured interview (Rubin and Rubin 1995).

However, it is also worth emphasizing that the data that we use, both primary and secondary, have been generated using small samples or non-replicable methods, or derive from a particular set of accounts in constructing a picture of the events at hand. In some respects this leaves our approach open to criticism because the data are, in the scientific sense, not generalizable – the stories that they tell may be relevant only to the individuals involved, and to their specific social context. Nonetheless, our contention is that, in order to develop a nuanced insight into others' experiences, it is crucial that we accept, respect and seek to examine them as individuals as opposed to taking their experiences as somehow representative of life in a wider social group to which we have decided, *a priori*, that these men and women belong. Indeed, one of our primary objectives is to explore the ways in which individuals interact with, live out or resist prevailing discursive constructions which imply, for example, that sex offenders are necessarily difficult or distressing to deal with or that all prostitutes are chronically drug-addicted, vulnerable, helpless victims of patriarchy – and this means that the data we have employed were effectively the only viable sources available to us. As Sanger (1996: 20) puts it:

> It seems that here there might be a good starting point for the researcher who wants to observe with a different vision than that clouded by every day familiarity. Rather than observing people and objects as samples of larger groups in some presupposed classificatory system such as the common one for example, used to denote teaching style – didactic, child-centred, resource-based etc – examine them in their complex singularity. Build up the range of observations, seek those characteristics which are shared by them and thence evolve a classification from the data.

Relying on data from representative samples, selected according to the rules of statistical method, would have glossed over what turned out to be important differences between members of particular social categories – such as the way in which the various professionals interviewed for chapter 4 define failure at work – while at the same time ignoring what they share with those in other groupings – such as the career ambitions and entrepreneurial spirit exhibited by some of the sex workers who feature in part II of the book.

Moreover, we do not claim that our interpretation of these data is somehow a definitive or value-free reading. After all, every observation constructs the object of its attention simply by seeing it from that point of view, and reflexively it is impossible for any account to guarantee its own neutrality. Even being 'system-atic' only elaborates this problem and can, moreover, inculcate contextual insensitivity (Linstead 1994). Consequently, the data here, and our subsequent reading of it, have undoubtedly been generated at least in part by our own ways of being-in-the-world, such that its collection, analysis and reportage can only ever be a construction of what was actually said or done in the initial research situation (Silverman, D. 1993: 26–7; Knights 1995: 234–5). In the case of the secondary data, this construction has actually been several-fold – first, by the original researcher/s or author/s and, second, by ourselves. This is not, however, an apologia for a degree of subjectivity which we could have avoided had we been more rigorous in our approach – rather, it is an assertion that we see bias both as inevitable *and* as an essential part of making sense of reality, whether this is in academic research or everyday social negotiations and interactions. As Silverman and Jones (1976: 23–4, cited in Gowler and Legge 1983: 226) put it:

> It begins to look as though there is no 'neutral' ground from which to observe phenomena 'as they really are', or to judge the 'bias' of particular accounts. For each 'observation' constitutes the character of the phenomenon which it claims to speak 'about' … Rather than implying that accounts are 'biased' in particular ways by the social location of the speaker, [this] suggests that 'bias' (or a common system of accounting) is the only way in which reality may be apprehended. Without 'bias' there are no phenomena to be discussed.

To close this methodological discussion, it is also important to remark in more detail on the specific way in which we have built our argument in the second part of the book. Here we have chosen to focus primarily on material from the UK, the USA and Australia, given that these three countries are commonly regarded as sub-sets of the modern, Anglo-Saxon, English-speaking, late industrial 'West' and are therefore culturally, legally and politically commensurable.[4] It would be all too easy to draw dramatic contrasts between societies valuing the *ars erotica* – primarily the Orient – and those obsessed with *scientia sexualis* – the Occident (Foucault 1979), but it is crucial for our argument that, even in relatively similar contexts, wide variations in the experience and interpretation of sex work are not only possible but actually do occur. Additionally, while we accept that the sex industry is increasingly global and involves in many cases the international movement of women (Pheterson 1996: 100–8; Montgomery 1998; Murray

1998; Watanabe 1998; Wijers 1998), we look at some of the features that the sex industry may have in common with other mature industries, including stratification and market segmentation, as one means of explaining how this variety can and does occur.

We also focus in the main here on the dominant paradigm in sex work worldwide – male client–female prostitute – while fully recognizing that other forms of sex work (for example, child, male heterosexual/homosexual and transgender prostitution) exist and that they exhibit similarities to but also some very significant differences from heterosexual female prostitution. In terms of male prostitution, for example, the law is usually different, often down to the age of consent for the homosexual act, or even whether this act itself is legal; the market is different, as there are fewer female customers available, so heterosexual workers often have to entertain same sex clients in order to make ends meet (Prestage 1994: 181; McKeganey 1999); and conditions for homosexual male prostitutes can vary considerably from those for women in the same profession (Joseph 1997; Aggleton 1999). This affects employment opportunities and options accordingly, and support systems are also markedly different. In the UK, the USA and Australia, the gay community is very active in its support for male homosexual sex workers, but heterosexual sex workers have much less support (McKeganey 1999). Moreover, it is apparent that information about male prostitution in our core context forms only a small part of what is available, although we should also note that we do address this, child and transgender prostitution where relevant. Race is another significant dimension of prostitution, and of the choices, experiences and meanings available to prostitutes within Western society. Here, simply being a member of a non-white ethnic group – even one which is culturally well established – changes the prostitute's situation, as Chapkis's (1997: 207–9) interview with Gloria Lockett makes clear. However, space does not permit extended discussion of racialized differences between prostitutes in the locations which our data cover.

Furthermore, our data stem largely from sex workers who could be considered to be 'free'. That is to say, our discussion concentrates on prostitutes who are not explicitly coerced into working in the sex industry as child prostitutes or those who are trafficked commonly are, although we also accept Chapkis's (1997: 51–3) qualification of the use of terms like 'free choice' prostitution. She argues that there are of course differences between, say, those who are trafficked and those who are not, but that 'free choice' may still be a misnomer in the sense that the lack of realistic alternatives from which to choose often means that not all consensual prostitution is necessarily 'free'. Chapkis gives the example of migratory prostitution from Eastern Europe to illustrate her point, saying that sexual, racial and class inequality may, when coupled with differences of wealth within and between nation states, generate 'tremendous pressure on women to engage in any available form of employment, including sex work' (Chapkis 1997: 52). This is what O'Connell Davidson (1995a: 7) refers to as the 'dull economic compulsion' of prostitution – although it is also worth noting the considerable evidence that 'free choice' prostitution may be exactly that, a choice to enter a profession which offers opportunities for either short-term financial gain, self-development and/or entrepreneurialism and career progression.

Moreover, Doezema (1998), whose position is supported by Bishop and Robinson's (1998: 218–49) extended analysis, argues that there is a need to move beyond the 'free' versus 'forced' dichotomy, because each of these concepts has a moral baggage which comes with it – those forced into the work being immediately cast as 'innocent', those freely choosing it as 'guilty' or 'tainted'. As an example of this, some legal systems refuse to support exploited and abused women who may have been trafficked if they were known to have been prostitutes before their migration. Less specifically, this imported morality affects the rights and resources available to all prostitutes, and prevents offences such as slavery and confinement from being treated as offences in their own right, regardless of the character or occupation of the victim, as well as denying prostitutes' subjective agency.

Key concepts

Finally, we should also point out that there are certain key concepts underpinning our analysis here which provide the theoretical bolt-holes for our explorations. In what follows, then, we will briefly outline our understanding of organization, economy and work, desire, abjection, sexuality, the erotic and eroticization.

Organization

The term organization is most commonly used as a noun referring either to organizations – sites where complex systems coalesce to produce goods or services – or to the arrangements which are made for the organization of production. But organizing is a process which extends much more broadly into our lives, even down to the organization of consciousness and identity. Indeed, our focus here is almost the reverse of the traditional concern with how production is organized – instead we are concerned with how a particular sense of organization is produced, specifically our sense of ourselves as sexual beings, and how this is both carried into and emerges from our involvement in organized work activities. In this sense, sex work is of particular interest because it occupies a pivotal moment between sexuality and organization. Despite moral condemnations of professionalized sex work, its very existence constantly troubles normalized sexual relations by reminding us that there is something within them that remains unfulfilled, which is positioned as a special case of those relations. Moreover, even where moral condemnation is withheld, the discourse of organizing ignores prostitution because, in its trading on sexual desire, it seems to confound such important organizational principles as differentiation, order, regulation, standardization, stability and even size. However, our discussion suggests that prostitution also returns to haunt the boundaries of organizing in the sense that differentiation, order, regulation, standardization and stability are all visible in this highly organized industry which is global in its scale.

Economy and work

If we move outwards from our thinking on organization, on the one level, we have the macro dimension of economy, on the other, the more focused issue of work. Yet as Bataille argues, to conceptualize 'economy' only in terms of organization, regulation, order and exchange, in terms of work, the labour process, profit and loss, is only to pay attention to one side of the argument and to ignore what should be, for human beings, the most important side. Where Foucault asks the Nietzschean question, 'What does it mean to be human?', Bataille asks 'What is it that makes us human? What do we do that defines us as human?'. His answers are interesting. Beginning from the observation that energy flows from the sun, that 'Solar energy is the source of life's exuberant development' (Bataille 1991: 28), he notes that it is always in excess of what is needed. That is to say, there is no such thing as scarcity on a global scale. Energy is in the first instance employed for the purposes of subsistence and survival of all organisms and, second, for their growth. This is not inconsistent with Freud, or even Maslow, the primate researcher and development psychologist recently rediscovered as a management guru. However, Bataille posits that growth is always limited by the fact that we inhabit what he calls the biosphere – a circumscribed mass of land and water – so that 'life occupies all the available space' (Bataille 1991: 30). Therefore no organism can continue to expand indefinitely – even if it grows in such a way that it is able to displace its immediate neighbours and occupy larger and larger areas of space, this growth is always proscribed by the physical limits of the spherical earth. Bataille's earth, then, is bursting full of energy which will, he maintains, surge outward to be spent, regardless of return. It is how we spend, or waste, energy in this 'economy of excess', or what he refers to as a *general economy* – through emotional expression, dance, laughter, poetry, drunkenness, gluttony, orgiastic behaviour and even murder – that is the measure of our humanity, not how we hoard, contain and ration energy through the *restricted economy* of work. When we discuss 'economy' in this book, we will bear in mind both definitions, but will be particularly concerned with what happens to the excess, the 'accursed share' of desire, when it clashes with the restricted economy (see chapters 3, 4 and 6 especially).

Desire

What, then, do we consider to be desire? Although we will discuss this in more detail later in the book, we will observe here that the recent history of the concept of desire – a history heavily influenced by Hegel and Freud – has tended to construct desire as a 'lack' of something – some characteristic or object, which produces a motivational drive to acquire the object, characteristic, or a suitable substitute. Lacan operates a subtle change in this line of thinking by noting that desire is better thought of as the desire to be desired, the desire for the desire of the other, for which the object may stand as sign or guarantor. Yet even though this formulation has considerable explanatory power, it remains too closely engaged with a restricted view of bodily economy. Drawing more from Nietzsche than Hegel, Bataille argues that desire in fact operates without an object, that it can be best understood as a fluid, formless energy than a motivated drive towards an understood goal. This more improvisational understanding of desire is one whose implications we explore here – indeed, a key theme in our argument, as already stated, is that current understandings of the sexuality of organization and of sex work suffer from their reliance on an implicit but essentially Freudian understanding of desire (see chapters 6 and 7 in particular for further discussion).

Abjection

Another associated concept which can be traced back to Bataille via Kristeva is that of the abject, the dark side of desire. The basic concept is that in human self-understanding there is always some aspect of the self, some aspect of our desire or our past experiences, that we find unacceptable – whether because of individual guilt or social censure. Desire may be the desire for death just as much as the desire for life. This unacceptable part of experience we reject or suppress – some of it quite successfully, and we don't find ourselves troubled by it. But the abject is that which always returns to haunt us, often drawing us towards it in fascination. It is something which was so close to us that we can never create a strong enough boundary or prohibition to overcome its power – which is what Bataille and Kristeva call the power of horror, forcing us to look on when we know we should look away. In this book we examine several instances of the abject for individuals – violence in the first chapter, sexuality in the second chapter, sexual harassment in the third chapter, sexual offences in the fourth chapter, sadomasochism in the fifth chapter, and prostitution as socially abject category throughout the second part. It is also worth noting that it is still the case in some societies that even the discussion of sexuality is a confrontation with the abject.

Sexuality

The concepts which we have discussed above underpin our understanding of, and approach to, sexuality. For us, sexuality is not synonymous with biological sex (that is, being male or female), gender (that is, being masculine or feminine) or sexual practice (that is, being heterosexual, bisexual or homosexual). It is a matter of constantly, and often subtly, shifting relationships between bodies, emotions, desires, selves and others, in contexts where understanding is discursively and semiotically shaped. Our sexuality is not, therefore, something which is purely individual and reserved for sexual relations – it is a social field through which desire moves and which affects all of our behaviour. As we have already intimated, organizations, structured as a part of the restricted economy, often set themselves to restrict or censure the kind of actions – fluid, improvised, expressive, unpredictable, passionate – which are a recognized part of conventional sexuality. This we discuss at length in chapter 6.

The erotic and eroticization

The force which moves sexuality, desire as a life force, a force of attraction, we call the erotic. But our reading of Bataille alerts us to the electrifying tension – the *erotic* tension – between life and death. Where work for Bataille involves both the avoidance and the embodiment of death in its countless restrictions and denials (see chapters 3 and 4 for discussion), death itself – in the form of sacrifice – can be life-affirming, as a gift that demands no reciprocation. For Bataille it is the element of the unknown, of risk, of passionate exploration which characterizes the erotic – balanced often on the edge between good and evil. Moreover, and as we suggested at the beginning of this Introduction, it is this sense of the dark side of the erotic which we find missing from most of the work that has been done on the eroticization of organizations, particularly as it is influenced by Reich and Marcuse (both contemporaries of Bataille), which seeks to unpick some of the constraints and taboos around the expression and release of emotion and sexual feeling in organizations. We also find that sex work provides fertile ground for exploration of the positive and negative sides of eroticism.

The above having been established, at this stage it only remains for us to point out that the Conclusion, in summarizing the arguments presented in the book, returns to the three questions which inform our discussion throughout. That is to say, why study sexuality in the work context? To what extent is it possible to re-eroticize organizations? In what ways might the study of sex work shed light on more mainstream organizing, and can we identify aspects of this mainstream organizing in sex work as an industry?

Part I

Reading sex into organization

1 Violence, masculinity and management

Introduction

Death, as we have implied in our introductory chapter, inhabits sexuality and organization. It both drives and frustrates desire – it is simultaneously and paradoxically the desired release from desire and the loss against which desire is set. Indeed, in pursuing fulfilment desire actively pursues its own extinction. This inhabitation of death and desire is not simply a pathological variant of the modern imagination but, as Dollimore (1998) argues, a crucial element of the intellectual and imaginative formation of Western culture over 3,000 years or more. Sievers (1995) has also noted the complicity of organizing with death, organizing being concerned with the punctuation and control of movement, process and change (Chia 1996) to the point at which time might become suspended and the organization itself immortal. Not only are such attempts to stop the clock illusory, but they are only accomplished by activities of division, separation and repression in the name of productivity and progress – activities which are themselves *violent*. Chia (1996 – also see Cooper 1989; Linstead and Grafton Small 1992) has noted with Derrida that the ordering and spacing strategies which produce our sense of organization are themselves linguistic practices – more specifically, practices of *writing*, of inscribing experience. Language must exclude and repress that which it does not seek to express, and in doing this it does violence to the flow of the process of experience, and creates a residual element which is always outside it, but always present. As Lecercle (1990) puts it, the significance of language lies powerfully in the way in which it inscribes violence into the ways in which we think about and represent experiential reality – into consciousness itself. Violence, then, is woven deeply into both the practice of organizing and our experience of organization, yet it is only rarely acknowledged as such. But for men in particular the experience of violence – ontically the world experienced as 'violent'- is an even more powerful shaping force on identity. Although violence signifies death, it is pressed into the service of desire, making them what they are taught to feel they must be, shaping the world and the Other to their will. Where weakness is encountered as an interiority it is violently suppressed and cast out, resulting in a self-obsession which psychoanalysis would regard as narcissism. Yet those who suffer at the hands of violent narcissists often violently repress their own emotions towards violence, control, discipline and power, and lose the ability to respond naturally to events around them, social, organizational or erotic. Violence towards others may even be a consequence of such narcissism. While we need to be able to recognize and come to terms with the paradoxes of sexuality and power, death and desire, love and suffering, violent experiences may pervert our ability to do this.

Organizations are violent places, sites of violence: but they are not its only source nor the most influential, as we have implied above. In this chapter we explore some case material to consider how identity-forming non-organizational experiences of violence can shape subsequent behaviour within organizations. These connections are not commonly considered either in the study of organizational behaviour or of managerial practice, because behaviours from other arenas, cathexes, adaptations and responses, can be reproduced many years away from the original source of anxiety. These behaviours are widespread, patterned, cyclical and carry an inevitability about them that cannot be modified simply by changing behaviour alone. We concentrate on examples where the extent of pathological behaviour is easily seen, but the processes which surface are common mechanisms of 'ordinary' human behaviour and more attenuated experiences of violence within organizations operate similarly. Going somewhat against Foucault's (1979) rejection of psychoanalysis at this point, we discuss these processes through the work of post-Freudian object relations theorists, Julia Kristeva, and recent theorists of masculinity. Accordingly, we argue that bureaucracies operate by ignoring the emotions at work in our behaviour and our decision-making, which renders emotion itself abject, never admitted to but always there. Men are caught up in this web of societal and organizational denial because of their traditional dominance in formal organizations and the historical association of masculinity and rationality, compounded by the dynamics of male psychology. However, traditional symbolic associations between men and physical violence introduce a problematic contradiction, and societal, cultural and organizational arrangements tend to support and facilitate the psychodynamics of denial which deals with this contradiction by producing narcissistic and addictive responses. This we illustrate by a discussion of biographical, film and novel data. We conclude by arguing that men in organizations need to learn to live with the unacceptable in themselves and their experience so as to put an end to this vicious circle of damaging and dysfunctional behaviour.

Men, violence and management

Violent behaviour can take many forms – extremely physical, sexual, intimidatory, psychological, intense, infrequent, impulsive, sustained, planned, ritualized, official, encultured, verbal, cognitive, emotional, linguistic, visual and representational among them (Lecercle 1990; Hearn 1994: 735). It constrains both the violent and the victim in thought, word and subsequent interaction. Its effects spill over into areas of life beyond the initial arena of violence, and can last a lifetime. It produces anger (as well as being a product of anger) and perpetuates itself; it affects world-views, the ability to dream and to envision the future; it affects the perspective of self-worth, and the ability to cope with success and failure; it affects the ability to grow and develop and to deal with such growth in other persons and institutions; and it affects the ability to relate to self and others. The victims, the abused, not only may carry the scars and damage of violence for the rest of their lives, but ironically often find themselves reproducing those behaviours which have caused them pain in their dealings with others.

Men are the primary offenders in the overwhelming majority of violence cases and, although women are certainly capable of all forms of violent behaviour, they are not normally under pressure to embrace and incorporate violence into their gender identity in the way that males are compelled to deal with violence as a condition of masculinity (Polk 1994). That is to say, being male requires that the subject develops an attitude towards violence, whether in sport, society, the military etc., in order to be recognized as masculine; men tend to have stylized means of behaving violently; and the management of Western organizations remains overwhelmingly male.[1] This chapter focuses on the men of one family as a case study of how intergenerational violence can affect men's development as managers, drawing on psychoanalytic theory and cultural theory in arguing that pathological behaviour is shaped by the combination of individual ego-defences and societal images of different masculinities, as well as organizational experience and circumstance.

In what follows we will first develop a theoretical background for the consideration of violent behaviour, which is grounded in psychoanalytic and particularly object relations theory as reworked by Donald Winnicott and Julia Kristeva. This centres around the concepts of narcissism and the abject, which is, as we established in the Introduction, essentially denied experience that cannot be fully suppressed by the subject. The defence against the abject is bolstered by symbolic investment in the ego-ideal, which may embody stylized or exaggerated ideas of masculinity or femininity, and the ways in which men may draw on such symbolic resources is examined through a consideration of films. Addictive behaviour as a parallel defence against the inherent self-loathing of narcissism is discussed through both personal interview data and material drawn from a novel by Alan Duff. Examples of the effects of violent behaviour on individuals are discussed based again on personal interview data and from a recent biography of a victim of child abuse. Finally, we consider some of the possible consequences for organizations.

We should emphasize here that in this chapter we do not claim that the explanation of the emergence of masculinist organizational cultures can be reduced to a description of individual psychopathology. However, in a tradition which can be traced back to Freud if not to Plato, we suggest that the study of pathological behaviours reveals processes which are at work in the 'normal' or 'healthy' psyche and helps us to identify tensions which are common and widespread, though they may not be in crisis everywhere – that is to say, there are 'normal pathologies' (Simon 1996: 100). The difference between the normal and the pathological is primarily one of degree, of a loss of a sense of limits which enables the socially adjusted personality to co-operate with others.[2] However, the existence of these differences should be a signal, not to reproduce the expulsion of the maladjusted and console ourselves with the thought that most people can cope with their problems without becoming dysfunctional, but to reflect on the fact that personality formation is never finished and fully formed but is constantly recursively shaped, reconstructed, reviewed and refined, as contradictions and unresolved tensions re-emerge and as new situations unfold. Social and cultural forms, discursive practices and power relations also form a shifting context, an intertext which crosses the site of subjectivity, making personality and identity perpetually emergent and incomplete projects. It is the processes at work throughout ordinary or everyday relations which the study of the abnormal helps to reveal, and to remind us of the fragility of 'normal' subjectivities within the field of forces helping to shape them.

Additionally, although 'healthy' personalities may come to operate social arrangements without undue catastrophe, there remains the possibility that extreme stress or crisis might yet produce regression to earlier and more primitive coping mechanisms for ensuring psychological survival. It is characteristic of organizations that their performative, 'problem-solving' orientation tends to address such issues only when they emerge as problematic, and those approaches which seek to identify and surface potential problems are often accused of creating needless difficulties for practitioners. Nevertheless, if we are to attempt to properly understand the range of influences on managerial and organizational behaviour we cannot afford to assume that what is *apparently* not broken does not need fixing. The interplay between individuals' early and non-organizational experience, socio-cultural influences, career emergence and development, organizational culture and managerial behaviour remains imperfectly appreciated, and suggests some important social and psychological processes which are worthy of further attention and research.

The promise of violence

Violent behaviour often takes the form of a denial of promise, a snatching away of something almost attained, the cancellation of a project which seemed to be going well, the destruction of something of value, or the theft of a deserved reward. Frequently it is unpredictable and shocking, taking the victim by surprise, but it can also be the result of a systematic abuse of their position by those in power, and may also be a combination of both. Where the violence is a by-product of official social or organizational structures, the powerful often explicitly justify their abuse by placing the guilt and responsibility on the victim's head, constructing the violence either as a necessary rite of passage or as a dutiful purging of the victim which will ensure redemption.[3] Either way, the violence becomes more profound in denying the victim the right to define, and hence oppose, it as injustice. The capricious and explosive form of violence intimidates and invades our everyday consciousness by virtue of its possibility; the organized and ritualized form by virtue of its inevitability and its claimed necessity. Both forms affect organization as a process and organizations as institutions, but in different ways. The possibility of capricious violence causes victims and potential victims to organize their lives around this possibility, to become more self-conscious, and to learn to cope with its eventual eruption and lessen the damage of its impact. Violence which is embedded in organizational practices may be less whimsical but exerts a constant pressure on others to behave in particular ways. In fact, bureaucratic violence is the inversion of random and unpredictable violence. We might thus extend Albrow's (1992) observation that Weber's conceptualization of bureaucracy makes emotion its central organizing principle, given that it is constructed specifically to banish sentiment, passion, favouritism, coercion, violence, indiscipline, unpredictability and their resultant disorder from the operations of the organization – an argument which we develop further in chapters 5 and 6. However, as Weber implies, the iron cage may be cool, but it is still oppressive.

The everyday experiences of individuals also affect their behaviour in organizations. Organizations, from both Marxian and radical Weberian perspectives, can be understood as structures of domination, which institutionalize violence in their structures of authority and command. Where organizational members are abused by the system, they can be expected to display future characteristics which are typical of the survivors of other forms of abuse and are frequently detrimental to organizational survival, being antithetical to organizational learning. These behaviours include dependence/counter-dependence, aggressiveness and a punitive approach to authority, excessively tight control or a converse inability to control, inability to manage growth, unwitting reproduction of past abusive patterns, and a tendency towards narcissistic 'addictive' behaviour in attachments to corporate forms of the 'ego-ideal'. Corporate culture change, business process re-engineering and total quality initiatives, for example, may be seen to be expressive if superficial forms of the latter (Schwartz 1990). However, let us suspend our discussion of theory for a moment in order to examine some examples of everyday experiences which have shaped the life and organizational behaviour of one particular manager.

Like a bat out of hell ...

> It took me the best part of the following day to piece together the story from neighbours and my grandmother, who lived across the road, and despite my phlegmatic approach to his endeavours it took a little imagination even for my fertile 14-year-old brain. I knew he was drunk even at five o'clock the previous day, as I found him on the cold-stone of the pantry eating baked beans from the tin – he was incapable of understanding that there was a meal in the oven for him. Or perhaps he resented its presence at the hand of someone other than his wife. It wouldn't have been the first time he'd stomped on his dinner and ground the vegetables into the carpet with his foot because they weren't 'made with love'

as he put it. He left his car in the garage and went out for the night, which was unusual for him as he habitually drove when intoxicated to incoherence. However, I expected that he would have no stomach for trouble when he returned, and I went to bed early so that, in case he did, I would be asleep and he might not bother to wake me. It was a tactic I employed every night, praying for sleep as the fear crept over me, praying for my suffering mother, my brother, and sometimes even for death – mine, his, ours – but mostly for peace and for the three of us to be left alone.

Thus begins a narrative of one of several incidents recounted by an informant we will call Allan,[4] a manager in his forties. Allan's story displays some features which we think are significant for the consideration of violence in the context of organized life and organizations. One of these is that it was not only Allan's father who had become enveloped in a distorted reality but, in complementarity, so had Allan (and for that matter his mother and brother, although they were on holiday during the incident he describes here). They *organized* their lives around his father's violence, which they regarded as inevitable, although it was never predictable what precise form it would take. They developed tactics for avoiding it, delaying it, trying to shut their ears to it. They even avoided bringing their friends to the house if they knew he was at home. Yet perhaps inevitably the violence pursued them into unexpected corners of their lives. Allan continues:

Astonishingly, I slept through a night which was riotous. My father had returned home at around midnight, and had dozed in an armchair for an hour until wakened by a telephone call from his mistress, who had been observed by her husband when with my father earlier. The husband had armed himself with a bread knife and was presently pursuing her around the housing estate with a vocally professed intent on her life. My father leapt into action, only to discover that he could not find the key to the garage. Furious, he stormed across the street to where he accused my grandmother of hiding the key to frustrate his possible intentions. Some of the other residents were quite willing to call the police, two of whom lived in the same block as the old lady, so he returned home, where a neighbour spotted him breaking the window at the rear of the garage and attempting to climb through it. Shortly afterward, the doors burst open as he drove his almost new and very expensive car, Hollywood-style, out into the street, shards of glass and splintered wood scattering in clouds.

He careened about 100 metres before he realized that he had severely gashed his ankle in gaining access through the window. Fortunately, he was able to recognize the seriousness of his injury, being a trained first-aider, applied a tourniquet to it and sat out the next four hours until he was sober enough to call the first available taxi for the hospital, where his injury was repaired. During this time, his wound oozed on to the soft furnishings and he had just completed his clean-up job when I greeted him the following morning.

For Allan, the violence he experienced was primarily a private matter, kept within the walls of his home and only surfacing on the outside in verbal or other symbolic forms. Despite the fact that all the family often experienced verbal humiliations, and many conversations were poised and tense, his father's violence rarely displayed itself on such a public stage. This incident, however, alerted the neighbours, and in the process brought the family some support, underlining the absurdity of their situation and the depths of abjection to which the father had sunk. It was also apparently one of the few occasions when the merest flicker of guilt, a glint of self-loathing which was so important to Allan's father's condition, was visible behind the bluster, the arrogance, the bullying and the blaming of everyone else for any imperfections which he happened to notice in everyday circumstances. It also serves to remind us of the link between alcohol and violence or, more precisely, between addictive behaviour, narcissism, masculinity and violence. We look at some of the processes through which these links become visible before we discuss specific examples from case material in more depth.

Introducing the abject

> Abject. It is something rejected from which one does not part, from which one does not protect oneself as from an object. Imaginary uncanniness and real threat, it beckons to us and ends up engulfing us.
>
> (Kristeva 1982: 4)

In *Tristes Tropiques* (1989 [1955]) Lévi-Strauss argues that primitive societies deal with strangeness in a way which differs from that of civilized societies. Difference, he suggests, equals danger: strangers are therefore dangerous. Primitive 'anthropophagic' societies devour, ingest and consume strangers to absorb their special magic and power into themselves. Civilized 'anthropoemic' societies, on the other hand, reject them, cast them out, drive them away, exclude them. As Bauman (1993: 165–7) argues, Lévi-Strauss, perhaps seduced by nostalgia and the crispness of the binary divide (also see Derrida 1978: 278–93), fails to recognize that these processes are inseparable. They are indispensable twin mechanisms of social spacing, in every society and at every level.

These social spacing strategies, however, when metaphorically extended from societies which physically ingest the Other, can be seen also to be psychological strategies. They are the means by which our sense of self is manufactured and positioned, subject and object differentiated, waste defined and rejected, order inserted into the system. Yet in so doing, these strategies also produce an in-between category, neither one nor the other, neither filth nor purity, which is not rejected yet is not acceptable either, and which irritates the system. This, as already established, Kristeva calls the abject.[5]

It is not lack of cleanliness or health that causes abjection but what disturbs identity, system, order. What does not respect borders, positions, rules. The in-between, the ambiguous, the composite ... Abjection ... is immoral, sinister, scheming, and shady: a terror that dissembles, a hatred that smiles, a passion that uses the body for barter instead of inflaming it, a debtor who sells you up, a friend who stabs you ...

(Kristeva 1982: 4)

This paradoxical relationship becomes central to the understanding of several types of behaviour, including the reproduction of violent behaviour by former victims, addictive behaviour and substance abuse. In each case, the subject attempts to suppress, deny or reject complex but uncomfortable experiences by casting them out of consciousness. The subject may even develop an obsession with determining boundaries and delineating margins in other areas of their life, driven by the need to separate the unacceptable part of themselves (the sufferer, the helpless victim, the shame and guilt felt by all survivors of trauma) from their real self. The criteria for exclusion, however, have to appear objective, principled and not arbitrary, ones over which the individual can claim no discretion, if the strength of the barriers is to be maintained. The feeling of the unworthiness of the self is also one of the defining conditions of narcissism, and of course the abject, loathed and denied part of the self continually flows back into the subject's experience, prompting ever more extreme forms of escapism and denial (which in narcissism often appears as a self-obsession ironically interpreted as self-love).

Narcissistic behaviour, then, offers a useful model for understanding the behaviour of Allan's father, such that we continue by examining some of the key concepts used in the explanation and analysis of narcissism by psychoanalytic theorists.[6]

Narcissism, the ego-ideal and the superego

The psychoanalytic understanding of narcissism is grounded in the earliest experiences of the infant, when psychological mechanisms which persist throughout adult life can be formed. At the beginning of life, the child is not separate from its mother, and psychologically this separation is not achieved until well after the physical separation of birth and the cutting of the umbilical cord. The child experiences what Freud calls 'primary narcissism', seeing itself as the centre of a loving world, the focus of its mother's devotion. To itself, it appears omnipotent. When it needs food, it hallucinates a breast (or surrogate) and the breast appears, such that it appears to the child that it has created the desired object of its own volition. The hallucination is, of course, initially quite vague but it is enriched by real experiences of feeding so that the infant gradually acquires the ability to visualize and conjure up what is *actually* available (Winnicott 1945: 152–3). Winnicott argues that it is necessary for the child's development for the mother to make sure that the infant does indeed have these reinforcing and confirming experiences (by anticipating and responding rapidly to the child's needs), and Kohut (1977) too believes that a prolonged experience of omnipotence is essential for healthy psychic development. The mother must ensure that her reactions and responses correlate closely to the child's needs and wants, reflecting and mirroring its experience and gestures and confirming its sense of its own existence. The environment is, for a time, a close to perfect reflection of the child's needs. As Winnicott (1948: 246) puts it, 'The mind has a root, perhaps its most important root, in the need of the individual, at the core of the self, for a perfect environment.'

Klein (1975) argues that the child idealizes its positive experiences of feeding into an image of a 'good breast' (a metonym for the mother), and its negative experiences of blockage and difficulty into the 'bad breast'. This splitting technique is a defence against the painful reality of having to recognize that the mother has other things to do, and other people who compete for her attention, and that the child is not the centre of her world. For Winnicott, the mother's role is crucial in managing the whole situation, the feeding response, and the comfort after feeding. For him the critical dimension is that of the relationship itself, not the object of the relationship, which is Klein's focus. In Winnicott's scheme of things, other objects besides the mother and father assume importance. Winnicott further emphasizes the importance of the mother managing the process of gradual withdrawal, as the child and she enter into a system of communication by gesture and signals rather than physical contact, in which the mother's previously immediate adaptation to the child's needs becomes deferred, and the child develops the ability to separate, differentiate and realize for itself. In other words, we do not know that we are an individual, or even a human being, until someone else tells us so, and it is the manner and timing of this de-centring telling that is critical to functional psychic development. This could also be seen to correspond with the development of self as the moment of the child's entry into language, its fitting in to the system of others, as in Lacan's (1977) concept of the 'mirror-stage' in personality development.

The splitting of the good breast (all our positive experiences) from the bad (all our negative experiences) Klein calls the paranoid–schizoid position. The child fantasizes an omnipotent mother who loves it completely and responds to its every whim, which is not entirely a fantasy as we have seen, but clings on to this ideal of a return to fusion with the mother. Freud refers to this as the ego-ideal, or the imago. As Schwartz notes, Chasseguet-Smirgel (1985, 1986) argues that the ego-ideal represents the satisfaction of our desires. We become 'perfectly at home in the world, without anxiety or shame, sure of ourselves, certain of the validity of our behaviour without doubt or marginality' (Schwartz 1994: 3). Of course, this version of the world would entail the lives of all others revolving around us, and the very recognition of the independent existence of others occasions the anxiety inherent in becoming aware of our own de-centredness, contingency and the general indifference of the world to our needs. This Klein calls the depressive position. In this situation, we come to understand that others do not construct their lives around us. We learn to take the good with the bad.

We recognize that we, and others, are free to form relations as we wish, and we begin to become 'socialized'. The rules that we must learn in order to be socialized are presented to us through the 'paternal function', which is the main influence on the formation of the superego.

The superego is, in essence, the 'good father' corresponding to the ego-ideal's 'good mother'. The good father principle as the agent of society within the family leads the child to internalize its discipline, taking the perspective of the Other and punishing itself when the father would otherwise have punished it. The child begins to understand that it must at times do what it does not want to do, and learns how to fit in with the demands of others without becoming alienated from its own desire by the need for deferral. It becomes aware that there is a world outside its own imagination and that to be part of it entails certain obligations. In sum, the superego lays down the rules and enables us to fall in with the symbolic systems of others; the ego-ideal is a projection of our imaginary world (Lacan 1977):

> The superego provides the basis both of concrete achievement (Rothman, Lichter, and Lichter 1992) and for the renunciation of immediate gratification. The ego ideal is represented both as a developmental emotional bedrock and as a promise of what will happen if one fulfils one's obligations.
>
> (Schwartz 1994: 4)

Problems in the formation of the superego, in this schema, may lead to 'secondary narcissism'. The child feels angry and rejected when it realizes that others do not return its love, and appear to have abandoned it. It fantasizes itself merging with the good mother, to create the wished-for love relationship, in attempting to re-establish the state of primary and undifferentiated narcissism. This also entails the suppression of anxiety and guilt aroused by its frustration with the disappointing real object, that which fails to return its love (Lasch 1991 [1979]: 36).

The importance of the proper development of the ego-ideal is emphasized in Winnicott's work. He argues that, if the formation of the ego-ideal, the 'perfect' relationship with the mother, is impinged upon by others making demands and interrupting, the child loses touch with its spontaneous needs and impulses and its experience fragments. It avoids the possibility of being ignored, of expression without response, and the 'true self' goes into hiding. The 'false self' develops as a reflection of the demands of the mother and the environment, as the child strives to become the mother's image of it, reproducing only rewarded behaviours. Winnicott also argues that, with the inevitable disruption of the ego-ideal, the child often focuses on transitional objects, such as a teddy bear or security blanket, to represent the missing 'good mother', a 'developmental way station between hallucinatory omnipotence and the recognition of objective reality' (Greenberg and Mitchell 1983: 194–5). Adults as well as children constantly vacillate between these states. People, things, or organizational arrangements may all become transitional objects given that the key aspect is the relationship between subject and object, not the objective qualities of the thing itself.

The splitting in response to anxiety that we have discussed in relation to Klein and Winnicott's work is also addressed by Kristeva (1982: 6–7), who argues that, in addition to those strategies of negation (neutralizing) and denial that are characteristic of such neurotic and psychotic responses, there is also a strategy of exclusion. Here the object is recognized and identified as powerful, but ruled out of order and unacceptable in a normal existence. Because this element remains on the edge of awareness, it requires a defensive position to be established and constantly threatens the prevailing order. At the societal level, this is represented by rules of purity and pollution, as we have already remarked (Kristeva 1982: 65–79). The person who generates the abject Kristeva calls the deject – a person constantly obsessed with situating himself/herself relative to the acceptable/ unacceptable.

> A deviser of territories, languages, works, the *deject* never stops demarcating his universe whose fluid confines – for they are constituted of the non-object, the abject – constantly question his solidity and impel him to start afresh. A tireless builder, the deject is in short a *stray*.
>
> (Kristeva 1982: 8)

Significantly, and as we would expect from earlier discussion, Kristeva (1982: 56, 64) cites Bataille who argues that 'Abjection … is merely the inability to assume with sufficient strength the imperative act of excluding abject things (and that act establishes the foundations of collective existence).' In other words, abjection is founded on the weakness of the prohibition that forms the basis of social arrangements for the recognition of the sacred/profane, pure/impure and proper/improper. The abject remains to undermine these arrangements and categories. If we then apply this concept to the functioning of the superego, we can see that the improperly formed superego (where it is lax, repressive or punitive, therefore making it difficult for the child to integrate properly with society) will produce a personality which is constantly seeking order and stability by creating and re-creating rules and regulations to guarantee itself, but will nevertheless have a fascination with those things it seeks to exclude and which constantly leak back to threaten it. Lasch (1991 [1979]: 178–9) also notes the connection between the harsh and punishing superego and *thanatos*, the death/ destructive instinct. Moreover, he remarks on the tendency for restlessness, discontent, depressive moods, and a craving for substitute satisfactions associated with this connection.

From a child with developmental problems in maternal and paternal formations, we can therefore expect both a shifting ego-ideal and a fluctuating superego. A series of transitional objects may become important as the child and even the adult, in the absence of a clearly imagined ideal relationship, continues to search for substitutes. We might also expect a paradoxical arrogance, a deep hunger for affection and admiration, yet a contempt for those who provide it, and a hunger for emotional experiences to fill the inner void which might include sexual promiscuity. This might also include other forms of risk taking, craving after excitement, or excessive bids for the attention of others. Where a critical and punitive parental influence has shaped the superego, particularly one which appears capricious, we might expect the deject's insistent searching for order and rules, coupled with addictive tendencies. Alcohol in particular may be used to weaken the imperatives of the superego (Schwartz 1990: 129) which then progressively leads to a slide into abjection, accompanied by depressive moods, self-loathing, self-pity and dejection. We might also predict a lack of a capacity to mourn, grieve, apologize or even acknowledge error because of the intensity of rage against the parental figures. Close involvements are avoided by such an individual or, where they occur, often end up releasing intense rage and violence (Lasch 1991 [1979]: 37–9). Additionally, we might anticipate an element of sadism, and a belief in the right to exploit others, yet this might conflict with values embodied in the ego-ideal. In particular, we would expect the search for the ego-ideal to be influenced by societal images which promise to perform the ontological function (Schwartz 1990: 32) – an easy answer to the question 'Who should I be?' which provides an acceptable sense of identity for members of that society.

Masculinities and violence

The theoretical context having been established, we now consider in particular some widespread and important images of male identity which established support for the ego-ideal of men like Allan, his father and grandfather, and miti-gated against the fragmentation of the masculine self in the first half of the twentieth century. Levin comments that:

> The modern self, the self which appears in the metaphysical texts of moder-nity, is a self deeply divided, a self in which reason is split off from feeling, from sensibility, and from the innate wisdom of the body. It is also a self moved by the will to dominate. Even our self-knowledge must assume this character: the self exists in self-mastery and in the self-possession of the immediacy of certain knowledge.
>
> (Levin 1988: 20)

As Levin implies, the modern idea of self is one which is predicated on violence, on struggle, on persistence in the face of the inevitable and the pathos of brico-lage ranged against the ruin of a fragmented self; or, rather, the inescapable recognition that the hard-won 'unity' of that self was only ever partial and hence illusory. Each 'one' of us is a piece of violent self-creation, a tussle denying the openness to experience that Heidegger (1967) recognized as Being. As we have suggested, Lecercle (1990) recognizes that this mental violence operates even within language as it claims for itself domination over the province of 'meaning', negating and denying the operation of the 'remainder', that which language leaves behind glowing like one of Derrida's (1991) cinders and which, though silent, is constantly active and necessary for meaning to take place at all, the smoking gun of the modern positive project.

The symbolic struggle for Western modern identity has often been projected, sometimes romantically and sometimes not, on to the American West in story and film. The frontiersman alone against the unformed, unordered elements which threatened to physically fragment him; the Indian fighter against the superstitious and mercurial savage; the lone lawman striding out on to the main street at high noon against the dark forces of disorder. These were images which shaped Allan's childhood, and that of his father's generation before him. They clamoured too for the attention of the minds of his grandfather's generation, who may have been only dimly aware of the actual circumstances of life and death in the Wild West, but knew that the pioneer's story represented their struggle against their own harsh frontier, although here cobblestones replaced tumbleweed. The powerful, self-confident characters of the Western battled through adversity and doubt to tame the wilderness, yet usually in a spirit of self-sacrifice that might even entail self-destruction. Like Davy Crockett at the Alamo, these were compelling metaphors for the early twentieth-century struggle for masculine consciousness, and the film actors who played these heroes developed and embodied important role models for the man in the street, as Simon (1996: 99–100) notes. In fact, Simon argues that the significance of the audience has been neglected in cultural criticism, which is particularly unfortunate for contemporary cultural forms such as feature film, because as Freud first pointed out the dramatic medium exploits intrapsychic conflict within the hero, a conflict of contradictory wishes of which the hero may be unaware. Freud's main insight here, which Simon takes up, is that dramatic representations are only effective in locating real, fluid and often elusive emotions 'when the audience shares to some degree the same unconscious conflicts, elements of the same psychopathology' (Simon 1996: 100). For Simon, the importance of this genre is in locating the 'normal pathologies' resulting from Western male adolescence and their continuing residues in the lives of male adults, the genre of historical fantasy metaphorically allowing the emphasis of characteristics not normally acknowledged in more contemporary or realistic expressions of everyday life.

Masculinity itself has been regarded as problematic since (and possibly even before the onset of) Ancient Greek civilization. However as both Bordo (1986) and Horrocks (1994: 7) point out, what T.S. Eliot refers to as a 'dissociation of sensibility', associated with a separation of mind and body, rational and non-rational, intellect and feeling, science and spirit, did not set in until the late Renaissance. Masculinity became associated with the first element in each dualism, femininity with the latter, and the connection of mind and intellect to the public, political and economic sphere, and of feeling and emotion to the private, domestic sphere, exacerbated these processes of social division. Men became dominant in the former arena, women in the latter, and, as Horrocks (1994: 26–8) argues, each therefore became powerful within their demarcated zones of influence – men economically and politically, women emotionally and psychologically. Horrocks discusses the novels of D. H. Lawrence and the American Western in this regard as a defensive reaction to the spiritual domination of the female in nineteenth century America (Horrocks 1994: 6–8, 42–3, 151–4, see also Tompkins 1992). In a similar vein, Wright (1975, 1994: 123–6) identifies the mythic narrative structures of the classic Western, with sixteen key functions, three character groups (heroes, villains and society), and four binary oppositions (inside/outside; good/bad; strong/weak; and wilderness/civilization) which define these characters and their points of conflict and opposition. We now consider one such film which, as Simon (1996: 100) points out, has received considerable critical attention despite its apparently conventional and even regressive qualities, but which deploys the dimensions discussed above in a way which illuminates their provision of symbolic reference points for the identities of men of Allan and his father's generation.

The Man Who Shot Liberty Valance is a 1962 film, directed by John Ford. A studio production with no location shots, it has little visual compulsion. It is thematically interesting in that it plays, in a modest way, with the four binary dimensions referred to above, featuring two heroes, each of whom is flawed and each of whom carries a burden on behalf of society. One of the heroes ultimately stays physically within the society but is rejected by it to die in obscurity; the other moves on to greater glory but remains its hero and most famous son. The film also narratively places what would more conventionally be its climax, the fight, about two-thirds of the way through the story in order to explore the moral problems of living on. In contra-distinction, a traditional Western such as *Shane* explicitly avoids such engagement, with lines like 'there's no living with a killing' (Wright 1994: 125), whereas lesser works often assume that, despite the preceding carnage, there are no tensions involved in settling down and living happily ever after. The central theme of *Liberty Valance*, from a Freudian perspective, is that of castration.

Allan remembers this film as having been almost the last one he saw with his father, who identified closely with Tom Doniphin, the rancher character played by John Wayne. Tough and able, streetwise but unschooled, hard-working but unsophisticated, Doniphin is honest but practical, a pragmatist and survivor who will fight if threatened, but not for his principles alone. Ransome Stoddard, the character played by James Stewart, is a lawyer – thoughtful, intelligent, full of enlightenment values, gentle but morally as uncompromising as Doniphin is physically – who unwittingly robs Doniphin of his simple dream. In fact, Doniphin effectively gifts this to him, along with his glittering future (Stoddard goes on to become Senator and Ambassador to the Court of St James), in two unselfish acts. One is the shooting of Liberty Valance (Lee Marvin), the local bad guy, in the process saving Stoddard's life and allowing him to take the credit for the deed, so that he becomes a local hero; the second is disclosing these facts only privately to Stoddard at the right time when, believing himself to be a killer, Stoddard undergoes a moral crisis and is about to withdraw his candidature for Congress. Doniphin's double-barrelled burden of this secret, guilty truth and the loss of his dream destroys him and he embraces both failure and the bottle, burning down the ranch-house he was building for the girl (Hallie) who has now gone away with Stoddard, and ultimately dying, unremembered by anyone except as the town drunk.[7]

Simon (1996: 100–1) identifies three types of narcissism embodied in the characters of Valance, Doniphin and Stoddard. Valance embodies narcissistic grandiosity – the idealization of personal ambition, the 'dark side of over-masculinized individualism' (Simon 1996: 101), the refusal to submit the values of adolescence to the more practical demands of social life, a 'cruel' and 'sadistic' version of 'the last legacy of childhood' (Simon 1996: 104). He wants what he wants and, with few exceptions, has no need to defer gratification. Doniphin embodies narcissistic honour – which entails preserving a more precarious equilibrium between personal ambitions and desires and the social mores which constrain them. Doniphin's increasing maturity is indicated by his desire to marry and his building of the ranch-house, his continuing immaturity by his inability to articulate this effectively to the object of his affections and his difficulty in abandoning the '"heroic" postures so antagonistic to the life of domesticity' (Simon 1996: 101) – a man's still gotta do what a man's gotta do, even if he is virtually engaged to be married. Stoddard embodies social honour – a developed sense of the 'ought', a submission of control over behaviour to the collective code, a transformation of what the adolescent bully would see as snivelling weakness into heroic self-sacrifice. Stoddard represents men, not as masters of literal violence, but as masters of symbolic violence – the rules of the games that need to be played in order for men to be thought successful. As Simon notes, those who are successful game players – whether in winning, appearing to have won, or appearing not to have lost – often promote the ideology that these games are more than just games, the result of something more than just superficial cleverness. Honour emerges where there is a conflict between desires, between morality and practicality, between self and reality.

Valance plays his own game, and loses because he is cheated, although in his personal code this is not problematic – you rig the game because the stakes are the highest, triumph or death. Doniphin knows this game, and can play it, yet recognizes that there are some rules – the unwritten 'code of the West' that you don't shoot a man in the back, for example – as well as seeing something more important than these simple rules. He technically violates one code by shooting Valance from a backstreet in order to preserve what Stoddard stands for. Then he is unable to reveal the truth because this would expose Stoddard as an unwitting fraud, and himself as a cowardly code-breaker. In acting as he did, Doniphin is neither a winner nor a loser – just irrelevant (Simon 1996: 108). He is unhappy with the game he understands, yet doesn't understand how to play any other game properly, whether it be politics or domesticity.

Elements of narcissistic grandiosity, which all men must at some point renounce even if only to the realm of the abject, and aspirations for or attempts at social honour with success are familiar to those struggling with the demands of contemporary masculinity. Yet it is the area of conflict which characterizes narcissistic honour which is probably most familiar – where the penis must be abandoned for the phallus, at the risk of castration or impotence. Thus the critical similarity between Allan's father and Doniphin, which the former perhaps intuitively recognized in his identification with the latter, lies in Doniphin's response to his failure to achieve his personal dream which is, of course, the American Dream. Allan's father loved to feel himself the maker of the decisive intervention in a situation, especially if it was one which was unappreciated by the general population, which would give him more emotional ammunition as the victim, the one who took on everyone else's problems without thanks. He identified with Doniphin's self-sacrifice more than with any other aspect of his character. He would also have applauded Stoddard's enduring guilt, even at the end of a long and successful career in which he had achieved the American Dream in all but peace of mind, because he needed the winners to acknowledge that life is not fair.[8] But most of all, when Doniphin realizes that the dream is not to be his, because he didn't understand the rules of the game he needed to play in order to get it, he captures the moment of dread, when we ourselves realize as inevitably we must that we all fall short of the ego-ideal. Doniphin's self-loathing at that moment propels itself into violence and anger, the dark rebelliousness of narcissistic grandiosity turned against itself, as his punitive superego castigates him. One effective way to relax a punitive superego is of course to drink alcohol, but that as we have argued also risks letting the demons of repressed anger against the parents – who didn't demonstrate how to play the game, or demonstrated the wrong game, or were losers themselves – out of Pandora's box. This appears to be exactly what happened with Allan's father. As he began to find that his dream was not being attained according to its specifications, as he both continuously set impossible moral standards for his family yet nevertheless sought compensatory alternative experiences through promiscuity which inevitably produced even more guilt, unworthiness and self-loathing, he attempted to let up on his internal self-humiliation through increasing his drinking, which released even more repressed anger, against himself and others. Ultimately, like Doniphin, he metaphorically burned his own ranch-house down, in his case because in effect it needed a coat of paint.

The sting of deprivation

We have already discussed the problems that a punitive superego can create in setting impossible standards and eroding self-confidence through constant introspective criticism, such that the self is reflexively being constantly found wanting. The superego can also pass on those punitive imperatives under which it is most uncomfortable, and in this section we would like to consider the effects of such a reproduction in relation to Allan's experiences.

> Those most beset by commands are children. It is a miracle that they ever survive the pressure and do not collapse under the burden of the commands laid on them by their parents and teachers. That they in turn, and in an equally cruel form, should give identical commands to their children is as

natural as mastication or speech. What is surprising is the way in which commands are retained intact and unaltered from the earliest childhood, ready to be used again as soon as the next generation provides victims. ... The depth of the impression which commands make on children and the tenacity and fidelity with which they are preserved owe nothing to the qualities of the individual child; intelligence or exceptional gifts have nothing to do with it. No child, not even the most ordinary, forgets or forgives a single one of the commands inflicted on it ... the new situation which releases the command must be the exact replica of the situation in which it was received. This reproduction of earlier situations, but *in reverse*, is one of the chief sources of energy.

(Canetti 1987: 354–5)

Consistent with Canetti's argument, it is characteristic that, when love is withheld from those who most crave it, they lose the ability to give it themselves, as 'love rejected turns back on the self as hatred' (Kernberg 1975, cited in Lasch 1991 [1979]: 35). Allan's recounted experience of relations with his father is one of constant frustration, of being expected to be first in all things, his modest sporting achievements being ridiculed, his academic excellence always being found capable of improvement, his career preferences being challenged violently, his friends, music, and opinions being contested, scorned, belittled and dismissed. Promises of reward were made and not honoured, because Allan was always accused of misinterpreting the undertaking, or having done something which was not up to his father's ever-shifting mark. From Allan's later discussions with his grandparents (his father disclosed very little about his past life, and Allan believes that much of it must have given him pain), it was clear that his father had craved affection and been denied it; indeed, the more he craved it, the more weakness he was deemed to show, and the more was affection denied. Allan's father was geographically moved around frequently, from school to school, and was unable to form enduring and redeeming friendships. His father and mother had children from previous marriages, and he was frequently left alone by both of them. Allan's grandmother repeatedly left his grandfather on account of his violence, and Allan's father would return home from school to find himself locked out of the house. He therefore developed a fear of locked doors: when he encountered them as a child, it meant his mother had abandoned him and soon another of his father's mistresses would be moving in. In his craving for a good and loving, stable relationship, he attributed these characteristics of love and permanence to his own relationships too readily. He then blamed his all too human partners for the failure to measure up to his ever more exacting standards, these in themselves driven by his innate fear of intimacy, a destructive drive that was almost frustrated by his second marriage, to Allan's mother (of twenty-two years). After they split up, he continued his womanizing by moving a married woman into the house, which he perversely justified by accusing Allan's mother of abandoning him. This of course, according to his lights, was what had happened and was also unforgivable, making him no longer responsible for his actions. Indeed, he seemed to be incapable of living on his own and entered into a series of dubious and short-lived relationships in order to satisfy his thirst for companionship, all of which he publicly flaunted to the puzzlement of his associates and the embarrassment of his family. His behaviour was typically narcissistic, moving from an immense arrogance and cruel independence which was but a thin mask of his self-pity and self-loathing, to a palpable and demanding dependency on others, friends, lovers or colleagues. Yet despite his enormous need for affection, no one did more to alienate others, which is entirely consistent with narcissism.

Moreover, Allan's father's attempts to get close to people often seemed to embarrass him and turned into a form of manipulation, ultimately resulting in the humiliation of the person who had responded to his apparent generosity or vulnerability. Here again a pattern from his own early life was endlessly repeated. A gift, which would later turn out to have had conditions, was a major token of his expression of concern for his loved ones, but inevitably turned into an expression of contempt for their weakness and dependence when they accepted it. As Allan tells it:

> When my father was in his thirties, he was saving up for his first car. His father urged him to borrow the money from him, which my father was reluctant to do, but he was persuaded that he could give his father lifts occasionally when needed, that it wouldn't be so much of a loan after all, and that it was better than making repayments to a bank. Soon, however, he was being required to run his father all over town, and whilst standing at the bar (for his father never went anywhere else) he would be ridiculed as a chauffeur, put down as having only half a car, suddenly required to produce money and told 'I'll knock it off what you owe.' Eventually he sold the vehicle and repaid the money to his father of his own volition as he could not stand the humiliation.

Despite the mortifying effect this behaviour had on him, Allan's father was unable to come to terms with it. Allan in fact only found out about this incident from his mother, as his father never spoke about it, although it had happened during Allan's childhood and he had often wondered what had happened to their little car in the family photographs. Yet, consistent with our understanding of abjection, he repeated the pattern in his relations with Allan:

> When I was sixteen my father bought me a motorcycle (I had wanted a scooter like my friends, but he insisted as he had a mate with a motorbike shop) as a reward for my examination performance. The following year, I arranged to sell it and buy a small car. I sold the bike on Friday evening, and was to collect and pay for the car on Saturday morning. I put the money in a big blue vase in the dining room, but my mother warned me that my father would take it from me if he found it. I couldn't believe that he would do it, but he came right in and snatched it out of the vase. 'I bought the

bike, so it's my money – you own nothing,' he said. I was left with the humiliation of pulling out of the deal, and being left without transport into the bargain. Some years later he visited my house and stayed for a few days, but claimed that the cooker was not good enough for my wife to use (although this did not reflect the actual division of household duties). He insisted that I order a new one, which he would pay for. I insisted that I could not afford to pay him back and would not accept it. Nevertheless he said that it did not matter and he wrote out a cheque for the cooker. Two years later we were in a public bar with other friends and relatives when he loudly interrogated 'When am I going to get that 300 quid I lent you for the cooker?'

The tendency or, as Canetti notes, the inevitability of harsh authoritarian parents to so firmly imprint their behaviour on the psyches of their children that they repeat it themselves seems to be well illustrated here. Repressed but not banished, under house arrest, it still exerts its pull, its call to action. It can remain dormant for years, as it did in Allan's father's case, and then return to destroy a life. It falls into the category of the abject, and Allan's father's response was a gradual but accelerating descent into abjection which he was never totally able to repudiate. Moreover, he reportedly continues in a much subdued way to reproduce those behaviours which he abhors. As Canetti also points out, a similar pattern can occur within any authoritarian structure of command, and though the 'sting' may not go so deep, we can nevertheless expect that victims of organizational abuse and bad practice will, however unwittingly and with whatever elaborate legitimating rationale, reproduce such behaviours unless they are made specifically aware of what is happening and take action to prevent it.[9] If those behaviours are the result of parental abuse and not simply institutional mistreatment, they are likely to be much harder to repudiate. But even if the behaviours are renounced the victim remains disadvantaged, for their own historical abuse robs them of a sense of balance. Having been repeatedly wounded by authority it is difficult to develop a model of its responsible exercise. Thus, as Lasch (1991 [1979]: 176–80) notes, authority is often abdicated by those who are uncomfortable in exercising control, who cannot plot a path between self-critical punishment and self-indulgence. Often they oscillate, sometimes violently, between the two.

Violence and addictive behaviour

> One way and another we compromise in tiny steps until we come to realise –
> perhaps with a shock – we are standing on alien ground. To make such discoveries, and retrace our steps, it is essential not to be willingly caught up in an
> illusion of truth-telling. It is hard enough without it.
>
> (Farber, cited in Greenberg and Mitchell 1983: 188)

We have already remarked on the connections between narcissism, addictive behaviour and violence, and some of the images of masculinity which support them. However, masculinity is also shaped by a sense, or conversely a lack, of ethnic or class identity. Some of the contours of alcohol addiction, violence and male working-class consciousness which parallel Allan's father's existence are explored in a remarkable novel by Alan Duff (which has also been adapted into a 1994 film). *Once Were Warriors* (1994) tells the story of a Maori family, the Hekes, living in Pine Block estate in Two Lakes, New Zealand. Of the advanced economies, New Zealand boasts the greatest divide between rich and poor, according to the OECD. The Maori are dislocated – working people who can't work, warriors who can't fight, people without history who no longer understand their heritage or their traditional language, a community which first turns upon itself with rage and then to itself for comfort, its sorrows lubricated by alcohol, the liquid bars on the prison of despair.

Jake Heke is the man with big muscles, the toughest guy, the man with the biggest 'rep' (reputation) for fighting in town. Unemployed for two years, he lives off the drinks others are willing to buy him to stay on his good side, just in case. Nevertheless he considers himself to be an enlightened modern male as he gives his wife fully half of his money – from which she only has to pay the bills, feed and clothe his five children and entertain his friends. Jake's only perspective on the world is through violence. His self-love is of course fragile, and the drink that he uses to fuel and preserve it leads him, incrementally, to greater and greater despicability, without his being able to acknowledge it. For example, he rejects his 15-year-old son, Boogie, because he can't fight.

> His own kid. And being disowned because he couldn't fight. What about Boogie's other qualities? Always near the top of the class, very kind, and *very* sensitive to the kids that everyone else forgets about, or scorns. Nope, you got to be able to fight first.
>
> (Duff 1994: 23)

Boogie then seeks his father's admiration through criminal non-conformity and is taken away from the family. Both parents, separately, are so drunk that they don't even make the court hearing. Similarly, Nig, the 17-year-old eldest, wants to be like his father. Not embracing the comfort of drink, he thinks he finds the family he needs in the Brown Fist gang. Testing his loyalty, his new family force him to miss the funeral of his sister, Grace, who hanged herself in the garden of a rich family after her drunken father raped her. Jake's descent means that he also misses the funeral of his daughter, in his case because he is drunk. Beth, his wife, ejects him as a result, and in the process he is downed with one punch by an old friend who has returned to town. His reputation gone, he is still able to work as a bouncer until he viciously assaults someone. The drinks stop coming, he lives with the winos until they throw him out of the house, and he then lives rough in the park. Meeting a neglected child also living rough, Jake finally begins to discover some vestigial human tenderness inside himself by befriending the waif, but he is still so outcast, so abject, that he has to watch Nig's funeral (he has been killed in a gang fight) from the distant safety of some trees.

Beth, the battered wife, is the character who descends into and then emerges from the maelstrom. Her story is, for the first part of the novel, Jake's – drawn by love and her own demons, she drinks and smokes her life away, her life structured by the fear of his violence. She hides changes of clothing around the house for those occasions when she wants to sneak out without disturbing him – as much in fear of his preferred form of reconciliation (sex) as his renewed anger. Spurred by self-reflection and Boogie's being taken into care, she kicks the drink, and eventually manages to save enough money to buy a big picnic and hire a car so that Jake can take the whole family to visit him. Jake drives around town, lording it with the car, and gradually the day slips away. He drops into the bar for 'one drink'. Eventually Beth goes in to fetch him and is lured into joining them until the day is gone. She returns to the car and sends the disappointed kids to buy some food and play:

> A woman sitting there watching her kids, four ofem anyrate, troop off into the dusk. The fast-gathering dusk. And all she can do is sit here feeling like nuthin' on earth ready to pounce on that picnic soon as they're out of sight. And kids runnin around the place. Little buggers. Horrible little buggers. Least mine've got a decent mother who ... who *cares* about em (I do. I truly do). But feeling as if she was being driven by some force greater than herself. Watching ... watching them disappear so she could jump, like a thief in the night, the almost night, onto what was theirs, her children's, their food, their treat, sposed to be their day.
>
> (Duff 1994: 110)

That night, the drunks return to the Heke home and eat the kids' picnic. Mark (Boogie) waits in the home for his visitors who never arrive, and Grace stands in the garden of the idealized Trambert family, gazing longingly at what secure and caring family life is like. Seeing a father lovingly bid his daughter goodnight, she climbs the nearest tree and hangs herself.

Beth, fired by the note which Grace left about being raped by her father, and with the help of friends, throws Jake out, reclaims her home and, aided by the elders, reclaims her cultural history. There is no room in this society for the brawler or the killer. But there are other qualities of the warrior culture which are noble and redeeming, and Beth is able to rediscover her racial identity and with it her self-respect. The house becomes the centre of the neighbourhood regeneration, Boogie gets the education he deserves, but Nig still has to die before the final redemption can be won. And Jake, still struggling with his own demons, an outcast on the edge of society, teeters on the edge of enlightenment.

As Schwartz notes:

> for the alcoholic, drinking is a way to induce a manic defence. Within this analysis, one has become an alcoholic when the self-centred world as seen

within the intoxicated state is taken as one's real world. Hence, one needs to drink in order to resume contact with and verify one's own reality. It follows from this that, as one comes to take one's narcissistic fantasies as reality, the more out of touch with the real world one becomes, hence the more one needs to drink in order to 'verify' one's fantasies, and again, the further out of touch one becomes. Within this logic we can see the progressive element of the alcoholic's disease.

(1990: 129)

Both Jake and Beth beautifully illustrate this progression of self-deception in the passage of their lives from dissolution to tragedy, and even greater tragedy, at each step constructing another rationalization, another excuse. In fact Jake's illness is so far advanced that he has barely a glimpse of the possibility of a return to reality. Similarly, Allan's father's intoxicated version of reality placed him firmly at the centre of a world in which he was unloved, neglected, and unappreciated. Everything he did was done for others who failed to acknowledge the fact of his selflessness, and the answer to this predicament, as the family were repeatedly informed, was for them to 'get your minds sorted out'. They were loved, they were often told in the aftermath of some horror, but they didn't love him, didn't do anything for him, didn't realize how horrible life would be without him. Against the harrowing dissonance of everyday experience, they were all pushed to the edge of psychosis.

> As recently as a couple of years ago he told me that he never touched my mother more than a couple of times, and even then it was 'only a love tap'. He remains so deep in denial that, had I not seen the bruises, seen the door off its hinges where she had careened into it after a blow, heard the screams as he hauled her sleeping form out of bed by the pubic hair, even been threatened and struck myself (on one occasion only that I recall) I could almost have believed it.

Allan's father lived in a world in which he was entirely justified. The progressive commitment to this fantastic version of reality was also exhibited in other ways. He frequently said or did things to others which were outrageous, insulting or tactless. In order to demonstrate that he meant no harm by it, that it was innocuous, and that it truly was their problem, he would then do it again. This would just widen the escalating gulf between the worlds – in his escalating commitment to his fantasy world he would be confirmed in his view that his behaviour was harmless as it was so easily repeatable, but his victim would be doubly outraged. He would often hit Allan's mother twice to emphasize that the first one was inoffensive. Moreover, his imagined isolation quickly became a reality – he could at that point have relinquished drink entirely as his fantasies of abandonment had become concrete.

However, in contrast to the story of Jake Heke, the anger, the aggression and the fantasy of the frustrated warrior had nothing to offer Allan's father by way of solace. Although he had a working-class street-fighting past he had always been found wanting by his own father despite his pugilistic successes on the spoil-heaps of the 1930s – *his* father had been a professional boxer, and a renowned champion. He alternately proudly embraced his past, then rejected it in shame. His version of the working-class ethic became a degenerate one, a romanticized notion of fellowship which he coupled with a rather petulant ideal of individual self-help. But in this scheme there was no middle ground, no existential aware-ness of the family except as an extension of his *need* of a family, not as a collection of real individuals with their own wants, gifts, faults and aspirations. His lack of a happy family background led him to incorporate the idea of a family as part of his narcissistic ego-ideal, and his real family had to mirror this fantasy. When they fell short, when they demonstrated they had needs, demands and dreams, abilities and career plans which did not coincide with his own construction of their place in his scheme, he of course blamed reality, not the false ideal. The family was no reconciling structure that would help him to locate an identity other than that of the frustrated, isolated, unappreciated warrior, that would allow him to grow and develop to give and return affection within the family without guilt or shame. As it did not fit his ideal, it had to be changed or destroyed. He destroyed it.

Victims living on

Duff's novel leaves us with both tragedy and hope, but we are left to imagine for ourselves how the family will fare in the future after its traumas.[10] But for our argument here we need to consider what happens to those who survive violence in similar circumstances, and examine what sort of scars are left. We must also begin to consider how this affects adult lives in organizations. Let us then look at a further example that has recently come to light after over fifty years of suppres-sion. This concerns an organization created by and run through violence but which ironically, until 1990, was regarded as an unequivocal triumph of the Christian spirit, and whose crimes have only, as recently as 1996, been denounced by the Catholic Church.

Bindoon Boys' Town is an impressive structure. Its entrance is dominated by a huge stone statue of Brother Paul Francis Keaney, 'The Orphan's Friend' who masterminded its construction. Sixty miles north of Perth, Western Australia, it is a sister institution to Castledare and Clontarf, to the south of Perth, and Tardun, about 210 miles further north. All these institutions are run by the Christian Brothers, founded in Ireland by Edmund Rice in 1809, and who came to Australia in 1869, founding their first orphanage in 1894. Bindoon covers 17,000 cleared acres. It consists of seven very large and ornate colonial-style buildings, two to three storeys high with towers in addition, boasting under-ground water tanks, hundreds of miles of fencing, dams and bores, and cultivated paddocks of wheat with flourishing orchards and vineyards. It is even more remarkable to think that the whole edifice was constructed by boys between the ages of eight and eighteen, without proper tools or machinery, even without underwear, pyjamas, shoes or socks, sleeping in tents under a single army blanket until they built their own quarters, between 1942 and 1954. As one survivor recalls:

> Boulders and stones had to be collected and stockpiled, ready for the foundations of stage two of the planned building project. To accomplish the mammoth task, the boys carried, rolled or dragged the stones and boulders to the sled they had been given to use. The sleds consisted of two wooden bearers rounded at the front end, with a wooden platform laid across them. A rope was attached to the front end of the bearers and this was used to drag the sled. The boys would heave and strain to get the sleds across the paddocks to the area from which they were to collect the boulders, then they dragged their onerous load all the way back to the intended building site.
>
> Day after bloody, back-breaking day, week after week, in all weathers, the work went on. Shoulders were rubbed raw from the ropes, feet cut and bleeding. Yet still Brother Keaney roared, '*Pull*, you lazy shits. Come on, you good-for-nothing bastards. PULL ...'
>
> (Davies, K. 1994: 97)

The boys here were not only slaves, subjected to a strict disciplinary regime and deprived of both affection and physical comforts, but they were also depersonalized objects which the brothers used for entertainment in mock sporting contests such as blindfold boxing tournaments. The boys were, moreover, useful devices on whom they vented their anger in frequent criminal assaults, regardless of whether the targeted boy had done anything to occasion or even merit their displeasure:

> Sadistic Keaney thrust with direct force a bloody stick with a bullet-shaped metal casing on the end, right up my rectum and lower bowel, causing immediate acute, prolonged pain, shock, bleeding and a dreadful feeling of degradation. And to think it happened at a building site at approximately 3.30 pm on a very hot stinking day, where I had been working almost non-stop from seven o'clock that morning. Brother Keaney had difficulty removing the stick, and a few minutes later he examined me to see what damage had been done. Without any word of sympathy or regret, the sadistic bastard Keaney told me to go and clean myself up and get back to work.
>
> (Davies, K. 1994: 170)

But violence of this nature was not the only form of abuse in which the Brothers indulged. The place most dreaded was the dairy, where one of the Brothers enjoyed showing them 'a different way to make cream', as he put it. Even in their dormitory beds the boys weren't safe, because the Brothers had a power over their lives which reached from the City Mayor and magistrates right down to their most private moments. Not only was flight pointless, as the eyes and ears of the Brothers stretched right across Western Australia, but even after the inmates reached adulthood and were discharged from the orphanage, their experiences went with them. As another victim reflects:

> I've been married for thirty years. I've got my own house. I've had the same job for thirty years. I've got children and grandchildren. I don't owe anybody anything.
>
> To look at me, anyone would think I have achieved the Australian dream. But when I was eight years old, I was called into this Brother's room at bedtime. Here was this man who looked about ten feet tall in his black robes. He made me suck him off. He made me do that twice a week for six or seven weeks until he got sick of me and got another boy. The point of the story is that not one day of my life goes by when that doesn't come back to haunt me. The older I get the worse it gets. I get terrible flashbacks. Maybe when I'm playing with my grandchildren or when I'm at work or I wake up in the middle of the night. You can't just tell people to forget it and then get on with their lives.
>
> (Davies, K. 1994: 171)

Many of the other Bindoon orphans interviewed by Davies developed common responses to assuage this torment and bolster their sense of self-worth. Typical was workaholism, the drug to which they had been exposed in childhood, their young life of forced hard labour becoming their self-inflicted adult habit. Typical also was intolerance of a lack of the same obsessive work ethic in others, which made these others easy to blame. Survivors also reported difficulty in tolerating children simply being children, as they had themselves been robbed of a normal childhood. Starved of affection for so long, they found difficulty in giving it. In some of them, this did not emerge until their own children began to show signs of being independent and occasionally truculent as they entered their teens, which brought out an authoritarian reaction in their parents. Subtle approaches to natural emotional problems they found particularly problematic. For many, workaholism was a route to success, and they found this easiest working on their own behalf or in a succession of jobs involving travel and rootlessness. They worked hard, even incessantly, feeling guilty if they didn't work on any given day, and frequently pushed their family lives to the brink of collapse by their immersion in work, which was often carried out recklessly and with scant regard for safety. Many families were, unsurprisingly, unable to take the strain of this obsessiveness.

Even the successful like Karl 'Skinny' Davies, who founded and sold up several prosperous businesses, found it difficult to work for others and felt extremely sensitive to being pushed around by even the most minimal exercise of authority. Karl always felt that someone or something would take what he had, and was constantly moving on from place to place, constantly winding up a good thing, finding it difficult to make a commitment and often, for no apparent reason, disappearing completely only to turn up again after a few weeks or months – indeed, this pattern extended right through into his later life. Although he was never physically violent, his tongue was his lash and his family soon learned when to avoid discussion. Karl also suffered from recurrent nightmares, tormented by a sense of shame that, if his true background were ever found out, he would lose the respect and love of those he most cared for.

Work behaviour and the legacy of violence

The unhappy experiences which these men had of violence in their early lives clearly affected them in their later organizational lives as managers and co-workers, and their behaviours affected those of their colleagues. To return to our consideration of Allan and his family, we find a unique opportunity for comparison, as Allan's father took over the job of Allan's grandfather when he died in post, although at the time they did not work for the same organization and the job was subject to a public election. Each of them held the post for twenty-five years, and in the case of Allan's father it precipitated a cycle of repetitive and destructive behaviour which, six years on, cost him his marriage to Allan's mother. Despite his technical excellence in the job, his authoritarian style and violent tongue often made him enemies and ultimately cost him advancement to a national post.

The job both men held was unusual, being that of permanent general secretary to a group of some 200 co-operative businesses in the hospitality and leisure industries. The group was run by a committee which was elected and which it was Allan's father's job to service. The committee was exclusively made up of men from the same violent working-class sub-culture as Allan's father. Many of them were out to settle old scores, several did not fully understand the job and their role, some resented the fact that Allan's father had been able to move out of the areas they came from yet still depended on them for his expensive suits and flashy car, and some just did not like being told what to do by an 'expert'. Allan's father found it difficult to cope with his lack of success in this verbally violent sub-committee, and being forced to carry out decisions with which he disagreed. The committee placed many of the same constraints upon him as his father had, yet the very tools and procedures he had for dealing with this were those he had acquired from his father. Despite the combative street-corner atmosphere to much of his work, however, it did have an associated other side.

Buchbinder (1994: 38–9) notes that working-class co-operative groups offer a haven of 'mateship', often ludicrously nostalgic and sentimental even in its emotional autism, and perhaps also melancholic. Nonetheless, the highly rivalrous nature of men's relations with other men, as is visible in Westley's (1990) and Collinson's (1988, 1992) accounts, also emerges in these areas of comfort. Stories of sexual exploits, fast living and hard drinking, and frequent real-world attempts to live up to them, are used to warrant the underlying fantasy of masculinity and what it means to be male in such a society. Allan recalls that drink and drinking were constant themes in his father's life, and that even as a boy he learned to direct strangers by the names of public houses and licensed premises rather than the more usual landmarks. He also recounts that drinking with his father was always an intense and competitive affair (Mangham 1996), and that there was even competition regarding who should pay for the round of drinks, an oppression through gift-giving which is familiar to anthropologists. Because of the nature of the business of the co-operatives, Allan's father found himself constantly 'in the field', which could entail three- or four-hour drinking sessions at lunchtime and again in the evening, on as many as seven days a week. Several independent commentators have studied the relationship between drinking, the pub/club environment and violence and have found positive links (Boyatzis 1974; Gibbs 1986; Homel and Tomsen 1993; Polk 1994). They note that the act of drinking deadens the effect of the competitiveness of the drinking sessions themselves, which of course are usually intended to be a release of the tension and aggression of the working atmosphere. Indeed, all Allan's father appeared to be able to do in these circumstances was to reproduce the very machismo he detested in the local sub-culture and his governing body. He reproduced it in his own office organization, and staff deserted him; he reproduced it in his field consultations with his clients, and lost political support; he reproduced it at national level where he was a representative, and as a consequence failed in bids to become both President and General Secretary; and, of course, he reproduced it in his own domestic life. Drink became an addiction for him, and so did those behaviours which, even when sober, he appeared compelled to reproduce.

Given what we have already observed about narcissism, the abject and Allan's father's own background, we could expect his behaviour to shift between a constantly shifting ego-ideal and a fluctuating self-image – between extremes of self-indulgence and self-denial. In the office he was certainly obsessed with order and system, tight controls, prescriptions and procedures, whereas outside he displayed little self-control, although he was still determined to control others, especially when his usual rigidities were relaxed by alcohol. This is typical of abjection in its inability to distinguish boundaries between the acceptable or appropriate and the unacceptable or inappropriate in the absence of rigid prescriptions, and the associated obsession with rules, order and models. Allan's father also attached himself to a series of transitional objects, both human and material, who were distinguished only by the purpose they played in his scheme of things and not by their personal and individual qualities. He always had a 'best mate' – who changed periodically – to function as a substitute for real relationships with his family and colleagues. These best mates eventually withdrew from the scene as the pressures of bearing what was projected on to them grew too claustrophobic and they found it impossible to be themselves in his company. The range of substitutes also included members of the opposite sex, with whom, as we have already noted, he formed a series of restless and turbulent liaisons, which were equally competitive and violently confrontational. These relationships illustrated the converse side of Allan's father's violence and, of course, its root – a desperate need to be loved which emerged as a mawkish sentimentality about 'mateship' in general. Organizationally, this destroyed his political credibility as he was unable to build alliances with others, being unable to comprehend the real reasons why people made them. His approach was either to bully others into submission (intellectually or psychologically) or to morally impugn them for inconstancy and flatly demand loyalty. He found it very diffi-cult to win people over through rational persuasion as he regarded every issue as being decidable either through the requirements of friendship or by trial of strength. His resulting failures to achieve greater work-related goals – his two defeats in national elections were numbing rejections by the organization of the love he offered it – rebounded on him and redoubled his self-loathing, making his problems even more intractable.

Allan, and to a lesser extent his brother, are struggling to be good managers against this legacy. They work in different industries and are both currently enjoying success, but they both claim to be driven by a sense that someone is going to take away what they have achieved. They have both changed jobs frequently – indeed, Allan has not held a single job for more than three years. Both report the perceived need to keep a potentially violent temper in check, although they are patient and successful negotiators. They both work long hours and bring work home, and they both report that their decision-making tends to alternate between periods of tight control and great relaxation without any reli-able middle ground. These characteristics are very similar to those displayed by the Bindoon Boys, and other victims of violence. However, although both Allan and his brother report that they have worked for superiors who were abusive in the same way as their father, they do claim to have been fortunate enough to learn many positive skills from good managers they have worked for. In fact Allan reported that one of his guiding criteria in considering whether to accept any new position was whether he felt that he could learn, and would be comfort-able learning, from his new superior.

Conclusion

Despite the important work of Hearn (1994) and others in developing our understanding of organizational violence through grounded theoretical frame-works and cross-organizational examples, this area demands further and more detailed exploration of specific cases to show the extent to which non-organiza-tional experiences of violence can shape subsequent behaviour within organizations. As we have suggested, given that violent behaviour may be repro-duced at a temporal and spatial distance from its origins, organizational analysis tends not to acknowledge such connections. The impact of petty tyranny (Ashforth 1994) and violent, combative organizational cultures (Westley 1990) have both been illuminated in behavioural terms. Ashforth (1994: 770) notes the vicious circle that can be enacted – the manager attributes subordinates' successes to him/herself, develops an inflated sense of self-worth, prefers and maintains greater psychological distance from subordinates and consequently views them as objects to be manipulated. Dependent subordinates accordingly learn to be more dependent and reinforce this process. Westley (1990) illustrates how managers feel constrained to use violent and abusive behaviour because it is culturally expected of them, and they will be politically disadvantaged if they publicly appear to be weak. Yet although these observations are certainly consistent with what we have observed of narcissism and abjection, they warrant a greater depth of explanation than simple apparent causality. Their breadth, pattern, cyclical character, indeed their inevitability, as we have also noted above, cannot be changed solely by modifications at the behavioural level. Nonetheless, the way to change them must involve sustained direct contact with reality at the level of action rather than the fantasy world which generates these behaviours.

Organizations themselves have their own structures of abjection. As Lévi-Strauss argues, human societies have two basic defences against otherness – incorporation and expulsion. Modern organizations display both. Bureaucracy, as Weber argued and Albrow (1992) penetratingly reminds us, revolves around emotion. Its central purpose is to remove and suppress the unpredictable behaviour which is an outcome of emotional drives, and make the organizational world safe for rationality. Organizations therefore seek to deny the ways in which emotions form part of behaviour and decision-making (which paradoxically becomes an emotional commitment to the idea of rationality). But, of course, this merely creates emotion as an abject phenomenon, denied but present, ever potentially resurgent, never addressed as reality. Most recently Schwartz (1990) in particular has demonstrated that organizations have begun to recognize the power of suppressed emotion by, in effect, seeking to supplant the ego-ideal with the organizational ideal, cementing a love for the corporation. As he argues, this is the pattern of addictive behaviour. Of course, the corporation legitimates one type of emotional attachment, but this is predominantly one way as it cannot return each individual's love equally, either through reward systems or, in these days of flattened hierarchies, promotion – just as the bottle cannot love the alcoholic, whatever he or she may think. Love of the team then becomes the only reward. This makes it very difficult for the organization to deal with difference adequately, and reveals a deeper dimension to the problems of managing diversity which are currently identified as the management challenge of the moment. The consequent frustrations and rejections that occur every day rebound on both the individual and the organization, and produce dejection.

At least in part because of their historical domination of formal organizations, men are entwined in this net of denial. This is reinforced by the splitting of emotion and rationality and the association of masculinity and rationality after Descartes, and compounded by the dynamics of male psychology (Bordo 1986). Social associations between men and physical violence add another dimension to the problem, which is turned yet again by the conflict and crises in modern masculinities. Men, then, are particularly vulnerable to the return of the abject, the denied and unacceptable part of the self, containing experiences, traumas, desires and memories. As we have seen, it affects both aggressors and victims, but in different ways. It waits in the wings ready to emerge on stage, often to our great bewilderment. Societal, cultural and organizational arrangements have a tendency to underpin and make possible the psychological processes of narcissism, denial, rejection, abjection and dejection that we have observed. Yet that which is rejected before it is understood remains hypnotic and compelling. It exudes, as we suggested earlier, the power of horror – the fascination of the repulsive. Men in organizations therefore need to come to terms with the unacceptable in themselves and their experience in order to break this cycle, especially in organizations which remain patriarchal, masculinist and phallogocentric. Otherwise they will remain condemned to reproduce behaviours and patterns of relations which they recognize and despise, but do not understand and cannot explain.

In sum, if our organizations abuse the people who work in them, either through individual agency or systematic policy, there is strong evidence to suggest that many of the victims will turn out to be abusers and reproducers of behaviour they know to be abhorrent in time – they will not learn how to control, grow and develop their organizations in an appropriate balance when they are constantly thrust into adopting defensive routines, displaying anger and demonstrating aggression. They will find it impossible to motivate subordinates while denying their competence and setting ever-increasing standards. They will find it difficult to lead when deeply unsure of their own self-worth. It is what is so compelling about violence and the abject that causes it to resurface even against the will of those who both suffer and come to practise violent and abusive behaviour that puzzles and perplexes us, and offers a rich, if perturbing, field for further investigation. However, the influence of the anxiety which produces the abject as a response affects behaviour more widely than where it (re)surfaces as violent behaviour, and particularly powerfully where it engages with sexuality in organizations. Masculinity and femininity develop together, and in terms of one another, rather than in isolation from each other, which our exclusive concentration in this chapter on the construction of masculinity might be taken to imply. In the next chapter, then, we will look at a case in which the masculine anxiety of a group of airline managers was forced to confront a stylized version of the feminine which represented its own abject, and sexualized, creation. However, far from being dispossessed and submissive, this version of the feminine was proving disobedient and subversive, openly challenging the disciplinary gaze of management, and in public too. We will examine the ways in which masculine anxiety increasingly, and for the worse, determined the strategy which management pursued in what became a major industrial relations dispute, and a public relations disaster for the company concerned.

2 Power, gender and industrial relations

Introduction

'It's wonderful isn't it?' a female bystander said as she watched the women march towards Caritas House ... 'Who would have thought that Cathay girls would have done this?'

'Yes,' said her exuberant male companion, 'I hope they stick it right up Cathay.'

(*South China Morning Post*)

The practices of femininity can readily function, in certain contexts that are diffi-cult to ascertain in advance, as modes of guerrilla subversion of patriarchal codes, although the line between compliance and subversion is always a fine one, difficult to draw with any certainty.

(Grosz 1994: 144)

In this chapter we develop our previous argument that masculinity exerts a powerful effect on behaviour in the workplace, although it is largely formed from influences which are historically and contextually external to organizations. We argue that the interplay of masculinity as a social construction, masculinism as an ideology, and patriarchy as a political system is grounded in the ontic condi-tion of anxiety as a response to undecidability. Gender differences initiate a desire to try to resolve the ambiguities and incompletenesses experienced through the experience of the Other as lack – as mysterious and inaccessible. In phallogocentrism this means the masculinist claim to epistemological legislation – the fixing of meaning for others, the removal, denial or solving of ambiguity. This resolution is, of course, artificial and embodies within it fear and anxiety because of its own contingency. Fear and anxiety then emerge in particular situ-ations and events where the resolution of ambiguity is problematic, and may be especially piquant where sexuality is involved. In this chapter we explore the managerial problems experienced during a strike by Cathay Pacific Airways flight attendants as an example of such a situation. Tensions between emotional display and rational argumentation in the strike turned the status quo on its head. Management mounted an emotional defence of its position in language which evoked rationality but which was not itself a rational argument, revealing its origins in anxiety and the true fragility of its position. Flight attendants turned the seductive skills which their company training had developed into an effective weapon to mobilize public opinion. Management were faced, not by the look or averted gaze of the normally supine stewardesses, but the committed, articulate, organized and consolidated stare of rebellious employees who had re-eroticized the workplace as a power play.

Background to Hong Kong's airline

Hong Kong's Cathay Pacific is the world's third most profitable airline. It is a signal success in a recession-hit industry in which many major players have recorded massive losses in recent years; indeed, at the time of the case outlined above the effects of recession were particularly severe. Hong Kong has been perhaps a paradigm case of the free market economy, distinguished by its Confucian avoidance of overt conflict in industrial relations and lack of work-force organization (Bond 1986; Redding and Wong 1986; Hofstede and Bond 1988; Redding 1990; Kirkbride *et al.* 1991). However, in January 1993, the company was disrupted by a strike by the airline's cabin crew, which the company estimated to have cost it HK$240 million (approximately £20 million, or US$31 million) in extra costs and lost revenues (*South China Morning Post* [*SCMP*], 26 August 1993). Though lasting only seventeen days, it prompted action by the Hong Kong Legislative Council (Legco) to protect workers' rights and review employment legislation in the territory. The disruption of the customary familial and quasi-familial relations of Chinese capitalism led to accusations of collusion between the government and the territory's major 'hongs' (large and historically dominant British-owned corporations of which Cathay's parent, Swire, is one) with influential voices on the Executive Council (Exco). Questions and fears also emerged about the likely human resource policies of large and/or foreign-owned companies operating in the territory in the light of anxious anticipation of the reversion to rule by the People's Republic of China (PRC) in 1997, and the possibility of increasing industrial conflict in the coming years as other groups of workers would be likely to take a similar plunge into industrial action. As Cathay's managing director, Rod Eddington, observed of the need to review the framework of industrial legislation before 1977, 'What is this company, and others like us, to do?' (*SCMP*, 30 January 1993). Those other companies, mindful of 'the growing disparity between profits and pay' were 'fearful that there may be trouble to come on their own shop floors' (Gittings and Wilson 1993: 9). They therefore hoped that the problems of Cathay Pacific would prove instructive (Abdoolcarim 1993: 41).

Moreover, manufacturing by 1993 was no longer the dominant sector in Hong Kong's economy. As the relocation of manufacturing capacity across the PRC border into Shenzen and Guangdong increased, Hong Kong was coming to depend on its service industries as a staple of employment. No longer a cheap city even by international standards, running inflation at 10 per cent per annum, the territory was finding itself having to compete on service quality rather than price. Service standards in Hong Kong were at this time highest in the hotel industry, where on occasion the best international standards were being achieved; however, far more frequently they were not. Service in stores, further-more, was at best disinterested and at worst the indecisive customer had been known to be subjected to a torrent of abuse and vilification (Vittachi 1993; Martin 1994). How to improve and maintain service quality in this cultural context therefore became of great interest to Hong Kong businesses, so when an acknowledged industry leader like Cathay Pacific had problems with its key customer contact staff, all of the territory took notice.

The Cathay Pacific strike provides the opportunity for us to examine several emerging trends in Asian business, among which gender issues were, and remain, very prominent. The strike was not the first time that it had been pointed out that Asian women, particularly in the more advanced Asian economies, were prepared to become more assertive and were beginning to demand more say and more involvement in the spheres in which they were active. Nor, given the turbu-lent atmosphere leading up to 1997, in which claims were being staked for the future, was it surprising that Hong Kong would be the first place for these aspira-tions to emerge in the form of militancy. However, not only were Cathay Pacific management surprised by the strike, they seemed to experience great difficulty in dealing with it, and were ultimately, by their own acknowledgement, culpable in prolonging the action.

The quote which begins this chapter, with its ironically pro-feminist deploy-ment of the phallocentric metaphor, is more than a humorous gesture of support for the strikers. It illustrates that, even in everyday utterances, at a common-sense level, aspects of masculinity and femininity remain ambiguous, are not easily or naturally separable and are deployed metaphorically together without loss of meaning. The hope that the Cathay 'girls' will 'stick it right up' their employer recognizes that these women, traditionally thought of as carrying a prominent and public image of gentle, caring femininity, have acted here in a way more associated with the masculine – vocal, determined, collective, tough and polit-ical. With Foucault (1980), it recognizes that gender issues are inevitably power issues, and that overturning dominant metaphors is not just a means of reversal but of recognition of the duality, flow and interdependence of terms. As such, masculinity and femininity are always present, in tension, in balance or imbal-ance or, following Derrida (1978), in supplementarity. At least one thread of the resistance and inflexibility displayed by Cathay management in the strike – and in the face of a sexualized ambiguity – was enravelled with issues of masculinity and femininity which were publicly raised and widely debated in the media. This offers us a means of empirically illustrating and advancing our earlier arguments on the psycho-social dynamics of organizational sexuality.

A case study of the Cathay Pacific flight attendants' strike

What follows is an interpretive anthropology (Gowler and Legge 1983: 225). It is a personal account of experiences in which one of us (Stephen Linstead) was immersed, largely as a member of the public, partly in contact with Cathay Pacific as an academic attempting to research the strike, and partly through personal and professional contacts with various departments in Cathay Pacific. This study began somewhat serendipitously, as he was asked for comments by the media as an 'expert' on the global airline industry. In the interests of doing an accurate and credible job, he began his research with no theoretical objectives other than to determine as fully as possible the various facets of the case as they emerged. In the process, particular elements were explored because they seemed significant (Gowler and Legge 1983: 226), and because of the unusually high level of media exposure and public interest which was generated in certain issues by the strike. This was not an abandoning of method, although a case could be argued for that approach (Phillips 1973; Feyerabend 1978), but a search for as full a variety of responses to the situation as the natural unfolding of events made available. It was at the very earliest stages possible to obtain interviews from company representatives but, as the dispute went on and negotiations became more sensitive, both sides withdrew from any discussion outside of press conferences. After the strike, both sides agreed not to talk on the matter any further except within the company, and all subsequent approaches led to the response that the subject was considered 'too sensitive'. The main thrust of the research, then, was to comb all published accounts of the strike over the relevant period, with some reports of problems emerging before it took place and retro-spectives appearing after the settlement was reached. This comprised all editions of the English language press on all days of the week, and included reports, leaders, letters to the editor and extended interviews with representatives of both parties. Translations of certain articles in the Chinese language press were obtained, although in this respect the coverage was far from comprehensive. In addition, several hours of television footage, including two half-hour specials on local television, were consulted. This produced a picture which was as balanced and complete a representation as was possible in the immediate context of the dispute. However, it has to be acknowledged that these accounts are necessarily selective and are motivated constructions, even where they feature verbatim and unedited speech by the protagonists.

The outline of the events of the strike which follows is based on summaries which appeared in the *South China Morning Post* and *The Standard*, the only Hong Kong English language press at the time, on 30 January 1993, and press releases issued by Cathay Pacific and the Flight Attendants' Union during the strike. Press releases of course were constructed by public relations professionals to maximize their beneficial effects for the client, and the emphasis in presenting this account has been placed upon facts or interpretations of the facts which were not disputed by either party. Where it is necessary briefly to present one party's position, this has been based on their own published account of that position. Where there were conflicting or divergent personal accounts emerging from within either party, the account given by official spokespersons has been followed. Nevertheless, this is not a partial attempt to eradicate 'bias' for, as already suggested in the Introduction, there can be no final or correct version of events which is therefore deserving of priority. Although where a reasonably common account emerges it is sensible to give it, this should not be taken to imply that this account deserves priority, finality or represents testable truth; other readers of and participants in the strike would certainly have different emphases in their accounts.

Outline of events

The origins of the 1993 Cathay Pacific flight attendants' strike were argued by some union members to have been rooted in a change in the company's policies towards its workforce in the preceding years (*SCMP*, 30 January 1993), but this account will concentrate on the specific events which precipitated the taking of this industrial action. On 18 December 1992, three Singapore-based first class pursers were sacked for refusing to work a flight as junior flight attendants. They claimed that they were maintaining a work-to-rule campaign initiated by the Flight Attendants' Union (FAU). This had been instigated as a protest against staff shortages and a recent increase in the practice of senior staff being asked to 'work out of position' in downgraded jobs. Flight attendants did not suffer financially by this practice. The following day, the union executive claimed to have considered, but rejected, the idea of industrial action over Christmas and the New Year. Discussions began with Cathay Pacific management on the question of reinstatement of the dismissed crew. Meanwhile, union and management were also in discussions over the annual wage round. As we have noted, Hong Kong had inflation running at approximately 10 per cent at the time, and it was the practice for the government to award civil servants, public officials, education and related employees a cost of living increase, with most private sector employers following suit. However, by 13 January 1993, talks over staffing levels and the wage round had become deadlocked, and the company postponed a decision on the reinstatement of the dismissed crew. The FAU, irritated by what it viewed as repeated stalling by the company, took a strike vote from those of its members present at Kai Tak Airport and called its 3,700 members out on strike at 10 pm. This disrupted late flights to London and Johannesburg. Later, both the company and the FAU were to declare themselves as having been unprepared for the strike.

The following day, 14 January, saw severe disruption and dramatic demonstrations at Kai Tak airport as thirteen of Cathay Pacific's forty-one departures were cancelled. Five flights were chartered from other airlines, but only twenty-three flights operated normally. Striking flight attendants set up picket lines outside Cathay Pacific offices and, as a result, twenty-nine attendants were suspended, facing possible dismissal. Amidst considerable media attention the flight attendants mounted very effective demonstrations at the airport and were successful in persuading many non-striking attendants to join the action. By 15 January, 2,100 (out of a total 4,000) attendants had joined the strike, and the Government Labour Department set up talks between the parties. These talks began in the early afternoon of the following day, ending in deadlock in the early morning. The FAU argued for the three attendants to be reinstated, staffing levels reviewed, and a 3 per cent pay rise on top of a cost of living increase. Cathay Pacific was estimated to be losing HK$20 million in revenues per day (£1.8 million; US$2.6 million) as a result of the strike and, as established, later estimated its total losses to be HK$240 million (£20 million; US$31 million). It chartered flights from Taiwan's China Airlines as a temporary measure, but on 17 January China Airlines warned it would not be able to provide extra flights over the coming Chinese (Lunar) New Year period due to heavy demand on its own routes. This is the major Chinese holiday of the year and record numbers of passengers were expected to fly throughout the region between 20 and 25 January. Talks between Cathay management and the union then resumed, but on 18 January they again broke down. At this point, management rejected an FAU proposal to organize staff for selected flights on condition that negotiations continued as being 'impractical'. Management then, under pressure in a press conference, made an ill-considered offer which it later described as a 'blunder'. This was to donate all profits for the coming seven days (HK$35 million) to the Hong Kong Community Chest (a group charity) if the union agreed to suspend both negotiations and industrial action. The FAU was quick to respond and described the offer as 'emotional blackmail'.

On 19 January, however, there appeared to be some movement. Management offered to reinstate the sacked pursers and review staffing levels, but argued that the pay issue was only introduced after the strike began and should be discussed separately. However, the FAU did not agree. On 20 January management printed an open letter to shareholders in newspapers setting out its position and its objections to the FAU position. Both sides then agreed to restart negotiations, but talks failed on the 21 January after thirteen hours. One of the stumbling blocks appeared to be Cathay's insistence on its right to discipline those 'actively' involved in the strike. This raised questions about an ambiguity in Hong Kong employment law which diverges from UK employment law (on which it is modelled), and in some respects from international principles, in challenging the workers' right to strike. Cathay Pacific claimed that this, and other issues including the conduct of strike ballots, should be dealt with through what it called the 'proper channels'. However, the question of the principles involved now sparked the interest of local politicians and legislators, and as the New Year holiday began on 22 January the picket line moved to Government House, the governor's residence, in the early morning. Some 1,000 strikers and three legislative councillors appealed to the Governor, Chris Patten, to intervene. Patten, however, was on holiday in Bali and chose not to return. The stake-out endured through the night of 23 January while negotiations continued without success. Significantly, no flights were cancelled.

On the 24 January, claiming that it needed to prepare its rosters for February, Cathay management set a deadline for striking staff to return to work by midnight on 27 January. Crew who were not registered for work by that time would have their contracts frozen and would have to apply in writing to be considered for further duties. A coalition of thirty-four groups including trade unions, community and religious groups was formed in support of the flight attendants and claimed that the company's threat to discipline strikers violated workers' rights. Again no flights were cancelled. On 25 January the apparent broadening of the strike continued. The union claimed international support would result in a boycott by overseas trade unions and threatened to take its case on the right to strike to the International Court of Justice in The Hague. The strikers' vigil was moved peacefully in response to police instructions from Government House to Central Government Offices. Continuing negotiations still failed to reach agreement and both parties, in apparent frustration, printed open letters to the public.

By the following day, 26 January, it was becoming clear that support for the strike was waning. The FAU publicly admitted that some strikers were leaving the picket line and returning to work, and twenty-three legislative councillors rejected the FAU's call for them to intervene in mediating the dispute. The International Transport Workers Federation stated that overseas unions had expressed support for the strike but none of them had committed to industrial action. As the company's 27 January deadline approached, 1,000 workers signed a pledge not to return to work before the end of the dispute, but splits in the FAU leadership were occurring. Shortly before the deadline, the union's official spokesperson Rachel Varghese, with other leading members, dramatically resigned from the Union Committee in order to return to work. By 28 January, 90 per cent of the cabin crew had joined her. Some 300 remained outside the Central Government Offices. Cathay Pacific itself remained adamant on its right to discipline strikers and claimed that the FAU was no longer representative of Cathay cabin crew. In the early hours of the morning of 29 January the picket lines packed up and left for home. The strike had coincided with the coldest period of the year in Hong Kong and the pickets had endured some very uncomfortable nights. The Legislative Council then set up a fourteen-member monitoring committee to examine post-strike action by Cathay Pacific, and urged the Governor to create a board of inquiry into the strike. The union officially called off the action at a meeting attended by 700 crew, although Cathay Pacific claimed at the time that only eighty were still on strike. As the company were using non-rostered (that is, on rest) crew, management, trainee crew, and crew and aircraft contracted from other airlines to meet their commitments, it is impossible to get an accurate picture of what the true situation was at any point in the strike. However, both sides of the dispute pointed out that considerable conciliatory work was necessary in order to rebuild the Cathay Pacific culture in the wake of the dispute.

The occupational gendering of flight attendants

The job of the flight attendant is frequently used as an archetype of a conspicuously gendered occupation yet, as Albert Mills (1994) observes, the occupation originated in a quasi-military model in the 1930s which was exclusively male. Cathay Pacific inherited this model, but stopped recruiting males in the mid-1970s after industrial action led management to believe that local men were more politicized (Gittings and Wilson 1993). By the time of the strike, only 15 per cent of the cabin crew were male, although some attendants within the airline felt that they 'still dominate the thinking of the union ... despite the fact that the impression is that it is run by a group of militant women' (flight attendant, quoted in Gittings and Wilson 1993: 9).

   Along with the structural gendering of the occupation comes its definition as feminine work, as it involves service, caring, nurturing and a mild but overt sexuality (Hearn 1993; Kerfoot and Knights 1993). Hochschild (1983) identified these tensions as part of the demands of 'emotional labour', in which the job-holder not only has to manage the demands of the task, but also their own sense of self. Along with debt collectors, Hochschild studied flight attendants as a paradigm case of an occupation where a public self has to be adopted and the individual's own emotions backgrounded and suppressed. In the case of female flight attendants, Hochschild also noted the curious and contradictory combination of femininities as 'proto-mother' and 'sex-queen' in the occupation, nurture and seduction being simultaneously demanded of these staff. Airlines themselves make no secret of their wish to entice a predominantly male clientele on board in the lucrative first and business sectors by using gently erotic evocations (Grafton Small and Linstead 1989). Consequently, airlines with a growing female business clientele have experienced difficulty in making their product sufficiently flexible to appeal. A recent internal semiotic survey by consultants to a major world carrier did not advance matters by suggesting that the role of flight attendant was symbolically compromised as the cabin represented a womb to the passenger (a symbol of nurture and submission) but the aircraft itself was an airborne phallus (a symbol of power and domination):

> Simply by virtue of the phallic shape of planes, flying sets up a male metaphorical structure. This could, however, be offset by the womb-like interior were it not for the connotations of power, hierarchy and chain of command set up by the pervasive symbolism of uniforms and uniformity.
>
>   (anonymous report, cited in Burrell 1997: 230)[1]

As Burrell notes in discussing this report, the female flight attendant's 'attributes of caring and serving are made to stand in for her complete being' (Burrell 1997: 231). Meanwhile, 'the corporate imagination which so informs airline design is clearly male ... [drawing] all its symbolic reference points from a patriarchal – almost tribal – power structure in which traditionally women have no role' (Burrell 1997: 231). The Cathay Pacific managers had so much difficulty with the strike because they were immersed in this taken-for-granted patriarchic domination. They found the flight attendants' attempts to break out of their synecdochical confinement so as to be taken for who they were rather than what they signified to constitute a direct attack on their (management's) most cherished myths. Management therefore saw themselves with no alternative but to defend themselves.

Discipline and appearance

The gendering of the flight attendant's occupation entails an implicit model of 'normal' sexuality which needs to be constructed and maintained, both symbolically and practically, in everyday life (also see discussion in chapters 3, 4 and 5). The divisionalizing practices which define what is normal or deviant, legitimate or illegitimate, in thought or deed are not self-sustaining, or challenge to such divisions would be almost impossible. As Foucault (1977) insists, they have to be policed. The historical passage from pre-modernity to post-modernity, if it can be thought of in such terms without distortion, can be understood in terms of a move from direct, physical control (for example, torture, flogging, corporal punishment), through rules-based, rational–legal control (for example, industrial bureaucracy) where control is external, to a means of control where individuals, aided by powerful socialization processes, internalize beliefs which generate action that can be seen to be 'in-accordance-with-a-rule'. This occurs without the need for specific orders or instructions, advance specifications or direct supervision. The technology which epitomizes this shift Foucault identifies in the well-known example of Bentham's Panopticon. The significant element in the disciplinary 'gaze' is that those subject to discipline believe in the *possibility* of their being watched (not even its actuality). Imagining this ocular intrusion into their world, they behave in response to it. Discipline may not be externally imposed but the source of discipline is imagined to be external. However, as de Certeau (1984) notes, the response to the gaze is the 'look', the management of impressions by the disciplined so that they appear to be controlled. Behind the look, myriad resistances, an alternate microphysics of power, come into being and provide the ground for subversion and change.

In the airline industry, the look is represented by the 'smile'. Flight attendants and other customer contact staff are trained to reproduce the smile in response to or anticipation of the gaze of the customer, which is symbolic of the gaze of the corporation. The internalization element is explicit here, as flight attendants are assessed on their sincerity and are exhorted to smile 'from the inside'. Hochschild's (1983) important study, which first made this observation, has been well digested by both academics and practitioners, and responses of Cathay Pacific flight attendants to the press confirm the insistence on the smile:

They are always telling us that we are pretty and intelligent and that we are a very important part of the company and then they treat us as if we clean the toilets AND no matter what happens we must always SMILE.

(flight attendant, quoted in McGee 1993: 1)

'The flight (to Taipei) takes 55 minutes, an hour at the most and there are more and more of these flights all the time. In that time we have to do a full meal service. Drinks, dinner, coffee, tea, everything. The aircraft flies to Taipei, we run there,' she said.

'And we must SMILE,' said another with grim irony.

(McGee 1993: 1)

Cathay Pacific, like most Asian airlines,[2] featured in its advertisements beautiful, demure and sensual stewardesses, whose only apparent wish was to serve, typically smiling, but averting their gaze in respectful submission. However, this aversion of the gaze is a response to the disciplinary gaze of the (male) client, who demands reassurance that his every need will be met, his every wish fulfilled, and that he will not be met by a challenging counter-gaze. These things will be cheerfully carried out, as though delighting the customer, in Total Quality Management terminology, delights the server as well.

Similar problems of dissonance in the occupation are reported in Höpfl and Linstead (1991, 1993; see also Höpfl 1993). Rafaeli and Sutton (1989: 37), in their discussion of research on emotional display in organizations, claim to extend Hochschild's work by identifying conditions in which the ubiquitous smile, or similar prescribed behaviour, is faked in good faith; for example, where the performer doesn't feel like giving the behaviour but acknowledges its legitimacy as part of doing the job properly – an element of professionalism. In contrast, greater dissonance to the point of exit occurs if the behaviour is faked in bad faith; the performer does not believe in or see the point of the behaviour. Watson (1994: 184), supported by Höpfl and Linstead, identifies the phenomenon of the 'honest con'. Here the 'faker' believes the faking is either good for both parties, or offers potential benefits for both, and at the least causes no harm to either. A dishonest con would occur where the object is deliberately to disadvantage or defraud the other party. The combination of the individual Kantian dimension of faking in good faith and the social recognition of the honest con characterizes much of the reality of corporate culture change (Anthony 1989, 1994; Linstead and Grafton Small 1992; Höpfl 1993). In the Cathay Pacific case, it helps to explain the eventual translation of resistance into collective action in the face of exploitation. More common, however, is the possibility that the honest con may become self-deception as it masks the exploitation of the performer by the organization, resulting in a simulacrum of commitment (Anthony 1994).

Anxiety and discipline

The sexual dimension of the occupation of flight attendant also produces the tension of anxiety. Existential gender differences themselves initiate the desire to resolve the ambiguities and incompleteness experienced and embodied by the lack of the Other. In phallogocentrism, as we have noted, this translates into the masculinist claim to dominate epistemologically – to determine meaning for others and to resolve, deny or banish ambiguity. Any such resolution is nonetheless false, containing fear and anxiety because of its own unacknowledged but inescapable contingency. That Cathay Pacific management were anxious that their celebrated crew had not fully internalized discipline, in a business in which for both safety and commercial reasons a high measure of order and reliability is important, is clear from their reported style of crew management. Under the pressure of worldwide recession and downturn in the airline industry, they launched Operation Better Shape in order to restructure and cut costs. At around the same time, crew 'noticed a change in the management practices of a company already acknowledged within the industry as a stringent employer' (McGee 1993: 1). With increasing frequency 'cabin crew were reprimanded and disciplined for misdemeanours which had not attracted penalties in the past' (McGee 1993: 1), and without appeal. These penalties were extensive, ranging from withdrawal of free flight privileges to dismissal, and were applied to activities as diverse as late arrival at briefings and oversights in grooming through to missing a flight. The approach, it was argued by the attendants, came from the assumption that 'all flight attendants are capable of calling in sick, when they are not, because they want to go to the hottest party in town on Saturday night' (McGee 1993: 1). Crew move through disciplinary stages, but so stringently have the rules been applied that 'We say we are all entertainers now because everyone is on stage' (McGee 1993: 1). For management, however, such discipline was seen as essential, and non-negotiable. Said Rod Eddington, Cathay Pacific Managing Director:

> We have to reserve the right to discipline our employees ... to take disciplinary action against those who have acted against the interests of the company. This dispute remains, as it has from the beginning, about a company's right to manage its affairs in the interests of all parties – our customers, our staff, and our shareholders.
>
> (McGee 1993: 1)

Management here made a naked bid for the centre of power – to dominate 'in the name of' all other parties, becoming in itself transparent as it made reflexive acknowledgement of the interests of management. Masculinist ideology would of course have management dutifully bearing this burden, as of right, in an objective and unselfish manner. In truth, the only way that management can effectively prevent itself from being judged and found wanting by any one of these separate parties is to claim to act in the best interests of them all, and having effectively laid claim to this organizing central position it can further (logocentrically) claim that only management has the ability to perceive (know) all other interests in view of its privileged vantage point. In circularity, power becomes knowledge which in turn preserves power. Management's anxiety therefore is that, should one of these parties break away from this consensus, its house of cards would collapse. The 'is', having successfully laboured to become the 'ought', does not wish to subside into the possibilities of the 'could'.

The pornographic gaze

Male experience of organizations, as is evident even in the very moment of its denial, is not unemotional. On the contrary, it is characteristic of masculinity, though not masculinism, that domination brings fear of being dominated, control brings fear of losing control, collectivism brings fear of losing individuality, independence and competition bring fear of losing solidarity and fellowship, aggression brings fear of being hurt and often signals that, cognitively at least, the battle has already been lost (Hearn 1993). Males feel a full range of emotion but are only allowed to display a small part of this – such as triumph, or anger which is often rationalized as uncompromising commitment to a goal or standard. Denial is deeply complicit in masculine discourse. Perhaps as a result, during the strike, male management did not appear to possess the symbolic vocabulary to (e)motivate support (Höpfl and Linstead 1993).

This organizational anxiety has an important analogy in the pattern of male responses to pornography (Kaite 1988, 1995). In pornography, especially soft-core pornography, the secret or forbidden desire (the desire to be subordinated, to become vulnerable or to be taken advantage of) is often explicitly acknowledged. Pornography shocks but deadens – its most profound effect is that it desensitizes as it de-eroticizes (Burrell 1992a). But it also plays on weakness. It seduces the observer by creating a false object, an image of femininity which is unattainable precisely because it has no real world referent – it is a simulacrum. This in turn motivates the reader's recognition of the self-encounter in the image, a reflexive recognition of a real vulnerability, a real inadequacy to be acknowledged. Women in pornography assume provocative come-hither poses which challenge – do your best/worst, satisfy me if you can, I'm yours if you're man enough – and this is often supported by accompanying text (Kaite 1988). Bataille (1982, 1985) would argue in this regard that the viewer's gaze is reciprocated, the object looks back at the observer. This cuts through to the fear of the observer, the fear of inadequacy in the face of demand, possibly the fear of attraction to the forbidden, but also of an unreachable standard being imposed from outside. It is an ocular 'penetration' which mirrors and reverses the imagined physical 'penetration' of the observer's fantasized sexual act with the image. In everyday life, which is not as easy to control as the image, the feeling of being in power – of sovereignty – can only be achieved through a kitschistic simulacrum of control through a display of conspicuous waste, excessive behaviour, continually going too far, the construction of an apparent surplus of power, fertility, creativity or even destructive energy – an imagined surplus which para-doxically represents a real lack. This form of power would be termed excremental by Bataille (1985) and Baudrillard (1983a), controlling by giving, spending and destroying, but is not to be confused with the genuine excess of energy and exuberance which characterizes creative desire and which is at the heart of genuine sovereignty – this power is heart*less*. Authority is imagined to be symbolically derived from these externally directed actions, but the feeling of inadequacy remains gnawing within. Pornography motivates and relies on this tension between the image and the observed, the spent and the unspent, the hollow moment of inadequacy in the face of the return of the abject in the returned gaze, and this anxiety provides the excitement, the psychic energy to drive a response.

This tension is paralleled in much of the textual and visual responses to the flight attendants' strike. Hochschild's proto-mother sex-queens were not only returning the gaze, but challenging and over-turning its right to view:

> In the advertisements, the Cathay girls fix a sultry smile then avert their faces with Asian humility. But in the past three days this servile image has been smashed by the perfumed picket line which has shown itself to be tough, resilient and well orchestrated.
>
> Hundreds of glamorous women, more accustomed to serving cham-pagne than shouting strike slogans, are braving the wintry conditions to brandish banners which scream their demands in bold coloured ink.
>
> (Nott 1993: 2)

The strikers seduced the public and disturbed their management. Public interest in the dispute was highly charged and unashamedly sexual. Management, however, gave the impression of being furtive little boys caught in the closet, ashamed and unsure of their own responses. The inflexibility of their declared position reflected their inability to examine their management practices in the context of patriarchy, the shrewd and street-wise boardroom versus the beautiful bimbos in the cabin. Not only did management find that the image they had calculatingly helped to create was tremendously effective, but also that it belied its substance. They gazed, as some of the public defenders of the hard-line management stance also gazed, on what was no longer the eye-lid fluttering look or the averted gaze of the passive stewardesses, but the vocal, determined and unblinking stare of resistant workers who had imported the erotic into their workplace as a tool of power (Burrell 1992a). The image was real enough, and it was staring, even screaming right back at the seat of power; and the seat of power was squirming. The 'girls' were clearly crossing boundaries, becoming ambiguous, a literal abomination (Bailey 1977; Gowler and Legge 1981). Management's response to this disturbing object was horror, as Bataille and Kristeva (1982) would have predicted. What drove their pursuit of the action to its climax/conclusion in a reassertion of material patriarchy was their fear of their own fear – the return of the abject. The fear was not solely of vulnerability, but of gleefully succumbing to that vulnerability, of admitting it and giving in to the attractive side of the case, of becoming 'soft', and finding that it wasn't an altogether unacceptable option. The same anxiety drives homophobia. But in this case the object itself more powerfully implicated the observer as it was so conventionally seductive. Similarly, the reader of transvestite pornography realizes with that ambiguous excitement poised between horror and attraction that these beautiful desirable women literally have *balls*. As a consequence the masculinity behind the gaze is called, hauntingly, irrevocably, into question. The 'gaze' of the powerful becomes the guilty 'peek' of the schoolboy.

Masculinity and desire

It is possible to emphasize this further. Masculinity, as co-emergent in supplementarity with femininity, is oxymoronic at the ontological level. That is to say, there are no guarantees of what it means to be masculine. It is therefore to be expected that contradictions, non sequiturs, ambiguities and paradoxes will be generated at the epistemological level as we try to determine what we know about being a man. As Ryan (1982: 215) reminds us, where we encounter sites of ambiguity, this can only be resolved by wielding some sort of authority (temporary yet often pretending to be absolute) to legislate for one determination or another. Masculinism is constructed to resolve these discrepancies.

However, it is often necessary to preserve or create ambiguities, to blur definitional boundaries, deflecting and conflating meaning in order to preserve the material objects of the discourse when they might become unsustainable in the light of too much clarity (Golding 1980, 1991, 1996a, 1996b). Cathay Pacific management felt this strain. Masculinity as an ideology lays claim to the foundational ordering principle – the *logos* – in phallogocentrism, a physical embodiment of the 'word of the law'. This is consistent with Kerfoot and Knights' (1993) argument that the emergence of the New Man of the 1990s, who adds caring and sensitivity towards partners and children to the panoply of male virtues, was not an overturning of male domination but an elaboration and extension of it (also see Moore 1988: 187–8; Brittan 1989: 184–7; Elliott *et al.* 1993; Brewis 1996: 337–45). Ironically the adoption of certain perceived-as-masculine virtues by women who seek to be taken seriously in the business world is not usually regarded as a similar extension of feminine repertoires, but a further example of the same to the extent that it involves a renunciation of the feminine (Grosz 1994: 144). The image allows the colonization of certain attractive parts of femininity in order to re-centre rather than de-centre masculinity, and to further marginalize the feminine by creating a more 'complete' version of masculinity. This drive for completeness is the working through of desire as desire for the Other, the will to power (over the Other) as a means to sovereignty, which is not just a behavioural option but a fundamental drive organizing human consciousness (Cooper 1983). As Derrida (1978) argues, this proceeds in modernism by in effect acknowledging the failure of its own project, by pursuing divisionalizing, standardizing and spatializing practices in language and thought which include and normalize the 'controllable', while marginalizing and excluding the ephemeral, mysterious, problematic or paradoxical. Masculinist extensions of this logic disavow the corporeality – the subjection to natural physical forces which are constructed as excessive, uncontrollable, fluid, expansive, disruptive and irrational – that is commonly attributed to women (Grosz 1994: 200). Foucault (1967, 1973, 1977, 1979) identifies some of the social mechanisms through which such boundaries and margins are created and preserved, and through which power flows, linking, as we established earlier, practice and language in his concept of discourse. Nevertheless, flow can also lead to dissolution, which is the ultimate threat of corporeality. By association, femininity becomes ambivalent and subversive, and invites repression. As Daudi (1983) observes, every culture is aware of that which it does not want to know, and in a masculinist society this is the uncertainty of acknowledging its own femininity.

The Cathay Pacific strike brought this dualistic tension into focus in a dramatic way. The unsettling of taken-for-granted assumptions about masculinity and femininity came at a time and in a place where the pace of change, the realization of existing social contradictions, the uncertainties of the future, the uneasy blending of traditional culture and hypermodernity, east and west, and the apprehensions of all sections of the community over the fruition of their aspirations was disrupting subjectivity. It was hard to find one's subjective 'place' in contemporary Hong Kong at that time, hard to establish it in any comfortably sustainable sense. This, as Fairclough (1992) argues, was reflected in the heterogeneity of discourses which increases at the time of social upheaval. The aspirations of the Cathay 'girls', their awkward and self-conscious insistence on pursuing a course which was unfamiliar (which they repeatedly reported in press and media interviews both during and after the strike), and their highly publicized use of some of their more traditional stereotypically feminine tools (which they also happily and self-consciously publicly acknowledged) to exploit the modern media exhibited this. So too did the anxious insistence of the 'macho' Cathay management on the letter of the law, their image of competitiveness, determination, rationality, and emotional distance deriving from the fear of intimacy that comes with the desire for power. The gender aspects of the Cathay strike therefore encompass much more than a small group of female flight attendants behaving out of character and being defeated in a minor industrial action while nevertheless simultaneously denting management's image (Abdoolcarim 1993).

The textual discourse of the strike drew attention, perhaps predictably in a culture of *feng shui* which is highly aware of issues of image and design, to stylistic elements of the strike. This was supported by visual discourse:

Chic Campaign on the Perfumed Picket Line (headline, Nott 1993: 2)

As industrial disputes go the Cathay Pacific flight attendants' strike has to rank as the most glamorous in the world. Day in, day out, the public has been treated to yards of gorgeous young things stretched arm-in-arm in picket lines intent on doing, in industrial terms, what had once been unthinkable ... It was enough to melt the hearts of every hot-blooded male in town, and it worked, mentally the males signed up in droves and the 'girls', as they are so patronizingly called by the rest of the world, milked the good will for all it was worth.

Bundled up against the seasonal cold in their best leggings, appropriate silk and wool clothes and the essential shades, they acknowledged the motorists' wolf whistles and the victory signs with their trade-mark come-hither style.

There were poses all round as the photogenic strikers accommodated the media with 'picture opportunities' that got the photographers snapping as they had rarely done before

(McGee 1993: 1)

Elsewhere the press was littered with references to 'silk and cashmere' and a 'dainty leather and fur gloved hand'. The attendants were obviously successful at winning exposure – they turned the very symbols of their submissiveness, performance tools which company training had given them, against their bosses. They were sensual, and now available for the symbolic consumption, not just of the privileged Cathay Pacific clientele, but of anyone who cared to look. Branding in the airline business is all about power, and power brings with it access to this exclusive surrogate relationship with cabin crew. Out on the street, however, the criteria are different, and business class frequent flyers are reminded of their own mortality. Not only were management damaged by this display, in not getting attention paid to their case, but the customers were also hurt as an exclusive product became public property. Textually, there was also evidence of gender discrimination being a factor in the dispute.

They think just because we are young and we are girls we won't question them. They think they can carry on using us as dupes, they think we are dumb, we are bimbos, that we will accept everything they throw at us.

(Nott 1993: 2)

Suddenly a normally conciliatory group of glamorous women was at war with a finely honed machine of experts, trained in one of the shrewdest boardrooms in the world.

(McGee 1993: 1)

The image of gentle, glamorous 'guerrillas' pitted against tough, calculating and unfeeling males was reinforced visually with shots of men and women in opposition, of management looking insouciant, and of women expressing emotion in various ways: joy, sadness, welcoming friends with tears of relief, expressed in a natural uninhibited way which frequently dominates common-sense constructions of feminine emotional expression in organizations (Hearn 1993). Management of course, unmoved but clearly anxious both about power and popularity, repeated its hard line, emphasizing the legalistic and apparently rational underpinnings of their position.

Masculinity and rationality

In recent years it has become much more common for commentators to acknowledge the problematic nature of masculinity. Some studies have considered 'what it means to be a man' in the context of both male and mixed work settings, laying emphasis on emergent themes in organizational talk (Collinson 1988; Collinson and Hearn 1996). Masculinity is typically displayed as a concern for strength, physicality and sexual prowess, and is associated with horseplay, ritualized degradation, humiliation and put-downs which importantly do not diminish as the stakes get higher and one moves up the management hierarchy (Golding 1991, 1996b; and chapter 1). Kerfoot and Knights (1993), following Brittan (1989), take off from this ground to consider how relations between available expressive forms of masculinity and specific work settings produce a distinctive discourse of masculinism. Masculinity here is of course not a biological category but a socially defined one. It emerges historically, within specific settings, and is socially constructed. As it is constantly shifting, constantly emergent and negotiated, it reflects its intertextual nature. Masculinities are multiple, and are constantly in struggle over the 'possession' of signification – what it means, for example to be a 'real man', 'one's own man', 'a man's man', 'a ladies' man' or 'one of the boys'. These multiple masculinities are not entirely dissociable, but do to some extent compete with one another. However, they are also inextricably defined in contrast to a nexus of multiple femininities. They are in themselves alternative attempts to define and resolve this ontological discontinuity (a recognition of the feminine Other).

As Derrida (1978) reminds us, language is at its root a power relationship as terms assert themselves above the supplement which is both necessary to sustain them and is also more than simply a response to the prioritized term. It may be seen, in the overturning moment of deconstruction, as the prior condition to which the dominant term is a response. As Derrida goes on to argue, a more accurate representation is to see the two terms as being co-determining, existing in constant movement between themselves, a condition of difference/*différance*, a play of 'metaphorization', one constantly collapsing into the other (Cooper 1989; Linstead and Grafton Small 1992; Chia 1996). Masculinity cannot do other than imply femininity, and does this more emphatically the more it attempts to suppress it. Kerfoot and Knights (1993: 663) argue that:

> where masculinism justifies and naturalizes male domination, we regard this domination occurring as an effect of the interplay of sexual power relations within and between particular practices, rather than as existing *a priori* to those relations and practices in which it is continually reconstituted.

Male domination, then, does not flow from pre-existing social relations of patri-archy, but is immanent in localized forms and practices. That is not to say that historical patterns of relations and individual reproductions of those relations are not in tension, but the shaping of the latter by the former is not inevitable. Kerfoot and Knights do, however, point out that in specific contexts individuals may in effect have no option other than to reproduce existing relations. As Grosz (1994: 144) puts it:

> All of us, men as much as women, are caught up in modes of self-produc-tion and self-observation; these modes may entwine us in various networks of power, but never do they render us merely passive and compliant. They are constitutive of both bodies and subjects ... Women are no more subject to this system of corporeal production than men; they are no more cultural, no more natural than men. Patriarchal power relations do not function to make women the objects of disciplinary control while men remain outside of disciplinary surveillance.

It is perhaps important for us to remember this in our discussion of the specific responses made by Cathay Pacific management to the action of the flight atten-dants; they may well have experienced themselves as having no alternative. In the Cathay Pacific events, both traditional Western and Asian definitions of masculinity and their associated forms of patriarchy formed an important part of the context in their permeation of both business and social life even as they were disrupted and brought into play.

Self-exposure and manipulation in public

This context was not fixed, as we have argued, but constantly in play, and the establishment and preservation of a consensus in the world at large were impor-tant to both management and strikers. Public relations thus became a critical issue. The early stages of the strike were described by Cathay as a 'communica-tions disaster', and an independent consultancy, Forrest International, was brought in to handle media relations as a consequence (*The Standard*, 7 February 1993). They arranged smaller and more intimate briefings, press releases, open letters and press advertisements which had a noticeable effect on public opinion and softened the tough, aggressive and unpopular corporate stance. The original company approach seemed to have been a typically masculinist one, that the only way to win was to knock the ball right out of the ground. This shifted into an approach which adopted the position that, if you argued with the umpires for long enough, the spectators would lose interest, the challengers heart and the trophy, after all, can't change hands on the basis of a draw. So issues were made more ambiguous and meaning less crisp, except in the area where management made its final, rather punitive and, in terms of PR, most damaging stand on the treatment of strikers after their return to work. Nevertheless, despite the airline's obvious willingness to exploit PR artifice and rhetorical sophistication, they were highly critical of the techniques and motivations of the media and importantly chose to gender their arguments.

> Public relations headaches had come from television coverage: managers in suits had failed to compete with the Hong Kong rarity of a picket line and the almost universal rarity of a photogenic picket line.
>
> Mr. [Nick] Rhodes [Swire Group Public Affairs Director] dubbed television 'an impossible medium to do well in'. He said: 'visually the picket lines and strikers were far more appealing to the cameras than our managing directors [*sic*] in a press conference, and we took a bit of a beating as far as objective reporting [was concerned].'
>
> 'That was a great shame because we organized press conferences on a daily basis. The Managing Director ran them. He was very open, honest and answered all the questions.'
>
> 'But we got five or ten seconds, and they would pick on the most difficult question or pick a moment when the managing director looked defensive, and he came across badly as a result ...'
>
> (*The Standard*, 7 February 1993: 4)

For the PR director here public image and public opinion become synonymous. Any critical capacity possessed by the general public is at least backgrounded if not negated in this argument, which has the effect of diverting attention from the company's failure in terms of its policies. Cathay lost public sympathy, and patronage (though not universally) because of its actions, not because the managing director was less physically attractive than his cabin crew. The purpose of the account, then, is to move attention away from the content issues of the strike to focus on gender inequality, in a physical sense, as being a key determinant of public perceptions of the strike. This comforting autocommunicative reversal is not entirely belied by an examination of the attention given to both sides in the media, and the company did get a substantial treatment of its views in all local dailies, albeit on the inside pages. The managing director, here exposing himself to the public via the press, sought to make his apparent vulnerability a winning tactic. However, despite his public self-manipulation, he discovered that vulnerability is just that, and is not predictable. Although he had his metaphorical trousers down, the press preferred a head and shoulders shot. Nevertheless, this unfortunate setback should not be allowed to obscure the fact that, even though it was heart-warming, emotion presented *qua* emotion by the flight attendants did not win the day. Emotion, or anxiety, suppressed behind quasi-rational discourse, was ultimately sustained, stirred but not shaken.

Though management kept its specific expressions fairly restrained when under pressure, and although openly using sex as an explanation for its lack of success did not overplay that particular hand, supporters of management writing to the press clearly revealed the underlying worries of the male managements of other Hong Kong companies. Masculinist anxiety was clearly and deeply dispersed throughout the business community. J. D. Lawrence, Director of Matheson PFC (a very successful finance and investment house) wrote:

> As an expatriate who has lived in Hong Kong for 15 years and flown back to the UK at least two to three times per year always on Cathay Pacific, I am completely at a loss and disillusioned as to why the Flight Attendants Union has called a strike at this time. Its members are one of the most privileged workforces in Hong Kong. They are paid top rates, I believe equal to or better than any other Asian airline, they and their families have the perks of subsidized travel, days off and numerous other benefits. For every girl who wishes to resign there are 20 to 30 clamouring for their jobs. Don't they realise that every company has to have a bottom line which shows a profit, look at airlines in the States which have gone into the red, gone bankrupt, what is the future? ... This is economics and anyone living and working in Hong Kong should understand this. It is said that an active minority can always hold sway over a passive majority. I would say to you girls who are being led astray – think very, very carefully about your futures.
>
> (*SCMP*, 20 January 1993)

Mr Lawrence begins by characterizing himself as a reasonable person with relevant knowledge through seniority which immediately distances him from the youth of the attendants ('15 years ... two or three times a year'), followed by the cognitive extension of this distance into dumbfounded amazement at the irrationality of the strike (note later the patronizing apostrophization of 'you girls' – despite 11 per cent of the crew being male). This gulf, having been opened up, is followed by a series of mystifications. As Burke (1969) argues, mystification occurs when one or two elements of an account are specified and the recipient is encouraged to 'fill in the blanks' and formulate other elements as being consistent. The likelihood of those elements being connected in the desired way is increased if they invoke discursive themes already familiar to the reader. Mr Lawrence draws on several interlinked themes, or, as Salaman (1979) calls them, 'ideologies', that are familiar in rationalist managerialist discourse. These are now invoked on the masculinist side of the gulf, and have the effect of being mutually supporting. It is thus an advantage that the specified elements here are ill-defined. To borrow Salaman's terminology, these elements can be seen as:

1   the *welfaristic* emphasis on the benefits and rates paid to Cathay crew (who do have the highest basic salary of the major Asian airlines, but also the lowest allowances), implying that the attendants are spoiled and overprivileged and therefore not tough and independent;

2   the *psychologism* of the threat of replacement of those workers who do not have the right level of performance or the correct attitude by selection of others from the reserve army of envious workers (there is a shortage of labour in Hong Kong so this 'reserve army' is already part of the domestic labour market).[3] This places responsibility firmly at the individual level in

the face of action by the collective, which is another feature of masculinism;

3   the *structuralist* invocation of US airlines who failed to respond to the imperatives of the environment, despite rather different circumstances, which yet again invokes the masculinist pioneering myth of valiant struggle against the hostile elements.

However, Lawrence continues to imply that these self-evident facts will speak for themselves, although the very existence of his letter to the press on the subject tends to belie this fact. The naturalism of his argument is augmented by an attempt at scientism in the form of an appeal to economics. The success of this appeal depends on the reader accepting that the writer's statement is in fact economics and not ideology, whatever the level of analysis or specificity of evidence. Why is Lawrence so insistent? It is possible to begin to perceive the threat of the Other here, the deflationary flaccidity of the phallus, the collapse of the order painstakingly achieved by everyone following the rules, bowing to the laws of nature as interpreted through neo-classical economics and pursuing their own individual interests, which will eventually turn out to be in everyone's best interests. The danger of subversive collectivism is incipient, as an 'active minority can always hold sway over a passive majority'. As this is only the third dispute in Cathay's history, a naïve reader might mistakenly assume this active minority to be the Cathay board, but the unspecified Other here is the militant, possibly Marxist, certainly irrational union leadership. The naïve 'girls' are being 'led astray' by the popular folk-devil of seductive and persuasive activists, but the solution to the problem remains obvious. All they have to do is think very, very carefully (and, later in the letter, about 'priorities', another rational divisionalizing and distancing practice). This phrase, with the rhythmic emphatic doubling of 'very', now has the aesthetic form of a threat, and utilizes a common structure for giving a final warning to a miscreant. Evocatively, perhaps even unconsciously, a legalistic theme becomes discernible, harmonizing with a widely held public suspicion that the Cathay management were intent on exacting a punitive revenge upon the strikers. Mr Lawrence has not, despite his protestations, attempted to reason with his readers, but to bully them. Masculinism here mounts an emotional defence of its position in language which evokes rationality, but which is not itself a rational argument, thus revealing its own auspices in anxiety and the true fragility of its position.

Conclusion

The Cathay Pacific strike is certainly instructive, if not conclusive. At the discursive level, it underscores the necessity to construct gender identity through discourse, but also that these discourses are mixed, inconsistent and often contradictory. This has a social ostensive referent, in that in turbulent and changing times such as Hong Kong was and is experiencing, subjectivity becomes disrupted and this increases heterogeneity and inconsistency in discourse. Even in stable social conditions, however, language itself is not fixed. To the extent that the terms constituting masculinity and masculinism depend on supplementary concepts to sustain them, they can be deconstructed and subverted. Masculinist discourse, no matter how positive and self-assured, is always at risk.

In terms of social power, gender relations are not all one way. Femininity can be deployed in a form of 'guerrilla warfare' to subvert masculinism. Males can be trapped within particular versions of masculinity, especially rationalist and in this case post-colonialist ones, to the extent that they appear to have little alternative other than to reproduce them. Nevertheless, despite the success of the cabin crew winning a moral victory, the real victory fell to the status quo. Although this victory was somewhat Pyrrhic, management reaffirmed their traditional right to manage; but the extent to which they could also dominate was put into question. Rationality, however, was ultimately the more powerful discursive influence on public decision-making, especially in a business-dominated society. Nevertheless, the fact that rationality is often a mask for emotional forces in organizations emerges strongly from this analysis. Emotion packaged as rationality tends to win arguments. Emotion presented as emotion, though more honest, at this point wins only sympathy.

Although socially sustained, the masculinist position begins to look fragile as never before. Managerial responses to the strike were deeply, and inevitably, driven by anxiety. The existential issues opened up by the strike were not to be easily resolved, and ultimately the working through of these issues led to a fuller recognition of the changing role of men and women in the corporation, although this remains an ongoing project for the company. Managerial repertoires had to change, because of the nature of the service industry and the need to address the Other in the form of the customer. The thin line between compliance and subversion is particularly critical in this industry, and makes it very vulnerable to changing social expectations. This may eventually extend to greater self-reflection and increased reliance on trust rather than control on the part of managers.

In a limited way, the strike was something of a manifestation of bio-power and resistance to it. We might allow ourselves a final ontological reflection here. The interplay of masculinity as a social construction, masculinity as an ideology, and ultimately patriarchy as a political system is rooted in the ontic condition of anxiety as a response to undecidability. We have already noted the relations between sexuality, power and the body, and the entanglement of creation and negation, of sex with death. The gendered struggle of the Cathay Pacific strike gently but firmly reaffirms that the anxieties of masculinity, of loss of identity and the power to act from a base of certainty, of the liberating repression of subjectivity, are but reminders of our own mortality – and that we are what we fear most.

3 Sexual harassment

Introduction

The term 'sexual harassment', standing for a particular set of unwelcome sexualized behaviours in the organizational context, could be seen to have passed into the common argot in the West following Williams v. Saxbe (1976) – the first harassment complaint to succeed in an American court (Faley 1982: 585–6). However, this relatively recent 'recognition' notwithstanding, harassment is widely understood to be a phenomenon that has existed throughout time, albeit one that has only come to public attention during the last three decades of the twentieth century:

> Women have been sexually harassed on the job for as long as they have been in the workplace. Yet it has only been within the past few years that the public and professional community have identified sexual harassment as a serious problem.
>
> (Malovich and Stake 1990: 63)

> Did the relations that constitute sexual harassment [not] exist before they were named, and did the women in those relations [not] have an experience? Is not that pre-discursive experience the reason that women wanted to take the personally risky and politically fundamental step of giving the experience a name?
>
> (Cain 1993: 89)

> In the past, sexual harassment was an invisible problem. Sexual harassment had no name and organizations were not responsible for it if it occurred. Today, it not only is very visible but has achieved a certain amount of notoriety.
>
> (Gutek 1996: 272)

Similarly, MacKinnon claims that, prior to Williams, sexual harassment was 'literally unspeakable, which made a generalized, shared and social definition of it impossible' (MacKinnon, cited in Benson and Thomson 1982: 236). Her point is that, while harassment pre-existed its definition as such, it was not until a vocabulary was developed that allowed its precise delineation that we have become able to address its problematic effects. Indeed, Hoffman (1986), in her analysis of harassment in academia, goes so far as to credit herself and her fellow harassment commentators with its discovery. In so doing, she emphasizes that this *was* a discovery: of something that 'lay in wait' for the astute observer, able to cut a swathe through the obfuscatory mire of organizational reality so as to reveal the truth about gender relations therein (also see Brewer and Berk 1982; Maypole and Skaine 1983; Taubman 1986; Ross and England 1987; Ellis *et al.* 1991). Moreover, now that harassment has achieved the status of public problem (Weeks *et al.* 1986), commentators such as these position themselves as able to work to push understanding forward, as beginning to build real foundations for the eradication (or at least reduction) of harassment in the modern organization.

The notion that harassment has an objective existence which researchers have only relatively recently identified is where our argument in this chapter, which continues to explore the exploitative potential of sexuality in the organizational context, takes off. Here we critically engage with the discourse which structures and constitutes 'sexual harassment', which presents and simultaneously constructs it as an irrevocably gendered form of *bad* sex, sex-without-desire, sex as an abuse of power, which has adverse implications for those members of organizations who are its targets. That is to say, we read harassment in a similar way to that in which Foucault reads sex itself. He accepts that we are corporeal beings who, in certain stimulating circumstances, experience particular and commonly understandable physical sensations and pleasures, but he rejects the representation of these sensations as an objective unity called 'sex', a definable and essential human property which is to be carefully managed and properly expressed only in certain ways. Instead, Foucault argues that:

> the [discursive] notion of 'sex' made it possible to group together, in an artificial unity, anatomical elements, biological functions, conducts, sensations and pleasures, and it enabled one to make use of this fictitious unity as a causal principle, an omnipresent meaning, a secret to be discovered elsewhere: sex was thus able to function as a unique signifier and as a universal signified.
>
> (Foucault 1979: 154)

Similarly, harassment as we see it is a discursive product – the discourse of harassment is what generates the understood phenomenon of harassment, what establishes its meaning, its identity and coherence, and what, most significantly, delineates it from 'acceptable' forms of sexuality and/or of organizational behaviour. A germane example of this process of construction is that a behaviour which in some contexts might not be unacceptable in itself – such as a man complimenting a woman's appearance while they are drinking in a bar – becomes unacceptable by virtue of its being labelled harassment, usually in another context (the work, or educational, organization). That is to agree with Foucault that 'discourse is not *about* objects, rather discourse *constitutes* them' (Foucault, cited in Sheridan 1980: 98, emphasis added).

The relationship that Foucault (1980, 1982) posits between discourse and identity suggests that we are subject to, and made subject by, discourse because of our common need to believe in some foundational and enduring truth of human existence. As a consequence, we willingly reproduce the various discourses to which we are subject *as if* they were true, because we want to and may come to believe that they are true. That is to say, human behaviour has the *effect* of constituting discourse to appear to be true and of according it the status of truth, rather than such 'truth' being attained through the collection of empirical and direct evidence of an object world. What we 'know' of ourselves as human beings is therefore generated by discourse. From this standpoint, contemporary discourses act to invest us with, among other things, certain understandings of natural, normal and appropriate sexual activity, and its means of conduct. In so far as we fail to see the workings of discourse as they are, we are compelled to signify and act out these understandings as though they were our 'nature', part of our 'essence', our 'inner truth' (Butler 1990), and come as a result to take for granted that certain sexual behaviours are acceptable while others, such as harassment, are not.

Based on the above, then, we start here by rejecting the premise that sexual harassment has been 'discovered' because, as Foucault rejects the idea of sex as an *a priori* human property, so we reject the notion of harassment as an *a priori* set of dysfunctional sexual behaviours in the organization. This is not to say that 'sexual harassment' as event does not exist, that men (or women) do not engage in sexualized behaviours which their female (or male) colleagues in organizations find unsettling.[1] In fact, the existing empirical data depict harassment as 'a pandemic problem' (Saal 1996: 67) in organizations, a claim well illustrated by David's (1998) overview of European and US statistics on harassment:

> The ILO [International Labour Office] estimates that more than one Dutch woman in two, nearly one Austrian woman in three and more than one French woman in four have been victims of serious incidents of sexual harassment. If all forms of sexual harassment are included, from the least serious to the most serious cases, reported cases amount to 74% of British women. In the United States, one woman in two is subjected to one form or another of sexual harassment during her student years or working life.

Instead, we wish to emphasize the ways in which harassment has come to loom large in the collective modern Western consciousness – to reveal 'the workings of discourse as they are'. What we take aim at in this chapter, then, is not the truth status of harassment discourse but the consequences of the discursive production of harassment as a phenomenon. We focus on the ways in which harassment is framed and made abject by this discourse and draw the conclusion that the very process of its constitution guarantees that it will always reappear. In other words, our claim here is that the production of sexual harassment as dysfunctional, derogatory and discriminatory sets the scene for its inevitable return to, and disruption of, the organization.

Harassment, the passions and the abject

Given that we have dismissed the idea that somehow there is transcendentally 'good' sex and transcendentally 'bad' sex, and that harassment forms part of the latter category, why then is harassment *constructed* as dysfunctional? Sexuality more generally is depicted within harassment discourse as essential to healthy human existence, whereas harassment itself is presented as an intrusion into organizational behaviour, given that it represents a warping of or deviation from functional sexual activity, and therefore causes distress to those abiding by these norms.[2] We contend, therefore, that harassment is one form of the return of the abject: that it may be usefully considered to fall into the category of those behaviours which are considered threatening because they remind us that we are subject to natural forces, instincts, processes and passions which are beyond our control. These emerge through behaviours which can be managed and contained through their being labelled as harassment and positioned within the broader discourse which prescribes what is to be done about them, once labelled, in terms of such things as prevention, cure, discipline, punishment and reparation. Thus it is not harassment itself which is the true object of the discourse which speaks it. Indeed, although within normalizing discourse the normal is often naturalized, and nature, natural or primitive behaviours are paradoxically constituted as abnormal and hence *un*natural, this is only possible because of the ontological subordination of nature to culture which this discourse implies.

This de-ontologizing is not new, as Linstead (forthcoming) notes, but has taken on a new dimension since the eighteenth century and the rise of modernity when the passions became particularly problematic for the emerging colonialist and commercial, yet liberalizing, democracies (also see chapter 6). Hirschman (1977) examines works of political and social theorists and economists from this early modern period. These sought to establish a moral climate supportive of capitalism which took adequate account of both 'passions' and 'interests'. Early arguments were that human beings were driven by desires and passions – greed, avarice, aggression, lust – which needed to be controlled, subdued or channelled in order to prevent them breaking out into war, crime or promiscuity which would destroy the stability of society. For many years the debate was primarily over which passions could be used to countervail or cancel out other passions – avarice against aggression, lust against greed – identifying positive and negative passions and the most propitious and productive pairings. However, during the eighteenth century the idea of 'objective interests' became the favoured argument, entailing the Panglossian assumption that each individual pursuing their own best interests for commercial gain would lead to overall calm, co-operation and world peace. Commerce was seen to be value-neutral, and the distinction was commonly made between the savage ruled by passion and the civilized merchant ruled by reason. In this revision, the interests counteracted the passions rather than the passions themselves performing such a function. Moreover, despite the Romantic backlash against neo-classical rationality during the nineteenth century, the world of economics remained relatively untroubled as Adam Smith provided an effective solution to the dilemma – interests were the practical working out of the passions. The passions therefore needed to be properly channelled in order to turn 'dangerous human proclivities'

> into comparatively harmless channels by the existence of the opportunity for money-making and private wealth, which, if they cannot be satisfied in this way, may find their outlet in cruelty, the reckless pursuit of personal power and authority, and other forms of self-aggrandizement.
>
> (Keynes 1936: 374, cited in Hirschman 1977: 134)

Smith displays a modern sensibility in providing the compromise which allows for the channelling of those passions which classical rationality had rendered abject. Problems, however, then presented themselves in two forms: first, the question of whether all the passions were capable of metamorphosis into positive and utilitarian channels; and, second, the more radical question of whether the utilitarian approach was not altogether inimical to a passionate ontology, which is the thesis advanced by Bataille in his ironic theory of general economy, as sketched out in our Introduction. It is this last which is of most relevance to our purposes here. Because of the endless circuit of sun-given energy which lies at the heart of this thesis, the general economy as developed by Bataille posits a fundamental connection between all matter on the earth. That is to say:

> If one thinks of a particular object, it is easy to distinguish matter from form, and an analogous distinction can be made with regard to organic beings, with form taking on the value of the unity of being and of its individual existence. But if things as a whole are taken into account, transposed distinctions of this kind become arbitrary and even unintelligible.
>
> (Bataille 1985: 45)

Bataille talks, in fact, of nature as a continuous and '*concrete totality*' (Bataille 1997: 268), from which the birth of a human being itself represents only a temporary break, one that always and unfailingly ends in death, in our *rejoining* 'abject nature and the purulence of anonymous, infinite life' (Bataille 1997: 244), in a 'rupture of the discontinuous individualities to which we cleave in terror' (Bataille, cited in Dollimore 1998: 257). Our general tendency to deny this communion with abject nature, emerging in our construction of ourselves as independent, autonomous, separate, limited, unitary and self-contained individuals, derives from our reluctance to acknowledge the inevitability of death, already implied in chapter 1. That is to say, '[an] abhorrence of nature [is] built into our essence' (Bataille, cited in Dollimore 1998: 251) because we '[contemplate] the idea of not existing with horror' (Richardson 1994: 37). While this is effective as a survival instinct, it leads us to construct ourselves as human individuals on the basis of a series of disavowals and separations:

> Not wanting to depend on anything, abandoning the place of our carnal birth, revolting intimately against the fact of *dying*, generally mistrusting the body, that is, having a deep mistrust of what is accidental, natural, perishable – that appears to be *for each one of us* the sense of the movement which leads us *to represent* man independently of filth, of the sexual functions and of death.
>
> (Bataille 1997: 249)

Taboos for Bataille, then, are all variants on the death taboo and are a matter of we humans establishing that we are something more than animal, possessing a certain dignity, a certain autonomy from the 'natural given' and 'animal avidity' (Bataille 1997: 250). Indeed, it is one of the characteristics which distinguishes humans from animals (the ability to look into the future and contemplate one's own death) which leads to the construction of social life as a means of avoiding, postponing and preventing death. 'The flight from death' is therefore 'the beginning of servitude' (Bataille 1997: 317), the beginning of what we referred to in chapter 1 as attempts to stop the clock, of our drive to save ourselves for as long as possible (even for eternity) by working, by producing, and by subordinating ourselves to particular goals or ends. Such efforts, for Bataille, ensure that we have an identity, an individuality, because they erect for us a past, present and future:[3]

> In efficacious activity man becomes the equivalent of a tool, which produces; he is like the thing the tool is, being itself a product … the tool's meaning is given by the future, in what the tool will produce, in the future utilization of the product; like the tool, he who serves – who works – *has the value of that which will be later, not that which is* … The fear of death appears linked from the start to the projection of oneself into a future time, which, being an effect of the positing of oneself as a thing, is at the same time the precondition for conscious individualization … death prevents man from attaining himself.
>
> (Bataille 1997: 316, emphasis added)

However, despite our attempts to render things otherwise, and as also noted in chapter 1, this hard work of ours is pointless because we always know that we will die one day. We cannot escape the loss of self, the restorative return to 'concrete totality', that death represents – it will always catch up with us and, although it represents a cessation of life, it is also a cessation of struggle, a moment of relaxation and reconciliation. Consequently it is always something to be desired at the same time as it is contemplated with horror. Similarly, the abject – all that reminds us of our inevitable death (such as filth), all that brings us close to death (risks, accidents, injuries) and all that causes us to be forgetful of or unconscious of self (such as the ecstatic, oblivious *petit mort* of the orgasm) – also promises to relieve us of the burden of selfhood and therefore exerts both attraction and repulsion, such that it can never be satisfactorily rejected even though it may bring us to the edge of madness (as also discussed in detail in chapter 1).

Psychological, social and organizational 'normality', then, Bataille's 'profane' everyday world of home, work, practical activity and education, the character- istic core of homogeneous society, seeks to delimit and drive out the abject – it cannot abide it. But we have already seen that the abject always returns to haunt the boundaries of normality through some impassioned insurgence of love or lust, greed or gift, sex, power or charity. Bataille suggests that the abject can be cathartically expelled from the profane via rapid, violent, brutal but pleasurable 'rupture', or rendered homogeneous, useful, rational and moderate. Expulsion consists of our satisfying of orgiastic, self-shattering impulses, of giving in to the combination of fascination and horror which attends our inevitable death – it is, in fact, an end in itself, a burning out of abject desire by indulgence, which allows the possibility of moving beyond it. Appropriation, on the other hand, is the establishing of an identity between oneself and the abject so that it is subor- dinated to 'future necessities' (Bataille 1985: 99), always deferred to some form of utility or external and separate end. Bataille's argument suggests overall that the prohibitions which exist around the abject attempt to appropriate the associated passions, to 'socially channel and regularize' them and hold them at bay, but in so doing these prohibitions 'betray' our real need for redemptive expulsion such that this need always returns until properly confronted (Bataille 1985: 96). In other words, the social regulation of the abject must fail because all profane prohibitions of powerful human drives are rendered fragile against the range and strength of the drives themselves.

Read through Bataille, then, via the identification and exegesis of sexual harassment, and the development of policies, regulations and laws which will apparently eradicate it from the organization (or at least reduce it) so as to ensure that only healthy and functional forms of behaviour exist therein, the discourse on harassment seeks to appropriate this form of impassioned behaviour, to regu- late it, and to render it homogeneous with the utility-producing organizations which are the site of its occurrence. Put simply, this could, we suggest, be seen as an attempt to neutralize harassment as an expression of uncontrollable passions, as a reminder of the power of natural forces, and of the inevitability of death which always lurks beyond the abject. The real threat here of course is that, despite the best efforts of organizations to render themselves immune to the effects of the mortality of their individual members, unless they can master the forces of nature they will not themselves be immortal (Sievers 1995). Here, however, as should by now be clear, we contend that this effort is always doomed to fail – that the abject (as represented by harassment) will inevitably return to threaten the boundaries of organization precisely because of its constitution (and/or rejection) as abject and the failure to confront the passions – light or dark – which lie behind it. This failure to satisfy the need for expulsion in the discursive appropriation of harassment precisely represents our substantive argument – that the effects of the production of harassment in fact contribute to the conditions of (re)production of harassment itself. That is to say, the social regulation of harassment as a form of the abject provides a focal arena for the abject to return to trouble the boundaries of 'normal' sexual behaviour, and of 'normal' organizing, so that in seeking to control and contain harassment, to eradicate or at least reduce it, harassment discourse arguably (re-)creates a context ripe for its emergence or, in Bataille's terms, its expulsion.

Having established *why* harassment is constructed as dysfunctional, as abject, we now examine the ways in which this dysfunctionality is produced – that is to say, *how* is harassment constructed as dysfunctional?

Power and sexual harassment

> The other component [in sexual harassment in the City of London] is competition. The motivation here is not sexual, it is to do with rivalry and dominance. Because of the sums of money at stake, the competition, especially on trading floors, is intense. The encroachment of women into what was traditionally a male monopoly has exposed [male traders] to that competition. If a man loses a large sum of money, very often, more than his professional competence is threatened. His job is closely tied up with his identity. The link between money and power and sex becomes inverted when some male traders lose money; they feel impotent. One of the quickest solutions is to force their sexual persona on to female colleagues, by propositioning them, by making offensive sexual references.
>
> (Davies, L. 1994: 6)[4]

Sexual harassment is categorized by harassment discourse as a perversion, a sexual deviation or misdemeanour. This is because it is seen not to derive from 'real' sexual desire, but rather from a compulsion to dominate, to preserve power differentials through a denigration and undermining of its targets; that is, harassment is represented as an abuse of power. For example, Bratton claims that harassment is 'not about sex, [but] about power ... it supports and perpetuates a system in which one class of persons is systematically disempowered' (Bratton, cited in Van Tol 1991: 160).[5] Similarly, Tangri *et al.* (1982) suggest that harassment does not conform to the usual pattern of sexual courtship – that is to say, harasser and recipient are often not of similar age, social status, ethnic origin and so on – which implies that there is less likelihood of the recipient being genuinely attracted to the harasser. Rubenstein (1991), likewise, argues that there is no reason to expect harassment only to happen to attractive women. An evocative empirical instance of the abuse of power seen to be inherent in harassment is provided by Yount (1991), who states that the men in the US coal mine that she studied consolidated their domination of their female colleagues through sexualized behaviours including the stripping and greasing of these unfortunate women. Such behaviour, Yount claims, sent a clear message to the female miners that the pit was a male environment in which they remained only on sufferance. Another example is the experience of Michelle Vinson (Meritor Savings Bank v. Vinson 1986). Sidney Taylor, the vice president who hired Vinson as a trainee teller in the first instance, had, during the four years of her employment, constantly asked her to have sex with him. Although Vinson initially refused, she capitulated in the end, claiming that she feared losing her job. As well as between forty and fifty instances of intercourse, the harassment Vinson endured also included Taylor fondling her in public, exposing himself to her, following her into the toilets and raping her (Koen 1989: 291–2; Paetzold and O'Leary-Kelly 1996: 87–8). These two cases, then, speak evocatively of the discursive construction of harassment as always and already 'bad' sex, the intention of which is only ever to derogate its target.

Michelle Vinson's response to Taylor's behaviour – failing to make an official complaint because she was frightened of him – also illustrates a vicious circle that is commonly identified within harassment discourse, that the abuse of power which harassment represents means that its recipients are often reluctant to complain. Renick (1980), for example, suggests that power differentials render harassment 'inaudible'. A typical empirical claim in this regard is made by Stockdale (1991), who found that (a) 50 per cent of the 160 incidents of harassment reported by her respondents involved a male 'superior' harassing his female 'subordinate'; and (b) all of these incidents went unreported because of the status differential between harasser and recipient. This apparent harasser 'immunity', moreover, is identified as more pronounced in organizations where junior members are directly dependent on their seniors' good will for favourable assessment, career progression, continued employment, and so on. Maypole (1986), for instance, discusses the 'stranglehold' that their managers have over social workers, in terms of the former's control of employment conditions, assignments, promotion, assessment, salary and redundancies. This is argued to provide a series of levers for harassing behaviours. Education – and higher education in particular – also tends to be identified as a likely breeding ground for harassment, given the high degree of dependency of students on staff members in this context (Benson and Thomson 1982; Reilly *et al.* 1982; Hoffman 1986; Fitzgerald *et al.* 1988; Dziech and Weiner 1990; Bremer *et al.* 1991; Fitzgerald and Ormerod 1991; Barak *et al.* 1992), and there is an abundance of empirical data to support this claim. For example, in 27.7 per cent of the American secondary schools that Wishnietsky (1991) studied, disciplinary action had been taken as a result of teacher–pupil harassment – and he points out that this figure does not take account of unreported incidents. Similarly, Grauerholz's (1996: 30) overview of the available data from the US university sector indicates that 'one out of every two or three undergraduate women students, and a slightly greater proportion of women graduate students, have experienced some type of sexual harassment or sexually inappropriate behavior', and Schneider's (1987) survey of female postgraduate students, in the same context, saw something of the order of 60 per cent of the sample reporting that they had experienced harassment from their supervisors. Indeed, because of the pronounced character of power differentials in education, some of those who write about sexual harassment in this regard suggest that the only way to address the problem is to introduce anti-fraternization policies, which define sexual relationships between those of unequal power as automatic disciplinary offences on the part of the senior person involved (Schover *et al.* 1983; Hoffman 1986; Schneider 1987).

As Ellis *et al.*'s (1991) meta-analysis suggests, then, the overall organizational picture appears to be one in which sexual harassment is far more frequent in a relationship involving a power differential than it is between those of equal status – and it is true to say that the emphasis on power in the harassment discourse as a whole cannot be overstated. Indeed, as Benson and Thomson (1982: 247) explain, 'it is important ... to clarify that the issue of sexual harassment does not derive from a moralistic concern with sexual activity per se'. The discursive attention paid to harassment does not, it appears, stem from some notion that sex between members of organizations is morally unacceptable, but from a concern deriving from what are identified as the abusive roots of harassing behaviours.

Finally, it is also important to remark on the fact that many Western organizations have adopted some form of sexual harassment policy, as well as noting that unwelcome sexualized behaviour in the organization may now be considered legally actionable under the banner of sex discrimination – in both the US (Title VII of the Civil Rights Acts of 1964 and 1991) and the UK (the Sex Discrimination Acts of 1975 and 1986, for example). Prior to Williams v. Saxbe, by way of contrast, complaints of harassment (for example, Barnes v. Train 1974; Corne v. Bausch & Lomb, Inc. 1975; Miller v. Bank of America 1976) were dismissed by US courts on the basis that the behaviour concerned was seen *not* to consist of a discriminatory misuse of power. Rather, it was defined as the result of misunderstandings, of badly thought out sexual advances from one person to another. In most harassment complaints prior to Williams, then, the behaviour at the centre of the complaint was read to represent a private problem in which neither the legal system nor employers had the remit to interfere. The behaviour in the case of Barnes, for example, was seen by the court as evidence of a poor working relationship. The plaintiffs in Corne were told that their supervisor's unwanted sexualized behaviour was merely a proclivity or mannerism rather than anything more serious. Similarly, the Miller verdict attributed the behaviour at the centre of this complaint to the 'natural' sexual attraction of one sex to another (Koen 1989: 290–1). Williams, however, established harassment as an abuse of power, and the equivalent UK case (Strathclyde Regional Council v. Porcelli 1986) followed some ten years later.

The above review illustrates the division that harassment discourse constructs between sex which is healthy, consensual and contributes to the overall human good and sex which is unhealthy, non-consensual, tainted by an abuse of power and inevitably hurts or damages its targets.[6] This established, we contend that consensual sex is 'made good' by harassment discourse in the sense that it comes to represent a functional release of normal desires, a *mutual* expunging of sexual instincts, a means to an end. Mutuality, indeed, is crucial here – each party to the 'good' sexual relationship is constructed as having *individually decided* that they desire the other person and wish to have sex with them. Thus, even as they meet in the sexual embrace, they are constituted as and remain separate, autonomous monads who are parties to an emotional transaction – a very different representation of this interaction from that offered by Bataille:

> the totality of what is (the universe) swallows me (physically), and if it swallows me, or since it swallows me, I can't distinguish myself from it; nothing remains, except this or that, which are less meaningful than nothing. In a sense it is unbearable and I seem to be dying. It is at this cost, no doubt, that I am no longer myself, but an infinity in which I am lost.
>
> (Bataille 1997: 267)

> In a word, the object of desire is the universe in the form of him who, in the embrace, is the mirror in which we ourselves are reflected. In the most live instant of fusion, the pure splendor of light, like an unexpected bolt of lightening [*sic*], illuminates the field of possibilities.
>
> (Bataille, cited in Rella 1994: 99)

The Bataillian embrace, then, does not afford the participants purchase on each other as they are, in some natural and objective sense, but instead allows them to see each other in a way which simultaneously reflects back to the viewer aspects of themselves, and renders each party indistinguishable from and a product of the relationship between them. Identity, for Bataille, was located in this connectedness rather than in individuality, and he expressed this idea in a critique of an 'ontology of nudity' (Richardson 1994: 37). Bataille argued that nudity was not a natural condition but one in which we lose an element of our personalities (signified in our clothes, jewellery, cosmetic enhancements, and so on) and therefore experience a certain vertigo, a sense of anguish at the discontinuity with the natural world and other people, triggered by the loss of both functionality and stylistic congruence which we experience in undressing and 'a laceration, a terrifying shattering of our being' (Richardson 1994: 38) as we come face to face with our own stripped-down reality. That is, nakedness brings home the disconnection from and lack of the other, of continuity and community, which lies at the heart of our individuality. Thus for Bataille, 'The idea of there being a natural state [of nudity] from which we are separated by social conventions and which can be recovered by laying ourselves bare is a particularly pernicious form of puritanism' (Richardson 1994: 38), whereas the construction of 'good' sex in harassment discourse seems to suggest precisely the opposite, to evoke the nakedness which is commonly part of consensual sexual relations as a 'getting back to basics', a *rediscovering* of our connectedness, a pure and entirely natural form of human expression. In fact, 'good' sex, as produced by harassment discourse, seems analogous with the scenario conjured by Habermas's (1979) ideal speech situation – sexual interaction free from hidden agendas or implied coercion. Sexual harassment, on the other hand, in its lack of respect for individuality or autonomy, is 'bad' sex – and marks off the territory of 'good' sex in harassment discourse. It therefore becomes, alongside other 'perversions' like rape and sexual abuse, an important device in the social regulation of sexuality.

To extend this argument further, the abjection which underlies harassment contains both the threat of dominant behaviour (by the other or over the other) and the threat of not being loved (by, or not loving, the other). In other words, the set of problems to which harassment discourse is one response is characterized by the fact that we are as actors simultaneously tempted by those activities to which we do not want to fall victim. Anyone who has ever had sex with someone they did not love should know this tension intimately. We need to remember here that the abject is a denied part of ourselves which constantly threatens return, and that identifying and classifying our own motives for particular acts, as well as those of others, are just as important as constraining others. Guilt as well as blame are equal partners in the scrutinizing operations of Foucault's (1985) 'hermeneutics of the self'. Both of these concerns permeate 'normal' relationships, although the latter is more frequently voiced as a concern within them. While these dimensions are often viewed as being exclusive (that is, power kills love through killing reciprocity; love levels all power relationships), the reality of human relationships suggests that there is considerable interpenetrating between them. In contra-distinction, harassment discourse could be seen to imply, and even depend upon, the existence of what Giddens (1991) calls 'the pure relationship' – the relationship in and for itself as it emerges over time – in which the relationship as relationship takes priority over any of its elements, whether these be lust, shared work activity, common social interests, intellectual affinity or anything else. This idealized relationship is grounded in the principle of self-denial – individual drives, desires or interests are always subordinated to the preservation of the quality of the relationship, however that is defined by the parties, and any resurgence of them is taken to threaten the relationship accordingly. Ironically, although this 'velvet cage' model of the relationship might appear to be a romantic reaction to the transactional and interest-based approach to relationships represented by the recent extension of neo-classical economic thought into the human sphere in the work of such thinkers as Gary Becker, in reality it simply reincorporates them through the idea of 'working at our relationship' with its supporting industry of counsellors and divorce lawyers, and the technologies of family therapy and pre-nuptial agreements. For Bataille, however, and for Foucault in his extension of Bataille's work into the discursive, there is no 'self' outside the relationship, no self whose interests and desires are formed and sustained independent of that relationship, no self whose interests and desires can be separated and, if necessary excluded, from it.[7] Consequently, no relationship can ever be 'pure' even in the attenuated sense in which Giddens uses the term. Self is both lost in and formed by the relationship. The 'pure' relationship is a myth in that there can be no relationship which is free from the operations of power and desire, forces over which we are never fully in control.

In constituting harassment as a signifier of the *perversion* of power in a relationship, harassment discourse establishes the illusion that the abject has been identified and eliminated, that we are safe from unruly power and desire as long as we are free from harassment as discursively defined; and, in casting doubt over those relationships which might be seen to be 'motivated' in some way, it also feeds our anxiety over our connectivity with others through preserving the myth of the 'pure' relationship.

Indeed, Foucault (1980, 1982) observes that to see power as something which allows one person to hold sway over or coerce another is to see power as a 'zero-sum' game, as a possession which some have and some do not. What follows from this is the assumption that those who have power are at liberty to exploit those who do not without limits – to use and abuse them for their own self-serving ends, regardless of the other's 'rights' and 'needs' as an 'individual'. Power here becomes something that can work on and warp 'natural' human experience – like the 'pure' relationship – such that its abuse represents a significant challenge to the identities of those subjected to it because it ignores or dismisses their individual licence. That is to say, 'power is bad, ugly, poor, sterile, monotonous and dead; and what power is exercised upon is right, good and rich' (Foucault 1988: 120). Harassment discourse, then, constitutes the belief that, in engaging in 'good' sex, we are:

> affirming the rights of our sex against all power, when in fact we are fastened to the discourse on sex that has lifted up from deep within us a sort of mirage in which we think we see ourselves reflected – the dark shimmer of sex.
>
> (Foucault 1979: 157)

Consequently, we see power as working upon sex to shape and deform it only because we are subject to, and have been made subject by, the operations of discourses such as those surrounding marriage, courtship, adultery – and sexual harassment. We come to believe in the possibility of sex-without-power, 'good' sex (as an element of the 'pure' relationship), and strive to engage (or to convince ourselves that we engage) only in this form of sex. Foucault contends instead that this power-free sex is impossible, because sex does not exist outside of the powerful effects of discourse. Thus there can be no such thing as 'good' sex, because there is no sexual *logos* against which sexual *eros* can be evaluated. Sexual harassment is not the frontier at which power acting on sex begins because all that we know of sex has come about as a result of power, and so we cannot achieve sexual emancipation as we have been constituted to believe in it, as a state of erotic existence free from power. Indeed, 'One must not suppose there exists a certain sphere of sexuality ... were it not the object of mechanisms of prohibition brought to bear by the economic or ideological requirements of power' (Foucault 1979: 98).

Consequently, when we engage in what we perceive to be 'good' sex, the kind of sex good subjects and good citizens enjoy, we reveal only our subjection through a broader discursive regime of sexuality of which harassment discourse is part. In coming to define certain acts as harassment, we may seek to eradicate them but the ideal of 'good' sex will continue to elude us because there is no such thing. As long as we strive for 'good' sex, moreover, we will continue to experience 'bad' sex – because there can never be 'good' sex. We remain trapped in the anxious quest for something which does not exist, something which is a historical contingency alone. In reproducing 'good' or 'pure' sexual arrangements (dating, co-habitation, marriage), we therefore enmesh ourselves further in the conviction that consensual sex is crucial to us as healthy human beings. We continue to subject ourselves to power (Minson 1986) such that our sexual choices can be seen actually to reinforce the operations of power over and through us, while we believe that we are working to free ourselves from power, 'affirming the rights of our sex against all power'. In both Foucault and Bataille's terms, we are labouring in this regard to preserve our individuality, to consolidate our sense of ourselves as beings with a set of inalienable rights, with dignity, with choices to be made and autonomy to be exercised. The abject of sexual harassment, however, must inevitably return because, although we cannot tolerate it within our vision of what it is to be human and what it is to organize, the fragility of the boundaries between 'good' and 'bad' sex – or, put another way, between discontinuous individuality and continuous totality – ensures that, in engaging in the former, we will always have the latter.

Women and sexual harassment

As well as emphasizing that harassment is sex-without-desire, sex-and-power, harassment discourse also constructs this set of behaviours as deriving from a man and directed at a woman. Harassment is coded as dysfunctional in this regard because it apparently speaks of and, perhaps more significantly, seeks to preserve gendered power differentials. Although many commentators do make the effort to state that harassment is not something which *exclusively* happens to women, to acknowledge that harassers and recipients can be of either gender, it would be inaccurate to say that the discourse *actually succeeds* in producing harassment as a non-gendered phenomenon. Its overweening message is, first of all, that harassment is proof of male social privilege as reflected in male power in the organization; that men harass because they are dominant, socially and organizationally. In fact, MacKinnon places societal gender power above organizational power in her explanation of sexual harassment, which she defines as 'a clear manifestation of the privilege incarnated in the male sex role that supports coercive sexuality, reinforced by male power over the job' (MacKinnon 1979: 107). Tangri *et al.* (1982) agree that the origins of harassment lie beyond the organization, that organizational power derives at least in part from societal power and that organizations are microcosms of power relations in the wider society. In a similar vein, Stringer *et al.* (1990: 45) suggest that:

Gender power makes women with achieved power particularly vulnerable to sexual harassment. Even when a woman has role, information or money power in an organization, she does not have access to the societal value placed on the male gender.

Perhaps most emphatically in this regard, Grauerholz (1989, 1996) discusses the phenomenon of 'contrapower harassment' – junior men (students, in her research) harassing senior women (members of academic staff) by virtue of their superior social status *and regardless of their inferior organizational status*. Second, harassment is also constructed as a male attempt to *maintain* dominance by 'intimidating, discouraging or precipitating the removal of women from work' (Tangri *et al.* 1982: 40). We have already referred to Yount's (1991) study of US coal mining in this regard, and Collinson and Collinson's (1989: 99–103, 107–9) account of the experiences of a woman who was elected to the previously all-male executive committee of a company-based trade union division makes much the same point. After complaining of sustained harassment from other men in the union, Sue was told by another male colleague simply to quit her job if she could not take the pressure.

This gendering of harassment is widespread throughout the discourse, whether explicitly or implicitly. We should certainly note that there are some commentators who will not accept that a woman harassing a man is analogous to the reverse, on the basis that women do not enjoy the same social power as men and therefore cannot intimidate men in the same way as men can women. Hoffman, for example, comments that 'sex-neutral institutional policy may contribute to the elimination of sexual harassment. It leaves unchallenged, however, central assumptions about male and female sexuality and reduces the problem of sexual harassment to an inappropriate use of sexuality' (Hoffman 1986: 111 – see also Benson and Thomson 1982; Fain and Anderton 1987; Ehrenreich 1990).

In terms of the more implicit aspects of the gendering process, some published empirical findings concerning perceptions or experiences of harassment do derive from mixed gender respondent groups (for example, Jensen and Gutek 1982; Lott *et al.* 1982; Reilly *et al.* 1982; Weber-Burdin and Rossi 1982; Maypole 1986; Terpstra and Baker 1987; Saal *et al.* 1989; Baker *et al.* 1990; Malovich and Stake 1990), but it is worth noting that the critical incidents which often form part of data gathering in harassment research usually follow the script of a powerless woman being harassed by a powerful man. For example, Saal (1990) asked his subjects to respond to several vignettes including the following:

- A male supervisor asks a female employee personal questions about her sex life.
- A male executive and his female associate are planning a business trip, and he reserves only one hotel room.

- A manager tells his female secretary that she must sleep with him because it is his right – he pays her salary.

(Saal 1990, cited in Saal 1996: 76)

Furthermore, the use of the female third person pronoun when referring to the recipients of harassment is so widespread in the discourse as to almost escape detection. Same sex harassment also tends to be ignored and, if it is acknowledged, may be considered to consist in the haranguing of homosexual men by heterosexual men, such as on the subject of AIDS (Smith, M.L. 1992). When research deals with homosexual women, it tends to focus on their reactions to being harassed by *men* (for example, Schneider 1982). We have been unable to locate any discussion of women sexually harassing each other.

Likewise, certain legal provisions enshrine the principle that it is men who harass women – there are numerous cases that have succeeded on what might be seen to be an assumption of men's greater social power, even in the absence of any organizational power differentials. For example:

- Strathclyde Regional Council v. Porcelli (UK, 1986) – a female technician was harassed by her male colleagues, their behaviour included suggestive remarks and forcing her to brush up against them in order to walk by.
- Hall v. Gus Construction Co. (US, 1988) – one female worker was called 'herpes' by her male colleagues, who also urinated in her car's petrol tank. A fellow plaintiff had been sexually propositioned, insulted and touched on the breasts and the thighs.
- Robinson v. Jacksonville Shipyards (US, 1991) – this case involved a woman complaining of male colleagues displaying pictures of nude and partially nude women and making sexually derogatory remarks and jokes.
- Salmon v. David and others (UK, 1998) – workers openly reading pornographic magazines and engaging in sexual banter was seen to represent harassment of a female colleague.

It is also worth noting the application of the 'reasonable woman' standard in cases of hostile environment harassment, discussed in more detail later in this chapter, by certain US courts. That is to say, the rule that has been used in these instances is whether a 'reasonable woman' would see the behaviour concerned as hostile or abusive. This is so as to adjudge whether, in an objective sense, harassing behaviour has so detrimentally affected the plaintiff's working environment that it can be seen as actionable. The use of the reasonable woman standard is underpinned by the belief 'that using the reasonable person standard [may] risk enforcing the prevailing level of discrimination because that standard would be male biased' (*West Legal Directory*), given considerable evidence that 'women and men view harassing conduct differently (i.e., that what is perceived as offensive by some women may not be viewed as offensive by some men)' (Paetzold and O'Leary-Kelly 1996: 95). Ellison v. Brady (1991, involving a man making repeated requests of a female colleague for dates, sending her unsolicited love letters and loitering around her desk) was one of the first, alongside the Robinson case described above, to establish this precedent.[8]

Why though is harassment deemed to be specifically *sexual* in its apparent efforts to keep women down in organizations? Gutek and Morasch (1982; see also Gutek 1985; Konrad and Gutek 1986; Gutek *et al.* 1990; Gutek and Cohen 1992) attribute this to what they call 'sex role spillover'. When the sex ratio in a particular working context is skewed in one direction or the other, spillover is seen to occur. That is to say, when there are many more women than men, such as in nursing, the job in question becomes 'feminized' (i.e. it is seen to demand specifically 'feminine' characteristics); when there are many more men than women, such as in the construction industry, women simply stand out by virtue of their sex. Thus in both cases women are treated as women as opposed to workers by their male colleagues. Such treatment may well include harassment, or so Gutek and colleagues claim, given that the stereotype of the female sex role is, at least in part, one of women as sexual objects. Moreover, this belief that women are sexually attractive *and* sexually available is argued within harassment discourse to generate two further effects: the first when women who complain of harassment are seen to be disingenuous, as having at least welcomed if not actively invited the behaviour, and the second in that women who are the recipients of harassment tend to assume that they must in some way have been responsible for the behaviour.[9] Phelps and Winternitz's (1992) account of the Clarence Thomas–Anita Hill case provides an example in the first regard. One of the claims made in the Senate hearings by Thomas's team was that Hill was an erotomaniac, that she craved male sexual attention to the extent that she was often forced to imagine it. In labelling Hill in this way, the double implication was that (a) had the alleged behaviour actually taken place, she would certainly have welcomed it, indeed had probably incited it; and (b) the likelihood was that she had invented the allegations in their entirety in any case. Evidence presented to support this 'diagnosis' included the so-called 'pube affidavit'. This document, signed by a former student of Hill's at Oral Roberts University, claimed that, when she returned graded term papers to the class, she had inserted pubic hairs between the pages. On the second issue, both Renick (1980) and Grauerholz (1989) argue that women often understand themselves as little more than objects for men's sexual relief, and Bremer *et al.* (1991) similarly have it that women, especially younger women, may feel confused as to whether the revulsion they experience in instances of harassment is actually an appropriate way to react, or whether in fact they are over-reacting to behaviour which they themselves have (albeit unintentionally) provoked. Women may also be depicted as failing to recognize harassment for what it is, and a gap is commonly identified between 'objective' and 'subjective' definitions of these behaviours. For example, Fitzgerald and Ormerod, focusing specifically on female students, suggest that:

> One of the consequences of the confusion surrounding the concept of harassment is the consistent finding that, although a limited number of both graduate and undergraduate female students report that they experience

obviously harassing behaviours such as touching, fondling, and proposing, only a small percentage of these same women indicate that they believe they have been sexually harassed.

(Fitzgerald and Ormerod 1991: 283, emphasis added)

In a similar vein, Barak *et al.* (1992) cite the fact that, while 57.8 per cent of the female students in their sample had experienced objective sexual harassment behaviours, only 4.3 per cent of this same group saw themselves as actually having been harassed (also see Collins and Blodgett 1981; Bremer *et al.* 1991; Brooks and Perot 1991).

In sum, harassment is discursively constructed as men sexually degrading women in organizations largely because of the gendered (hence unequal) distribution of power in wider society, and as part of their attempt to preserve this inequality. Harassers are understood to be (socially and/or organizationally) powerful men, recipients powerless and hapless women who require special protection from harassment, given that (a) it stems from power differentials which are beyond their individual control; and (b) their sex role constructs them as sexually available in any case. For example, in discussing organizational measures to combat harassment, the European Commission's Code of Practice recommends that:

employers should designate someone to provide advice and assistance to employees subjected to sexual harassment, where possible, with responsibilities to assist in the resolution of any problems, whether through informal or formal means ... Often such a role may be provided by someone from the employee's trade union or by *women's support groups*.

(European Commission 1991: 15, emphasis added)

Rubenstein and De Vries (1993: 67), in their guide to implementing the Code further suggest that it is important to ensure that the harassment contacts who are appointed are trusted by female employees. Similarly, Brighton Borough Council (UK), which dubs its all-female contacts 'sympathetic friends', was told during the first review of this system that it was very difficult

for recipients [of harassment] to acquire information about whom to contact about their problems without heralding to all concerned that they were seeking this information. It was suggested that information about the names and extension numbers of sympathetic friends should be displayed in the *women's toilets* in the Council.

(Wilkinson 1991: 13, emphasis added)

The harassment dynamic presented here could, however, be seen to map on to conservative heterosexist understandings present in wider society: (a) that heterosexual sex is the only 'real' form of sex; and (b) that, in sexual activity, men are active and women passive. Women are also constructed here as *victims*, of sexual attention that they do not want, but do not necessarily recognize as harassment, and need assistance in withstanding. The female subject constituted here is helpless in the face of such attention from her male colleagues; there is a certain 'hysterization' of female sexuality, a construction of this sexuality as peculiarly, even pathologically, vulnerable (Foucault 1979: 104). We would suggest that such a hysterization may translate into women understanding themselves as unable to fight back against unwanted sexual attention experienced in organizations, because to adopt the female subject position constructed within harassment discourse implies a learned helplessness, an understood inability to prevent or even understand men's behaviours towards them and an understood dependency on others. Moreover, if women come to see themselves in this way, this allows those men who choose to harass their female colleagues greater licence to (continue to) do so.

To be sure, the argument that discourse produces gendered subject positions such that women may come to see, think, feel, act, talk and behave differently from men is not one that appears in Foucault's work to any significant degree. The brief acknowledgement that women's sexuality is constituted as especially fragile through the operations of modern discourse on sexuality is scarcely developed elsewhere in his work. Consequently, Bartky, for one, asks 'Where is the account of the disciplinary practices that engender the "docile bodies" of women, more docile than the bodies of men? ... [Foucault] is blind to those disciplines which produce a modality of embodiment which is peculiarly feminine' (Bartky, cited in Ramazanoğlu and Holland, 1993: 250). However, we agree with McNay (1992: 32–8) that Foucault's inattention to gender as a discursive regime arguably represents an excusable (when we consider that his primary interests lay elsewhere) lacuna in his work rather than a serious theoretical difficulty. That is to say, it is entirely possible to give a Foucauldian account of the ways in which the human subject becomes masculine or feminine – of us constituted not simply as subjects-with-a-sexuality but at the same time as *gendered* subjects (see, for example, Butler 1990, 1993; Kerfoot and Knights 1993, 1996; Brewis *et al.* 1997a; Kerfoot 1999; Moodley 1999) – and to discuss their implications without departing from the original Foucault in any substantive way. Indeed, gendered subject positions, the textual roles of masculinity and femininity, are offered to us in such an impactful way that we tend to strive to live up to our 'genderedness', to reproduce whichever half of the prevailing binary is 'rightfully ours', as seamlessly as we can in everyday life. As a consequence, although women may never attain the relevant discursive version of femininity (nor men the corresponding ideal of masculinity), these images to some degree mould the lives of millions of real members of both sexes (Hearn 1987: 98; Horrocks 1994: 143–5). It is in *extending* Foucault, therefore, that we can argue that men and women may be differentially constituted by harassment discourse and, further, that the positioning of women's desires as inevitably subordinate to those of men in this discourse may be seen to create/perpetuate the conditions of (re)production of sexual harassment. Discussion in a later section of this chapter, moreover, focuses on the particular ways in which harassment discourse can be seen to constitute men.

We should also point out that the argument that harassment discourse makes victims of women has been echoed elsewhere. The so-called 'power feminists' criticize harassment discourse precisely for its assumption that women need special concessions to enable them to cope with the rigours of organizational life, that they are always helpless and hapless. These commentators agree that women are the primary *recipients* of sexual harassment – but they do not see this to mean that women are necessarily *victims*, or that strategies for dealing with harassment should be so paternalistic as to actually render women victims. For example:

> [There is] a tension between creating a sanctuary and constituting a political space; between protecting the vulnerable and binding up their wounds, and politicizing those same individuals in an avowedly feminist direction and sending them forward to challenge that same status quo.
>
> (Elshtain, cited in Hoffman 1986: 114)

> Rules and laws based on the premise that all women need protection from all men, because they are so much weaker, serve only to reinforce the image of women as powerless.
>
> (Roiphe 1994: 89–90)

Elshtain implies that the protectionism represented as necessary by harassment discourse means that women can only continue to be helpless, hapless victims, that they will only continue to need protection because of a consequent belief that they are incapable of fighting back against harassment on their own. She, by way of contrast, rejects such protectionism in favour of a consciousness-raising empowerment, an effort to restore full organizational citizenship to women. Here, then, Elshtain argues that women *are* capable of confronting harassment on their own terms and that efforts to tackle harassment should be targeted at developing this capacity in them. Like Elshtain, Roiphe argues that for women to take refuge behind arguments of the omnipotence of men is to do themselves few favours; that if they cower behind the protection of others they will only consolidate their victimhood and become yet more psychologically fragile. She suggests that the way in which harassment discourse confers victimhood on women may in fact constitute women as incapable of coping effectively with any instance of unwanted sexualized behaviour.

In a similar vein, Strossen, talking of the tension between ensuring equality of employment opportunity and free speech, suggests that:

> Throughout US history, measures designed to 'protect' women in the workforce have undermined women's full and equal participation. Overly 'protective' restrictions of sexually explicit speech in the workplace would follow in this tradition … Protectionist legislation assumes that women

cannot make informed plans or decisions on their own. Regardless of the benevolent intent of such measures, they reflect and reinforce a patronising, paternalistic view of women's sexuality that is inconsistent with their full equality and works to their detriment.

(Strossen 1993: 8)[10]

As our earlier analysis suggests, we are in sympathy with these arguments that it is potentially problematic to make heavy weather of the sexual victimization of women by men, given that to persuade women of their essential vulnerability is probably to ensure that they are unlikely to take any steps against harassment in their own organizational contexts. Nonetheless, we disagree with power feminism to the extent that it constitutes women as self-reliant across the board, the behaviour of their male friends and colleagues notwithstanding. Roiphe suggests that:

> Instead of learning that men have no right to do these terrible things to us, we should be learning to deal with individuals with strength and confidence. If someone bothers us, we should be able to put him in his place without crying into our pillow or screaming for help or counseling ... we should at least be able to handle petty instances [of harassment] like ogling, leering and sexual innuendo on the personal level.

(Roiphe 1994: 101–2)

What Roiphe implies here is that women ought to be able to consciously control not only their own behaviour but that of others – that is to say, men's – as well. Here the organizational woman is charged with a particular set of responsibilities: she is constituted as the polar opposite of the victim which harassment discourse constructs. Therefore, while power feminism does go some way towards questioning the certainties of harassment discourse, it immediately replaces these certainties with its own – that women must be accountable for their own behaviour *and* the behaviour of others towards them. Consequently, an individual woman's relationship to self as constituted by power feminism can also be seen as problematic, fraught as it would be with what Dews (1984: 84) refers to as 'the stifling anguish of responsibility'. An evocative example of this is to be found in the details offered by MacCannell and MacCannell (1993) of an incident in New York's Central Park. The woman involved had mistakenly caught the wrong bus and had therefore alighted at the opposite side of the park to her home. The account of what subsequently happened is reported here by someone else:

> She got out and realised her mistake. It was about five o'clock in the afternoon. She decided to walk through the park. On the way she met this gang of boys, about five or six of them, aged ten to maybe eighteen. They all successively raped her. She got raped like a few times by that gang. Then she started to run after they were done and got stopped another time by this

huge guy. He raped her. And she ran the rest of the way home … It was written up in the *Spectator*. She was interviewed about a week later. She said it didn't bother her. She just realised what the situation was, and she was in the wrong. She wasn't traumatised by it at all. She said 'I was in the wrong place at the wrong time. I made a mistake and this weird thing happened to me.'

(reported in Wachs 1988: 118, cited in MacCannell and MacCannell 1993: 208)

Here, the woman who was raped apparently assimilated the trauma of a gang rape followed by a second rape, a deeply traumatic and disturbing experience by contemporary discursive standards, as *her own fault* for deciding to take a particular route home. She does not question the behaviour of the rapists, preferring to see herself as to blame for their behaviour towards her. This somewhat extreme instance of taking full and active responsibility for one's own sexual experiences arguably illustrates the 'stifling anguish' to which Dews refers – having to attribute all sexual experiences as resulting from one's own actions, however discomfiting or frightening those experiences might be. Here, on the one hand, this woman had to deal with the after-effects of the rapes and, on the other, also coped with the belief that, through more 'careful' conduct, she could have avoided the experience altogether. Indeed, this sort of response is a form of denial, not of the experience but of the causes of the experience, in that it refuses recognition as such of formless, capricious and unpredictable forces outside the control of the individual and consequently suppresses the abject such that it will always return.

It seems, in summary, that the discourses of sexual harassment and of power feminism may constitute women in equally problematic ways. Harassment, on the one hand, becomes understood as an inevitable consequence of gendered power differentials and the prevailing female sex role, and therefore as something with which women cannot cope alone; on the other, it is constructed as something for which women can and therefore should assume responsibility. Either way, it is arguable that these discursive representations seem to create/perpetuate conditions for the (re)production of harassment – in the continuing construction of the weak and helpless female victim, or the constitution of the female subject who can only blame herself if harassment continues, indeed if it occurs *per se*. Thus to some extent they may be seen to assure the return of this particular organizational abject, even in their apparent remit to eradicate or reduce its prevalence.

Men and sexual harassment

We have already established that sex occupies a position of prime importance in harassment discourse, in that harassment, because it is characterized as sex-and-power, is considered always and already to be 'bad' sex. Sex, it is implied, must be 'good', because it lies so close to the heart of what it is to be human.[11] This positioning of sex is consolidated within harassment discourse in its focus on the *sexual* element of harassing behaviours; the most striking evidence of which is the emphasis on the negative consequences of the experience of harassment itself. While the tangible consequences of harassment are often noted (such as losing one's job or being refused a promotion as a result of rejecting sexual advances, or having to submit to such advances to keep a position or ensure career progression), the psychological consequences of being a recipient are also writ large across the discourse. Research (see, for example, Frazier and Cohen 1992; Gutek and Koss 1993) into the specific consequences of sexual harassment for the individual reports that being harassed causes anger, frustration, anxiety and depression, even post-traumatic stress disorder, because (it is implied) of its sexually punitive character. Likewise, commentators such as Vinciguerra (1989) point to the need not to uphold economic or career-related detriment over mental hurt resulting from harassment. Harassment is therefore constructed not only as discriminatory against but also as peculiarly degrading of the women who experience it. It is presented as causing distress above and beyond the kind of problems caused by other forms of sex-based discrimination, such as asking questions about childcare arrangements or geographical mobility only of women at interview. Another point at which this problematization of the sex in harassment is clearly manifest is the argument against understanding harassment as a sex discrimination issue only. Certain writers argue that characterizing harassment as discrimination alone to some extent neutralizes the noxiousness of the conduct involved. They imply that there is more to harassment than discrimination – that is, that its sexual element renders it especially serious – although they may simultaneously argue that expedience necessitates presenting harassment as primarily discriminatory in order to have it publicly problematized at all. In other words, the claim is that it may be easier to ensure a recognition of organizational sex discrimination than of psychologically injurious sexual abuse in that same organization or, as Weeks *et al.* (1986: 448) put it: 'Viewing sexual harassment as simply another form of sex discrimination narrows the scope to a "role equity" issue which is less controversial since it only involves extending to some women the rights enjoyed by other groups.'

Moreover, harassment discourse tends to construct harassment as consisting of a wide range of behaviours. Many (if not most) forms of interaction are presented as sexualized and, consequently, as potentially unwelcome and upsetting. Crocker (1983), Schneider (1987) and Stockdale (1991) all identify, for example, a need to recognize non-physical behaviours like jokes, verbal advances or posters as possibly representing harassment. Organizational policies also frequently allow for 'milder' instances of behaviour to be defined as harassing. For example, in the UK, the Royal Mail's policy defines harassment as follows: 'the key issue is whether [the behaviour] is unwanted by the recipient or undermines people's dignity at work' (Royal Mail sexual harassment policy, cited in *Bargaining Report* 1992: 5). In the list of examples of possibly harassing behaviours which follows, the policy includes sexually suggestive or explicit posters. Moreover, it is often stated (by, for instance, Brandenburg 1982 and Hoffman 1986) that organizational sexual harassment policies should be related to but separate from broader equal opportunities policies, in order to underline the special significance of *sexual* harassment.

Legal provisions also demonstrate this understanding of harassment as disturbing in and of itself because of its sexual character. The US Civil Rights Act (1964, 1991) and the UK Sex Discrimination Act (1975, 1986) both allow for cases of harassment to be brought which have not necessarily resulted in *quid pro quo* loss (/gain – in a situation where the recipient complies with the advances). This is the aforementioned concept of hostile environment harassment, as sanctioned by the US Supreme Court in Meritor. Harassment, then, can be assumed in American legal terms to be discriminatory[12] *on its own*:

> For [hostile environment] sexual harassment to be actionable it must be sufficiently severe or pervasive to alter the conditions of the victim's working employment and create an abusive working environment.
>
> (US Supreme Court, cited in Koen 1989: 292)

> Sexual harassment also occurs when sexual conduct or communication 'unreasonably interfer[es] with an individual's work performance.' Tangible loss of pay, benefits or the job itself is not required for sexual harassment to be claimed and proven.
>
> (*West Legal Directory*)[13]

> [Hostile environment harassment] involves a situation in which sexual conduct has the purpose or effect of unreasonably interfering with an individual's work performance or creating an intimidating, hostile, or offensive work environment.
>
> (Paetzold and O'Leary-Kelly 1996: 86)

Hostile environment is also a permissible claim under the UK Sex Discrimination Act. Here sex discrimination is considered to be any action which (a) consists of less favourable treatment of one sex than another; (b) is based on sex; and (c) represents an employment 'detriment' to the applicant (IDS Employment Law Handbook 1993). This detriment can be dismissal, denial of employment opportunity or, as Rubenstein (1991: 35) explains, 'although the words "sexual harassment" do not appear in the Sex Discrimination Act, it is "legal shorthand for activity which is easily recognizable as 'subjecting her to any other detriment'"' within the meaning of the Act'. Further, it has been established elsewhere that detriment simply means 'putting under a disadvantage' (Lord Justice Brandon, in Jeremiah v. Ministry of Defence, cited in *IRS Employment Trends* 1992b: 10). Again, then, harassment, if seen to have had a sufficiently negative impact on the recipient's working environment, can be considered to constitute a disadvantage to that recipient merely by virtue of having taken place; 'there is no need for the offending behaviour to result in concrete developments such as a transfer or disciplinary action, or for it to amount to grounds for constructive dismissal' (*IRS Employment Trends* 1992b: 10).

An example is provided in Salmon v. David and others (1998), as discussed earlier. Applicant Salmon won her claim of sex discrimination on the basis that her employers, the Prison Service, allowed a hostile working environment to persist. In this instance, the tribunal (cited in Equal Opportunities Review 1998: 6) ruled that:

> The explicit approval of and delight in women as creatures for the provision of sexual gratification for men by prison officers was bound to have the effect of creating a humiliating working environment for women officers, especially one such as the applicant who had chosen the Prison Service with a view to advancing her career therein.

Moreover, the UK case of Insitu Cleaning and anor[14] v. Heads (1995) demonstrates that unwanted sexualized behaviour need not be particularly severe or indeed pervasive in the usual understanding of these terms in order to be legally actionable. Heads, employed by Insitu as an area supervisor, attended a meeting with a director and a manager of the company. The manager, who entered the meeting late, greeted her with the remark 'Hiya big tits'. Heads succeeded in her complaint of sex discrimination. Furthermore, when the case went to appeal, the Employment Appeal Tribunal (EAT) also awarded in her favour; these two decisions despite the behaviour only having taken place once and being verbal alone. EAT said that the original tribunal

> had been entitled to find on the facts that H[eads] had suffered a detriment. The fact that B [the manager involved] was the bosses' son and had made the remark to a female employee twice his age was bound to cause distress and was unacceptable behaviour. The European Commission Code of Practice on measures to combat sexual harassment makes it clear that such conduct is likely to create an intimidating, hostile and humiliating work environment for the victim.
>
> (*IDS Brief* 1995: 4–5)[15]

As we have already seen, however, for Foucault (1979), modern discourse on sexuality lends sex a false unity, and thereby an artificial importance. We could therefore argue that, because harassment has a sexual character, this explains why it has been discursively constructed as problematic in other ways than its economic and career-related consequences, and as potentially consisting of a wide range of behaviours. Furthermore, it is suggested here that the understanding among human subjects that a 'healthy', self-governed sex life is crucial to human happiness, as constituted by the operations of discourses such as that of sexual harassment, may again create/perpetuate the conditions of (re)production of sexual harassment in particular ways. This understanding that one's sexuality is peculiarly important is visible, for example, in the current proliferation of self-help sex manuals and videos in the West (Giddens 1991; Hawkes 1996). Indeed, as Brewis and Grey (1994: 74) point out, 'The notion of sexual healthiness is a profoundly disciplinary one … one of the legacies of the "sexual revolution" of the 1960s is a constant, anxious self-surveillance of sex.' If we understand sex as centrally important, and it seems that we do, this can be argued to simultaneously subject us to particular imperatives regarding our sex lives, such that we are aware to a highly attenuated degree of the 'significance' of our sexuality and may therefore labour to ensure that our sexual 'requirements' are met.[16]

Further to this, it has been established already that harassment discourse constructs harassment as heterosexual; as taking place between an active man and a passive woman. This heterosexism, which as we have suggested is a widespread discursive phenomenon, can be argued to privilege the man over the woman as the initiator of sexual activity, by and large. The woman, consenting or otherwise, is the recipient/receptacle of the man's advances. Thus it is possible to suggest that the understanding that one's sex life is crucially important is generally more powerful for men. Indeed, Hollway (1989) emphasizes that what she refers to as the 'male sexual drive' discourse is prevalent amongst modern men – that many believe that they *need* to have frequent sex.[17] It is argued here, therefore, that the operations of harassment discourse may serve to produce or consolidate the understanding on the part of men that they are necessarily sexually aggressive *as well as* necessarily sexually needy, having to instigate and engage in sexual activity at all costs, with or without the consent of the chosen woman. Just as the emphasis on female passivity may create/perpetuate the subject position of victim-woman, and women come to understand themselves as helpless in the face of unwanted male sexual attention, the heterosexist privileging of sex in harassment discourse could be argued to make harassers of men, or at least to perpetuate this kind of behaviour. Furthermore, those men who experience difficulty in sustaining a masculine identity by more conventional means – that is to say, attracting and engaging in sex with a willing woman – are perhaps particularly vulnerable in this respect.[18] In fact, our discussion in chapter 1, as well as other literature on masculinity (see, for example, Brittan 1989; Seidler 1989, 1997; Stoltenberg 1990; Kerfoot and Knights 1993, 1996; Kerfoot and Whitehead 1996; Kerfoot 1999), points to the consequences – such as sexual violence – which may result from men settling themselves into the subject position of the macho, predatory male. Ironically, then, while harassment discourse seeks on the whole to challenge the 'myth' of uncontrollable male libido (for example, Tangri *et al.* 1982), as well as constructing 'good' sex as taking place between individuals of equal status and equal capacity to choose what unfolds within the sexual encounter, its emphasis on the importance of sex *and* its heterosexism may serve to perpetuate the active male–passive female paradigm, thereby arguably contributing to the maintenance of sexually aggressive behaviours. That is to say, in constructing men as aggressors who need and must have sex, the rapid, violent and brutal 'rupture' of 'normal' relations which harassment might be seen to entail is always made understandable and hence possible. While men come to believe in themselves as needing to have sex to preserve their 'humanness', harassment might be seen in terms of Bataille's arguments as a form of expulsion which actually represents precisely the indulgence of the out-of-control, orgiastic, self-shattering impulses which we both fear and desire, because they remind us of our own mortality.

Conclusion

Our argument here has concentrated on addressing the consequences of the social regulation of the abject of sexual harassment – one element of that which organizations cannot tolerate but which will always return to disturb their self-definition as rational, productive, utility-generating and co-operative efforts. We have used both Foucault and Bataille to make a number of important suggestions about the discourse which comprises our talk, writing, behaving, organizing and acting with regard to sexual harassment, and to reveal the fragility of the boundaries of organization, as well as of 'normal' sexuality. First, sexual harassment is arguably an important issue for organizational analysis in the current climate, given the prevailing discursive construction of sex and sexuality. However, it is also important to acknowledge that social problems are historically constituted according to the preoccupations of the period. Therefore the existence of a behavioural pattern dubbed sexual harassment should be recognized to be a product of its time and place in those discursive practices which centre on this phenomenon. The discussion here also points to the need for us to consider the conceptualization of power as currently presented by harassment discourse. This kind of critique may reduce the self-perpetuating anxiety which compels continual monitoring of sexual activity to ensure that it is 'good'. The chapter also points to the need to address the heterosexism of harassment discourse, so as to question the depiction of women as victims and also to undermine the possible production/perpetuation of the subject position of the necessarily active male initiator of sex.

4 Working with sex offenders

Introduction

> sexuality as such, in the body, has a preponderant place, the sexual organ isn't like a hand, hair or a nose. It therefore has to be protected, surrounded, invested in any case with legislation that isn't pertaining to the rest of the body.
>
> (Foucault 1988: 202)

In chapter 1, we examined the workings of the abject in the psychology of the individual manager; in chapter 2, we considered a collective manifestation of and response to it; and, in chapter 3, we looked at an example of the social regulation of the abject and its effects. In this chapter, we focus again on the abject and the ways in which it disturbs the boundaries of 'normal' organizing, but here we look at the labour of those individuals who have to work with it beyond the point of prohibition. Such work, located as it is in the space of the abject, raises important issues for our overall argument given that, according to Bataille and as established earlier, work more generally is part of the process by which we (ultimately unsuccessfully) 'flee' from death. The abject therefore has no legitimate place in work, because it is the abject which reminds us of, or brings us close to, the experience of death, the point at which we plunge back into the 'concrete totality' from which we originally emerged, losing self, individuality, meaning, role and function in the process.

However, what of occupations like the ones we have referred to above, those which require their members to confront the abject, even work within it, on a daily basis, those which are usefully captured by the aphorism 'it's a dirty job, but someone's gotta do it'? The 'dirtiness' or 'taint' of such work can be physical – jobs which deal with death, rubbish, waste, the body etc. or apparently require labour under difficult or risky conditions; social – jobs which necessitate interaction with stigmatized groups or seem to involve being servile to others; or moral – jobs viewed as somehow sinful or as drawing on techniques which themselves are dubious, such as cheating (Ashforth and Kreiner 1999: 414–15, following Hughes 1958: 122). 'Dirty' therefore speaks directly of the presence of the abject within such work and the ways in which jobs like these make the accomplishment of the fragile and ultimately doomed disavowals and separations which lie at the heart of productive activity much more onerous. That is to say, they illuminate the difficulties faced by incumbents in avoiding the blurring of the identity 'between being and non-being, between the living and the death-stricken being' (Bataille 1997: 225). These incumbents are therefore faced with the specific challenge of somehow reconciling their notion of themselves as autonomous, bounded individuals with the fact that their employment requires them to behave in ways which may contradict such a 'truth'.

Prostitution, analysed in detail in part II of this book, is an apposite example of such an occupation, because it consists of the sale of sexuality, the commodification of something which normalizing discursive regimes, as we have already seen, construct as properly inviolate, deeply personal and only to be exchanged within the confines of a mutually desiring, non-commercial relationship. It is, using Ashforth and Kreiner's development of Hughes, both physically and morally tainted, involving selling one's body in a very literal way and being viewed as unseemly or unworthy. As Bataille (1985: 70) puts it, the brothel is 'the place that most offends polite society'. Selling sex, then, is always and already abject and our discussion of the masks which prostitutes may adopt to enable them to keep professional and personal identities apart makes this abundantly clear (see chapter 8 in particular).[1]

Another occupation which is relevant here is that of the abattoir worker (Ackroyd and Crowdy 1990), given that it entails the bringing about of death and is therefore physically tainted. To kill another living being is one of the societal prohibitions to which Bataille specifically refers, and he notes in particular that 'murder is regarded as awful, unthinkable' (Bataille 1997: 255). The work of the slaughterman, then, offends the sensibilities of Western populations who in the main continue to eat meat but are still sentimentally reluctant to fully acknowledge the circumstances of the killing that is necessary for that diet. Ackroyd and Crowdy (1990: 4) suggest this presents a dilemma for those working at the abattoir which they studied.[2] However, in reconciling this dilemma, these men in fact choose to 'reject the common view' (Ackroyd and Crowdy 1990: 9), having collectively renegotiated discourse concerning life and death to provide themselves with a sense of pride in their work, rather than one of disgust, shame or terror. They report their perceptions of slaughtering as a noble and heroic occupation, requiring physical strength and a strong disposition; asserting, for example, that 'Only one in a thousand has the stomach for this job' or 'Most people would throw up all over the shop if they tried what I am doing now' (abattoir workers, quoted in Ackroyd and Crowdy 1990: 8). Indeed, 'the single act that is most easily identified with killing' (Ackroyd and Crowdy 1990: 6) – severing the blood vessels in the animal's neck and beginning preparation of its carcass, known as 'sticking' – is the highest status task in the working cycle. Moreover, the men also make great play of the epiphenomena – blood, excrement, internal organs – of their work, using them in games and rituals such as filling a work colleague's boots with blood, hurling entrails across the 'shopfloor', shoving a carcass along the overhead line on which they are transported into 'the path of a worker momentarily in the wrong place' (Ackroyd and Crowdy 1990: 6), or deliberately splashing themselves with blood before leaving to walk home. For these workers, then, killing is courageous, it demonstrates guts[3] which few others possess; in bringing about death, they are *positively affirming* their identities, their individuality, their humanity. As such, they have redefined what is commonly held to be true regarding life and death and, consequently, appear to experience little tension between their own understandings of themselves as human individuals and the performance of their jobs.

This could be described as aggressive (Knights and Willmott 1989: 549), or perhaps proactive, identity work, given that here there is an active renegotiation of/resistance to discursive 'truths' which otherwise might be damaging to one's sense of self. An alternative term is infusing, 'where the [occupational] stigma is imbued with positive value, thus transforming it into a badge of honor' (Ashforth and Kreiner 1999: 421). The denial that any 'immoral, strange, or untoward' activity is involved in the work of the slaughterman also represents a particular form of 'motive talk', a recasting of behaviour to defuse 'identity-threatening situations' (Arluke and Hafferty 1996: 201). The specific type of motive talk in which the slaughtermen appear to engage is what are known as justifications; these involve the actor taking responsibility for the apparently deviant or morally dubious behaviour, but denying that any wrongdoing has actually been committed.[4] In general, moreover, this reversal of conventional mores regarding life and death among members of a specific occupational group can be usefully contrasted to the aforementioned separation which many prostitutes seek to establish and maintain between their professional and personal identities – a more defensive or reactive form of identity work[5] – although it is also important to point out that the discursive renegotiation (/resistance) demonstrated by the slaughtermen is also visible in empirical accounts of prostitution as an occupation, as part II, and chapter 9 especially, also emphasize. However, whichever form of identity work or motive talk is employed, this labour takes 'the judgmental sting out of behavior that is perceived as dirty work or deviant … cushion[ing] the burden of a negative conception of self by creating one that is more respectable' (Arluke and Hafferty 1996: 222), and it is also worth noting Ashforth and Kreiner's (1999: 421, 429) point that such 'ideologies' may be more to do with securing '*internal* rather than *external* legitimacy'. That is to say, identity work in this regard is more likely to provide someone in a dirty job with a functional and healthy sense of themselves than it is to persuade others of this job's essential value or that those who participate in it are not moral reprobates.

The occupations which we take as our focus in this chapter, of those professionals who act for, supervise, support or treat sex offenders, are also 'dirty' in key respects. Despite the fact that sexual offences are legally and morally prohibited, like sexual harassment they always exist because they are abject, speaking evocatively of forces and passions which we cannot control and so try (unsuccessfully) to suppress. Therefore they represent an ever-present problematic for 'normal' society. Moreover, sex offenders cannot simply be eliminated, nor for that matter forgotten about. Instead they have to be represented, guarded and cared for, counselled and, if possible, rehabilitated – that is to say, efforts are commonly made to appropriate the form of the abject that these offenders represent, to render it socially useful, to neutralize it (Bataille 1985: 99). This emphasis on appropriation is evident even from a cursory glance at the psychiatric, jurisprudential, criminological and social policy literature on sex offenders, at the centre of which appear to be the questions of (a) whether various efforts in this regard are successful; and (b) how they can be improved. For example, one strand in recent research emphasizes cognitive, psychological, experiential and behavioural differences between types of sex offenders, and tends to argue as a corollary that different treatment/rehabilitation approaches therefore need to be used with different groups (Miner *et al.* 1995; Miner and Dwyer 1997; Zgourides *et al.* 1997; Blumenthal *et al.* 1999; Marques 1999). Another evaluates different legislative approaches – such as the various forms of incarceration, registration and/or supervision in the wider community as an alternative to or following incarceration, or civil commitment of sex offenders after they have served a prison sentence (Bedarf 1995; Berliner *et al.* 1995; Brannon and Troyer 1995; Winick 1998) – and still another assesses various forms of treatment (Roys 1997; Quinsey *et al.* 1998). A further category of work examines the measurement and prediction of recidivism, and the practical implications thereof (Prentky *et al.* 1997; Doren 1998; Hanson 1998); and, finally, a good deal of research discusses the aetiology of sexual offences, again usually with the intention of drawing conclusions for treatment (Freund and Kuban 1994; Spaccarelli *et al.* 1997; Anechiarico 1998; Barbaree *et al.* 1998).

However, our contention here is that the particular discursive emphasis placed on sexuality, as discussed at length in chapter 3, translates into the construction of sexual offences in such a way as to conflate offence and offender, and relegate both to the abject (which often means literal incarceration in the case of those convicted for offences designated as criminal). The general public therefore harbour a special loathing for sex offenders, as well as tending to mistrust any claim that these individuals could ever lead 'normal' and 'productive' lives. They keep a watchful eye on any effort at counselling or rehabilitation, seemingly much more so than they do with regard to the treatment of thieves or even murderers. Indeed they may even take matters into their own hands. For example, Brooks (1999) notes the April 1998 publication of an ACPO (the UK Association of Chief Officers of Probation) dossier which contained information on forty cases in which community action against known sex offenders had resulted in violence, or the individual in question either leaving the area or going into hiding. Likewise, Cramb (1999) reports on the case of six-times-convicted George Belmonte, forced out of his home near Kirkcudbright by a local action group; this after two similar experiences in other locations in South West Scotland. In a similar vein, Victor, who was released from a UK prison in 1996 after serving eighteen months for child abuse, talks of the reaction he expected when he was set free:

> You feel absolute stark terror ... You're coming out into a society that you
> know hates you, that treats you with loathing and contempt. You expect
> abuse, you expect to be ostracised at best, beaten up at worst. And you're
> terrified of yourself.
>
> (Victor, quoted in Brooks 1999)

Moreover, since the introduction of the requirement in the UK for such
offenders to register their name, whereabouts and date of birth with the police,
as enshrined in Part 1 of the Sex Offenders Act (1997), pressure has mounted for
this information to be more widely available. At present, it is released only 'in
extreme circumstances' – that is to say, when the offender in question is considered to pose a particular risk to the community (Brooks 1999). This is in contrast
to the USA, where, since the federal Megan's Law[6] was passed in 1996, there
has been what Laurence (1997 – emphasis added) describes as 'a legal requirement for the *public* notification of the identity and address of any convicted sex
offender, for life, so that communities may know the threat and take steps to
defend themselves'. Indeed, many states have taken this initiative on board in the
form of Internet sites which the public can search to see whether a particular
individual is resident in their area, and which sometimes include photographs of
the offenders.

Sex offenders, then, are discursively positioned as a peculiarly awful menace
who should not, even after 'serving their time', enjoy the same rights as those
who conduct themselves in a sexually 'appropriate' way; and constructions such
as these pose particular problems for those members of 'normal' society – solici-
tors, warders, counsellors – who have to enter and manage this 'abnormal' world
and yet remain capable of smoothly reintegrating into normal society on a daily
basis. That is to say, these professionals are engaged in socially tainted work,
being 'in regular contact with people or groups that are themselves regarded as
stigmatized' (Ashforth and Kreiner 1999: 415). Like prostitution and abattoir
work, these occupations arguably place psychological demands on the people
who do them beyond the demands of the tasks themselves, are often not valued
by normal society and may even have stigma attached to them. Certainly their
incumbents are subjected to significant censure when they are perceived to have
made errors – as in the implication that social workers were partly to blame for
the sexually motivated murder of 11-year-old Wesley Neailey. Neailey was blud-
geoned to death in June 1998 by Dominic McKilligan, a convicted sex offender
whose court-imposed supervision order had expired ten months previously – and
one day before the UK sex offenders register was introduced.[7] Social workers
were described as having been duped and dodged by McKilligan, despite the
fact that, according to defence counsel Paddy Cosgrove, QC, reports produced
by 'various authorities' in 1994 and 1997 indicated his propensity to re-offend.
Cosgrove also criticized the relevant professionals for their failure to provide
adequate support for McKilligan following his release from a young offenders'
centre. Detective Sergeant Trevor Fordy, who led the investigation into Neailey's
death, called as a result of the case for changes in the law so that it becomes

mandatory for social workers to inform the police when sex offenders are released from custody (Hopkins 1999; Stokes 1999).

Nonetheless, it is true that, stigmatized or psychologically demanding though they may be, jobs like these cannot be directly compared with those of the prostitute or the abattoir worker, given that labour in this respect takes place in the space of the abject but does not involve the abject itself. Moreover, the prostitute's work is often illegal in itself or compels them to engage in illegal or sub-legal activities such as the advertising of sexual services,[8] and the slaughterman holds down a job which, although legal, is certainly low status. On the other hand, professionals such as those we discuss in this chapter do high status work which is fully legal (Arluke and Hafferty 1996: 201–2; see also Ashforth and Kreiner's (1999: 415–6, 430) discussion of occupational prestige) – and their experience of dirty work may therefore be somewhat attenuated. However, the discursive practices which demonize sexual offences and therefore those who commit them, effectively rendering offence and offender inextricable, still implicate and involve these workers, so how do they cope with their labour within this abject space, given that they are charged with improving the life situation of individuals who have apparently proved themselves 'inhuman'? What is it like labouring with those that society has designated, as one of our respondents put it, 'the lowest of the low'? Or, as another says, acting as one of 'society's refuse men … you put your refuse out on Monday morning or something and it's taken away; who gives a toss about it then? Unless he hasn't been or he's spilt half of [it] over your doorstep – then you're very concerned about the refuse man, but really you don't give a toss'?

In asking these questions, we aim not so much to *directly* engage with the prevailing discourse on sexuality, as we did in chapter 3, as to examine the consequences of this discourse *for one particular group working within it*. However, although critique is not our primary objective here, that is not to say that in pursuing other lines of enquiry we are somehow implicitly accepting its normalizing effects – not least because, as we have already suggested, it is possible to argue that these effects (re)produce the conditions of existence of sexual misdemeanours and offences. We therefore intend that a byproduct of our analysis of the impact of this regime on individual workers, of the ways in which they manage having to work in an abject space, is the telling of what Sawicki (1994: 309, 310) refers to as 'cautionary tales' of life as a modern subject; the underlying motif, as also emerged in chapter 3, being the *implications* of particular discursive understandings of self and others.

In this chapter, therefore, we employ qualitative interview data in order to provide some insights into what working life is like for professionals such as these. Their understandings of their role and of their relationship with their sex offender clients are examined in detail in order to ascertain any specific difficulties that arise, and to examine the related issue of identity work. If tensions exist, how do these individuals manage them? Have these professionals, like Ackroyd and Crowdy's slaughtermen, redefined discourse on sexuality to enable them to perform their work? Or do they rather, like many (if not all) prostitutes, labour to maintain some kind of separation between their 'real' selves and their working selves? Related themes include the level of organizational and institutional support available for these professionals, and whether or not that support is helpful in mitigating any tensions identified. The issue of whether or not working with sex offenders is more problematic than other aspects of the more general work that they do is also explored. Finally, a central concern of our discussion is to acknowledge and explore the implications of the different labour processes in which the professionals interviewed for this chapter are located. We conclude that these individuals find the most difficult aspect of their work with sex offenders, their daily confrontation with the abject and the threat to identity that this arguably poses, to be actually hearing about the crimes their clients have committed. Indeed, they display not inconsiderable sympathy for the offenders themselves, tending to construct them as damaged or abused. This division of the 'criminal' from the 'crime', the continuing suppression of the actual offence but re-presentation of the offender as 'recoverable', appears to be an important element in the labour that is described and also seems to indicate some measure of proactive identity work on the part of these professionals, given its subversion of prevailing discursive constructions.

A methodological aside

Three UK professionals who either currently work with sex offenders or have experience in this area were identified through our personal contacts. Identifying details have been altered or omitted to preserve their anonymity as far as possible. The three respondents were:

1   Martin, a social worker who runs a resettlement hostel which takes sex offenders who have either 'been released from custody or convicted of an offence within the last twelve months';
2   John, a solicitor who has experience of acting for alleged sex offenders, and whose firm had, at the time of the interviews, recently accepted the defence of an individual accused of serial sexual murders;
3   Peter, a clinical psychologist who was involved in the assessment of a sex offender as part of his training and now treats, among other clients, men and women with sexual problems such as erectile or orgasmic dysfunction, premature ejaculation, painful intercourse and vaginisimus.

Interviews were conducted in order to get some sense of how these professionals view their life-worlds, to establish what they '*have to do* to be (routinely, unremarkably, but recognisably and readily so) doing' their jobs (Sharrock and Watson, cited in Silverman, D. 1993: 29), and to avoid as far as possible common-sense reasoning about what it is like to work with sex offenders. All three respondents were male, which may of course have had some bearing on the data gathered, given the subject matter and the fact that the interviewer (Jo Brewis) was female. Gender may also figure in the responses in the sense that the majority of clients encountered by the interviewees were male (thus producing a male-on-male interaction in the work described), and that female professionals may very well hold different views, particularly given discursive constructions of the vulnerability of female sexuality and the prevailing understanding of sexual offences as gendered (see chapter 3). Moreover, as we argued in the Introduction, the data here have undoubtedly been produced at least in part by the researcher's identity, such that a degree of damage has inevitably been done to the respondents' own sense of their words through her interpretations and ordering. Overall, then, the analysis here cannot be said in any way to be independent of this particular research situation, or of this researcher, especially given the size of the sample. Nonetheless, again as intimated in the Introduction, generalizability in its strictest interpretation was sacrificed here in favour of achieving a detailed and informed sense of what working life is like for these three individuals, if not necessarily for others in their fields.

The role of the professional and the persona of the offender

In order to contextualize discussion of each of these respondents' professional roles, it is worth noting that they all three spoke of the ways in which discourse on sexuality constructs sexual crimes and those who commit them. For example, Martin, the social worker, suggested that:

> I think there is very little sympathy in society in general for anyone who does things to people, a rapist who has raped someone of your age [mid-twenties] or an older woman especially, I don't think there is a lot of sympathy. If I was looking for funds I'm on a sticky wicket … [given that] I need help to give a better daily environment to a murderer, to a man who kills, a better environment for a rapist.

Solicitor John was in broad agreement, commenting that, even among his other clients, there is a sense that:

> 'I'm alright, I'm a good honest villain. I might cause people grievous bodily harm or commit crimes against property which are very hurtful and damaging to people but at least I'm not a nonce, at least I don't interfere with children.'

Ashforth and Kreiner (1999: 425) suggest that such 'downward social comparisons' can be attributed to a need on the part of the actors involved to withstand challenges to their identity – in this case, the process of being labelled a criminal. Moreover, the attitude that John describes is widespread, as is amply demonstrated by the existence of Rule 43 in UK prisons. This provides for separate accommodation for vulnerable prisoners like those convicted of sexual offences so as to assure their safety from other inmates. The murder in prison of US paedophile, serial killer and cannibal Jeffrey Dahmer, who lured victims to his apartment for paid pornographic photography sessions and often had sex with their corpses, further illustrates the hatred that prevails for sex offenders even among their fellow criminals (Freedland 1994).

The respondents here also identified a 'hierarchy' of sexual offences, deeming rape, sexual assault and child abuse the most injurious. This ordering again could be argued to represent part of the popular discourse on sexuality, given that Foucault (1979: 104) points specifically to the discursive construction of children's sexuality such that it becomes a 'precious and perilous, dangerous and endangered sexual potential', and that women's sexuality is framed in much the same way, as already suggested in chapter 3. That is to say, rape, sexual assault (both usually considered to be crimes committed against women)[9] and child abuse are the sex offences which are perceived to prey on the most vulnerable, and thus are seen as the most despicable, the most damaging of such offences. Moreover, in John's explanation in particular, consent and the perceived invasiveness of the behaviour seem to be key factors. He notes activities such as cottaging or flashing[10] but does not classify these as particularly serious, seemingly because the first is consensual and the second, while it is performed without the consent of the onlookers, is deemed not to be particularly invasive. It is of course, as John also pointed out, a criminal offence in the UK to engage in homosexual sex in a public place (gross indecency), as it is to flash (indecent exposure). However, there seems little mileage in arguing that these behaviours are considered heinous in the same way as are rape, sexual assault or child abuse, and John certainly does not seem to think this is the case. Moreover, it is worth noting that Peter, like John, emphasized consent as a central issue in the defining of sexual offences. As he explains it: 'I think a sexual offence is a sexual act that is committed without mutual consent … I think that's an offence, and in most instances that might be a crime as well I should think.' His and John's ideas on the subject, then, also speak of the conventional discursive construction of 'good' sex as mutually desiring and non-hierarchical, again as discussed in chapter 3, and which John describes as 'a proper sexual relationship with an adult which [is] roughly equal in terms of its power distribution'.

It seems, then, that these professionals work or have worked with others who have committed *what they themselves agree* are particularly disturbing offences – so they acknowledge their labour in the space of the abject. As Ashforth and Kreiner (1999: 418) comment, this is not unusual among dirty workers, at least partly because they are as subject to broader discursive influences as anyone else. Moreover, even though John actually questioned prevailing discourse in this respect, asking 'Is rape worse than … murder, cutting somebody's throat, glassing them, disfiguring them for life?', he did not pursue the point, stating that it is something that women are more qualified to comment on (which again harks back to the construction of women's sexuality as especially fragile). This reluctance on his part to develop what undoubtedly is a controversial argument in contemporary terms seems to bear particular testimony to the powerful nature of modern discourse on sexuality, and to throw into relief the challenges these men therefore face in terms of working with those who do not conform to consequent discursive requirements.

What, then, do these three professionals actually understand themselves as doing with or to the sex offenders with whom they work, and what does this imply for their relationship with these individuals? Martin, first of all, emphasizes that his role with regard to the residents of the hostel is *not* one of constant surveillance to ensure that they do not re-offend. His primary concern is the resettlement process which, when carried out successfully, means residents leave the hostel having developed enhanced self-esteem and possessing the skills required to live independently. There is therefore a need to treat residents as responsible adults, to work with them in (as Martin puts it) an 'empowering' way. For example, he mentions the residents' committee, which operates to permit these men to discuss issues of concern regarding the running of the hostel, and he also suggests that therapy is only offered if individual residents are willing to discuss their problems. In this instance, then, contrary to popular understandings of offenders as somehow beyond the pale, residents are constructed as having the potential to be 'ordinary' human beings, as capable of rejecting their 'deformities' (Bataille 1985: 66), of working to reject their crimes by living life in functional and useful ways. The objective of developing self-worth is particularly significant in this regard, given our discussion in chapter 1 of how lack of such esteem (narcissism in its chronic form) may generate an obsession with establishing boundaries between the abject and the acceptable parts of self, such that the subsequent reappearance of the abject generates ever more pronounced efforts to restore these boundaries.

Moreover, Martin, while he does not see himself as a watchdog, also alluded to the fact that sex offenders perhaps warrant closer monitoring than most of his residents. He described them as experienced dissemblers who pay

> [a] very high degree of lip service to what you're saying to them, say all the right things, get you on their side … [so] you trust [them] or you give them the portrayal of trust and certainly respect for the individual but you never let your guard down [so] that, you know, everything that you're told is true you don't blindly trust.

Here Martin does not represent these offenders as brutish animals who have no concept of the threat that their behaviour poses, or who cannot see that what they have done is appalling to others. Instead he depicts them as being more than aware of the intense societal distaste for such behaviour and thus as working hard to conceal their personal compulsions so as to be able, in the kind of instance he describes at least, to continue offending. As Martin says, then, a sex offender may seem to be 'playing the game' as far as the hostel demands it, but in reality he is perhaps planning his next rape or episode of abuse, just as Goffman's (1961: 64–5) mental hospital inmates choose to 'play it cool', behaving tractably and co-operatively with the staff of the institution so as to keep out of trouble, but in reality faking this acceptance of their required incarceration. For example, a falsely enthusiastic attitude to therapy might be displayed by patients, given the widespread belief that 'willingness to participate ... would bring the therapist over to their side in their efforts to improve their living conditions in the hospital or to get a discharge' (Goffman 1961: 225–6). Indeed, during a discussion of how he planned to secure his release, one man told a fellow inmate that 'Man, I'm gonna attend everything' (mental hospital inmate, quoted in Goffman 1961: 226). Although this kind of behaviour may partly explain why sex offenders are seen as impossible to rehabilitate, Martin is in fact at pains here to emphasize that many of his clients are intelligent individuals who have had the misfortune to be 'born on the wrong side of the lines'. In other words, he suggests that they would, given the right environment, never have offended at all, and that they can, given their abilities, learn not to do so again.

Peter's description of his role echoes the rehabilitation process that Martin describes in that he (Peter) says he aims to a large extent to effect a cure for his patients, but that this cure is not something he can perform alone and unaided. As he comments, 'therapy isn't something that the therapist performs on a passive patient ... I hope they see me as somebody that they can explore their problems with in a collaborative, mutual, non-threatening way'. Both Martin and Peter, then, seem to see themselves as collaboratively restoring the people they work with to their fullest potential, and treating them as equals; there is no sense here of practising *on* others, dysfunctional though these others may be in whatever ways. The occupational ideologies reported here therefore involve a (re-)construction of the sex offender as a human being rather than a dangerous or abject savage, prone to excess, to lack of restraint, to animal behaviour. Indeed, Martin states explicitly that he tries to interact with the residents as people first and offenders second, trying not to dwell on the nature of their crimes – in other words, there is a deliberate displacement of the crime as 'master status', as something which necessarily pervades and colours every other aspect of the person who commits it (Becker 1973).

There are also some similarities between John's and Martin's perceptions of their roles in that John describes himself as an advocate, as arguing the case for his clients and making sure justice gets done, and Martin comments that there is an element of advocacy in his job, such as ensuring residents receive their due benefits, fighting to get them 'move on' accommodation and accompanying them to court. Nonetheless, John suggests a rather different relationship with his clients in other respects to that which Martin and Peter outline. He seems to see himself largely as an expert guide, as someone who can illuminate the confusing and often intimidating process of criminal justice, as an 'advisor to the masses' (Kritzman 1988: xii). Indeed, John's conceptualization of his expertise seems to involve him protecting, even saving, his clients, and certainly dispensing knowledge to them:

> In [a police] interview I think your role is two-fold – firstly I think to prevent any oppressive, unfair behaviour by the police and that is quite common-

place. The second role is, to a degree I suppose it depends on your philosophy, certainly my boss would say that part of your job is to save your client from themselves and, you know, people [clients] agree that under the circumstances it would be wiser not to answer any questions because you can never really lose by making that decision and then they start talking and people do find it quite difficult [to remain silent]. I mean the police are becoming, less so uniformed police but certainly detectives, they have courses in the psychology of interviews, they know how to leave pregnant pauses, make it difficult, uncomfortable for people to remain silent ... there's a degree to which I think it's my role to intervene occasionally and say 'I remind you that my advice was ... and you do not have to answer these questions'.[11]

Thus the legal client is, for John at least, typically more passive in their relationship with him than the hostel resident is in their dealings with Martin, or the clinical psychology patient with Peter. Moreover, although John also remarks that he is involved in social work to some extent with the more minor offenders, he defines this somewhat differently from Martin, talking of the 'management of inadequacy' and being a 'damage limiter' where his clients have strayed 'over the line of legality in a desperate attempt to survive'. In a similar vein, he describes certain sex offenders as 'cases of monumental ... desperation, unsophistication insofar as [they exhibit] a complete failure to read sexual signals from somebody else'. John, then, does not see himself as restoring such individuals to their full potential in the way that Martin and Peter do; rather, he implies that they are somehow fundamentally incapable of running their own lives satisfactorily. However, although he does not see these clients as equals, and although he does not believe in them to the extent that Martin and Peter do in theirs, again John does not label them as intrinsically dangerous or threatening as far as he sees it. Rather, they are inadequates who need help in and protection from a system that they do not understand and who, if they receive the right kind of help and protection, can continue to live fairly functional lives, at least for the time being.

Moreover, all three respondents commented to the effect that their work has taught them to view dysfunctional behaviour as rather less unusual than they may have previously supposed. In describing the process of listening to patients' accounts of their anti-social predilections and behaviours, Peter says that:

It affects your view of the world because you learn over time very quickly that people are very much capable of doing horrible things to one another and it happens with astonishing frequency ... Really, people are capable of absolutely anything and that changes your view of people and any concepts you might have had of human kindness and fairness, because there isn't any fairness and there isn't any inherent human kindness because it can change rapidly under different circumstances. So it does challenge your view of things.

Martin and John, on the same issue, suggest that one's adult behaviour is partially shaped by one's circumstances, or one's experiences as a child. As Simon (1996: 127–9) points out, the latter is a common explanation of paedophilia in particular – indeed, we have already discussed the ways in which psychoanalytic theories explain the connection between childhood socialization and adult dysfunction (see chapter 1). Martin is especially emphatic on this point, stating that '99.9 per cent' of the sex offenders he comes into contact with originate in an abusive family, having experienced either sexual abuse or some form of emotional neglect. This, he argues, often translates into later offending, and he goes on to say that he feels himself lucky to have had a stable upbringing himself, clearly implying that, if he hadn't, he too may have gone on to commit such crimes (his 'wrong side of the lines' argument, as quoted above). Peter, talking of those who abuse children specifically, agrees: 'I mean a lot of abusers have themselves been abused and they're just sort of repeating the cycle, they're passing on the cycle … '. John also said most of the child abusers he has encountered had undergone some kind of negative formative experience, and he added that:

> I think I'm not very judgmental of people, that's the other thing. I think that I think quite a lot 'There but for the grace of God', I suppose … of course not in cases of rape and serious assault, but certainly, you know, in terms of the workaday people I deal with, people down on their luck who have, you know, been involved in petty thefts and all the rest of it. These people are not playing on a level playing field.

However, as the above implies, John is less convinced than Martin that sexual crimes are mainly if not entirely the product of experience and therefore that, if he had been brought up in different circumstances, he might have become a sex offender himself. He suggests that, while there are those who have come from damaged backgrounds, there are also simply 'evil, amoral' individuals who do not distinguish between sexual offences and normal behaviour. This second category of sex offender, then, is much closer to the popular perspective that sees sex offenders as incorrigible and aberrant monsters, as the very epitome of disease and dysfunction. Nonetheless, Martin's and Peter's accounts, and John's to a lesser extent, vividly conjure the spectre of the abject, the uncontrollable forces, instincts, processes and passions which haunt the boundaries of *all* human beings, and suggest that particular types of experiences may make us less able to work to exclude it.

Here, then, there is a partial renegotiation of/resistance to prevailing discourse that constructs sex offenders as 'the lowest of the low' because of the crimes they have committed. It is less far-reaching than Ackroyd and Crowdy's slaughtermen's reversal of the relative values of bringing life and bringing death but there is a sense in which the definition of sex offenders as potentially functional human beings, as inadequates, as victims of abuse themselves, represents a form of aggressive or proactive identity work, such that all three professionals here to some extent separate the offender from the offence in their construction and performance of their professional roles. The offence remains in an abject space, whereas the offender is (re)presented as damaged, abused, a victim themselves, someone who may have the potential to function normally, someone who may not in actuality be very different from the 'average' individual. As already suggested, this might be seen to be a crucial element in assimilating the challenges of working within the space of the abject because of its subversion of the prevailing construction of sex-offender-as-monster. However, the point at which this separation apparently becomes most difficult is when these professionals are required to discuss details of the offence with its perpetrator.

Confronting the crime

All three respondents reported that they found talking about sexual offences difficult, which relates of course to their construction of these crimes as discussed above. Martin comments, for example, that:

> Sometimes the offences you hear [about] and you just feel, ah, nauseous and, you know, if your sexuality's straight and you're listening to someone describe fantasies or little kids and I've got, you know, I've got a little girl of ten and peculiarly then would go along with the hang 'em and then worse brigade.

Martin here suggests that his understanding of himself as a father can conflict with and intrude upon his understanding of himself as a professional, especially when he is required to absorb details of child abuse. As he says himself, this is a 'peculiar' reaction, given the construction he operates by in his professional life of sex offenders as separate from their crimes, as candidates for rehabilitation, as violated and defiled themselves. In Martin's identity as a father, then, there is a heightening of his reaction to the abject of sexual offences, an opening out on to 'a certain vista of anguish, upon a certain lacerating consciousness of distress' (Bataille 1997: 224), and, importantly, a repositioning of the offence *squarely back on to* the offender (hence the urge towards capital punishment). These tensions between different elements of his identity project reveal the different discursive regimes to which he is subject. Indeed, as Knights and Vurdubakis explain:

> it is worth remembering that [power/knowledge practices and relations] are diverse and their demands complex and inconsistent. Accordingly, the routine discourses and practices through which subjects are constituted (and constitute themselves) as, for instance, unitary autonomous individuals, are fraught with contradictions. Self-identity can therefore be realized only as a constant struggle against the experience of tension, fragmentation and discord. Subject positions are made available in a number of competing discourses ... Identity is thus of necessity always a project rather than an achievement.
>
> (Knights and Vurdubakis 1994: 185)

John also describes a physical revulsion towards one particular client, an alleged child abuser. He says of this individual that he 'sticks in my mind' because he was

> a gentleman whose persona made my flesh crawl in the sense that he used to dress in a very funereal fashion, had a very unfortunate leery smile and was really probably, you know, most people's unfortunate stereotype of a sex offender.

This individual's dress and general demeanour had served to continually remind John, his legal representative, of the crimes that he had been accused of committing – again, the repositioning of the crime back on to the (alleged) offender is visible here. Moreover, as we imply above, the sensations which John describes – of his flesh crawling – are echoed in Martin's comment that hearing about sexual offences sometimes makes him feel sick. This not only illustrates how deep the discursive understanding of sexuality as inviolate runs in both of these men's identities, to the extent that confronting sexual offences actually has negative physical repercussions, but also speaks directly of Bataille's claim that the abject 'which arouse[s] in us the dread of death, sometimes introduces us into a kind of nauseous state which hurts more cruelly than pain. Those sensations associated with the supreme giving-way, the final collapse, are unbearable' (Bataille 1997: 225). That is to say, it is so deeply distressing (if also and at the same time fascinating) to come face to face with the abject, to be so forcibly reminded of our 'final appointment', that it makes us feel literally sick, as in the case where one is forced to listen to details of sexual offences.

To deal with the emotional and physical sensations experienced when listening to such accounts, then, the respondents all alluded to the need for emotional labour, to what Hochschild (1983: 7) describes as 'the management of feeling to create a publicly observable and bodily display' (also see chapter 2). There are, moreover, echoes here of Goffman's dramaturgical analogy, his discussion of

> the way in which the individual in ordinary work situations presents himself and his activity to others, the ways in which he guides and controls the impression they form of him, and the kinds of things he may and may not do while sustaining his performance before them.
>
> (Goffman 1971: i)

That is to say, we see here the taking on of another identity, another role, when in one's professional guise or, in Goffman's terminology, when one is in a 'front region'. This professional mask conceals the feelings of the 'real' person 'backstage' – the father, the upright citizen, the 'normal' human being – and is similar in form, if not necessarily in content or degree, to that employed by many prostitutes in the bodily and emotional separations that they effect between public and private selves (see chapter 8). Peter describes this labour as follows:

most people employ coping mechanisms like this which involve some sort of intellectualization and distancing. If you're involved with people that have been exposed to terrible trauma in the past and they tell you about it in therapy, then the likelihood is that you'd employ some sort of distancing or coping mechanism way of dealing with it. If you get somebody telling you about things that they've done which are sort of sexual criminal things then again you're likely to employ these sort of coping tactics.

Martin also remarks, as we might have expected from his comments above about feeling nauseous when confronted with details of such crimes, that the process is not always easy; 'Sometimes because of the nature of the offence you really have to struggle to maintain, put on a semi-professional front because ... you can't allow emotional things to get in the way of a professional approach, you know.'

The fragility of the professional self in the 'dirty' job is also something that is evident in accounts from prostitutes, as discussed in chapters 8 and 11; and Martin's comment about the need to maintain 'a semi-professional front' for the sake of doing a good job is, likewise, echoed in discussion there. That is to say, the performance of such 'dirty' jobs can be seen to necessitate two specific processes: first, the protection of one's private self from the rigours of working in or confronting the abject in the course of one's profession (as Peter's 'coping mechanisms' remark suggests) and, second, the maintenance of the professional role itself, the separation between public and private so that Martin's 'emotional things' do not intrude into the work that is actually done. This last is particularly pronounced in John's analysis of the exigencies of his own professional conduct:

> At the end of the day I have to say that I believe that there is a principle which is that of access to justice and that that is not divisible and that no matter how heinous the allegation everybody has a right to be represented, to be defended, to have what they say properly and confidently advanced to a body that will decide upon their guilt or innocence. I think that's where, I'm sure that's where I end up in fact, because I think once you start saying something's too horrible, I mean, where on earth do you stop? Do you then begin to endorse the behaviour engaged in by people who you *are* willing to defend – 'I'm not representing that rapist, but it's perfectly alright for somebody to beat somebody else to within an inch of their lives'?
>
> (emphasis added)

John says to a large extent that he has had to become 'numb' to sexual crimes, in other words that, while he does not in any way condone or endorse them, his professional persona has necessarily ceased to react to them. He illustrates this by drawing a comparison to doctors, saying that 'they don't faint at post-mortems – they've seen people's spleens before'. Thus in all three respondents' accounts, rationality (Peter's 'intellectualization') is seen as necessarily prevailing over the more emotive responses (Bataille's 'nauseous state') that would otherwise emerge in these situations. In fact, there is also a sense here that detachment and objectivity (which are, as we have suggested, discursively positioned at the heart of modern organizing processes) are even more necessary in a situation where the horrifying power of the abject is invoked simply by doing the job itself. It certainly seems that all three professionals here are concerned to do a good job; indeed, their emphasis on the importance of satisfactory professional performance became yet more visible when discussion turned to failure and its implications.

What does it mean to fail?

Work is, fairly obviously, one of the ways in which an individual might choose to secure his or her identity – to locate themselves as defined by their profession or occupation, using 'job title' as a 'prominent identity badge' (Ashforth and Kreiner 1999: 417). Indeed, according to Bataille, work is one of the most fundamental ways in which we separate ourselves from 'abject nature'. This attempt to secure a valid identity through work is clearly visible in accounts such as that offered by Knights and Morgan (1991) of insurance sales personnel, which talks specifically of the ways in which these workers internalize the demands of their organizational roles. The pressure of this close identification with work can also be seen in the levels of burnout in the profession:

> I haven't got many old-stagers – I used to have. One who has been with us for 12 years is off through depression – burnt out. Another has been a rep for 6 years – she's 90 per cent on the way to a nervous breakdown – burnt out. We lose the majority of our long serving reps because the pressure on a long term basis is very difficult to keep up – especially reps who don't see themselves going anywhere because they haven't managed to get into the management pool and are not likely to.
> (Area sales manager, quoted in Knights and Morgan 1991: 230)

Job performance for these individuals is inextricably tied up with maintaining their sense of self; indeed, they work exceedingly hard in order to preserve their identities. Perceiving oneself to have failed at work (for example, failing to secure promotion), then, has dramatic consequences for identity, as is visible in the instances of those in the sales teams who burn out. Moreover, as Peter points out:

> to some extent we're talking about personal identity; your own self-concept and what you do and how you come to do what you do constitutes the way you perceive yourself. Your own self-concept is influenced and determined by feedback you get from situations. It's not something you can have in a vacuum and so doing well at something might be particularly reinforcing, might make you feel good, lead to a positive appraisal about yourself. If you

have a whole series of negative appraisals then that might deleteriously affect your self-esteem and your self-concept. So obviously what you do, even on a very mundane level, affects the way you view yourself and the way you view yourself is an integral part of your personality.

Failure at work appears here to be an event which the individual might have to learn either to forestall, redefine or withstand, to avoid sustaining psychological damage. On the subject of what failure might be in his profession and how any such damage can be avoided, Peter went on to say that:

> if you're a therapist that believes that if a patient doesn't get better it's your fault then that's going to have personal repercussions because some patients don't improve in therapy and get better; and if you are one of these people that believes that this is a sign that you're a lousy therapist, then it's going to severely affect your self-esteem and your enjoyment of the job. I try not to believe that, although it's difficult not to believe it, but I think largely I don't believe that. I don't believe that if a patient doesn't get better it's entirely my fault.

Professional failure for Peter, then, means that symptoms initially presented by a patient do not disappear during therapy; thus, in the case of a sex offender, failure would result in re-offending. However, in line with his dictum that he does not practise *on* but rather *with* patients, he states that he doesn't believe that this kind of instance is wholly his responsibility. Nevertheless, it seems that this non-acceptance of blame may vary according to the perceived severity of the consequences of the failure:

> I suppose if I had somebody like that in therapy that was a sex offender and they went out and re-offended, in some ways I'd think that the treatment had failed. Whether or not I'd think that that was my fault I don't know. I might activate some defensive reaction at that point, say 'Well, this is part of that person's character and it's not my fault they've re-offended' and maybe I've got a double standard because, thinking about it, if I were to treat somebody with panic attacks and they were to have panic attacks after therapy, then I'd think 'Oh damn!', you know, 'Maybe it is all my fault'.

In other words, it is easier for Peter to accept responsibility for a failure which involves a recurrence of relatively minor symptoms, and in particular symptoms which have few consequences for anyone other than the client, than it would be to accept responsibility for a sex offender re-offending. Failure in the latter instance for him calls up the added difficulty of the nature of sexual offences, considered as they are to be peculiarly awful. So failing with sex offenders is likely to have a particularly 'deleterious' effect on Peter's self-esteem.

Martin, who also defines failure as a sex offender going on to re-offend, agrees that this does not necessarily mean that he will blame himself totally, which again reflects his understanding that he works *together with* his residents to facilitate successful resettlement. However, Martin does admit that these incidents are difficult to deal with – he talks of the frustration, guilt and anger that can follow – and says that he sometimes informally extends the professional relationship after residents have left the hostel as a result:

> if people want to drop in for a coffee, for a meal, scrounge a bag of sugar or a loaf of bread then, yeah, for as long as they want to, you know … Sometimes, especially when you've got somebody who is dodgy on whether or not they're going to make it … all we do then really is encourage them to come and have Sunday lunch every week, you know, little things like that.

Martin and Peter, as we have seen, share a conceptualization of their role as helping sex offenders to help themselves to stop committing sexual offences. Thus they profess themselves committed to stopping re-offending *with the help of the offender*. However, both recognize that this remit (however democratic or facilitative) presents particular challenges when a specific relationship is deemed to have failed. Further to the above, Martin comments that on occasion it is necessary to use 'heavy discipline', that he cannot let the residents 'totally take over' because of the reality of the situation that he and they are in, and in particular the need for continuity in the hostel week on week. The empowerment within the project is therefore incomplete, which may account for Martin's enduring sense that he and his staff are at least partially responsible for 'failures'. Again, then, as far as Peter and Martin are concerned at least, there is a partial renegotiation of or resistance to the popular discursive representation of professionals being to blame when sex offenders emerge from incarceration, therapy or supervision and continue to offend. However, the nagging sense of what Martin describes as 'if only this, if only that' persists for both men, suggesting that the popular discourse of professional accountability in such instances continues to exert considerable power at the same time as it is resisted by these professionals.

John, on the other hand, suggests that responsibility for the scenario in which someone accused of sexual crimes was acquitted and subsequently went on to offend would not be his. He says he thinks he would be 'unaffected by it', given that it is not him but a barrister who stands up in court and argues for the defendant's innocence, such that there is 'sufficient buffer between me and the result for me not to lose any sleep over it'. Indeed, even if he were at the 'sharp end', as he puts it, he thinks he would still try and remind himself that he didn't make the decision to acquit, although he does say that 'magistrates who release people on bail who then re-offend, you know, perhaps they're the ones who should lose the sleep, I dunno'.[12] Perhaps we can explain John's position in the sense that, if someone is acquitted of a crime and then goes on to commit precisely that crime, it is not re-offending in the *legal* sense – even if they in fact committed the original offence. Acquittal in the vast majority of cases means that a person's guilt or innocence regarding that offence is no longer an issue. Moreover, one's past record is not necessarily admissible in legal proceedings. As we saw in chapter 3, in rape trials in the UK, the defendant's previous crimes are often not admitted as evidence – and his past 'good behaviour' (which may include the *tabula rasa* produced by a series of acquittals)[13] can actually work in his favour. In Martin and Peter's occupations, on the other hand, sex offender clients are known to have offended at least once previously, such that going on to repeat such behaviour is understood as *re*-offending. This may therefore imply greater culpability for those involved in trying to prevent it. Overall, John is certainly more successful in resisting the discursive positioning of his profession as accountable for sexual offences committed by individuals who have already been 'processed' than either Martin or Peter – which suggests that this is a weapon in his identity work armoury that the others do not possess to the same extent.

Given the emphasis on professional competence in these data, and the ways in which it seems to intersect with questions of identity work, the next section discusses the extent to which occupational context – individual autonomy, training, codes of ethics, and so on – has a bearing on the challenges of working within the abject space that is sexual crime.

Occupational context

Mills and Murgatroyd (1991: 155) claim that 'through specialisms and professionalization, the occupant of the position operates through a complex set of rules in which they are compelled to undertake specific tasks but which also give the appearance of self-interest and autonomy' – that is to say, they argue that professionals operate within an environment that may be seen to constrain at the same time as it permits latitude. It is therefore instructive for the purposes of our discussion here to examine exactly what kind of autonomy Martin, Peter and John enjoy. Jurisdiction over one's work is of course identified as crucially important in labour process literature, and is most often discussed in terms of the difficulties that lack of discretion poses for the individual incumbent (see, for example, Willis 1977; Collinson 1988; Burawoy 1979; O'Connell Davidson 1994a). The issue here, however, is less whether these professionals feel themselves to be in control and autonomous at work *per se*, but rather whether they are able to control their work to the extent that they can (theoretically at least) minimize the challenges of the working day by reducing the numbers of potentially difficult clients such as sex offenders.

In fact, there appears to be a continuum in this regard, at one end of which John has no real control over his workload. He has to act for whoever comes his way, given that, as far as potential clients ringing for appointments is concerned, 'the boss of my firm would not allow it to turn away clients for both commercial and philosophical reasons', and, second, that:

> The other main source of work, you know, is via, you know ... the police station and there's no controlling the volume of that. I mean if the phone rings, it rings, and even if you're not in the bleep goes off.

John, then, does not have the opportunity to pick and choose his cases although, given his ideology regarding access to justice, it seems unlikely that he would employ this kind of tactic anyway. He in fact expressed disapproval of one instance where an individual in a particularly controversial case had been refused representation and also stated that 'the irony of it is in fact I think ... [that] when the allegation is at its most heinous [then] somebody most desperately needs proper representation.'

Somewhere in the middle of the scale is Martin, who has total jurisdiction over who he admits to the hostel, but does not tend to exercise this right of refusal very often. The only categories of offender who are 'in effect no way' – that is, whom he would always reject – are hard drug users who will not commit to attempting to give up and the 'overly violent'. The first type of offender, according to Martin, causes 'criminal problems', the second presents challenges for which the hostel is insufficiently resourced. These principles of admission also seem to make less of the crime committed than the individual committing it, in line with Martin's overall philosophy as reported above, and, moreover, do not exclude sex offenders out of hand.

In fact, it is Peter who possesses and actually exercises the most control over his client load. A full psychological screening is conducted for all potential patients to see whether or not they display disorders that he feels he can treat, albeit from a clinical point of view as opposed to a personal distaste for, say, sexual dysfunctions. However, Peter was also the only respondent who mentioned the possibility of manipulating client loading in order to safeguard his own health and well-being. Were he to have a high number of clients to see per week, he suggested that he would try and limit 'the most taxing and demanding patients. You'd want to take some easier ones to maintain the balance'.[14] This is because, as Peter points out, treating patients with severe psychological disorders is emotionally and mentally taxing. However, if he were to operate in this way, he would not abandon a prospective patient totally but would refer them elsewhere. For all three respondents, then, the issue of autonomy in terms of client loading seems to be tied to the issue of doing the job properly, such that to reject a potential client out of hand would be to contravene their sense of adequate performance. In sum, this is not a lever which is used by these professionals to avoid having to enter the abject space of sexual offences.

Respondents were also asked to comment on the value of their training in terms of enabling them to work within this space. Does training in any way enable the kind of masking skills discussed above? Or perhaps it imparts something in the way of 'truth' as to the 'real' origins of sex offenders' crimes? In short, does it in any way mitigate the challenge of working with sex offenders? Peter and Martin both insisted that training was indispensable to ensure that workers in their respective fields possessed the requisite skills. Nonetheless, Peter also commented that the training necessary to practise as a clinical psychologist (the Doctorate of Clinical Psychology) is in short supply in the UK and competition to obtain a place is fierce. Therefore, demand may exceed supply, just as it does in Martin's occupational context. Here the expense of training is prohibitive such that Martin has actually recommended that his staff receive training specifically to equip them to deal with sex offenders (how they tend to operate, that they are expert at dissembling, that they have often been abused themselves, and so on), but doubts this will be acted on. Moreover, he suggests that social work in the voluntary sector does not accord training a high enough priority in any case:

> I know with my current management, for example, they see training as, completely wrongly, they see training as junketing, opportunity for [a] cheapo holiday … there are organizations who do the job but very few orga- nizations really do more than pay lip service. Really it is vital that training is given.

Indeed, no qualifications are required to work within a project such as the one Martin runs, despite the potentially volatile and demanding nature of the job. However, as he further remarks, following the death of a former resident from heroin addiction, he has become yet more aware that 'our work is dealing with lives … [not] stacking shelves in Tesco's … [we should] give that resident the best chance rather than lumbering them with some untrained plonker who really shouldn't be doing it'. The general lack of training, then, can be seen to exacer- bate the challenges facing Martin's project in that staff may not necessarily be fully prepared for the work that they do, even though failure can have serious consequences for residents *and* staff.

By way of contrast, John, bound like Peter to possess certain qualifications, is dubious about the value of the training he has received in actually performing the job he is employed to do. He describes his legal training as far more academic than practical:

> Well, Law Society finals is [*sic*] quite good at teaching you the procedure. So I arrived at my present employers, you know, knowing the basics as to how a criminal case would proceed with the rules of evidence and so forth. In terms of how you deal with people … all the things that are really important in my job, it did not feature in my training at all.

Nonetheless, John did note that, since he qualified, a legal practice course has been introduced for trainee lawyers which is much more practical and includes skills of advocacy, and so on.

Training, then, is viewed for the most part as useful when it is available, but as Martin points out, it has to be quality training and not just training '*per se*'. Indeed, in his account it appears that this particular source of help can never be relied upon to make the job easier because of budgetary constraints. However, there is also a sense across these accounts in which training is important in enabling one to do the job properly from a customer service vantage point, as opposed to it necessarily being useful in terms of helping the incumbent adjust to and live within his or her occupational role. Moreover, all three respondents also suggest that it is only a particular kind of individual that would succeed in their jobs anyway, for example, Martin remarks that:

> there is that intuitive part of you that walks into a [dodgy] situation and I'm not saying you can't train that ... [but] I couldn't teach you to sense an atmosphere, to sense that when someone says 'I'm fine' that they're not, you know, and I think that is life, you know, your own experiences, your own judgement of things. You can't train that.

This kind of account seems similar to the 'one in a thousand' ideology of the slaughterhouse workers (Ackroyd and Crowdy 1990: 8), and the individual ability that it implies is also thematically present in what John, Martin and Peter had to say on the subject of professional ethics. The discipline required of the individual professional is here presented as an internalized discipline which, broadly speaking, *coincides* with existing professional guidelines – that is to say, a good clinical psychologist, solicitor or social worker ought to know how to conduct themselves *without* reference to externally imposed rules. For example, Peter is bounded by the Charter of Clinical Psychologists' code of ethics, which includes the dictum that the relationship between therapist and client should not be an abusive one, that there should be no relationship outside of the therapeutic one, and so on. He abides very strictly by these guidelines, but also says that rules such as these will likely make little difference to those who enter psychology for the wrong reasons, that professional morality is for the most part internal to the individual and that most clinical psychologists would be aware that there were lines across which one should not step in any case, even without the existence of the Charter. Moreover, although the distance required protects the patient from the therapist, it also protects the therapist from the patient – in the instance of transference, for example, as Peter himself points out.

John also, in making reference to the statutory and cultural guidelines regarding the relationship between client and legal representative (for example, that one is required to act in the best interests of one's client at all times without ever misleading the court in any way), suggests that maintaining some degree of professional distance is necessary in order that these regulations be observed. For example, he gives the instance of becoming close to a client and realizing as a result that they are in fact guilty, such that one would be forced either to with-draw from the case or lie to the court. However, John has a different interpretation from Peter as to the degree of distance which is necessary, saying that, for example, he would not object to having certain of his clients buy him a drink, because he is 'quite fond of' them. Nonetheless, these individuals are, as he also states, those who have committed relatively inoffensive crimes such as the violation of trading standards where 'it's difficult to see ... any real victim'. This suggests that, on the other hand, John would feel uncomfortable drinking with his sex offender clients, given that they are accused of committing crimes with very obvious victims, and with (as we have already seen) what he sees to be very damaging consequences for those victims. Again, then, there is a sense here in which one as an individual professional has to know where to draw the line, without it being spelled out in existing occupational codes.

Martin, by way of contrast, implied that the regulations governing his profession are not so much codified as informally shared. He also states that, in any case, he disagrees with the majority view in the profession:

> there are lots of people in the business who say you mustn't get too involved with your clients. Certainly you must never appear to condone them and cover for offending but I would certainly argue that you can't do the job unless you are involved in their life and you're going to take it warts and all. You can't be a distant presence behind a desk because you're not going to get that experience of trust.

Martin, then, shares some personal information with his clients – such as his own brief experience of homelessness or what he has done with his family at the weekend – and also says that part of the job involves taking the residents out to social events such as a local carnival. Getting close to the residents is therefore presented as a prerequisite of the job; indeed, to maintain the distance which John and especially Peter emphasize as central to performing their jobs adequately would be to jeopardize Martin's likely success, as far as he constructs it. Here, moreover, Martin actively overturns the precepts which many members of his profession subscribe to of such distance being necessary in social work, which once more points to this belief in the need for an individual to negotiate and develop a professional morality *for themselves*.

Overall, then, the respondents' comments concerning professional codes seem to conform to Mills and Murgatroyd's (1991: 60) suggestion that:

> The truce between workers and the 'rules' within which they are required to work is not fixed and static but is continually negotiated … the worker engages in a conversation … through which he or she processes the rules of the organization and establishes a relationship within them (the truce) which assuages personal, moral and emotional issues with which that worker confronts those rules for him or herself.

It is also true to say that this truce is, according to Peter, John and Martin, impossible if the individual does not in the first instance have the 'right' attitude to do the job. Although codes of professional ethics exist in all three cases, to more or less formal degrees, there is also a strong sense that one must establish one's own morality in order to manage the job properly. All three professionals report themselves as having set their own interactional boundaries according to how close they perceive it is safe to get for their performance (and to a lesser extent for their own identity – at least in Peter's case). In Martin's case, moreover, these individually set boundaries appear to differ from those held by the majority of his profession.

Conclusion

The professionals interviewed here certainly experience working in the abject space of sexual offences as challenging. It seems, furthermore, that possible sources of organizational or institutional support are not necessarily forthcoming – although all three of them do point out that the bottom line is one's individual professional capability. Would it therefore be true to say that working with sex offenders is the most difficult aspect of these respondents' occupations? Peter noted that, while treating patients with upsetting and complex disorders is one of the more stressful elements of his job, it is also that element which absorbs his fullest attention, and that any unpleasant narratives or anti-social behaviour that his patients tell or display are usually part of the pathologies from which they suffer. Thus he is duty bound to take these episodes in his stride, however difficult that may be. However, Peter also implies, in saying that he sometimes hankers after an occupation which is more practical and in which one can see the tangible results of one's work (such as carpentry), that there are jobs which are less challenging to one's sense of self than clinical psychology. It is also interesting that he gives the example of manual work with 'concrete' results, especially if we recall Bataille's thesis that work is inextricably bound up with the disavowal of nature and death:

> The being that work made individual is the anguished being. Man is always more or less in a state of anguish, because he is always in a state of anticipation, an anticipation that must be called anticipation of oneself. For he must apprehend himself in the future, through the anticipated results of his action ... A being that would exist only in the moment would not be separated in this way from itself in a kind of 'traumatism'. But subjectively this would not be an individual.
>
> (Bataille 1997: 316–17)

The kind of work by which Peter is occasionally tempted, then, because it has a visible consequence or product, is perhaps that which constructs and reinforces individuality most definitively, as opposed to that which generates less tangible results, and which therefore does not ensure as strong a disavowal of death. More than this, in his particular occupation he has at times been called upon, via his work with sex offenders, to confront the abject directly, arguably making this disavowal even harder to achieve.

For John, on the other hand, the biggest challenge is a combination of a heavy workload and the hours he has to work. He does several on-call slots a month as the duty solicitor for his firm, and remarks of these that:

> I love police station work ... but I don't enjoy anything any more at three o'clock in the morning and it is onerous and I don't like it ... I don't wake

up that easily, I don't get to sleep again that easily, and if you have to go out in the middle of the night on a winter's night it is deeply unpleasant.

Moreover, the fact that this work, as John perceives it, demands that he is alert conflicts with the requirement that he performs it at unsocial times, and in large quantities. The stress generated by the kind of hours that he works is, in fact, a common theme in empirical research. Air traffic controllers (Cobb and Rose 1973), oil-rig workers (Sutherland and Cooper 1987) and nurses (Tasto *et al.* 1978), all engaged in occupations where shift work is entailed, have been identified as suffering from stress as a result. Moreover, working at night has been argued by Carpentier and Cazamian (1977) to be stressful due to the fact that we are physiologically diurnal, and therefore phenomena such as digestion, breathing, blood pressure and so on are designed to slow down during the hours of darkness. Nightworkers, as a consequence, tend to suffer from high levels of fatigue 'due to the fact that they have to work in a state of nocturnal de-activation and to sleep in a state of diurnal re-activation' (Carpentier and Cazamian 1977: 24). It is therefore unsurprising that John identifies the physical demands of his work as particularly stressful, albeit less predictable that he emphasizes these rather than the content of the work itself.

Martin also finds his job stressful, but again does not attribute this solely to the nature of the work itself:

> Most of the stresses come from having to deal with people who don't understand the work, i.e., higher management, people not involved in [the work itself], dealing with funders and trying to argue ... dealing with residents, yeah there are, you know, sometimes I'd describe it like warfare. There are sometimes, there are long periods of sheer boredom then brief minutes of sheer terror but I don't know, no, [the] main stresses come from the people who have got the power to fight for you to get extra resources and won't or don't or aren't bothered or you can't get through that you really need this and that.

Here then another set of stressors are identified which do not emanate from the work itself, but from lack of support for that work. Martin has a sense that his work is misunderstood to a large extent (perhaps in part because of the issues we have discussed in this chapter), and it is these misunderstandings that make the job of project leader a difficult one. This may, indirectly, make the interaction with clients more challenging – for example, because of the lack of training discussed above – but it is not this interaction which represents the primary tension.

In sum, then, the specific occupations discussed here do present challenges to the individual incumbents in terms of their remit to resettle, treat or defend sex offenders. It has been established that there is a conflict for these men, at least when having to confront the crimes committed by sex offenders and thus that there is some need for a professional mask in order to perform competently. It must also be reiterated that the issues of success and failure are inextricably tied up with self-image for at least two of the individuals interviewed here, which arguably renders this masking even more important. However, there is also a sense that other individuals are partially responsible for the outcome of the client relationship – be it the client themselves or individuals in other capacities in the system. While the ability of each individual professional to persuade themselves of this varies, it can be seen to provide, in John's words, some form of psychological 'buffer'.

There is, moreover, no denial that sex offences are difficult and unpleasant to deal with, so these individuals do share prevailing understandings of the importance of sex in the human condition, and of the extreme abjection of sexual offences in particular. However, Martin, John and Peter also tend to differentiate between those who commit the acts and the acts themselves. Understanding and dealing with the offenders as damaged or violated individuals themselves to some extent perhaps mitigate the need for concealment or masking of 'real' feelings, because this strategy pushes the actual offence into the background. Here strategies both of distancing (defensive identity work) and redefinition (aggressive/proactive identity work) are employed to protect these professionals' sense of themselves, as well as to ensure that they do their jobs to the best of their ability.

It seems also that all three have a very strong sense of their own professional morality, which is at least partly informed by the work that they do. Their work-related strategies broadly speaking obey codes of professional ethics as set out in whatever ways, but on the whole emerge from their own sense of what doing the job entails. They also express a sense that individuals who enter professions like theirs must be able to develop such strategies or ethical standpoints and, further, that the ability to do this in some ways dictates the performance of the job, as well as how effectively the incumbent survives its demands. This therefore implies that these jobs are suitable only for those who can think through the implications of this kind of work, and be able to deal with the conflicts and tensions that it presents. Those who cannot undertake this kind of negotiation either compromise the client relationship and/or risk their own sense of identity. Self-discipline therefore emerges as one of the most significant elements of successful making out (Roy 1955; Burawoy 1979), *and* performing adequately, in the accounts given here at least.

The insights derived from these very personal accounts of working with sex offenders to some extent bear out the demands that the relevant occupations may be assumed to present to the individual worker. However, it is also clear that there are other elements of the job which prove equally difficult and demanding. Particularly significant is that for two of the three interviewees the *content* of the job itself – including their work with sex offenders – is not as frustrating or challenging as its *context*. In conclusion, then, it is interesting to consider these accounts of daily working life if only because to some extent they confound our expectations of that life, allowing us some perspective on how workers like these deal with their labour within an abject space. Moreover, as Ashforth and Kreiner (1999: 429) put it:

The management of taint transcends dirty work occupations, because all occupations and organizations face at least occasional threats to their identity-making and identity-sustaining activities ... the self-serving nature of identity construction ... may, to some extent, undergird all occupations and organizations.

That is to say, our discussion of those professions which involve working with sex offenders might also be seen to illuminate the social regulation of the abject more generally – our individual and organizational efforts to shun that which must inevitably return.

5 Sadomasochism and organization

Introduction

> I am not just a human being, I am a piece of meat.
>
> (Shiveley, cited in Hart 1998: 67)

This chapter draws together themes raised in the previous chapters – the psycho-dynamics of abjection and the regulation of social boundaries – in a discussion of sadomasochism (S/M), and the ways in which it might inform modern orga-nizing. We draw upon secondary data from empirical research into S/M and accounts by S/M practitioners to argue that this genre of sexual behaviour can be understood as allowing those who indulge to express forbidden and dangerous desires, to respond to the compulsive return of the abject. As Sellers argues, the drive emphasized and exaggerated through the 'lust' of sadists and masochists, 'by which we distinguish ourselves, is the lust for death whom we worship. Morbidly do we cultivate this instinct for what extinguishes itself' (Sellers 1992: 144–5). However, this apparent death-wish is the carrying further of a basic human instinct, rather than simply being an inversion of the lust for life. It has its own integrity. Moreover, playing it out enables participants to move towards and extend their individual physical and psychological limits – that is to say, S/M has the capacity to disorganize customary understandings of self, being, the body, desire and pleasure in the sense that it exposes their socially constituted nature by bringing them into a stark confrontation with corporeality.

In what ways, then, can S/M be described as disorganizing? First, it is a form of sex which revolves around humiliation of the powerless by the powerful, the infliction of degrees of pain and fetishism, none of which are conventionally considered to be sexually pleasurable. It may not, moreover, ever involve pene-tration or even orgasm. S/M is also highly ritualistic and theatrical – indeed, its emphasis on imagination, role playing and staging in sex reveals the post-Cartesian division between physical and mental states to be a discursively constituted fiction through grounding them in activity. Within modernity, as we have already implied, humanity is understood to be a continual and inevitable struggle between the demands of the insatiable passions and the calming logic of reason. As Bataille sees it, work (which epitomizes performative rationality) is therefore an instrument by which we persuade ourselves of our autonomy from 'abject nature' and the passions, excesses and ebullience which it represents. S/M, on the other hand, represents a challenge to this essentialist separation of reason and the passions, given that it seems to depend as much on the labour of the mind as it does on the labour of the body.

At the same time, however, the highly *organized* character of contemporary S/M means that the re-engagement with the abject we allude to above is possible without those involved experiencing self-annihilation, such that they are 'able to play as close as possible to the edge without invoking terror … as close as possible to the edge without falling' (Hart 1998: 155, 157). Here Hart implicitly evokes Bataille's construction of joy as the experience that permits us

> [to] draw near to the void, but not in order to fall into it. We want to be intoxicated with vertigo, and the image of the fall suffices for this. One might say rather precisely that true joy would require a movement to the point of death, but death would put an end to it! We will never know authentic joy … Moreover, death itself is not necessary. I believe that our strength fails us before life does: the moment that death approaches it creates a void in us that incapacitates us in advance. So not only is trickery necessary in order not to die, we must avoid dying if we wish to attain joy. Thus, only the fictitious approach of death … points to the joy that would fully gratify us … since if we were dead we would no longer be in a condition to be gratified.
>
> (Bataille 1997: 262)

S/M is therefore paradoxical, because it seeks to disorganize, to transgress, to shatter, *but in a disciplined and regulated fashion*. Such a free movement of desire, a satisfying of what Bataille describes as self-shattering impulses, may otherwise transport human beings not only towards *but also beyond* their physical and psychological limits. In Foucauldian terminology, S/M is a limit experience, within which practitioners 'reach that point of life which lies as close as possible to the impossibility of living' (Foucault, cited in Simons 1995: 99). Notably, and in line with his own theorizing, Foucault himself experimented with this form of sex, being an enthusiastic *habitué* of the sadomasochistic bars and bathhouses in San Francisco's Folsom Street, the epicentre of the city's gay S/M scene (Miller 1993: 259–62). Consequently, S/M, read through Bataille[1] and Foucault, involves challenging our sense of ourselves as bounded and limited, living as dangerously as we can *while still continuing to live*. It enacts

> the pathos of the impossibility of love, the conflict between desiring-fantasy's shattering of the self and the necessity for returning to a coherent self in order to take one's place in the symbolic order, and the persistent fantasy of something that exists beyond language.
>
> (Hart 1998: 159)

Precisely because S/M has this capacity to bring us 'to the point of death', but not to drag us over into its void, careful and attentive negotiation, preparation and co-operation – that is to say, organization – on the part of its practitioners are vital prior to and during each encounter. Trust is, as a result, a key theme in our discussion, being both the condition and the consequence of successful S/M sex.

It is this disorganizing *and* organizing character of S/M which is our central concern in this chapter. Indeed, in addition to an extended consideration of the various facets of the limit experience that is S/M, we discuss what it might teach us in terms of the modern organization, given the dialectical character of power relations in the S/M encounter. We also consider trust in this regard, suggesting that S/M both depends on and creates deep intimacies which stand in complete contrast to the shallow, truncated and instrumental bonds typical of the organization. Finally, we consider the challenge that S/M poses to the mind/body dualism, and thus, when extended, to the boundaries of organizations themselves. We begin, however, with an analysis of the ways in which this kind of sex reconfigures notions of pleasure.

Sadomasochism and pleasure

Because of the ways in which S/M practitioners pursue pleasure, it is a relatively simple matter to assert that their practices are sexually radical; that what constitutes S/M is not, in conventional discursive terms, defined as pleasurable. Sadomasochistic sexual play therefore represents a break with prevailing conceptualizations of the erotic. Indeed, Moser and Levitt (1987: 334 – emphasis added) found that 'Most of our respondents did not engage in an S/M activity, nor realize this inclination, until a relatively late age. *This might suggest that the [discursive] inhibitions surrounding S/M are more durable and may take longer to break down.*' One obvious riposte to this argument is that those who take part in S/M are perverted; their natural desires and instincts have somehow become twisted so that they cannot find pleasure in 'normal' sexual activity. However, as should now be clear, we prefer not to read sexuality in such an essentialist way; rather, we contend that sexuality is a matter of discourse, signification and simulation; that there is no sufficiently coherent and stable alignment of physical properties, psychological responses and resultant actions within us which merits the designation 'sexuality'; and that all that we know of ourselves as sexually desiring beings is produced by discourse and our emergent positioning within systems of signification. S/M, then, can be read as making possible new and renewed forms of pleasure, located outwith the discursively powerful model of genitally-based, heterosexual, penetrative sex; it consists of a refusal on the part of its practitioners to define themselves as (only) experiencing sexual pleasure through activities such as the encounter of a male penis and a female vagina.[2]

To understand more fully how engaging in S/M is resistant in this regard, it is necessary to examine its constituent behaviours. While there is, as Moser and Levitt (1987: 323), Harriss (1988: 13) and Hart (1998: 120) point out, no definitive or unambiguous list of sadomasochistic practices,[3] Townsend, author of *The Leatherman's Handbook*[4] defines this kind of sex as broadly characterized by the following features:

> 1) A dominant-submissive relationship. 2) A giving and receiving of pain which is pleasurable to both parties. 3) Fantasy and/or role playing on the part of one or both partners. 4) A conscious humbling of one partner by the other (humiliation). 5) Some form of fetish involvement. 6) The acting out of one or more ritualized interactions (bondage, flagellation, etc.).
>
> (Townsend, cited in Miller 1993: 264)

Several points follow from this. The first is that the hierarchy which is so explicit in S/M sex (Townsend's first and fourth points) goes against the grain of what is usually considered legitimately erotic because it relies on sexual partners being unequal in their ability to dictate how the encounter unfolds.[5] It is true that S/M aficionados may swap roles from encounter to encounter so that one partner plays the Top (Master/Mistress; Superior; Dominant) in one encounter and the Bottom (Slave; Submissive) in the next – indeed, we discuss this issue in more detail in the next section but the dominant/submissive hierarchy is preserved *within each encounter*. That is to say, 'The bottom doesn't compete with his master; he manages with his help to challenge his own limits' (Lotringer 1988: 22, cited in Simon 1996: 131). Second, S/M frequently (necessarily, according to Townsend) involves one partner inflicting pain on another. As Sellers, whose career as a dominatrix prostitute led to her writing what appears to be a hand-book for *The Correct Sadist*, comments, 'I and my slavish cohorts continue to suffer and create more suffering. This is our pastime, it makes us feel alive' (Sellers 1992: 144). S/M practices, then, utilize the body so that the recipient of pain (even if it is excruciating) finds it erotically pleasurable. Miller (1993: 266–8), for example, refers to sex involving cock-rings with pins embedded inside them to pierce the penis as it becomes erect; clamps, alligator clips, stretchers and genital harnesses with weights, hot wax and needles; fist-fucking; flogging; medical scenes where the nipple or the genitals are cut with lancets; suspension and crucifixion; and even castration (although he points out that this last is probably fantasy on the part of Townsend, who records it). Sellers (1992: 40) also implies how intense the pain in S/M sex can become in her discussion of the appro-priate kit for a torture session, which might include a needle and thread; a hammer, nails and a board; razor-blades; knives; liniment; pepper; electric current; fingernails; and even a dog's teeth. As she says, anything 'sharp and dangerous' can be 'brought into play'.[6] These descriptions, of course, contradict the Freudian division of *eros* and *thanatos*, of desire and the death instinct, as well as the associated notion that, because we instinctively shrink from pain and seek pleasure, pain and pleasure are opposite poles of the normal human range of experience. The quest for pleasure within/through/as physical pain, then, is inconceivable for the 'normal' modern subject, invested as we are with Freudian understandings of sexual pathology – and it is also significant that some

ultimate simulacra. They occupy the ontological status of the model, appropriate the privilege, and refuse to acknowledge a status outside their own self-reflexivity. They make claims to the real without submitting to 'truth'.

(Hart 1998: 123)

Therefore, what may appear to be imitative heterosexual (or, more accurately, masculine) icons in lesbian S/M can in fact be read as identical copies of an original that never existed (Baudrillard 1983a). Hart implies that the erotic appeal for gay women of wearing, or being penetrated by, a strap-on instrument has nothing to do with pretending to be a man or playing out the passivity of the heterosexual woman. Instead, she states that 'it has become common to speak of "watching her play with her dick" or "sucking her off" or "your dick find[ing] its way inside of me"' (Hart 1998: 100). Lesbian dicks as used in S/M play, then, are literally the real thing. There is a reverence for the dildo that is not connected with its physical similarity to the penis – it is not a 'substitute', 'parody', or 'prosthesis' (Hart 1998: 123). Thus it does not *add to* the Top's physiological capacity; this would be to assume that women's bodies are somehow fundamentally lacking. Rather, what is implied as happening in this kind of sex is a movement beyond physiology. The lesbian Top's body-with-dildo-strapped-on is not a flesh and blood body with an artificial instrument attached. Instead, it seemingly represents the construction of a body that cannot be understood by reference to any existing configuration of organs, any living organism. We might suggest, therefore, that the use of dildos by lesbians in S/M play, as Hart interprets it, approximates to the building of Deleuze and Guattari's (1987) Body-without-Organs.[8] There is also more than an echo here of Haraway's (1990, 1991) thesis that bodies with 'technological extensions' – that is to say, cyborgs – render 'thoroughly ambiguous the difference between natural and artificial, mind and body, self-developing and externally designed … physical and non-physical', as Hart's (1998: 99) citation of her work recognizes.

In sum, then, the fact that S/M is pleasurable for those who practise it can be taken to suggest that all that we 'know about' our bodies, our desires and our pleasures is a product of modern discourse of sex and sexuality. S/M therefore, as we have suggested, represents a (re)fashioning of bodies, desires and pleasures, a certain resistance to prevailing discourse, a disorganizing. Indeed, as Foucault suggests, S/M creates:

new possibilities of pleasure with strange parts of [the] body – through the eroticization of the body. I think it's a kind of creation, a creative enterprise, which has as one of its main features what I call the desexualization of pleasure. The idea that bodily pleasure should always come from sexual pleasure, and the idea that sexual pleasure is the root of *all* our possible pleasure – I think *that's* something quite wrong.

(Foucault, cited in Miller 1993: 263)

However, as we have already noted, whilst S/M practitioners re-invent and simultaneously deconstruct the body, desire and pleasure, this is neither haphazard nor chaotic. This deconstruction in fact has a ritualistic and imaginative character (Townsend's sixth point) which is highly organized. Moreover, successful S/M apparently relies as heavily on mental labour as it does on physical labour. Indeed, some commentators imply that the former is more important in this kind of sex, although (which is also significant) it is difficult to draw a distinction in S/M between the realm of the body and the realm of the mind. This extends to questioning the common understanding of the objective of sex being bodily orgasm, as has been indicated in our discussion of fist-fucking. Even where physical sensation does remain paramount, it seems fair to say that the imaginative staging of S/M provides a vital intensification of any physical interactions that take place, amplifying the erotic charge for both participants, while providing a structure which ensures that neither tumbles 'over the edge'.

Sadomasochism and ritual

As we suggested above, contemporary S/M practice enshrines the principle that every encounter must be preceded by careful negotiation between Top and Bottom. A strong element of contract, which is then adhered to during the scene itself, is recommended so as to ensure pleasure for both participants. Therefore, although S/M appears to offer absolute power to one party and only submission to the other, it is rather the case that:

> From the early stages of verbal humiliation through to the final acts of apparent degradation the whole scenario is controlled and performed within well defined limits. Every act, every response is choreographed with extreme precision. Choice exists and is being exercised.
>
> (Words 1992: iv)

Hart agrees:

> What is striking about many s/m narratives and testimonials is the extent to which the sexual act is determined in advance, rigorously negotiated, planned in excruciating detail. Even the reactions of the participants are anticipated and planned for as much as possible ... the negotiations of s/m are in the service of safety, both physical and emotional attempts to guarantee that the consent of the parties involved is secure.
>
> (Hart 1998: 151–2)[9]

Sadomasochism is not, therefore, about the Top lashing out at the Bottom in an uncontrolled frenzy but, and this is important, neither is it some kind of reversal within which the Bottom controls the Top. If this was the case then the Top would be unable to sustain their fantasy of omnipotence (Sellers 1992: 132–3). For both partners to derive pleasure from S/M play, it appears that agreement between them as to the limits of the activities within the encounter is required, given that, among those taking part in Weinberg *et al.*'s extensive data gathering at least, 'a person who was not consenting would be considered neither "into SM" nor sexually desirable' (Weinberg *et al.* 1984: 385). Indeed, as a practising sadomasochist (quoted in Giddens 1992: 143) comments, 'Everything we've done together has been totally consensual and the "bottom" (who it is varies) always has control, together with the illusion of being out of control.' The domination–submission dualism in S/M, then, is far from rigid or well defined – indeed, if it were, both participants would be at risk of succumbing entirely to Sellers's 'lust for death'.

With the encounter properly organized, the Bottom is able to give into 'the terrifying appeal of a loss of the ego, of a self-debasement' (Bersani, cited in Miller 1993: 259), to experience being entirely at the command of another, no longer being an autonomous individual or self – but with the guarantee that this will only be temporary. For Sellers, one of the most pronounced examples of this abandonment is identification as an animal during the S/M scene:

> The desire to revoke the power of one's will and allow another to supersede therein manifests itself not only as the compulsion to become a contemptible specimen of humanity, or a helpless child, but *in a further extremity of self-annihilation* the masochist will destroy the possibility of rational thought and the power to choose what might be better for him, by reverting to an identification with what possesses only instinct – the animal.
>
> (Sellers 1992: 85; emphasis added)[10]

In a similar vein, Hart (1998: 118) says of Jane DeLynn's 'The Duchess of LA', a fictional account of lesbian S/M, that what the women spanking the narrator

> take from [her] is language and her 'I' – that is, they begin to speak for her and of her in the third person: 'she's really wet … see how she wants it … she'd probably beg for it if we stopped'.

Importantly, language for Bataille is one of the ways in which we most fervently disavow our 'connection with the natural world … Language is culture *par excellence*' (Richardson 1994: 63). Thus if we are deprived of our language, we are deprived of our subjectivity, and we move closer to our carnal origins. Elsewhere Hart, speaking of another fiction, this time the Pat Califia story 'The Calyx of Isis', recounts how Alex requires that her lover Roxanne submit to an S/M ordeal that she (Alex) has scripted, as a test of

> the ability to give up, temporarily and under ritualized conditions, her notion of her "self" as an autonomous ego. Alex wants to know if Roxanne can withstand becoming 'dehumanized' – erase (her)self – *and trust that Alex and her accessories will bring her back to the ground that necessarily reasserts itself in reality.*
>
> (Hart 1998: 150; emphasis added)

Such 'letting go', moreover, is reported to be particularly pleasurable for those who normally exercise and seek to retain control, in a political, economic or psychological sense, in their everyday lives. An active lesbian feminist, for example, comments that 'It feels good (at times) just to be able to let go of the struggle to be powerful and just relax and give up all claim to that power' (Zoftig, cited in Harriss 1988: 14). Here, one woman, usually concerned to preserve the right to an autonomous, non-degraded subjective existence, creates with her partner(s) an erotic space in which she can happily enjoy the illusion of loss of control, of becoming object, of abandonment to abjection.

The Top in S/M, by the same token, is enabled through the contract to experience being (again temporarily) in complete control, where they also know they will be loved by the Bottom, even though they are visiting humiliation and often pain on their partner (Zoftig, cited in Harriss 1988: 15). They may even imagine themselves killing the Bottom which, as we have seen in chapter 4, is one of the ultimate prohibitions to which Bataille refers, those social regulations which have at their core the horror *and* fascination that we have for death. However, in fantasizing about murder, we arguably forestall the threat of the void, and are permitted instead to teeter on its edge, to be forcibly, terrifyingly and pleasurably reminded of it.

S/M participants may also change roles from encounter to encounter. For example, 44.2 per cent of Moser and Levitt's (1987: 328) sample of practitioners understood themselves as being both dominant and submissive, known in the S/M subculture as being 'switchable', 'dual' or 'middle' (also see Weinberg *et al.* 1984: 383–4). When roles are swapped in this way, both individuals have the opportunity to experience abandonment (Bottom) and omnipotence (Top). We could also argue that swapping acts as a safeguard against individuals 'over-identifying' with the submissiveness of the Bottom or the aggression of the Top and may help to preserve the organized, ritualistic and therefore pleasurable nature of the encounter. In addition, the less physically, socially or psychologically powerful partner can become the Top, therefore allowing them to experience sensations which they are denied in conventional day-to-day encounters. The reverse is also true, as Simon points out:

> The social segregation of the sexual ensures its limited claims upon larger, more visible identities; for example, it allows those who are professional aggressors in public contexts to become submissive children within the sexual script as it allows what are in public timid subordinates to become the most demanding despots.
>
> (Simon 1996: 132)

Hart (1998: 138; see also Harriss 1988; Giddens 1992), in a similar vein, points to 'the large, relatively hidden, subculture of highly successful, powerful, heterosexual men who regularly go to dominatrixes for masochistic play'.

As further evidence of the organization which is so central to S/M, the contract between participants usually also includes the use of code words so that the Bottom can put a stop to a particular form of sadistic play if he or she finds it too demanding. Since enjoyment for the Bottom is almost entirely reliant on a sense of being out of control, and vice versa for the Top, the Bottom pleading with the Top for mercy may well be part of the erotic charge of S/M for both parties because of the belief that the Top will not stop, even if beseeched to do so. Therefore, if the Bottom actually does want the Top to desist, the use of terms like 'stop' may be misunderstood by the Top to simply form part of the realization of the Bottom's desire to be unable to dictate what is happening to them. As a consequence, there is a need for a vocabulary to be developed so that the Bottom can bring the scene to an end if they genuinely cannot tolerate what is taking place – that is to say, if it brings them too close to the void. Weinberg *et al.*'s (1984: 385) respondents, for example, referred to 'safe-words' or 'key-words' such as 'pickle' (presumably used because of its incongruity in a sexual setting); indeed, one S/M group of male Tops and female Bottoms had established a universal system where 'red' meant 'stop immediately' and 'yellow' 'slow down or break' in all encounters. As White says, then, 'the freedom to start and stop a sex scene is part of almost every S&M contract' (White, cited in Miller 1993: 265).

The S/M encounter, in sum, is properly ritualistic, organized and negotiated from the outset so as to permit experience its fullest rein. Indeed, because practitioners often engage in role play, where they act out scenarios which involve a powerful character humiliating a powerless character in some way and thereby concretize their sub and dom sexual play (Townsend's third point), these encounters may even be scripted. Sellers offers several sample scripts for S/M scenarios, and what follows is an extract from her suggested dialogue between a Prison Warden (Top) and a Prisoner (Bottom):

[Prisoner]: I feel like I'm going to be here forever ... Are you going to keep me here forever ... ? Please keep me ... I'll do work for you.

[Warden]: Yes, the guards and I make all the prisoners in solitary work very hard for us.

... What do you make us do?

... You have to cater to our every need ... We check you all out for talent and give you jobs according to your abilities.

... Wipe your feet on me ... use me as a toilet ...

... We'll decide on it.

(Sellers 1992: 28)

The fantastic character of the S/M encounter may also be bolstered by the use of costumes and props to add to the veracity of the scene being played (such as a mock cell in the prison scene above). Further, and importantly, in some S/M activity, props such as whips, chains, ropes and so on may not be much more than props (Giddens 1992; Miller 1993: 265–6). S/M is, as our discussion hitherto implies, often very theatrical. It requires a distinct talent for impersonation, mimicry and masquerade (Silverman, K. 1988) but it is also true to say that it may rely much more on imagination for its sexual vibrancy than it does on physical experience such as the actual infliction or suffering of pain. Indeed, Weinberg *et al.* (1984: 382) state that 'In SM, it is the *appearance* of pain which is often most important; the *sensation* of pain may merely lend credence to a fantasy.' The fantasy, then, the notion that one could be giving oneself up to all kinds of unimaginable terrors or that one is able to inflict all kinds of unimaginable terrors, is crucial – and it may be the case that fantasy comes to supersede or replace physicality, that what Havelock Ellis refers to as the 'joy of emotional intoxication' (Ellis, cited in Thompson 1994: 33) is the real hub of erotic pleasure here. That is to say, the power of the fantasy, the idea or the possibility of transgressing socio-physical boundaries, matters perhaps more than engaging in the actual physical practices themselves. To be sure, unbounded S/M practice can 'brand, burn, mutilate and kill' (Brewis and Grey 1994: 78) – and the sadistic episodes described by Sade, in *Juliette* (1968) for example, on occasion involve murder. However, it is arguable that there is equal impact to be found in imagining the acting out or suffering of such brutalities, with the appropriate preparation, scripting and props, as there is in their actual occurrence. Therefore we contend that the role of imagination and the masquerade in S/M mean that a genuine challenge to physical limits (or indeed the testing of another's limits) need not form part of pleasurable S/M activity. Moreover, S/M's theatrical character may act as a further assurance to its participants that they will 'reach that point of life which lies as close as possible to the impossibility of living', *but will not go beyond it.*[11]

Moreover, we would also contend that the physical practices associated with S/M are problematic in ways other than their capacity to bring about death. The brutal physicality of certain forms of S/M may be accompanied by a celebration of machismo among its practitioners, particularly gay men, for whom participation in extreme S/M play could become a rite of passage, one which marks those involved as 'real men'.[12] As one individual (quoted in Weinberg *et al.* 1984: 387), whose face had been defecated upon, said, 'It's avant-garde, man. Other guys don't have the guts to do it. They just talk about it. I'm proud that I can do it and the other guys can't.' Another, a 19-year-old who had endured a clearly painful (and not pleasurable) fist-fucking, said afterwards that he did not stop the session because 'Everyone else can take it'; his friend, in a similar vein, referred to 'peer pressure' in situations of this type (both sources quoted in Weinberg *et al.* 1984: 387). Moreover, it is significant that these men did not classify their scatological sex play or fist-fucking as S/M, preferring to see such activities as proof of their 'masculinity and toughness' (Weinberg *et al.* 1984: 387). This kind of machismo is also illustrated in Townsend's claim, as cited above, that he has witnessed an actual castration, in which the Bottom's testicles were severed and then put in his mouth. Whether, as Miller (1993: 267) suggests, this is itself a fantasy might be seen to be irrelevant; the important point is that Townsend actually makes such a claim. Sellers also notes that man-on-man S/M is frequently more brutal than other forms: 'Gay men have made a cult of fist and foot-fucking, these limbs magically taking on the aspect of phalluses. The slave prides himself on how agreeably huge his anus can grow, how well-drilled he can become' (Sellers 1992: 48–9).

The extreme nature of these descriptions implies a pressure among certain of its practitioners to escalate S/M activity, and not necessarily for reasons of pleasure. Additionally, if we accept that these ultra-macho identifications – which Bersani (cited in Hart 1998: 91) refers to as 'unqualified and uncontrollable complicities with ... a brutal and misogynous ideal of masculinity' – are not necessarily confined to men, then it is conceivable that women could equally become obsessed with their own ability to inflict or endure pain and humiliation above and beyond the actual pleasure that they derive from the activities themselves. Such behaviours imply the existence of a particular pathology in the S/M subculture where the sex is quite different from the organized and ritualistic masquerade discussed above.

Thus far, we have suggested that S/M offers possibilities for new and renewed forms of pleasure, both through the actual transgression of socio-physical boundaries, such as the infliction or reception of pain as part of sex, and/or in the masquerade, where one can imagine that one is engaging in all manner of transgressions through the use of scripts, role plays and props. It can also be argued that S/M depends on, and simultaneously creates, new and renewed forms of intimacy between sexual partners.

Sadomasochism and intimacy

The *non*-consensual infliction of violence or humiliation by one individual upon another within an intimate relationship can be argued to have a particularly destructive impact on the victim; to intervene in their psyche in such a way as to come to constitute an important component of their self-image, as we have already established in chapter 1. Discussing this kind of abuse, MacCannell and MacCannell (1993) suggest that it has two specific effects. First, it means the victim 'continue[s] to associate sexual pleasure and love with violent abuse to the point that they miss the violence and have difficulty experiencing intense pleasure without it' (MacCannell and MacCannell 1993: 225), for example, imagining the face of a sexually abusive parent in order to achieve orgasm. Second, such violence means that the victim may lose the foundation for intimate relationships except with the individual who has been violent in the past, individuals who are presently violent or may be violent in the future, or potential victims whom they themselves can abuse. In sum, then, the victim of abuse inflicted by an intimate is said to sustain what MacCannell and MacCannell refer to as subjective damage, to experience a 're-organization' or 'disruption' of their very personality (MacCannell and MacCannell 1993: 209, 221). Indeed, as one victim of domestic abuse reports, 'When I got married I thought that it was someone to look after me and provide for me and I would have a good happy life. You know, that I had someone that really cared for me and would put me first' (Elizabeth, quoted in Evason 1982: 63–4). Elizabeth, then, was forced to accommodate the fact that her husband did not look after her, provide for her, give her a happy life, care for her or put her first. In fact he did quite the reverse, beating and sexually abusing her throughout their marriage. Her expectations of him, then, have arguably rebounded on her sense of herself; we could suggest that she has 'learnt' that she does not deserve to enjoy any of the things she expected from her marriage, having introjected a sense of her own unworthiness. A similar account is offered by Jane, who states that her physically, sexually and psychologically abusive husband

> keeps saying that I am a slag and I am not fit to be the mother of my children. He tries to destroy my confidence, my pride and my dignity. I used to look after myself and I used to have a pride in my appearance, but now I mean look at me. It is because of what he has done to me, just because of what he has done.
>
> (Jane, quoted in Edwards 1989: 162)

Jane has 'learnt' the same 'lesson' as Elizabeth – that she is unworthy and despicable, so unworthy in fact that even her husband apparently cannot stand the sight of her. Her experience is also a useful example of how damaging non-consensual psychological violence (which often co-exists with, or may even take the place of, non-consensual physical or sexual violence) can be.

Clearly, then, for there to be erotic pleasure for both parties in S/M, there is a need for consensus between them. Trust is the key to successful S/M – if the Top fails to comply with the wishes of the Bottom, then the Bottom cannot derive pleasure from the encounter, and if the Bottom won't 'play the game' of submission, the reverse is also true. In fact, as Weinberg *et al.* (1984: 386) state, violators of the contract were not welcomed by their S/M aficionados; men and women who continually went beyond agreed limits were exiled to an 'outer circle' where they experienced difficulty in finding partners. However, this should not be taken to suggest that the contract which is drawn up is necessarily rigid and restricting. This would probably mean that the Bottom's experience of a loss of control and the Top's experience of absolute omnipotence would be difficult to sustain. Instead, a situation often seems to exist in which limits are agreed, but in which there is also the assumption that the scene may escalate, perhaps even resulting in serious injury to the Bottom. Indeed it seems to be this assumption which forms at least part of the erotic character of S/M (Moser and Levitt 1987: 335; Hart 1998: 91). Moreover, what Weinberg *et al.* (1984: 385–6) refer to as 'pushing the limits' appeared to be fairly commonplace among their respondents. They give the example of a female Bottom who told her male Top not to slap her in the face. However, he chose to do exactly that, albeit lightly, and, when she responded positively, he slapped her harder and harder until she finally indicated that she had had enough. Afterwards, the Bottom was surprised by her own pleasurable reaction. In a similar vein, Sellers argues that the skilled Top can draw the Bottom beyond their limits, because:

This is not to deny that there are individuals who would fit more comfortably into the categories of sadist and masochist constructed by Sade and Sacher-Masoch. Those who engage in the kind of sexual brutality represented by lust murders, for example, such as some of the sex offenders discussed in chapter 4, would genuinely deserve to be called sadists, *à la* the Marquis himself, and they clearly go well beyond the kind of physical and psychological limits we have discussed throughout this chapter. However, it is not with individuals such as these that this chapter concerns itself. The discussion here focuses on those individuals who engage in consensual sadomasochism and who do not necessarily consider themselves to be predominantly dominant or submissive. Sadomasochism, then, is a simulacrum.

In sum, successful S/M seems to require what might be described as a peculiar level of intimacy, a level of intimacy which affords both participants a deeply shattering erotic experience, while at the same time assuring that they will not fall into the existential void, that the loss of self which S/M makes possible is only temporary.

Problematizing sadomasochism

Having argued that S/M represents 'a movement to the point of death', it is also important to reflect on the problems that it raises. First, can perfect contracts ever exist between human subjects? To assume that participants in S/M can achieve an inter-subjective agreement which represents complete consensus between them is to assume that communication between subjects can also be fully transparent – that Habermas's (1979) ideal speech situation, to which we alluded briefly in chapter 3, can become reality. Such a claim rests on a particular estimation of the potential of dialogue; on the idea that, by communicating freely, equally, for long enough and in sufficient depth, individuals can gain a genuine sense of each other's desires and motives:

> Central here is the anticipation in every speech act of a free dialogue in a nonauthoritarian society in which the potentials in language for questioning, checking, and arguing are freely utilized. Habermas assumed that, in principle, knowledge can be cleansed of power, and subjectivity emancipated, by achieving symmetry in its relations.
>
> (Alvesson and Willmott 1992: 441)

There has, however, been substantial criticism of this position, a good deal of it informed by the work of Foucault. Foucault rejects the idea that individuals can achieve the utopia of transparency of communication; he argues instead that knowledge can never be free of power, that interpretation is always an exercise of power, indeed that our ability to interpret at all relies on us having been quite literally made subject by the powerful operations of discourse (for development, see discussion of the relationship between discourse and identity in chapter 3). Following from this, we can suggest that interaction engages its participants in imposing an artificial closure on the other's sense of their own words. From this perspective, then, there is no way in which one person can capture what another wants and needs exactly, so that what others want and need remains to some extent closed to us; we cannot claim to be able to fully understand it. Instead we can only ever construct their desires and motives, working on a simulation of what we believe them to want and need as produced by our own way of being-in-the-world. Perhaps, therefore, it is naïve to assume that the S/M contract can ever be perfect or complete, without imperfections and misunderstandings.[14]

It is also worth reflecting on what might follow from being the Bottom in S/M sex, as illuminated through a consideration of the work of Canetti (1987), also discussed in chapter 1. Canetti (1987: 352) asserts that 'Beneath all commands glints the harshness of the death sentence.' That is to say, he sees the impetus to obey an order from another individual as being located within the 'oldest command' of capital punishment. Canetti acknowledges that this threat is only a 'glint' in contemporary society; that commands have become so formalized now, so well established within hierarchies of authority, that the fear of death (which we have already discussed at length) is perhaps only a fleeting atavistic dread. However, he also states that 'the threat and fear of [the death sentence] is always contained within [commands]; and the continued pronouncement and execution of real death sentences keeps alive the fear of every individual command and of commands in general' (Canetti 1987: 352). According to Canetti, we therefore possess a certain impulse to follow orders which derives from our desire to protect ourselves against the wrath of others. However, that is not to say that we fulfil these orders at no cost to ourselves – Canetti locates a sting within compliance whenever it causes discomfort. This gives rise to a desire either to reverse (that is, to give back to the person who has issued you with a command) or to pass on (to another individual, a future subordinate) the discomfiture one has experienced through being subjected in this way. There is, Canetti suggests, an 'ontological desire' to reassert symmetry between oneself and the individual who exercises power over one; the sting, in sum, is the individual's objection to being subjected. Moreover, the deeper the sting and more unpleasant the command, the longer any reversal or passing on takes (Linstead 1997: 71).

If this analysis is transposed on to the hierarchy which exists within S/M, it is possible to suggest that a sting may lurk within this form of sexual activity. Certainly, S/M is, or at least should be, consensual, so the Bottom is receiving commands to which he or she has agreed to submit, to which he or she should take pleasure in submitting. However, the issue of reciprocity (Linstead 1997: 77) makes Canetti's analysis relevant here in some degree, in that an S/M command relationship in which there is insufficient reciprocity, in which the Bottom does not experience pleasure, or does not experience the requisite degree of pleasure, and yet has been subjected to humiliation, violence, pain, even injury, will probably produce a sting which awaits return. Sellers's (1992: 44) aforementioned warning that a Bottom will seek to escape and may even resort to violence against the Top if the Top inflicts too much pain too fast upon them is especially

The fact that the dealer here is permitted to choose the colours of the items that are taken to each party *but not the items themselves* again suggests that an illusion of autonomy is being fostered here, as opposed to a situation in which the employee has genuine, and possibly difficult, decisions to make.

However, in contra-distinction to the above scenario, in which power is constructed as something that is 'given' by managers to workers, and even then only in reduced and insignificant ways, power relations in S/M consist of Top and Bottom being dialectically dependent on each other, are founded on a mutually negotiated contract, and may also involve the person acting as Top changing from encounter to encounter, because it is understood that individual scenes are always and already temporary. It is also worth noting Gherardi's (1995: 60–2) findings suggesting the existence of such relationships *within organizations* – as well as her coda that they may be difficult to admit to. She writes that, in two offices where in her role as consultant she was asked to develop levels of employee involvement,

> The boss frequently indulged in violent temper tantrums which exceeded the bounds of acceptable behaviour: he abused the workers and belittled their professional competence and moral integrity. Those who worked in the office lived in fear of his daily moods: they never know what to expect when he arrived in the morning, they worked as if he was breathing down their necks when he was present, and did absolutely nothing when he was absent.
> (Gherardi 1995: 60)

The interesting issue here is that the staff made little effort to prevent their boss's behaviour – indeed, they tended to do the reverse. That is to say, instead of solving such problems as they were able to alone, they would consciously alert him to the relevant issue which 'only served to reinforce the boss's opinion that he was dealing with "cretins" (as he called them in public)' (Gherardi 1995: 61). Moreover, although the boss's arrival had created significant demand for transfers, new staff tended to leave quickly and no one elsewhere in the organization wanted to transfer in, those who had been there for some time (a) showed no desire to leave; and (b) saw Gherardi's efforts to create a more participative culture as threatening. The boss was also, despite his behaviour towards them, apparently satisfied with his team. As Gherardi (1995: 61) notes, the abuse he meted out, as well as the submissive response apparent on the part of the workers, certainly 'called to mind the sexual fantasies of the slave/master' – especially given the seeming reluctance on either side to put a stop to the relationship – and she was also intrigued to discover that, in discussing her findings, others recognized the situation she had described. Nonetheless, it is important to point out that, though jokes were made about the boss's behaviour being sadistic, much less was said about the 'reciprocal dependence and collusion' (Gherardi 1995: 61) which existed, although, as Gherardi (1995: 62) also states, if the situation had been more overtly abusive, then many more staff would have been prompted to leave. Although she does not speculate on the reasons for this, we might argue that the very nature of organizational hierarchies, whilst creating super-subordinate relations, also installs dialectical relations of dependency – although the fact that there *are* superiors and subordinates may obscure this fact, constructing superiors as all-powerful. Kerfoot (1999: 191) refers to this as the 'day-to-day practice of hierarchical management and the unquestioning autonomy exemplified in maxims such as management's "right to manage" '. Therefore what Gherardi (1995: 62) calls the 'erotic bond of reciprocity' between manager and staff in this organization was, in the final analysis, difficult for anyone involved to openly discuss.

The dialectical, contractual character of power relationships, by way of contrast, is explicit in S/M as we have analysed it in this chapter. Indeed, S/M can only succeed if the Top is aware that his or her control over the Bottom, and therefore his or her sexual pleasure, is entirely dependent on the Bottom's willing and enthusiastic submission, which in turn means that the Bottom must trust and respect the Top enough to believe that they are psychologically and physically safe during the S/M scene. We have spoken at length of the sting that may result from S/M relationships and, although the revenge that may be exacted within organizations by subordinates who have been forced to defer to others against their will may be less impactful than the ire of an unhappy Bottom, it is true that the consequences can be less than pleasant for the manager at fault. Here we might recall the tale told by Willis's (1977: 55) car engine operative about a colleague:

> the gaffers asked X to make the tea. Well it's fifteen years he's been there and they say 'go and make the tea'. He goes up the toilet, he wets in the tea pot, then makes the tea … He says, you know, 'I'll piss in it if I mek it, if they've asked me to mek it' … so he goes up, wees in the pot, then he puts the tea bag [in], then he puts the hot water in … He told them after and they called him for everything, 'You ain't makin' our tea no more'. He says, 'I know I ain't not now'.

More recently, Radio Five's *Drive* programme (broadcast on 21 July 1999) listed some of the ways in which employees have sought to reverse the sting created by their relationships with their managers. Inspired by the story of a disgruntled footman at Buckingham Palace who put whisky and gin in food for the Queen's corgis, these were all phoned in by listeners and included the emptying of a hoover bag into the manager's supply of custard creams, the ordering of supplies of incontinence pads and hearing aids for another hapless boss, and an individual who was ordered to water the office plants at a weekend, and so decided to use water from a just-boiled kettle. A real and deep-rooted awareness of the dialectics of power relations, sensitivity to the unspoken contract of power in organizations (more usually referred to as the psychological contract) and the realization that they themselves are far from irreplaceable on the part of managers, such as the Top always and necessarily possesses, may therefore help to forestall the workplace sting, as well as moving organizations

Conclusion

Reflecting on the organized practice of S/M, then, helps to reveal the dialectical character of power relations, as well as illuminating possibilities for human intimacy and problematizing the mind/body – reason/passions – public/private dualism. Moreover, doing all of this also enables us to consider new models of organizing *per se*. But the extent to which we can really hope to 'reach that point of life which lies as close as possible to the impossibility of living' within organizations – that is to say, to *dis*organize fully and completely – is debatable. For Bataille (1985: 101), economic and political organizations, being structures devoted to the generation of utility, cannot co-exist with 'orgiastic participation in different forms of destruction ... the violent excitation that results from the expulsion of heterogeneous elements', because this form of organization belongs firmly within the realm of the profane, the sphere of our activity in which we labour to disavow our carnal origins, to produce as opposed to consuming. That is:

> *the free 'subject', unsubordinated to the 'real' order and occupied only with the present* ... leaves its own domain and subordinates itself to the *objects* of the *real* order as soon as it becomes concerned for the future. For the subject is consumption insofar as it is not tied down to work.
>
> (Bataille 1991: 58)

We develop this issue in more detail in what follows, but we should observe at this point that the glimpse of what lies beyond our limits which practices like S/M afford us would be, for Bataille, *impossible* within work organizations. The wasteful excesses, the confrontation with the abject, with death, which he sees as central to the achievement of joy, and which S/M conjures up, cannot take place in this context. A re-eroticized organization, if we follow the path indicated by Bataille, would necessarily be directionless, non-utility generating and quite literally useless, just as the festivals and sacrifices to which he devotes lengthy consideration are directionless, non-utility generating and useless. Sexuality pervades the modern organization, as we have argued in this first part of the book but, as explicitly stated in the Introduction, it tends to do so either such that it is appropriated in the name of utility or in ways that can, from a perspective informed by Bataille, only ever represent ruptures or 'wounds' (however deep) in the profane, returns of the abject to the world of rational and productive effort that is the modern workplace. Work itself, and the organization which supports it, cannot be eroticized. As we argue in the next chapter, such a process appears to imply the antithesis of everything that work and organization in the modern context stand for.

6 Re-eroticizing the organization

Introduction

As we observed in our introductory chapter, recent thought on the role of the erotic in organizations has broken with orthodox modernist accounts of the need to suppress sexuality and intimacy, urging instead that sex be recognized as an unavoidable feature of workplace life, and arguing that it can perhaps provide the basis for re-energized relationships between work colleagues (Pringle 1989; Burrell 1992a; Hines 1992; Gherardi 1995). In this body of thinking which, following Burrell, we term re-eroticization theory, the possibility of eroticized organizations emerges not just as a potential, but as a prescription. Although it has roots in the work of Reich (1969, 1972) and Marcuse (1968, 1969), such thought is also influenced by the more recent and arguably postmodernist theorizing of Cixous (1988) and Baudrillard (1990, 1993a, 1993b). In this chapter we aim to draw together these disparate sources so as to provide an outline of contemporary re-eroticization theory at the present time. We also identify its key theoretical flaws, but suggest that neither re-eroticization theory nor the criticisms that can be levelled at it explicitly address what we see as being the major tension underlying the different perspectives on eroticization – that is, their contrasting understandings of the nature of desire. Thus we outline in some detail our treatment of desire from a different theoretical perspective to the prevailing Freudian construction of desire as lack, one informed by the work of Bataille, Foucault and Deleuze and Guattari in particular. Importantly for our purposes here, this allows us to investigate the dark side of desire, especially as it pertains to organization, and the ways in which death and the erotic are inextricably linked through dynamics of growth, change and loss. It also permits us to address Burrell's (1997: 236) retrospective take on his own work in his statement that 'it is extremely difficult to see how re-eroticization could be progressed. Indeed it is not even clear that it should be progressed.' That is to say, in exploring the question of whether work organizations can ever be eroticized, we also ask whether they can ever be de-eroticized, and we do this through a consideration of the role of transgression in cultural formations of desire.

In order to establish a context for discussion in this chapter, we initially provide a brief overview of the more accepted current thinking on sex and organization. As Hearn and Parkin (1995: 7) argue: 'The idea that sexuality and "work" are somehow at odds with each other is widespread', and in this vein we discuss the discourse of scientific modernism (Geuss, cited in Brewis 1996: 66) which (dis)places sexuality and the erotic as irrational, marginal and feminine in contrast to the rational, masculine core of organization. We therefore suggest that mainstream theorizing on the place of sexuality and the erotic in organizations is accomplished through the modernist separation of reason and passion, and public and private (Burrell 1984; Hearn and Parkin 1995: 3–16).

Following this contextualization, we go on to discuss re-eroticization theory itself, drawing an initial distinction between the essentialist emancipatory appeals of Reich and Marcuse as they have informed such thinking, and the contemporary work of Cixous and Baudrillard, which proposes an anti-essentialist de-centring of the erotic and an overcoming of psychological repression in the dismantling of self-identity. However, we argue that, in complex ways, the latter may be guilty of a romantic essentialism of its own which renders it problematic in terms of claims such as Burrell's (1992a: 86) argument that 'If we remain true to the theory of pleasure ... then there is hope that our practice will be enriched by it.' We intend, therefore, to denote two kinds of difficulty within re-eroticization theory as it stands. First, we argue that some of the sources upon which re-eroticization theory draws entail an essentialism in their depiction of particular forms of desire which, while diversity is to some extent acknowledged, are nevertheless conceptualized naturalistically, as innately normal human attributes, to the exclusion of other more 'abnormal' or 'unnatural' forms such as homosexuality or sadomasochism. The emancipation afforded by re-eroticization here would, such sources claim, 'cure' society of these aberrations. Second, we contend that what re-eroticization theory depicts as 'missing' from organizational life (sexuality, the erotic and intimacy) represents, within certain postmodernist accounts specifically, a somewhat artificial and abstract version of the feminine. This does not mirror the complexity of actual female experience and thus the theory may not fulfil its radical political promises because it is not women as a heterogeneous group of individuals whose re-integration is proposed, but a standardized characterization of women: the feminine as a sign. The ways in which the feminine is understood to relate to the masculine in this strand of re-eroticization theory are also addressed, our argument being that, as the feminine cannot exist without the masculine (and vice versa), representing the feminine as destabilizing and subversive of the masculine is as problematic as defining it as simply what the masculine is not.

Modernity, rationality and sexuality

The notion of the public sphere as rational, universalistic and unemotional and the private sphere as affective, particularistic and ruled by the passions arguably derives from the disciplinary character of modernity (Weber 1968; Foucault 1977, 1980; O'Neill 1986). As human individuals came to believe that they could and should control their own destiny, they simultaneously came to fear the possibility of the other they carried around within themselves. As Bauman (1987: 54–5) puts it:

> The new perception of the relationship between (man-made) social order and nature – including the nature of man – found its expression in the notorious opposition between reason and the passions. The latter was seen increasingly as the 'natural equipment' of men, something men acquire with their birth, with no effort on their part and no assistance from other men. The former, reason, comes with knowledge, [and] must be 'passed over' by other people, who know the difference between good and evil, truth and falsity.

In order to create ourselves as independent, autonomous and enlightened, our capacity for reason was, from the late seventeenth-century inception of modernity, identified as paramount. By developing our reason, it was believed, we could begin to evaluate the world around us, to cease to take our reality for granted, to make it work for us and make it useful. As Easlea (1981) convincingly demonstrates, 'science' was argued to be unashamedly masculine, ravishing a feminine 'nature' for the hidden secrets of the world around us (Linstead forthcoming). Our 'naturally occurring' passions, on the other hand, were to be subdued, being understood as the instinctual, lower, wasteful and animalistic components of the human condition. While this separation may be seen as a general characteristic of modernity, several commentators from the eighteenth century onwards debated whether the passions could be productively channelled into the service of society (see Hirschman 1977 and chapter 3). Moreover, it was Freud who first fully acknowledged that this channelling has its costs, that a fundamental tension exists between properly organized social life and the unmediated passions. According to Freud, the collective Oedipal sublimation of natural sexual urges is necessary to achieve civilization. Operating on the reality principle, the practical yet rational ego must learn how to manage the instinctive and sensual id, which is governed by the pleasure principle, yet without overvaluing the prohibitions internalized by the superego. The civilized and emancipated modern social as imagined by Freud, then, is not one in which there are no restrictions on human conduct – such a wildly instinctive existence would not, he argues, be a free one because enslavement to the passions implies the concomitant lack of an ability to make properly reasoned choices. That is to say:

> The liberty of the individual is no gift of civilization. It was greatest before there was any kind of civilization though then, it is true, it had for the most part no value, since the individual was scarcely in a position to defend it. The development of civilization imposes restrictions on it, and justice demands that no one shall escape these restrictions.
>
> (Freud 1963a: 32–3)[1]

Within modernity, therefore, human existence

> instead of remaining a natural condition enjoyed by all though in many alternative forms, became … a skill to be learned, an end to a tortuous effort, which everyone had the duty to undertake, but few only were able to accomplish unassisted.
>
> (Bauman 1983: 36)

In order to take control of our destinies, we were understood as having to work upon ourselves, to develop the 'skill' of being human by repressing the passions and cultivating reason – to which Freud added the important qualification of not becoming so fixated by these restrictions as to become unable to act, to grow or to develop. As a corollary, most obviously in the nineteenth century, sexuality and the erotic were constructed as belonging within the private sphere, which provides a sharp contrast to the public celebration of the body in the Middle Ages. Burrell, for example, describes the medieval carnival as being typified by

> lewdness and vulgarity, with an emphasis on grotesque exaggeration and colourful clowning. There was a low level of control over bodily and natural forces. The tabooed and the fantastic were possible. Reciprocity and mutuality were expressed through the interdependence of carnival members trusting each other for mutual safety, well-being and pleasure.
>
> (Burrell 1992a: 80)

Indeed, these public events were gradually stamped out as part of the 'civilizing process' (Elias 1978) which swept through the West in the early years of modernity. What Turner (1992: 194) describes as their exuberance, naïveté, directness, intensity and communal spirit was redefined as problematic, as instrumental in 'unleashing passions and stifling the voice of reason' (Bauman 1987: 61). Indeed, Elias makes the point that this aggressive cultural levelling precisely embodied the fervent belief in the threat of the passions and in the work needed to maintain a 'proper' public arena, as constituted by scientific modernism.

In terms of organizations more specifically, we can also identify the construction of the public sphere on the basis of the expulsion of sex in the development of the bureaucratic order. Nothing here was to be left to chance, the possibility for human irrationality was designed out of organizational structures, and modernity therefore dismantled 'the world of non-productive consumption and handed the earth over to the men of production' (Bataille 1991: 127). Indeed, as Burrell and Hearn (1989: 12) remark, 'Doesn't the very success of productivity as a notion depend upon the reality principle and the suppression of libido in organizational contexts?' Sex, it seems, is allowed no legitimate place in the modern organization, although this is not of course to say that it never in fact 'intrudes', or is never appropriated for organizational ends, as our discussion so far has suggested. Moreover, there are clear and well documented implications for gender relations in this dichotomizing of sex and work. As a result of the biological division of labour in sexual reproduction, women have traditionally been considered to be more in touch with nature, to be somehow more organic than men – as Easlea's aforementioned reference to nature being seen as feminine suggests. Even menstruation has been likened to the phases of the moon, so that women's bodies are seen to move in time to age-old natural rhythms. Being closer to nature, however, apparently does not equip one for modern life where such a 'natural' state of being is depicted as undesirable, archaic and irrational, and not, as in some other societies, a source of spirituality or wisdom (Banks 1981: 28; McNeil 1987: 19; Martin 1989: 16). As a result, it is primarily women who have been disadvantaged by modernity, and the legacy of the Enlightenment can be seen as peculiarly masculinist. If modernity does not welcome sex into the public sphere, neither does it welcome women, as the considerable literature focusing on gender and organizations has argued (see, for example, Cockburn 1991; Marshall 1984, 1995; Mills and Tancred 1992; Nicolson 1996; Alvesson and Billing 1997).

It is against this backdrop – the scientific modernist emphasis that sex belongs at home because it upsets the rationality and pragmatism of organizational operations – that the claims of re-eroticization theory must be evaluated.

Let's get loved up

Re-eroticization theory, by way of contrast, recommends that we explicitly attempt to encourage sexuality and the erotic in organizations; indeed, it contends that only in so doing will we subvert relations of power which at present are both repressive and oppressive, particularly of women. The public–private boundary is to be eradicated through a freeing up of the libido and a reclamation of pleasure. Some of this thinking focuses on the boundary in a general way, but there is, as we have remarked above, a strand which takes the organization as its specific theme. One key argument here is that, as also implied above, the erotic is currently being assimilated into or appropriated by managerialist attempts to enhance control over employees and to maximize productivity, as is more generally visible in the emergence of forms of organizational totalitarianism such as corporate culture initiatives. As Burrell (1992a: 74) puts it:

> Management consultants such as Peters and Kanter have recognized the powerful forces locked within pleasure and seek to render them up for chief executives for organizational use … the need is expressed for 'change-masters' … not to suppress play but to use it for their own benefit. The point of production is seen as the legitimate place for such energy and adrenalin – otherwise it is wasted and change is not brought about.

Burrell, rightly in our view, seeks to critique these attempts instrumentally to channel sexuality into productivity such that re-eroticization of the organization involves posing an alternative – his 'third face of pleasure' – to the managerialist assimilation of sexuality. Re-eroticization recognizes, allows and plays with the

Sexual desire for Reich and Marcuse, then, is conceptualized as an innate and powerful force which we would do much better not to dam. It is only because, they suggest, we cannot express our desire freely and openly that frustration leads some to visit prostitutes, to seek pleasure in experiencing or inflicting pain, to rape, to sodomize, to desire others of the same sex, to molest or to have sex with members of their family (etc.). Modern society emerges as a milieu in which we are either perpetually at the mercy of our own repressed sexual desires or perpetually at the mercy of others who are expressing their repressed sexual desires in perverted ways. As a corollary of this stance, Reich and Marcuse also concur in affirming the positive operation of Freud's pleasure principle. They suggest that desire is self-regulating; that, in the absence of sexual repression, all such urges will be worked out in a healthy and appropriate fashion, so as to give us and our partners maximum pleasure:

> The vital energies, under natural conditions, regulate themselves sponta-
> neously, without compulsive duty or compulsive morality. The latter are a
> sure indication of the existence of antisocial tendencies. Antisocial behavior
> springs from secondary drives which owe their existence to the suppression
> of natural sexuality.
>
> (Reich, cited in Baker 1982)

Reich also rather naïvely deploys Malinowski's anthropological data on the sexual lives of the Trobriand Islanders to argue that 'The natural morality of the primitive matriarchal peoples, living in sexual freedom based on gratification, was infinitely superior to the morality of our age' (Reich 1972: 147). He contends, then, that we possess a natural sexual morality, that we are 'programmed' only to seek sex which is good for us and for others such that 'The essence of sex-economic regulation lies in the avoidance of any absolute norms or precepts and in the recognition of the will to life and pleasure in living as the regulators of social life' (Reich 1969: 28). This kind of regulation, Reich suggests, allows the body (which he suggests needs to be maintained in equilib-rium) to build up orgone energy (via eating, drinking and breathing), and then to release it naturally via growth, excretion, perspiration, emotion, thought or work but, most importantly, through the orgasm. Indeed, the key tenet of his argu-ment is that 'To maintain a stable, economic energy level, excess energy must be discharged at more or less regular intervals. This economic discharging of energy is the function of the orgasm' (Baker 1982).

Marcuse's stance is similar. While he appears to tend more towards a Freudian interpretation in his emphasis on the need to maintain a degree of sexual repression so as to assure societal stability, Marcuse carefully differentiates between basic and surplus repression. Indeed, he argues that we possess a 'libid-inal rationality', an instinctive capacity to channel our sexual desire in appropriate directions, so that basic (that is to say, necessary) repression is auto-matically achieved without the need for any external societal restrictions, just as it is in Reich's conceptualization of a natural sexual morality. In other words, 'sexuality can, under certain conditions, create highly civilized human relations without being subjected to the repressive organization which the established civilization has imposed upon the instinct' (Marcuse 1969: 165–6).

In sum, then, Reich and Marcuse both problematize the subjugation of the passions to reason. What others see as the development of human rationality to such a stage that it has civilized our baser desires, they see as repressive and anxiety-generating. Nevertheless, they do not agree on the issue of what kind of sex it is actually healthy to enjoy. Sex for Reich is essentially physical and located in the genitals. He makes a great deal of the 'genital embrace' (heterosexual penetrative intercourse) and the importance of 'orgastic potency', where the whole body orgasmically convulses, then:

> After the convulsions, the two organisms remain united for a time while the energy which has been concentrated at the genital flows back through the organism, which is experienced as gratification. Separation then occurs with relaxation, a tender, grateful attitude toward the partner, and sleep.
>
> (Baker 1982)

To develop or unblock this potency, Reich recommends that what he calls the armour –the muscular rigidity and constrained breathing that results from sociosexual repression, prohibits the flow of orgone energy through the body and therefore renders impossible its adequate discharge – be broken down through the use of vegetotherapy. Vegetotherapy works on the body itself as well as, like psychoanalysis, on the patient's character. It may therefore involve breathing exercises, deliberate gagging, revolving of the eyes or massage of 'spastic muscles' by the therapist, working from the head down and 'freeing' the pelvis last (Baker n.d.). As a result of this therapy, Reich suggests that we will become a good deal more responsive to our desire, a good deal more willing to indulge it, and hence a good deal more liberated. His liberation appears, then, to be a matter of having genitally-based sex as, when and where the fancy comes upon us. That is to say, Reich argues that, as our orgone energy builds up, so does tension within the body, until 'At a certain point, known as the lumination point, the tension is felt as sexual excitement in the healthy individual. Energy above the level of the lumination point may be looked upon as sexual energy or the libido, which Freud described' (Baker 1982). Sex in this situation therefore represents what Baker refers to as 'nature's safety valve'. Moreover, it is a naturally sporadic activity, episodes of which will be interspersed with episodes of other kinds of activity – such as work. Indeed, for Reich (1972: 165) one is only able to work efficiently and effectively if one is sexually sated: '[Sexual repression] paralyzes the intellectual critical powers and the initiative of the mass individual, for [it] uses up much bioenergy which otherwise would manifest itself intellectually and emotionally in a rational manner.'

Marcuse, by way of contrast, conceives of a rather different kind of re-eroticization of the public sphere. He differentiates between the 'genital embrace' and his preferred concept of Eros, arguing that an emphasis on the genitals in

Postmodernist re-eroticization theory

Cixous and Baudrillard, then, reject the idea that there is an essentially common core to human sexuality, that we possess a natural capacity and a natural desire for particular forms of sex. Instead, they posit that we come to think of ourselves in this way because we are constituted as individual subjects through the operations of prevailing discourses (which might of course include critical modernist re-eroticization theory). Furthermore, this understanding of ourselves, for Cixous and Baudrillard, serves to foreclose the field of energy which is all they will acknowledge as human. For Baudrillard in particular, the body is nothing but potential which we close off or open up through particular ways of relating to ourselves:

> Any body or part of the body can operate functionally in the same way, provided that it is subject to the same erotic discipline: it is necessary and sufficient that it be as closed and as smooth as possible, faultless, without orifice and 'lacking' nothing, every erogenous difference being conjured up by the structural bar, that will design(ate) the body (in the double sense of 'designate' and 'design') ... it then envelops the body like a second skin ... all these qualities (coolness, suppleness, transparency, one-piece) are qualities of closure, a zero degree resulting from the abnegation of ambivalent extremes.
>
> (Baudrillard 1993a: 104–5)

Elsewhere, he suggests, in a similar vein, that 'The state of sex's liberation is also that of its indetermination. No more want, no more prohibitions, and no more limits: it is the loss of every referential principle' (Baudrillard 1990: 5). Thus Baudrillard calls for the dismantling of sexual identity, of erotic individuality and of sensual self-expression, because, he claims, it is better to perish through the transgression of the limits of individuality, to be overcome by pure and self-dislocating pleasure and to 'cease to be' a subject, than it is to die as a result of physical or biological limitations (Baudrillard, cited in Gane 1991a: 7). For Irigaray, this dismantling of the self and the loss of discriminate identity also make the idea of property – and particularly the idea of being the sexual property of another person – impossible. However, for her this is characteristic of woman. Irigaray (1985b: 31, cited in Dollimore 1991: 230) talks of

> [a] nearness so pronounced that it makes all discrimination of identity, and thus all forms of property, impossible. Woman derives pleasure from what is so near that she cannot have it, nor have herself. She enters into a ceaseless exchange of herself with the other without any possibility of identifying either.

Cixous and Baudrillard part company with Irigaray's essentialism, while preserving much of her argument, as they imply that in dissolving our identity into that of the Other we cannot preserve our concept of gender – we must cease to conceive of ourselves as essentially gendered. Our sense of ourselves as gendered subjects, as masculine or feminine, is irretrievably connected here to the ways in which we understand ourselves to be sexual. 'Masculine' and 'feminine' are considered by Cixous and Baudrillard to be no more than terms denoting certain bundles of characteristics which are arbitrarily mapped on to biologically differentiated bodies. Certainly Cixous (1988: 289–90) is

> careful … to use the *qualifiers* of sexual difference, in order to avoid the confusion man/masculine, woman/feminine: for there are men who do not repress their femininity, women who more or less forcefully inscribe their masculinity. The difference is not, of course, distributed according to socially determined 'sexes' … We must guard against falling complacently or blindly into the essentialist ideological interpretation … the awesome thesis of a 'natural', anatomical determination of sexual difference-opposition.

As Gane (1991b: 109) points out, Baudrillard agrees, suggesting that 'the body does not in itself naturally distribute the terms masculine and feminine in rigid division'. Cixous and Baudrillard argue, then, that men and women, although biologically distinct, have an equal capacity to behave, think and feel in particular ways. Moreover, Cixous (1988: 287–9) posits that the dualism of masculine/feminine, because it is typically conflated with the biological dualism of man/woman, inevitably elevates the man above the woman as active subject, while the woman becomes passive object. This privileging of masculine over feminine, and therefore of men over women, is seen by Cixous also to map on to other dualisms such as public–private, so that it is masculine values (and men) that prevail in the all-important public sphere (Cixous 1988: especially 287, 291 – see also chapter 1). The feminine is, as a consequence, marginal, absent, an Other to the masculine Norm – her values are inferior and belong to the debased private sphere. Cixous suggests that the de-sexualization of the public sphere therefore specifically disadvantages women. That is to say, she suggests that women are understood and understand themselves as irrational and sexual and therefore as less capable than men of functioning in this area of the social.

In these postmodernist accounts, then, there is a certain association of sexuality and gender, and the corollary that, in order to free up our desire, we also have to reject what we know of ourselves as masculine or feminine. Cixous and Baudrillard have it that we each of us have the capacity to span the full continuum of sexual desire and affect, to fully eroticize our existence by experiencing it in a multiplicity of different ways, and therefore that we can and indeed should refuse to think of ourselves as innately sexual and at the same time innately gendered. As Cixous (1988: 292) puts it:

> There have always been those uncertain poetic beings who have not let themselves be reduced to the state of coded mannequins by the relentless

In fact, Baudrillard actually claims that liberation from a masculine universe, the subversion of what he sees as our stagnant gender/sexual relations, depends on the deployment of the feminine as unknowable abyss, as artifice. For him, sexual liberation turns not on authentication of feminine identity (as in the radical feminist project described above), nor on the breaking down of the gender dualism, but, rather, on the subversion of the existing totem of masculinity and a literal plunge into the feminine, into the unknown. Consequently, Baudrillard counsels women to concentrate on playing at being non-existent, to flirt, seduce and tease. For example, he bids us to 'Imagine a woman who faints: nothing is more beautiful, since it is always at one and the same time to be overwhelmed by pleasure and to escape pleasure, to seduce and to escape seduction' (Baudrillard, cited in Moore 1988: 183). For Baudrillard, women must renounce any quest for feminine authenticity and instead play out an identity that is not real, so as to make impossible conventionally masculine sexual relations, and to confound masculine forms of desire. The feminine here is reflexively self-deconstructive.

It seems, on the whole, that postmodernist re-eroticization theory as presented by Cixous and Baudrillard calls for a stretching of boundaries and a dismantling of identity, for human beings to cease to relate to themselves as sexual and gendered subjects. The emphasis is on a state of being beyond the limits of identity, being caught up in a polymorphous, amorphous flow of desire which does not emanate from static subjects or exhaust itself via a fixed set of practices. Indeed, despite his basic essentialism, Marcuse could be argued to edge closer to these theorists in his insistence on the repressiveness of genitally-based sexual expression. Reich, on the other hand, appears to retain the Freudian notion that the channelling of our infantile polymorphous sexuality is a necessary feature of the healthy human condition. We have already offered some indication of what these ideas might mean for the workplace. Eroticism spreads from the private sphere across into the public, so that the dualism between sex and reason, public and private, becomes an irrelevancy. The accepted mode of governance of relationships in the private sphere – intimacy, proximity, possibility – spills over into the public. Organizational hierarchies are dismantled, to be replaced by 'the growing number of alternative organizational forms now appearing, whether inspired by anarchism, syndicalism, the ecological movement, the co-operative movement, liberation communism, self-help groups, or … by feminism' (Burrell 1992a: 82). Clearly, therefore, the bureaucratic mode of organization does not sit well with re-eroticization, which is fundamentally about potential, playfulness, unpredictability, transgression and danger. In fact, because modern organization is almost synonymous with bureaucracy, re-eroticization theory has close affinities with what Burrell and Morgan call anti-organization theory, the three main themes of which are:

1   the repressive nature of modernity, understood as 'a form of totalitarianism based upon the all-pervasive influence and control of factors such as work, rationality, science and technology, which shape and, channel and control men's consciousness' (p. 317);

2   the return to nature and an abandoning of science as a way forward, a romanticizing of the pre-modern world or of Oriental/Eastern cultures;

3   the notion that what alienates us is a product of our own consciousness, our own socialization.

(Burrell and Morgan 1979)

The espousal of alternative forms of reality, as evoked by the Yaqui shaman's use of the drug peyote in Carlos Castaneda's *Don Juan* series, is the backbone of anti-organization theory; 'windmills not power stations, craftsmanship not work, Zen not instrumentality' (Burrell and Morgan 1979: 319). Humanity is to be restored to its fully potent, non-alienated state. Echoing Cixous in particular, Hines suggests that the organizational imbalance between the Yin (feminine) and the Yang (masculine) is

> antithetical to survival, growth and wholeness, psychologically, physically and spiritually. What is at stake in the debate … includes, but goes far beyond, the suppression of women, to embrace the suppression of the values, percep-tions and ways of thinking, feeling and acting that are associated with the Universal Feminine or Yin. This suppression … affects the lived experience of both men and women, and has resulted in serious consequences … for society … the answer would seem to lie in retrieving what is not selected, what is excluded and suppressed … a Yang world-view, unbalanced by the Yin, [has resulted] in asceticism associated with body (and especially sex and sensuality) versus spirit dualism, and a repression of the Yin realm.
>
> (Hines 1992: 314–15, 317)

Hines makes a specific plea for the values of the feminine to be reconsidered and absorbed (back) into modern organizations. In a slightly different take on re-eroticization, both Pringle (1989) and Gherardi (1995) argue that work is already sexualized – Pringle suggests, for instance, that the boss–secretary relation-ship often 'oozes' with sex – but that its sexual character is rarely if ever openly acknowledged because of the bureaucratic character of prevailing organiza-tional values. She also notes that, where organizational sexuality is discussed or remarked upon, it is usually within the confines of the discourse of sexual harassment. This discourse, as we have seen in chapter 3, has

> largely restricted sexuality to its coercive dimensions … If women experi-ence pleasure it is treated as 'coerced caring' … In these accounts either virtually all heterosexual activity may be labelled as sexual harassment or a line has to be drawn between what is harassment and what is 'acceptable'.
>
> (Pringle 1989: 165)

Pringle argues instead that we should challenge constructions of sex as an intruder at work (as present within scientific modernism) or as a source of exploitation (as present within sexual harassment discourse), and begin to recognize the ways in which it might allow women in particular to 'operate more on their own terms' at work. Indeed, she asserts that 'The question ... is which pleasures, if any, might threaten masculinity or disrupt rationality?' (Pringle 1989: 177). Gherardi, as we have seen, agrees that organizations are sexualized places. She suggests that work can and does provide a non-threatening environment in which employees are able to meet others and engage in eroticized interaction without there necessarily being an expectation that such interaction will end in physical sexual activity. For example, Gherardi (1995: 58) argues that secretaries can and do flirt with clients in ways which they would 'eschew' in other settings and that men and women can and do engage in sexualized banter at work in ways which they would not or could not in the supermarket. It is this kind of interaction, she posits, which makes work more enjoyable and more fulfilling – but she, like Pringle, also suggests that it is this kind of interaction that is often marginalized or ignored. In short, Gherardi (1995: 60) asks that we 'admit ... that we seek erotic gratification in our work, that organizations inhabit our sexual imaginations, and that we use organizations to fulfil our sexual fantasies'.

Re-eroticization theory, then, revolves around destabilization rather than division and advocates a very different form of organization to that evoked by scientific modernism. However, little real detail is given by the relevant theorists as to what the erotic workplace would actually look like and, although it is possible to speculate,[5] an obvious critical riposte would be to question the realism of this brand of thinking. Nonetheless, for our present purposes, we wish to note and expand upon two key difficulties within re-eroticization theory as it stands before going on to consider to what extent it is possible to reformulate its precepts to arrive at some notion of the re-eroticized organization.

Reich, Marcuse and the ordering of disorder

As we have seen, both Reich and Marcuse argue that the sexual repression which is characteristic of modernity produces thwarted forms of sexual desire and behaviour, such that the removal of this repression would allow for the onset of natural sexual regulation, bringing about the disappearance of the 'perversions'. This is clearly a highly naturalistic argument, in the sense that it relies on a definition of the use of prostitutes, sadomasochism, rape, sodomy, homosexuality, paedophilia, incest and so on as always and already problematic, as counter to 'normal' and 'essential' human instincts. Indeed, as Paul Robinson (1970: 55) puts it, it is surprising that 'Reich's utopia' is so 'puritanical'. Admittedly, Marcuse is slightly more forgiving of these forms of sexual behaviour because, as already noted, their latent value for him lies in their resistance to the 'genital tyranny' of modernity: 'The perversions ... express rebellion against the subjugation of sexuality under the order of procreation, and against institutions which guarantee this order' (Marcuse, cited in Robinson 1970: 207). However, while such 'perversions' apparently serve in a sexually repressive society to indicate the possibility of other forms of pleasure than would conventionally be tolerated, Marcuse believes them in their essence to be unnatural and so casts their usefulness as ceasing to exist come the onset of a genuinely eroticized public sphere.

Both Reich and Marcuse therefore privilege a realist, static ontology which begins from an *a priori* condition of sexual freedom, such that sexual relations like those Malinowski identified among the Trobrianders are far more 'pure', less 'tainted', than those in which we currently engage. Their analysis obscures the ways in which discourses have operated over time and across space to produce and consolidate particular interpretations of who we are and how we should live. By way of contrast, it is useful to note Foucault's analysis of the production of the homosexual-as-subject. He claims that the notion of hetero/homo(/bi)sexuality – given, fixed, immutable, compelling us to seek sex in certain ways with certain types of others – appeared during Victorian times. Prior to this, so Foucault's argument runs, sexual activity between individuals of the same sex (such as man-on-man sodomy), although problematized, was considered only to be one component of the range of sexual behaviours available to human beings:

> It is very interesting to see that before the 19th century forbidden behavior, even if it was very severely judged, was always considered to be an excess, a 'libertinage', as something too much. Homosexual behavior was only considered to be a kind of excess of natural behavior, an instinct that is difficult to keep within certain limits. From the 19th century on you see that behavior like homosexuality came to be considered an abnormality. [But w]hen I say that it was libertinage I don't say that it was tolerated.
>
> (Foucault 1988: 11)

Foucault suggests, then, that an individual's sexual behaviour was at other times in history understood to be a matter of ethical choice rather than a natural predilection:

> As defined by the ancient civil or canonical codes, sodomy was a category of forbidden acts; their perpetrator was nothing more than the juridical subject of them. The nineteenth century homosexual became a personage, a past, a case history, and a childhood, in addition to being a type of life, a life form, and a morphology, with an indiscreet anatomy and possibly a mysterious physiology … Nothing that went into his total composition was unaffected by his sexuality … Homosexuality appeared as one of the forms of sexuality when it was transposed from the practice of sodomy onto a kind of interior androgyny, a hermaphrodism of the soul.
>
> (Foucault 1979: 43)

In fact, Foucault suggests that homosexuality, and certain other sexual 'deviations', are actually constructions. That is to say, they are the result of a labelling of particular kinds of behaviour in particular ways by modern medical, legal, literary and psychiatric discourses such that these behaviours become 'recognized' as perverse and unnatural, begin to be associated with specific categories

characteristics and re-affirming those values characteristic of the feminine. Given that she sees this to offer specific benefits for women, buried somewhere in this analysis is the notion that woman = feminine, that women usually identify as feminine and therefore as passionate, sexual, sensual, and so on. Such a position arguably homogenizes lived female experience (Jaggar 1983; Hutcheon 1988; Moore 1988); it ignores the reality of being female, the ways in which women actually relate to themselves and to others, and makes a set of transcendental characteristics come to stand for all women. Here Cixous seemingly, and inaccurately, maps the feminine on to women and, if her dismantling of sexual and gender subjectivity was to come about, we could argue that it might not automatically benefit real female subjects – because real female subjects may not easily or necessarily identify with the feminine. Indeed, as we have argued elsewhere (Brewis *et al.* 1997a: especially 1284), women may find living up to the feminine a highly demanding project. Bartky (1988: 81), for example, describes:

> The woman who checks her make-up half a dozen times a day to see if her mascara has run, who worries that the wind or the rain may spoil her hair-do, who looks frequently to see if her stockings have bagged at the ankle or who, feeling fat, monitors everything she eats …

Moore (1994: 5) also underlines the amount of effort to which women may go to successfully pass to themselves and others as feminine, talking of waxing, dieting, exercise, skincare, making up, and so on. For many women, then, just being feminine actually represents a struggle. It is also germane to note Woodhouse's (1989) suggestion that female partners of transvestites often resent their men for being more feminine when 'dressed' than they themselves are in the normal course of events. Reactions like these again exemplify the fragile, indeed tense, relationship that women may have with the feminine. Consequently, Cixous's suggestion that feminine characteristics be re-affirmed as positive and valuable may only increase the anxiety to which these real women are already prone. That is to say, if we are right to argue that there is in fact a good deal of slippage between the characteristics of the feminine and the ways in which real women relate to themselves and others, then women may not experience the Cixousian utopia as particularly liberating.

Baudrillard's characterization of the feminine also becomes particularly contentious in his translation of it from an abstract ontological principle to the concrete lives of women. The feminine as not real, the woman as seductive and destabilizing in her very non-existence, can have problematic implications for real women. In the first instance, it is a moot point as to whether it would actually serve women to behave in the ways that Baudrillard prescribes, especially when we consider conventional constructions of women as essentially sexual, and that these constructions may lead to women being blamed for male acts of sexual aggression such as rape or sexual harassment.[6] Consequently, if women were to come to understand it as imperative that they behave as seductresses, it is possible to argue that they would actually render themselves fair game for male sexual attention. Baudrillard's recommendation that women deploy seduction as a strategy to destabilize and re-eroticize the public sphere, therefore, would seem potentially to have the effect of reinforcing the existing essentialist connections between women and sex, to constitute women to behave in ways which may actually put them at risk of sexual aggression from men. In any case, it is arguable that this kind of role playing on the part of women is unlikely to challenge the existing understanding that members of the female gender are sexual objects to be 'conquered' by men.

Baudrillard also asserts that 'Femininity ... is on the same side as madness. It is because madness secretly prevails that it must be normalized ... It is because femininity secretly prevails that it must be recycled and normalized (in sexual liberation in particular)' (Baudrillard 1990: 17). His argument is that femininity *is* subversion, and thus has always been a threat to masculinity – just as madness has always been a threat to reason – and that feminism, by failing to recognize this, is involuntarily colluding with patriarchy in its quest to real-ize the feminine. Here the feminine threatens the domination of the masculine in its nothingness, whereas normalization of the feminine defuses its destabilizing potential by concretizing it, making it real, constituting women as though a feminine identity truly existed.

Baudrillard here hits on one of the singular characteristics of postmodern thought, one which has often been overlooked by its critics, which is its concern with the extent to which language depends upon the inexpressible, that which constantly and inevitably escapes being ensnared in speech or writing, which can only trivialize and distort it. This concern is echoed, with varying but common emphases, by Lyotard, Foucault and Derrida. It is this unsayable element of human experience which Baudrillard is, nevertheless, trying to capture here under his term of the feminine – leaving the masculine as that impulse to name, to create labels for and hence make controllable, to order, define and *write* the world. Writing is a masculine activity, as it is for Derrida, but where Derrida considers and even attempts to create an *écriture féminine*, for Baudrillard the truly feminine impulse would find the ossification of inscription, even transgressive reinscription, abhorrent. Baudrillard's feminine simply reminds masculine representation of its own inadequacy in failing to capture that which it represents. His arguments here are not inconsistent with those he makes in *In the Shadow of the Silent Majorities* (1983b), and echo Adorno's discussion of how critique can avoid co-option into kitsch, in that silence may be the only possible form of resistance in a world of simulacra (Adorno 1999: 319–21). Unfortunately, where these principles of masculine/feminine take off from real men and women and real bodies, they leave behind the real problems of defining the practicalities of concrete everyday relationships between the terms, the pragmatics of their politics and the varieties of their acceptation.

Inevitably, then, and without trivializing the importance of engaging the inexpressible, we have to find it unhelpful to argue that it equates with the feminine even at an abstract level, even if it is allowed that men can embody it just as can women. This is because, in the everyday world, references to the feminine make no sense without references to the masculine. That is to say, both the feminine and the masculine as socially and culturally constructed are an effect of gender discourse, so that constructions of the feminine come to serve as one of the conditions of masculine dominance. No matter how effective the abstract 'feminine' may be in eluding masculinist definitions, that which is *labelled* 'feminine' will inevitably be the ground upon which relations are established and contested. As Derrida has made us aware, the supplement is the source of and what occasions the conception and constitution of the prioritized term (Cooper 1989; Linstead 1993; Chia 1994: 784) so that the feminine always represents the inferior term in the masculine/feminine dualism, while also allowing the masculine to stand as phallogocentric origin or first principle. The masculine claim to the Centre, then, depends for its power on the existence of the feminine Other, given that the latter stands in relation to the former as its inferior and marginalized opposite. It therefore seems problematic at least, dangerous at worst, to assert that playing upon the feminine represents a serious threat to patriarchy unless the terms can be overturned and metaphorized (the process of deconstruction). The feminine does not exist without some notion of the masculine, just as madness does not exist without some notion of sanity; they are power effects only, so to depict them as destructive can be seen to be inaccurate. Moreover, given that, for the masculine to continue to lay claim to the *logos*, the feminine has to be largely if not entirely silent in her meaning-giving function, to play upon her apparent non-existence would surely only strengthen what Cixous (1988: 289) calls 'the stability of the masculine edifice which passed itself off as eternalnatural'. Thus, ironically, Baudrillard's reading of the feminine as simulacrum, as not real, actually reinforces the marginalization, or rather the practical non-existence, of women, and manages to link the feminine indelibly to them. It is women who must play out the role of the feminine (even though it does not exist in positivity) in order to deconstruct the phallocracy which characterizes contemporary gender relations.

We have by now addressed re-eroticization theory in terms of its sexually essentialist tendencies (Reich and Marcuse), and its problematic readings of the feminine (Cixous and Baudrillard). Our contention is that this body of thought is unsatisfactory as it stands. But the question remains of whether re-eroticization theory can be reworked to provide a radical alternative for the future of organizations. Via a reconsideration of the nature of desire, it is this issue to which we turn in the section which follows and our concluding remarks.

Re-reading desire

What do organizations do? Organizations, in the most basic sense of the term, exist to generate utility – they are collectivities of individuals brought together for some kind of purpose. Although we do not wish to reify organizations, to see them 'solely in terms of structure, purpose, mission, and goals' (Brewis *et al.* 1997a: 1297), given that such phenomena have no meaning outside of their performance by human actors and cannot be said to be given or immutable, it is nevertheless the case that to organize human activity turns upon the notion of some kind of punctuated endpoint to that activity, where the achievement of something considered beneficial might be identified. Here, then, the activity of organizing itself is underpinned by a particular ontology of desire – the predominantly (and aforementioned) Freudian construction of desire as lack. Organization produces something – whether social order or sofas – that society otherwise would not have and could be deemed to need. Desire in this regard – and in particular the desire to organize – is motivated by the perceived lack of something useful, the absence of something which is needed, the urge to generate utility, improve upon our human environment and serve individual and collective interests. Organizing here stems from notions of scarcity, from what Bataille describes as the assumption that 'the development of productive forces [is] the ideal end of activity ... destruction ... has in every case the meaning of failure; it is experienced as a misfortune; in no way can it be presented as desirable' (Bataille 1991: 22).

The original source of this reading of desire as lack is, as Deleuze and Guattari (1984: 25) argue, found in the work of Plato, both in his explicit treatments of Eros in *The Symposium* (1994), where genders are drawn to their missing complement, and in his more general theory of forms outlined in the dialogues. As Dollimore (1998: 90–3) also notes, the sense of loss and yearning for a perfect, once possessed state of union is found in the 'fall' myth of Christianity (which is also present in other religions and spiritual systems). Indeed, the tension between self-identity and the requirement for the loss of self in order to rejoin with the other, the field of the erotic between life and death where desire is in play, has, as Dollimore remarks, been the subject of anguished contemplation in philosophy, theology and literature for centuries, certainly long before the advent of the 'modern' self. Nevertheless, it is Hegel's formulation of desire, subjectivity and subjection, and the relation of death and being in *The Phenomenology of Spirit* (1977) – particularly the chapter entitled 'The truth of self-certainty' – which has most left its mark on subsequent treatments, including Freud's critical extension of it into the unconscious. Hegel argues that consciousness is always and already *self*-consciousness, in that it involves the recognition that the subject *lacks* something – not simply the object (the other) but also the *consciousness* of the other. Freedom (to be one's self, to follow one's own purposes) also creates discontinuity between different self-consciousnesses. Hegel's project was to demonstrate how these separate beings, travelling through history in oppression and alienation, would be brought through *recognition* into continuity by the driving force of desire. Desire propels humankind through unfolding and inevitable, if often bloody, progress in a dialectical movement as a state of affairs turns into its opposite, then temporarily resolves into a third term. Ultimately, discontinuous human spirits will become continuous in attaining Absolute Spirit, at the end of history when no more progress remains to be made.

Hegel establishes the conceptual status of several important elements of this discussion – particularly in positioning desire as an ontological motivating force and recognizing the interdependence of opposites in the dialectic. Desire, Judith

Butler notes, drives on towards absolute knowledge because its objective is self-knowledge – the 'illumination of its own opacity, the expression of that aspect of the world that brought it into being', the preconditions of its own existence (Butler 1999 [1987]: 24). In this sense, what unfolds through the pursuit of desire for an object or other is self-discovery. However, following in part from Kant's distinction between the noumenal and the phenomenal, Hegel distinguishes between the arena of the Absolute and the arena of Understanding. Importantly for our discussion here, he argues that the Understanding is a practical consciousness concerned with mastery of the given, which cannot understand movement – the way that terms continually imply their opposite. It is always concerned to fix its object in the present, and continually mistakes stasis for truth. Hegel carries this discussion into the distance between continuity and discontinuity in Life – continuity represented by the breaking down and recombination of elements in Death, in loss of self. But self only recognizes itself as such by being aware of its own estrangement from Life, from the active flux of life, and can only look on with the gaze of the melancholic – a concept also developed by Freud (Butler 1997: 185–7).

Furthermore, if much of this discussion has echoes of more recent theory, such as deconstruction, this is no accident. Although Hegel is inverted through a subtle engagement by Derrida, it is, as Foucault argues, through engagement with Hegel (even where mediated by Marx and Nietzsche) that twentieth-century philosophy has taken shape, particularly in France (Foucault 1972: 235). Here, some of the seeds of postmodern thought were sown by Alexander Kojève's critical reading of Hegel (Pefanis 1991: 2). Bataille, Sartre and Lacan were among the audience for his lectures at the Sorbonne in the 1930s. As Kojève (1980: 139) puts it, 'Man is Desire directed towards another Desire – that is, Desire for Recognition', and often desires the conditions of his own subjection precisely because, even in oppression, some degree of recognition is afforded. Under the influence of Kojève, this issue of complicity in the relations of power and the importance of recognition recurs in the work of Lacan, Foucault and Bataille.[7]

For Bataille, desire operates within an anthropological system, both economic and symbolic, of accumulation and expenditure. Here life and death, as for Hegel, are opposed forces, but for Bataille they are culturally regulated by systems of taboos and transgressions (Bristow 1997: 127). Bataille's conception of the erotic involves assenting to life even in death, because it involves transgressing cultural rules which valorize the stultifying effects of work and acquisition, already implied in chapters 3, 4 and 5:

> Erotic conduct is the opposite of normal conduct as spending is the opposite of getting. If we follow the dictates of reason and try to acquire all kinds of goods, we work in order to try to increase the sum of our possessions and our knowledge, we use all means to get richer and to possess more. Our status in the social order is based on this sort of behaviour. But when the fever of sex seizes us we behave in the opposite way. We recklessly draw on our strength and sometimes in the violence of passion we squander consid-

erable resources to no real purpose. Pleasure is so close to ruinous waste ...
Anything that suggests erotic excess always implies disorder.

(Bataille 1986: 170)

Bataille, argues Bristow (1997: 124), differs from Hegel in locating the dialectic of
desire 'not just in the divide between self and other, but in the erotic mechanisms
that generate the tension between the two'. Here, as does Lacan, Bataille departs
from the Hegelian conflation of *eros* and *logos*, in which all desire is ultimately a
desire for knowledge. Indeed, Bataille sacrificially decapitates philosophy in his
emphasis on the irrational and abandonment to unknowing – what he calls
acephality. Moreover, Deleuze and Guattari suggest that it was Plato himself who
first distinguished between production and acquisition but that, when the West
appropriated his thought, production was identified with acquisition – and this
understanding also emerges in Bataille's aforementioned formulation of general
and restricted economy:

> The question of a general economy is located at the same level as that of
> political economy, but the science designated by the latter refers only to
> a *restricted* economy (market values). The general economy deals with the
> essential problem of the use of wealth. It underlines the fact that excess is
> produced that, by definition, cannot be employed in a utilitarian manner.
> Excess energy can only be lost, without the least concern for goal or objec-
> tive, and, therefore, without any meaning.
>
> (Bataille 1970–1979: 215–16, cited in Richman 1982: 69–70)

Bataille's attack on restricted economy, which saw desire as utilitarian and acquisitive, always in search of the object, was also an attack on reason. His desire is
fluid, energetic, a creative principle evident in expense and effervescence, and
stands squarely against the Hegelian and Freudian reading of desire as lack.

But if we understand desire as Hegel and Freud do, as a desire for the missing
object or other, and then posit the possibility of eroticized organizations, then
sex in such a reading is always and already subordinated to the creation of utility
in pursuit of unity. If we look, for example, at Burrell's discussion of the kinds of
organization that he sees as most closely approximating to the eroticized ideal
(those characteristic of anarchic, syndicalist, environmental, co-operative,
communist, self-help or feminist politics), then the rub is clear. All such organizations still have a conscious *purpose* – to preserve the planet's natural resources, to
develop more healthy and functional attitudes among their members, to emanci-
pate women, etc. In contra-distinction, and as we established earlier, Bataille has
it that the energy which animates life on earth always exceeds what is required
for subsistence and growth. Therefore our key challenge is not to produce but to
consume, to waste, to squander. It is the celebration of heterogeneity that makes
us human, not the suppression of difference in the service of homogeneity. To
illustrate this, he refers to the massive military–industrial expansion of the late
nineteenth century which culminated in World War I:

Recent history is the result of the soaring growth of industrial activity. At first this prolific growth restrained martial activity by absorbing the main part of the excess: The development of modern industry yielded the relative period of peace from 1815 to 1914 ... But in the long run the growth that the technical changes made possible became difficult to sustain. It became productive of an increased surplus itself.

(Bataille 1991: 24)

As a consequence of the 'failure' of industry to use up sufficient energy, indeed of its eventually being 'productive of an increased surplus itself', the necessary squandering of excess took the form of worldwide military conflict.[8]

Deleuze and Guattari (1984), here following Bataille (although elsewhere they argue against his identification of transgression of cultural taboos as a driver of desire), similarly talk of what Seem (1984: xviii) refers to as an 'economy of flows', flows of desire (Bataille's energy), in their reworking of Freud's interpretation of desire as lack. For Deleuze and Guattari, the conceptualization of humans as (desiring) selves, with individual wants and needs, is based on the Oedipal repression of 'desiring-machines', so that we have come to misinterpret the nature of desire. Indeed, as Bristow (1997: 130) argues, their very use of the term 'machines' is deliberately and specifically *anti-humanist*. They wish to irrevocably displace human consciousness from the centre of the (Hegelian) scheme of things and restore the importance of the physical, the emerging emphasis on the body and the conative (*conatus*) that they find in Spinoza.[9] Deleuze and Guattari (1984: 1) argue that the desiring-machines are 'at work everywhere', breathing, heating, eating, shitting, fucking. These machines are irretrievably connected with each other in that they receive their meaning from the particular system to which they are coupled at any one time – but these couplings do not contain desire, they only channel it as it flows through them. Desire 'couples continuous flows and partial objects that are by nature fragmentary and fragmented' (Deleuze and Guattari 1984: 5) in a constant entrepreneurial motion. 'Organ-machines' are plugged into 'energy-source-machines' from which they receive their life force (desire/energy), but are themselves energy-source-machines for other organ-machines, such that what is produced carries over into a new form of producing. Contrary to the conventional representation of machines, moreover, desiring-machines, suggest Deleuze and Guattari, work only by *breaking down* the flow of the process that they are intended to amplify: 'The machine produces an interruption of the flow [of desire/energy] only insofar as it is connected to another machine that supposedly produces the flow' (Deleuze and Guattari 1984: 36). Here, however, we might argue that this breaking down does not mean ceasing to work in the usual sense of the term. Instead it implies a process of extraction and interruption (removal, deduction or cutting in Deleuze and Guattari's terminology – also see Chia 1994: especially 795–801), to allow the desiring-machine to continue to subsist, and for its own flows of desire/energy to be appropriated by other desiring-machines – in other words, to give it, however temporarily, an object. To illustrate this, Deleuze and Guattari offer the example of the ways in which the desiring-machine of the anus uses the products of the desiring-machine of the intestine, which uses the products of the desiring machine of the stomach, which uses the products of the desiring-machine of the mouth, which uses the desiring-machine of the 'flow of milk of a herd of dairy cattle' (Deleuze and Guattari 1984: 36). There is no desiring *subject* here – merely an endless flow of desire/energy, of producing.[10] Desire, then, from Hegel onwards driven by the acquisitive principle of the subject in search of a lacking object, becomes a productive process with multiple objects but without any subject.

However, although for Deleuze and Guattari all life is production, it is simultaneously also consumption, because of the connections between the desiring-machines which mutually consume and transform each other's outputs. Like Bataille (1991: 20), who suggests that:

> productive activity as a whole [should] be considered in terms of the modifications it receives from its surroundings or brings about in its surroundings[,] ... [that there] is a need to study the system of human production and consumption within a much larger framework[,]

they do not separate what is commonly designated as production (which they call social production) from this circuit of desire:

> For the real truth of the matter – the glaring, sober truth that resides in delirium – is that there is no such thing as relatively independent spheres or circuits ... the truth of the matter is that *social production is purely and simply desiring-production itself under determinate conditions.*
>
> (Deleuze and Guattari 1984: 4, 29)

It is in the interconnectedness of all forms of life, the immanence of desire/energy, where Bataille's legacy is so apparent in Deleuze and Guattari's work. Desire here is radically reworked, not as a drive that is directed at the fulfilment of a need, a drive that works towards extinguishing lack, but as one that seeks to proliferate, to reproduce, to improvise, to diversify, to create or to explore, to be curious, to play. Moreover, the 'factitious unity' of 'a possessive or proprietary ego' (Deleuze and Guattari, 1984: 72), generated by the repressive mechanisms of psychoanalysis, has as its raw material what Deleuze and Guattari call Organs without a Body (OwB). OwB is the undifferentiated experience which a child has prior to the development of a reflexive self, before they 'recognize' that organs exist within a body, an *organ*ized body, before the construction of the I (and indeed the Me), of an identity which is monadic and teleological, which has needs and wants. Deleuze and Guattari's schizo, because he or she resists oedipalization, comes closest to this inarticulable state of being, comes closest to the reality of the human condition, which is nothing more and nothing less than an exuberant and wasteful circuit of energy:

is [oedipalization] sufficient to silence the outcry of desiring-production: We are all schizos! We are all perverts! We are all libidos that are too viscous and too fluid – and not by preference, but wherever we are carried by the deterritorialized flows.

(Deleuze and Guattari 1984: 67–8)

This is what Deleuze and Guattari mean when they claim that the subject only appears as the result of repression of the real nature of desire – as is also the case in Bataille. However, whereas Bataille emphasizes the cultural nature of prohibitions in arresting desire and the consequent significance of transgression, Deleuze and Guattari argue that desire is arrested by the Body without Organs (or BwO – Deleuze and Guattari 1987: especially chapters 6 and 10; Bristow 1997: 130–2; see also chapter 7). The BwO exists in many forms – full or empty, intense or exhausted – and without a specific image (although many images may be motivated by it). It may be any phenomenon that arrests or obstructs the free flow of desire – such that the BwO of the capitalist entrepreneur is *capital*. Desire, with all its productive power, becomes appropriated by capital.[11] The object of desire becomes capital itself, which allows its repositioning as the *origin* of production, rather than its surplus. Capital now appears as the productive power of life, not the desire which it channels, and at the present time, where global capitalism (in self-satisfied conjunction with liberal democracy) is tempted to view itself as triumphant – the ultimate BwO – we have a resurgence of the Hegelian arguments for the End of History (Fukuyama 1992; for a brief but trenchant critique see Sim 1999). Various forms of BwO, motivating different levels of associated imagery, position themselves in this way – abstractions (cf. Baudrillard's simulacra) posing as objects (i.e., the 'lost' object of Platonic–Hegelian desire) offering reconnection with collective Origin. As such, Deleuze and Guattari set themselves very firmly against the legacy of which Hegel is a prominent ancestor. Consequently, Bataille, as both a radical critic and somewhat idiosyncratic interpreter of Hegel, is both an inspiration for and the object of their critique.

On the positive side, it is worth noting the parallels between the schizo and Bataille's concept of self-loss, where 'being is given to us in an intolerable transcendence of being' (Bataille, cited in Lala 1995: 107). Baudrillard (1983c: 133), likewise, takes his inspiration from Bataille in his own definition of the schizo:

> The schizo is bereft of every sense, open to everything in spite of himself, living in the greatest confusion ... What characterizes him is less the loss of the real ... but, very much to the contrary, the absolute proximity, the total instantaneity of things, the feeling of no defense, no retreat.

Bataille's further influence is also visible in Cixous's (1988: 293) definition of *jouissance*, cited above (note in particular the reference to the 'sun of energy', a concept also found in both Baudrillard and Lyotard). Indeed, *jouissance* is a central concept in Bataille's own work and is usually translated as 'joy', although the English word (like the alternative translations of 'bliss', 'coming' or 'rapture') arguably does not do justice to what is evoked in the following extract from Bataille's poetry:

> the trumpets of joy
> ring insanely
> and burst with the whiteness of heaven.
>
> (Bataille, cited in Lala 1995: 108)

Yet, and importantly, Deleuze and Guattari set themselves *against* the Freudian death drive, and consequently present a rather one-sided view of desire as production/consumption, deliberately de-emphasizing destruction. Hegel's singular contribution here, on the other hand, was to establish the intimacy of the dialectic – the necessity of one term, life, for the other, death – which relational tension Bataille established as the field of the erotic. Bataille's view of our relationship with death is not by any means the Freudian death drive, but he extends Hegel's concern with the differentiation of the subject into collective continuity and discontinuity through a consideration of ecstasy and annihilation. As Dollimore (1998) documents, and as we have already pointed out, the repeated co-emergence of *thanatos* and *eros* throughout Western literature demonstrates that the recognition of their connectedness is not a recent phenomenon. However, the suppression of death, and its displacement into the abject realm of the unthinkable and unspeakable, are certainly a modern one. Death, magic, superstition, irrationality, bodily functions and pollution all become spirited away into the realm of the abject as rationality, abstraction and order are prioritized in the greater scheme of things.

Nevertheless, and as we already know, for Bataille, bodies, passions and their attendant problems cannot actually be suppressed in this way, for the abject remains part of the subject, part of that from which it is supposed to be separated. *Eros* and *thanatos* must therefore be considered to be part of each other; the erotic and the necrotic do not simply interpenetrate but are ontologically contiguous; we love because we hate, make peace because we are violent, receive because we lose, give because we steal. Deleuze and Guattari do not see, as Bataille does, both sides in the same vision.

Conclusion

In the foregoing chapters, we have examined the ways in which the missing dark side of desire remains present, as the abject, within organized and organizational relations. Although for Bataille organization for work is a dead hand on creativity – unfettered production aimed at acquisition not expenditure – it offers a simulacrum of abandonment to collective continuity. Bataille was influenced by Durkheim (on religion, the sacred and the profane) and Mauss (on the gift), and yet had his own distinctive and eccentric reading of each (Pefanis 1991: 39–58; Bristow 1997: 122–8; Dollimore 1998: 249–57). Despite inaugurating the anti-productivism found in Deleuze and Guattari, and despite opposing homogeneity with heterogeneity, he retains a sense of collective continuity which is experiential and grounded in the body, not purely abstract as it is in Hegel. Indeed, part of his project is to demonstrate the condition of impossibility of any thought. This distances him from the abstracted humanism of the surrealists, as he refuses to take himself seriously. As Pefanis (1991: 58) argues, Bataille moves beyond dialectic to set into play a third term beyond the habitual dualisms, such as life and death, in a paradoxical movement which simultaneously critiques criticism. But this life-and-death scenario is no mere game of writing for Bataille – it is a matter of life *and* death.

As already implied in chapter 5, moreover, it appears that organizations could not possibly co-exist with a recognition and unleashing of the form of desire that Bataille and others describe, because of its fundamentally disruptive characteristics. The kind of erotic destabilization theorized by Bataille, Deleuze and Guattari, Foucault, and indeed Cixous and Baudrillard, would render 'I' an impossible position to sustain over time. To organize, on the other hand, could be seen to depend on the existence of relatively stable 'I's', on the existence of human beings who relate to themselves as one thing or the other and strive to behave in ways which mirror that relationship to self. This is because organizing, as we have already established, demands purpose, foreclosure, exclusion, decision-making; all of which activities imply a singular relationship to self, a 'knowledge' among those who participate of 'who' and 'what' they 'are'. However shambolic and revolutionary, playful and chaotic, an organization may be, there arguably remains some notion of objectives, some idea of what the organization stands for and what it does not, even where this is contested. This simultaneously requires the possibility of relatively stable identities, of people relating to themselves in particular ways, in the same ways, over a period of time. Consequently, the further that we move towards suggesting that organizations be fully eroticized according to this understanding of desire, the closer we come to displacing organizing as purposeful activity, and to creating collectivities for the sake of simple, wasteful, pleasurable-in-itself eroticism. This kind of re-eroticization is not only emancipatory but transgressive, not just of organizational forms, but potentially of the idea of organization itself. In fact, Bataille argues that there are two phases in what he refers to as 'human emancipation'. The second, the 'postrevolutionary phase':

> implies the necessity of a division between the economic and political organization of society on the one hand, and on the other, an antireligious and asocial organization having as its goal orgiastic participation in different forms of destruction, in other words, the collective satisfaction of needs that correspond to the necessity of provoking the violent excitation that results from the expulsion of heterogeneous elements.
>
> (Bataille 1985: 101)

Furthermore, Hegel (1977: 355–63) attempts to account for the relation between absolute freedom and terror (which troubled him deeply) by asserting it abstractly – independent of morality or institutional arrangements. Kojève's reading of Hegel absolves his contemporaries of all historical responsibility, wars and revolutions – with all their attendant horror – being merely means of bringing the less advanced societies into line with those further on in their progress towards absolute and autonomous consciousness. That which history destroys has no place in history for Hegel – a view which influenced Darwin. Yet Bataille argues that all forms of political opposition (in his case, to fascism) only tend to produce the counter–image of that which they oppose, requiring as much repression in the service of establishing an *alternate* homogeneity as that which they seek to overturn. For this reason, Dollimore (1998: 257) observes that 'Any aesthetic, political or erotic project that privileges expenditure, and in particular the undoing or the subversion of repression above all else, is a non-starter in terms of radical social change.'

This perhaps is also the Achilles heel of re-eroticization as a project. In moving beyond the lingering essentialism, nostalgia and even romanticism of the re-eroticization literature, maybe into posterotics, we need to create what Bhabha (1988: 10–11, cited in Dollimore 1991: 230) calls:

> a space of 'translation': a place of hybridity, figuratively speaking, where the construction of a political object that is new, *neither the one nor the Other*, properly alienates our political expectations, and changes, as it must, the very forms of our recognition of the 'moment' of politics.

Therein lies the challenge – to recognize heterogeneity in eroticism, the creation of what we might call a *heterotics* that does not lose sight of its grounding in power relations and a commitment to change. In seeking to create such a space, we cannot ignore the dark side of sexuality in organizations, the perverse, the abject, and also the dark side of power and domination in sexuality. Foucault ceased to use the term desire because he was unable to extricate it from the idea of oppression, for the *desiring* subject is already inscribed in a discourse of normality, abnormality and qualification (Dollimore 1998: 306). He preferred to talk of pleasure (as does Burrell) but this alternative loses something of the formulations of desire in those libidinal works we have discussed,[12] which seek to reinscribe Hegel and Freud but without losing the recognition of the inseparability of desire and death. In the chapters thus far, we have exposed some of the interconnected effects of desire, power and sexuality, and the neglected abject in particular, already in position in working and organized lives. In further addressing the dynamics of the organized erotic in the second part of the book, we make an attempt at the creation of a space of translation; having read sex into work, we go on to read work into sex.

Part II

Reading organization into sex

predictable and hence anticipated and appropriated by the powerful – than is the traditional self made anxious by the obsolescence of its rootedness. The two are in tension – a tension which may be characterized by the differing ways in which they experience and realize desire. Indeed, as we shall discuss later, some commentators argue that the fragmentation of desire can be exploited as a strategy of resistance to capitalist forces of uniformity and control.

To summarize then, following Foucault, our understanding of sex work is always and inextricably linked to our understanding of sexuality, of masculinity and femininity, and their alternatives. This understanding is shaped by discourses which are, as we know from earlier discussion, primarily institutionalized textual formulations in legal reasoning, administrative and organizational rules, literary and journalistic accounts of those rules and their relation to everyday life, which have an impact on the ways in which people think, speak and act. These discourses vary temporally and spatially: so, as our understanding of sexuality, masculinity, femininity, normality and perversion changes, so too must our understanding of prostitution. Accordingly, what prostitutes are, and what they may become, may differ from one locale to the next. In building our discussion, therefore, we must next examine the key discourses that have influenced contemporary understandings of sexuality in the modern West.

Discursive sexuality across time and place

Understanding sexuality as significant within the human condition is not a recent phenomenon in the West. Foucault (1986a) claims, for example, that the Ancient Greeks saw healthy human existence as at least partly dependent on the way individuals engaged in sex. The prevailing discourse of the time pathologized any failure to control sexual appetite, and emphasized a 'tranquillity of the senses': giving in to the demands of one's sexual urges and/or letting oneself be overcome by pleasure were to be avoided. One worked in this way on the sexual self so that one could rule effectively – self-mastery being seen to be a necessary precondition of the mastery of others. Moreover, potential or actual leaders had always to take the active role in sex. Foucault (1986a: 219) suggests that the authority of an Ancient Greek leader who had once been an object of pleasure for someone else would be seriously undermined. Such men were demonized as having adopted the female role, which in its most extreme form was the *kinaidos* (Halperin 1997). This paradoxical emphasis on sexual asceticism in a context of sexual indulgence continued into the Graeco-Roman era, although 'the love of boys' was replaced by heterosexual, and more specifically conjugal, sexual activity as the proclaimed ideal (Foucault 1990: 41).

Nonetheless, Foucault suggests that sexuality did not assume its current importance until roughly the turn of the eighteenth century. The Ancients, in fact, placed diet at the centre of a healthy human existence (Foucault 1990: 141). Likewise, their medieval successors did not accord sexuality any central significance (Foucault 1986b: 340). As Poster argues, Foucault's project in his *Histories* (1979, 1986a, 1990) was therefore to reveal the convoluted path by which ancient individuals became modern subjects whose 'truth is their sexuality' (Poster 1986: 212). What is presented here is a gradual shift, in the West at least, into a discursive emphasis on sexuality, with the Middle Ages as a period of equilibrium: 'the West has managed ... to bring us almost entirely – our bodies, our minds, our individuality, our history – under the sway of a logic of concupiscence and desire' (Foucault 1979: 78).[2]

Sexuality, therefore, is temporally and spatially specific; it has been constructed and reconstructed in many different forms by discourses throughout history and across cultures. Moreover, discourses may be internally contradictory, as well as existing in multiplicity at any one moment in time. Hollway's (1989) outline of three key discourses which currently structure and inform sexual thoughts, feelings and activities in the modern West illustrates the latter precisely:

- the *male sexual drive* discourse, which posits the uncontrollable character of male sexual libido. One of Hollway's respondents illustrates this precisely in his claim that he 'needs' to 'fuck'. Here men (*and therefore not women*) are positioned as sexually insatiable, as driven to seek sex by their particular biological configuration.
- the *have/hold* discourse, emphasizing the marital bond and the patriarchal family, is also premised on a moral double standard – that sexual fidelity is far more important for women than it is for men.
- the *permissive* discourse, a product of the 1960s, challenged the have/hold discourse in its valorizing of sexual freedom. This discourse constitutes women as having the same sexual desires and drives as men, as well as positioning sex as something which can equally well take place between two men or two women, and which, moreover, does not necessarily consist of heterosexual penetrative intercourse.

Turning to prostitution, we can see the effects of male sexual drive discourse as emerging in this regard during the Enlightenment. Because it was seen as natural and healthy for men to seek to fulfil their sexual urges, prostitutes at this time walked and openly consorted in fashionable areas, being understood as an inevitable outgrowth of the male sexual drive (Hawkes 1996: 35–6). Similar effects are visible during the nineteenth century, in Freud's claim that women at this time were divided into two classes. First, there were respectable women who submitted to their husbands' sexual demands for the sake of procreation but did not find any pleasure in sex itself, and, second, there were those contemptible but ardent women who enjoyed sexual activity and acted as the safety valve for the frustrations of the mates of respectable women, but were otherwise censured and avoided. This tracing of the effects of the male sexual drive discourse through recent Western history also explains the enduring image of the female prostitute as a necessary but degraded receptacle for male desires which cannot be expunged in conjugal relationships.

The effects of the have/hold discourse can also be traced back across modern history. Indeed, from the late eighteenth century onwards, it was accepted that men might regard their wives as frigid and therefore visit prostitutes – although they affected in public to deplore those women on whom they were privately emotionally dependent (Laqueur 1990; Pheterson 1996: 48-9). This condition, where men cannot find desire and love in the same relationship, was identified by Freud as pathological: he argued that love and desire should, if sexual development is healthy, be fused in the same object. However, he also pointed out that:

> In only a very few people of culture are the two strains of culture and sensuality duly fused into one; the man always feels his sexual activity hampered by his respect for the woman and only develops full sexual potency when he finds himself in the presence of a lower type of sexual object; and this gain is partly conditioned by the circumstance that his sexual aims include those of perverse sexual components, which he does not like to gratify with a woman he respects.
>
> (Freud 1963b [1912], cited in Pheterson 1996: 53)

The double standard present within the have/hold discourse was criticized as far back as the nineteenth and early twentieth centuries (Bland and Mort 1997: 17; Hall 1997: 6), and has been the target of much contemporary feminist debate (for example, Roiphe 1994). Nonetheless, it has proved persistent. Connell (1997: 66) notes, on the one hand, that twentieth-century studies of sexuality report more sexual contact outside marriage and a greater number of partners in youth, as well as a general convergence of men and women's patterns of sexual activity. However, women are still 'less than half as likely to report coming to orgasm in intercourse, and more than five times as likely to report an experience of forced sex' (Connell 1997: 66). The trends described above, then, are gradual if anything; not to mention the fact that the last place the double standard is likely to be seriously challenged is in prostitution where, as one prostitute told Pheterson (1996: 48), she left the work because 'my friends in private [police officers, judges, politicians, clergy] were my enemies in public'. The stereotype of the prostitute as 'fallen woman' which, as Maggie O'Neill (1996: 4–5) makes clear, dates back at least as far as the earliest years of written language, is still pervasive, serving to draw the boundaries around 'respectable' female sexuality as well as demonizing prostitutes (Roberts 1992; Pile 1996; Hubbard 1998). Prostitution can therefore be seen as the dark, 'shadow' side of the have/hold discourse, and suffers accordingly as it complements, supports and consolidates the effects of the male sexual drive discourse.[3]

The effects of the permissive discourse as regards prostitution are, however, more complex; they might, on the one hand, be taken to explain the existence of the gigolo, the rent boy, the dominatrix, the prostitute who specializes in baby fantasies or enemas, and so on. However, if we accept O'Connell Davidson's (1995a: 6–7; 1996: 188) argument that prostitutes' clients pay to 'step outside' the complicated mores surrounding non-commercial sex, in that 'No desire is too "perverse", too insulting or too disgusting to be confessed to a prostitute (although, of course, some requests are refused)', then we should also assume that the effects of this discourse have not been particularly pervasive, given that those who indulge them can only do so, by and large, in the context of commercial sex. O'Connell Davidson (1995a: 9) also discusses a theme which is developed in McKeganey and Barnard's research into Glasgow street prostitution, that clients purchase sex at least in part because of 'the dare of doing it', 'the thrill of it being illicit' (McKeganey and Barnard 1996: 53). O'Connell Davidson therefore argues that destigmatizing the work of prostitutes might remove the demand for such services altogether – that is to say, if the permissive discourse was so powerful as to make all sorts of sex possible, acceptable and publicly admissible (including sex with a prostitute), then there would, ironically, be no need for prostitutes.[4] As she states:

> if it is right to suggest that the demand for prostitute's [*sic*] services stems in large part from the contradictory and repressive ideologies which surround human sexuality, then, paradoxically, the prostitute's livelihood actually depends on the maintenance of the very ideology which degrades her and makes her into a social outcast.
>
> (O'Connell Davidson 1995a: 9)[5]

If O'Connell Davidson is correct in her argument concerning clients 'stepping outside' conventional sexual frameworks, then the permissive discourse cannot have been powerful enough to promote radical changes in sexual behaviour by the majority of people, otherwise why would there be a need for the more exotic kinds of sexual service in particular to be provided by prostitutes? This suggests that these services are not readily available in non-commercial sexual relations, and may indeed be impossible for many couples even to discuss. Furthermore, it is difficult to explain why clients still visit prostitutes for 'the thrill' if the permissive discourse has indeed been powerful enough to constitute the legitimacy of whatever sexual desires and needs we may harbour. Indeed, the degree of sexual equality that has been achieved thus far in the modern West does not seem to have generated a large market for male heterosexual prostitution. As we noted in our Introduction, male prostitutes usually need a client base of both men and women if they are to attempt to survive on their earnings (Prestage 1994: 181; McKeganey 1999), and McRae (1992: 85) actually describes women buying sex as an 'oddity'. Male heterosexual prostitution is also less visible than its female counterpart, tending to be offered through escort services or, more recently, through the Internet.[6] For example, male prostitute Joel Ryan, who runs Heaven on Earth Escorts from his home in Melbourne, advertises in newspapers and magazines, thus making the services he and his staff provide less immediately conspicuous than those of female streetworkers (Brooks 1998; *Under the Sun* 1998). In contra-distinction, McKeganey and Barnard's (1996) data gathering with male users of street prostitutes suggests that the reputation which attaches to red light districts is what attracts punters to these locations – that is to say, men know where to look for prostitutes because particular geographical areas are understood to provide such a service (also see Hubbard 1997: 133). A woman wishing to buy sex must therefore engage in a more active and intelligent search than a man does in the same situation. Moreover, further to the theme of the different ways in which male and female desire appear still to be constituted, Joel Ryan states that paying for sex is something that many women would find difficult, and so offers a discounted 'introductory package' as a 'taster', which includes conversation as well as sex (Brooks 1998: 4). This all suggests that the effects of the permissive discourse have not (yet) constructed women's desires to be as powerful as those of men, and that these effects have not (yet) legitimated their commercial satisfaction. Therefore it appears that it is still socially more acceptable for men to buy sex from women than vice versa, which also implies that, if the female sex drive is as powerful as that of the male, women who need sex may have developed ways of satisfying that need without having recourse to the commercial sex market.

The fact that women are unlikely to be able to use the street to locate prostitutes' services also means that they tend to pay a premium for commercial sex compared to men who may pay as little as £15 for the services of a street worker. However, as London prostitute Docherty points out, female 'outworkers' who visit clients at their homes can 'add another thousand on' to his £250 rate for an all-night stay. He attributes this to the fact that many women are still economically dependent on men and so cannot justify spending large sums to their partners without anything to show for it, or do not earn enough to be able to afford his services if he were to charge what his female counterparts charge (McRae 1992: 85). Based on Docherty's claims, then, we might surmise that the market for male heterosexual prostitution is not only restricted because of the ways in which male and female desire are understood, but also as a result of gendered income and wage-earning patterns.

Nonetheless, one of Docherty's clients, Rachel, claims that 'there are *many more women than you'd ever imagine* doing the same thing as us' (Rachel, quoted in McRae 1992: 90; emphasis added). Rachel implies here that there are numerous women paying for the services of male prostitutes, so giving some credence to the claim that this has perhaps become more widespread as a result of the permissive discourse, as well as the greater economic independence of *some* women (see Prestage 1994: 181), whilst also pointing to the secretive nature of these transactions. Rachel also says that only Docherty can satisfy her sexual needs, and says she pays him for sex as opposed to the more 'traditional' extramarital affair, so as to avoid emotional hurt (Rachel, quoted in McRae 1992: 92–3). Her description of affairs as traditional may also be seen as telling in terms of the effects of the permissive discourse, and is supported by McKeganey and Barnard's (1996: 51-3) account of reasons given by the (male) clients involved in their research as to why they choose to visit prostitutes.

In a related argument, Illouz (1998) notes a postmodern turn in the development of the permissive discourse, claiming that postmodern sexuality is characterized by a transformation of the affair from romance to transaction. As she puts it: 'In its intrinsic transience and affirmation of pleasure, novelty and excitement, the affair may be dubbed a postmodern experience and contains a structure of feeling with affinities to the emotions and cultural values fostered by the sphere of consumption' (Illouz 1998: 176). For Illouz, the affair institutionalizes liminality, in that it usually takes place on geographical, institutional and temporal margins, outside the normal frameworks of jobs, families and homes – it therefore exists in a space where normal hierarchies and identities can be reversed and social, aesthetic and cultural boundaries blurred (Illouz 1998: 177). In effect, it seeks out and establishes a permissive space. Second, the affair is not simply the exercise of power by one sex over the other, but is just as likely to be sought by both parties to the encounter. Third, it no longer contains elements of transgression of a normalizing or moral imperative. And, finally, it is underpinned by a rationality based on lifestyle choices and consumer rationality. Indeed 'the affair characterises the romantic experience of those professionals and new cultural intermediaries, located in large urban centres, who are most proficient at switching between sexual pleasure and forms of economic activity' (Illouz 1998: 178).

However, while what Illouz describes may appear to be the morality of the fictional 'sexual anthropology' television series *Sex and the City* (1998), we would argue that the real world of contemporary sexual affairs is not quite as simple or as transactional, and that the question of morality still looms large here. Indeed, as Rachel's comments suggest, many people, both male and female, can accept the transactional nature of the sexual act but cannot disentangle themselves from the emotional baggage that comes with it.[7] Sexual philosophy here has difficulty in outstripping persistent sexual–cultural values, such that affairs may be seen, contrary to Illouz's reading of them as a choice moving those involved beyond conventional frameworks, as potentially involving *all* the emotions (and therefore possible hurt) associated with these frameworks. We would suggest instead that, for prostitutes themselves and for male and (a much smaller number of) female clients, it is prostitution which might represent a way of embracing the transactional and consumptional nature of sex and avoiding the emotional entanglements and moral strictures that might otherwise attend it. In this scenario, prostitution is a natural extension of the increasing commodification of normalized relations, and may be a means to perfect the pursuit of pleasure at a technical level with none of the problems of romance – again as is evident in what Rachel has to say. Consequently, if we hope to understand those ways in which postmodernity positions us between economic activity and sexual pleasure, and blurs the boundaries between them, then a closer examination of the contemporary nature and conditions of prostitution is essential.

This argument runs somewhat against O'Connell Davidson's claim that the destigmatizing of prostitution would lead to the removal of much of the demand for the services of the prostitute. We therefore suggest that, given the nature of the clients in her study (who mainly want specialist services such as domination), and indeed the nature of the clients in most of the available British studies of prostitution, this is not an untenable stance *within its locality*. Indeed, O'Connell

Davidson (1995a, 1996) expresses reservations about how typical her data are of prostitution more widely. Nonetheless, elsewhere she begins to look at how the mobility of the repressed male sexuality of certain users of Western prostitutes may be *exported internationally* through sex tourism, military movements, shipping and trucking activities, and may interact with local client demands, sustaining such phenomena as debt-bonding and child prostitution (O'Connell Davidson 1995b, 1997; O'Connell Davidson and Sanchez Taylor 1996). Here O'Connell Davidson offers some truly sickening data in starting to map this dark side of the sex industry, and the existence of these substantial areas of prostitution confirms that, although the permissive discourse may in some places and circumstances have made it easier to do and say certain things, it has not yet transformed the context in which they take place, nor has it enabled many people to talk about, act upon, and if necessary seek remedial treatment for, their desires openly. The effects of this discourse therefore remain hard to elucidate, and not only vary but, as O'Connell Davidson indicates, may impact *across* cultures with the whole-sale global exportation of perversion. Discursive variations across place which affect the shape of sex work should therefore not be underestimated.

Discourse, desire and prostitution

As we have seen, Hollway's three discourses do appear to affect the emergence and understanding of, as well as demand for, prostitution in form, content and degree. However, the nature and source of psychological repression are notori-ously difficult to determine, and may or may not derive directly from societal ideology, individual life history, or both. Wherever there is a pattern of desire and lack in human existence, and this, as Cooper (1983) points out, can be read as an ontological condition which structures our experience, it will emerge – through sexuality, business enterprise, the creative arts, military conquest, etc. In the absence of a world in which every human being finds their perfect partner, we can expect that there will be a mismatch between desire and the preferred or necessary means of its fulfilment. The market mechanism upon which prostitu-tion is founded is one means of coping with this imbalance. So, while we must acknowledge that prostitution in the modern West is inevitably shaped by soci-etal discourses and consequent taboos, we cannot assume that, if these discourses were to decline in their power, prostitution would simply fade away.

Additionally, as we have established in chapter 6 in particular, the Freudian construction of desire as lack is only one possible line of analysis. This under-standing of desire as a drive towards need satisfaction stemming from an experienced lack of the other as object is present, albeit implicitly, in most socio logical accounts of prostitution and, though wider in scope, also relates to the male sexual drive discourse. Yet Freudian psychoanalysis often refuses to take straightforward manifestations of desire as desire for the object, insisting on cathexis, where the desire (or its inversion, revulsion) manifested is merely a sublimated desire for (or fear of) something else. Freud's patient Dora (Ida Bauer), for example, reported that she was being sexually harassed by the husband of the woman with whom her father was having an affair – a situation complicated by the fact that this man was also one of her father's close friends. Freud goes to great and somewhat convoluted lengths to explain Dora's 'hysterical' reaction, implicating Dora as repressing the real desire she feels for both the harasser and his wife – although he does accept her version of events without contestation (Freud 1977; Billig 1997: 29-30). In recognizing that the true object of desire might not be the object that appears to present itself, Lacan, as noted earlier, extends Freud's argument in suggesting that desire is not simply desire for the other, but 'desire for the desire of the other' (Macey 1995: 78; Hollway 1996: 96), a problem of and need for recognition. Desire here is the desire to find a place of value in the symbolic world of the other, not necessarily to dominate that world. Prostitutes' clients often need such self-validation, even though they may realize that it is only a simulacrum of valorization that they receive. For example, as Blain's (1994: 336) biographical account of her life as a prostitute in Australia suggests, she offers her clients important non-sexual services such as companionship, kindness and advice; and Moira, working in the UK, says that: 'Some [clients] don't even want sex, but friendship' (Moira, quoted in O'Neill 1996: 24). One of Pheterson's (1996: 40) respondents agrees that reassuring the customer is important, and Goodley, in his discussion of male homosexual prostitution in Australia, concurs: 'Most often the typical client just wants affection … it is the basically good-looking boys who can show a lot of affection that get the repeat business' (Goodley 1994: 129). In the same vein, an anonymous contributor to the on-line magazine *SIN* (South Australia Sex Industry Network)[8] suggests that:

> I like being a sex worker because I am a member of an elite group of multi-talented professional workers. I am at different times a lover, psychiatrist, teacher, counsellor, educator, masseuse, therapist and sometimes all of these at once. I like role playing … I like that I am helping to lessen the loneliness of the many clients who see me. Some of these men are widowers, some find it difficult to sustain relationships, some have never had a relationship. It makes me feel good to share an intimate experience with these men that is warm, sensual and caring and hopefully they will carry some of that experience away with them.

Our Australian fieldwork produced similar accounts – Katrina said that she has become a world-class conversationalist on a wide range of subjects, an actress, a counsellor and psychoanalyst, paramedic, interior designer and decorator, in support of her clients' self-validation. Finally, the attempt to satisfy clients' desires for the desire of the other is also evident in the way in which 'sex therapist' Sara Dale (alias Kinky Miss Whiplash, who famously worked out of Norman Lamont's London home), approaches her work (McRae 1992: 97–111); New South Wales escort[9] Fiona's comment that the clients she services are mixed and don't necessarily just want sex of whatever type (Kerkham 1997: 108–9); and Layla (London) and Caroline's (Bournemouth) interviews in the UK television series *Vice: The Sex Trade*. Caroline says that her clients 'come to me for, like for sex. But ... they say "We do like a friendly woman, not just one who's gonna drag us in there, take our money and then ten minutes later, you know, kick us out".' Layla, similarly, suggests that: 'You are the perfect hostess; you are the counsellor; you are the friend; you are the psychiatrist. You are everything rolled in one when you're doing this type of work.' Indeed, most of Layla's clients are divorced, find it difficult to approach women or have been hurt in the past. In these instances, then, affection and intimacy are not ruled out of the client encounter as something that the prostitute is trying to avoid at all costs, as is often deemed to be the case in UK accounts of prostitution.[10]

The above demonstrates that what is being provided that is of value to prostitutes' clients is, at least in part, psychological recognition, and the more subtle and sophisticated the repertoire of means of provision of this recognition, the higher the value that may be placed on the services. Nevertheless, the Freudian structuring of desire still remains too closely related to the view of nature embodied in Darwin's work on evolution, a drive to survive in which nature 'knows' what it 'lacks' and 'wants', although this may be deflected in practice. Haraway (1991: 67) contests this interpretation of nature, suggesting that it is, in fact, something of an opportunist, a teaser rather than a tester, an improviser rather than an experimenter. Deleuze and Guattari's (1984, 1987) reworking of Lacanian desire echoes her argument in suggesting, as we have seen earlier, that desire may be more than a drive produced by lack, or indeed that the lack that we assume underpins desire is '*a countereffect of desire*; it is deposited, distributed, vacuolized, within a real that is natural and social' (Deleuze and Guattari 1984: 27; emphasis added). Deleuze and Guattari here are, again as already noted, heavily influenced by Bataille (1991), and in particular by his thesis of the general economy, outlined in more detail in the Introduction. Deleuze and Guattari's (1984) critique of the Freudian reading of desire as lack also revolves around flows of desire/energy which connect, as established in chapter 6, the desiring-machines. Like Bataille, Deleuze and Guattari also refuse to accept that the subject of desire exists *a priori*, arguing instead that all that exists prior to psychological repression is an endless circuit of flows of desire. The immanence of desire is therefore a key theme in Bataille and Deleuze and Guattari's work, and desire here is reconceptualized as creative, playful, exploratory, wide-ranging and unpredictable, as we also established earlier on. Moreover, just as the drive to possess the object, or for the desire of the other (psychological recognition), may find its object elusive and be easily derailed, so might a creative, restless and rhizomatic form of desire find itself down some unexpected and even dead-end tracks. Perhaps it is the working through of this form of desire, a form of discovery of both self and other rather than the desperate pursuit of a need, which leads an Italian prostitute to claim that 'Lots of married men prefer pre-operative trans-sexual prostitutes (men in the process of becoming women who have both breasts and a penis); they want gay sex without forfeiting heterosexual identity' (Pheterson 1996: 72). Former sex worker and Sydney transsexual Louise made a similar observation in our Australian fieldwork. Moreover, Joseph, placing an advert in a Sydney newspaper for 'Married or *de facto* men who do, or want to, have sex with other men' (Joseph 1997: 5) to be interviewed for research purposes, received 46 calls in three days. The responses were so rich and the phenomenon seemingly so widespread that a book has recently been published from the interviews. Indeed, the Sydney Outreach Project estimates that 40–60 per cent of men who use beats[11] or who sell sex to other men only do so occasionally, perhaps once every one or two months, and also do not identify as gay.[12] Joseph suggests, therefore, that male sexual duality is on the increase; and also makes the telling point that, even in a tolerant city such as Sydney, its conditioned suppression is 'exacting a huge toll from many seemingly ordinary people, both men and women' (Joseph 1997: 3–4).[13]

Bodies without Organs

The reformulation of the problem of desire in terms other than those of lack has not only been attempted by Deleuze and Guattari, to whose work we shall return shortly. Lyotard (1974) has also addressed desire in his work on libidinal economy. For Lyotard, desire has two forms: *desire-as-wish*, the Freudian construction of desire based on lack, and *desire-as-force*, the more creative drive to which Bataille and Deleuze and Guattari refer (Elliott 1994: 151-3). Although overall Lyotard's concept of desire is closer to Freud's, where Freud is concerned with the ways in which libidinal energy becomes embodied in the structure of the psychic apparatus, which then distorts and channels the flows of that energy in the here-and-now, Lyotard focuses on the cultural practices which shape the flow of what he calls libidinal or pulsional dispositives of desire, the intensities lodged in cultural representations and social meanings (Lash 1990: 90; Elliott 1994: 154). Moreover, in common with Deleuze and Guattari, Lyotard sees this flow as being one of levels of intensity rather than one structured in terms of depth and hierarchy. Where Freud sees libidinal investment in other bodies and persons as being symbolic, representative of underlying psychic investment in the primary family unit of father–mother, both Lyotard and Deleuze and Guattari argue that such investments should be seen as connections between the body and externality, with sensation occurring at the point of intersection, at the surface, on what Lyotard calls the libidinal band, and Deleuze and Guattari the Body without Organs (Lash 1990: 77; Elliott 1994: 152). For both Lyotard and Deleuze and Guattari, then, postmodern desire moves from signification to sensation.

Ecstavasia (1994) has applied the concept of the Body without Organs to escort prostitution in the United States. Both escort and client, she suggests, have a BwO, but it is one of this Body's chief characteristics that it can never be attained, realized or fulfilled, existing both 'inside and outside the concrete, inside and outside the abstract' (Deleuze and Guattari 1987: 150). The BwO, then, is not a literal body, but a figurative body which needs to be constructed from a variety of sources, and which relies on a variety of tools and techniques. First there is a blueprint, a set of 'already written rules and conditions by which it must be constructed', such that the BwO constitutes a programme, 'a limit which marks the edges of the plane of desire' (Ecstavasia 1994: 178). The escort thus becomes part of the cyborg assemblage – including the telephone, and telephone directories, the escort agency, the hotel/motel/client's home, pager, mobile phone, transport, the clock, money, fashion, cosmetics, images, vibrators, costumes, condoms, etc. – which enables her to become part of and to help construct the client's BwO (for example, through a submissive fantasy involving uniforms), while also engaged in the construction of her own BwO (for example, through a dream of earning enough money to retire to a country mansion). Because the BwO is unattainable, being a forever shifting emotional state, it is also unbounded, deterritorialized, and only attainable by proxy. For the escort, the BwO – desires for a particular lifestyle, freedom, security, the BMW, the big house, etc. – becomes reterritorialized on to the commodity form money. Indeed, researchers typically report that prostitutes get through difficult client encounters by thinking of the money, so that the day is punctuated by calculations of what has and could be earned, and what this represents – a new dress, a bill paid, a holiday, savings towards a deposit on a house or even licence to leave the profession. For example:

> And when you look [at your watch during a client encounter], you constantly think 'Well, that's such and such money, that's that paid off. Shit, I need another two jobs and then I'm finished. I'm out of here. I've made my money.'
> (Inga, Melbourne brothel worker, quoted in Cockington and Marlin 1995: 179)

One of Järvinen's Norwegian respondents made a similar point; 'I try to think of something else. Plan what I am going to do with the money.' (Järvinen 1993: 144, cited in Scambler 1997: 115). Similarly, the client's BwO, because he can't possess the fantasized construction (for example, he isn't *really* in a subordinate role, the escort isn't *really* a maid or on active service),[14] is reterritorialized on to orgasm, which becomes the object of the encounter – 'a mere fact, a rather deplorable one, in relation to desire in pursuit of its principle' (Deleuze and Guattari 1987: 156). Consequently, ejaculation, relative to the BwO, is always premature – and always demands its reconstruction at a later date.

The BwO is therefore always deferred, always, in Derrida's terms, in *différance*, an absent presence whose conditions and logic are based on fetishized fragments of other absent presences – girlfriend, mother, girl next door, ex-partner, girl in magazine, film star, stripper (Ecstavasia 1994: 186). An example is the fact that the first semi-naked women that many men see are in the underwear pages of their mother's home shopping catalogues – and we might speculate that this is part of the reason for the enduring yet ambivalent popularity of lingerie as a tool of the prostitute's trade. The BwO then is built from the past, from memory and media images, and is oriented towards the future, but can never exist in the present. It is always in tension until that tension is released through reterritorialization (for the client, through orgasm; for the prostitute, through getting paid).

The assemblage of images and fetishized representations of women as objects of desire – signifiers and a signifying system inscribed on the prostitute's body – reaches a plane of consistency:

> an achieved state in which desire no longer lacks anything but fills itself and constructs its own field of immanence ... [which] is like the absolute Outside that knows no Selves because interior and exterior are equally a part of the immanence in which they have fused.
>
> (Deleuze and Guattari 1987: 156)

Here it is the signifiers and the signifying system which are being fetishized, not the woman's body as such (Ecstavasia 1994: 186). The assemblage is therefore not complete – there are inconsistencies in its consistency, gaps, partiality and incompleteness, unfinished business in its articulations and allusions.

As well as signification, the BwO also entails activity. For the escort, 'Your BwO is my physical activity: fucking, sucking, spanking, bending, straddling, arching, moaning, gasping, etc. I am a material girl' (Ecstavasia 1994: 197). It also relies on the deployment of technology, both that which will rewrite the cultural order on the body – high heels, garters, fishnet stockings, painted toenails, jewellery, long fingernails – and those tools which in their use affect the type and quality of interminglings that are possible – vibrators, latex gloves, lubricant, bubble bath, massage oil, riding crops. It is this combination of bodily image, bodily activity and technological support which lends the assemblage its cyborg character as an articulation of human subject and technology (Haraway 1991).

Ecstavasia also implies that the client may have more than one BwO. Indeed, although there are many clients who like one particular combination, there are others who prefer to alternate between BwOs, and others who are in the process of exploration of different BwO elements, who want to be surprised and prefer a more fluid encounter. And there are always those who just want to talk, which constructs a different type of BwO. The gaps and differences between BwOs offer a point at which subjectivity, interest, desire and power relations may begin to be explored but we would also argue that the body itself should not be forgotten in this consideration. The prostitute may become part of the client's future BwO – her smile, a tattoo or mole, the softness of a patch of her skin, the shape of a nipple – but there may also be room for connections to develop which go beyond the simple injunction that the worker and her pleasure only exist as part of the client's fantasy: 'If he likes it I like it. That's part of his fantasy. It isn't even a question of whether I like it or not' (Ecstavasia 1994: 196; see also Desiree, quoted in O'Connell Davidson 1995a: 7; 1996: 189; Charlotte, quoted in Salvadori 1997: 120). Although Ecstavasia's claim would on the whole be true of most worker–punter encounters, there are sufficient exceptions where more complex relations develop for theory to need to take into account – as we have indicated above in our discussion of the role that affection and intimacy play in the prostitute–client encounter. Another concept which therefore presents itself for discussion is Deleuze and Guattari's (1987) differentiation of smooth space and striated space. Smooth space is private, where there are no rules, and fantasy may seamlessly merge with reality. Striated space is public space, where there are rules, regulations, tax officials, police, health standards, benefit agencies, social workers and all manner of other constraints on the interactants. The construction of the BwO takes place in order to create the illusion of smooth, unbounded and unregulated private space in the commercial sex encounter, which is nonetheless always and already striated – a public, time-bounded economic transaction.[15] The attempted articulation of the cyborg assemblage of the BwO (Ecstavasia 1994: 184–5) therefore offers a route for the exploration of the forces which shape public striations around the encounter, and of how those striations continue to penetrate it, as well as exploring the work done to create the illusion of relaxed private space.

As Ecstavasia's piece is at this stage only exploratory, criticism is perhaps premature as there are many avenues along which her work could develop. However, this developing theory, as we have said, does need to create room for the theorization of real bodies in articulation, as well as subject positions in discursive alignment and re-alignment. We would also urge an expansion of the concept of partial identities into one of multiple identities (see Stone 1995). Moreover, it is significant that Ecstavasia's analysis is couched in terms of US escort work, and we could and must expect different forms of BwO to be in process in other parts of the world, in line with our emphasis on spatial variation. Additionally, the intensification of global media vectors in the West has a relevant double effect. It both causes the world to rush in on those of us with access to technology, offering a bewildering variety of images for BwO creation, while at the same time driving us in on ourselves, disrupting human social relations, which must inevitably have an impact on emergent forms of local and global sexual subjectivity (including the proliferation of cybersex and sex tourism). What is necessary to extend work in this area is further investigation of what sort of BwOs are being constructed inside and outside prostitute–client encounters, how they are being constructed, and to what sort of reterritorializations they are being linked.

The power of desire

Ecstavasia clearly sees the need to link the analysis of the escort encounter to wider social and political effects, but in her analysis desire itself seems to lose some of the power which it has in Deleuze and Guattari's account, notwithstanding the fact that she seems to recognize that the BwO is a 'push' effect of the workings of desire, rather than the more Freudian view that the Other exerts a 'pull' effect through the recognition of lack (Ecstavasia 1994: 186; Deleuze and Guattari 1987: 154). Deleuze and Guattari argue, as implied in chapter 6, that 'push' desire does not flow freely enough in modern society, and therefore suggest that the prostitute can potentially perform a radical and politicized function, as desire circulates in opposition to capitalism even as it employs, combines and discards capitalist cultural forms – the boots, the stockings, the bustier – for the intensification of sensation. Simply being involved in sex work is therefore potentially liberating and transgressive. For Lyotard, however, this is not enough – desire can't be simply opposed to capitalism because, even more than the rhizomatic motion which Deleuze and Guattari describe, it circulates freely and endlessly around objects, bodies and surfaces. Late capitalism is itself one immense desiring system 'in which all social forms are colonised by the economic logic of exchange' (Elliott 1994: 154). Prostitution is certainly an example of the colonization and commodification of sexuality in this system. But for Lyotard the very fact that the circulation of desire can be recognized within systems which seek to colonize, commodify, or even deny it – whether these systems be economic exchange or organizational scientific rationality – is a means of subverting them. For Lyotard, the fragmentation of desire in so many directions is a means of intensifying lived experience, a recognition of the fragmented nature of identity and a means of undermining the attempts of capitalism to control individual subjectivity and authorize its own existence. The prostitute, in this formulation, is more of a resistance activist than Deleuze and Guattari's commando, but both can radically reinscribe the cultural representations of capitalism, and hence capitalism itself.

In our discussion of desire, which any theorization of prostitution must explicitly address, we do not have space to fully discuss the complex ideas of Castoriadis but they more than warrant mention. Castoriadis, in his attempt to rewrite Freud rather than break with him completely, stands at one remove from the postmodernists Lyotard and Deleuze and Guattari, despite his concern with the effects of what he sees as the modern uncoupling of socio-cultural forms from desire conceived of as creative imagination (Castoriadis 1987; Elliott 1994: 161-4). From this perspective, the prostitute can become part of the 'fetishization of reality by the dull repetition of the self-same' (Elliott 1994: 163-4) – the McDonaldization of sex (Ritzer 1996) – or, alternatively, provide for greater release of this imagination in recoupling individual creativity to the social. Here we have a relation which seems unresolved, at least in relation to prostitution, which is that between prostitution and kitsch. It seems, in the fetishization of popular signifiers, that the prostitute encounter creates kitsch sex – involving a sentimental participation in the collective through the deployment of media images, creating a shorthand for avoiding an authentic encounter with the other, erecting a defence against unwelcome self-knowledge. There are many reported prostitute–client encounters in the existing literature which seem to be pure kitsch (see, for example, Greta, quoted in McRae 1992: 254–61; O'Connell Davidson 1995a, 1996). Yet there is also something else at work; a possibility for creativity and individuation of the encounter, and for both parties to emerge with greater self-knowledge, and even some knowledge of the other. What is it, then, that keeps the prostitute–client encounter from falling on to the side of kitsch? For Deleuze and Guattari, the difference between desire and kitsch would turn on the one hand on intensity, and on the other on the locus of control – kitsch being externally determined, a conditioned response occasioned by a signifier rather than a creative and sensational relationship between body and image, a denial of self rather than a constructive realization of identity. Again, this issue needs to be pursued simultaneously through both empirical research into the micro-practices of the encounter and the further development and application of aesthetic theory.

It should also be clear by now that we do not regard Hollway's three discourses, no matter which theory of desire we may connect to them, as being the only possible avenues for understanding sex work. Discourses are partial, imaginary, dynamic, often contradictory, fraught with tensions and subject to many exceptions. Nevertheless, as Foucault (1980) suggests, and as we have already argued, identifying discursive formations, and appreciating their power/knowledge effects, allows us to see how particular interpretations and experiences of sex work are possible in Western modernity. Our representation of desire helps us to understand the energies circulating in prostitution, and their political implications, but examination of the discourses which form a context for the construction and negotiation of meaning and experience for prostitutes accounts for some of the prevailing definitions of the work and the variations in the way that it is performed, which we explore at length in chapters 8 and 9.

Conclusion

In this chapter we have focused on the first dimension of the double effect of placing on sex work: that of discursive positioning. As we have argued, any definition of prostitution will be partially governed by the prevailing discourses of the time and the place on sexuality, and the ways in which these discourses are underpinned by ontologies of human desire. We have also suggested that these ontologies of desire are more often than not conceived of as Freudian, such that they turn on a conceptualization of desire as lack. How desire is constructed and worked out in prostitution is perhaps for us the central theoretical challenge facing contemporary research in the area (although there are other challenges more oriented towards policy-making). This is especially so given that a shift towards understanding desire as immanent, endless, rhizomatic suggests a very different and (if we follow Bataille, Foucault, Deleuze and Guattari, Lyotard and Castoriadis) perhaps more positive conceptualization of prostitution than conceptualizations which turn on desire as lack, for example, the prostitute as outlet for male sexual frustration.

As our discussion has established, there is yet much work to do in continuing to theorize prostitution, as an occupation, as an industry, as an encounter, as a form of autonomy for women, as a mode of global domination, as a site for subjectivity. Prostitution offers a rich field for both detailed micro-study and global analysis. As we indicated in our Introduction, moreover, the challenges which are presented for theory are mirrored by empirical complexity. Methodologically, problems of gaining access and building trust are enormous in this field of research (see, for example, O'Connell Davidson and Layder 1994). Interviewing seems to be a particularly pallid form of investigation in an area which provokes such passion, both among and outwith the participants. However, audio or video taping encounters is not only difficult to do unobtrusively, but may generate problems in gaining ethical approval and legitimacy in the research community, and in avoiding more perverse associations. On the other hand, actual participation as either prostitute or client would certainly offer insights not otherwise available, but would be even more controversial given the degraded status of prostitution. In this regard, Lunsing (1997, 1999) offers thoughtful arguments based on his somewhat serendipitous induction into male prostitution as a means of conducting 'intimate interviewing' through pillow-talk. Whether Lunsing's arguments about gaining intimate knowledge through knowledgeable intimacy are accepted or not, he makes a relevant and more general point about the engagement, or lack of engagement, of the sexuality of the investigator with the subjects (or, more frequently, objects) of their study. The question posed by Lunsing, in asking whether researchers are not already to some unacknowledged degree prostitutes in conducting their research, could also be expressed in terms of our consideration of desire. What are the elements of the assemblage through which the researcher pursues their own BwO? Might it be constructed through the artefacts of journal publication, the symbols of career progression? Is the researcher already part of someone else's BwO (for example, the representatives of funding bodies) in carrying out the research? In becoming more explicitly part of a client's or a prostitute's BwO, and perhaps contributing to an alternate BwO of their own, does the researcher devalue their own research or challenge the discursive domination of the typical BwO (detached, objective, scientific) inscribed on to researchers by 'normal social science' methods? While many fields of social analysis have proved particularly fruitful ground for the exploration of power/knowledge relations, a style now regarded as 'conventional' Foucauldian analysis, the study of prostitution alerts us to the presence of the essential third term – an awareness obvious in Foucault, blatant and unavoidable in Bataille or Deleuze and Guattari – that of desire. Further tracing of the workings of desire, through prostitution as a phenomenon, through the researcher's self-reflexive engagement with their own sexuality in the process, and extending back more broadly into a consideration of the workings of desire in the social sciences, offers a tantalizing problematic for the future. A future which, to borrow from Foucault, may yet be called Deleuzian.

8 Consumption and the management of identity in sex work

Introduction

This chapter develops our theme of variety in the understanding and experiencing of prostitution by analysing the ways in which prostitutes negotiate and construct their sense of themselves. As such, it moves one stage beyond our analysis of the discursive positioning of sex work in chapter 7, focusing primarily on the micro-practices of identity which are discernible in prostitution in our core context (the UK, the USA and Australia). This allows us to suggest that individual workers' tactics for managing the contradictions of working as a prostitute and preserving self-esteem are both similar and different and, moreover, that not all prostitutes necessarily want to maintain a strict divide between work sex and non-work sex at all times. Moreover, even for those who do, the trials of maintaining the divide are considerable, as is the permeability of the boundaries. In chapter 9, we return to the consideration of the discursive context of these micro-practices, and suggest that where prostitutes locate themselves among or in resistance to particular discourses has an inevitable impact on their identity work and professional life.

Here, then, we concentrate on the interactional features of identity construction in sex work, given that the work itself, by its very nature, potentially exerts pressure on the relationship between personal and professional identities. The ways in which these pressures are handled (or even experienced) sheds light on the complexity of sex work and, by extension of this perspective from the margins, allows us an alternative purchase on the reflexive project of the self in modernity (Giddens 1991, 1992). The meaning of the sex act itself is what is at stake in interactions between prostitutes and clients, and the categorization of different types of sexual encounter – work, relational or recreational – may be important for the prostitute to maintain the proper distance from the emotional demands of the client encounter and to enable the maintenance of self-identity beneath the public, professional mask. However, although what we discuss in this chapter primarily falls into the category of professional sex, we shall see that the boundaries between categories are leaky, requiring constant attention, and that the mask is always in danger of slipping.

In the first instance, it is necessary to expand on what we mean by the pressures on identities that may attach to working as a prostitute in the modern West, which necessitates the corollary that the development of late industrial Western modernity has been broadly characterized by a reversal of the classic assumption that identity was defined by what the individual did or made, by their involvement in production. Identity is now more frequently located in how we consume and what is consumed, as the consumption process itself becomes a process of symbolic (re)production – the consumption of signs as much as commodities. Our consumption patterns, and what we actually consume, have become key markers organizing identity so that the boundaries between work and leisure have become blurred by more ambiguous considerations of lifestyle (Giddens 1991, 1992; Hawkes 1996: 113–23). How then has this process unfolded, and what might it tell us about prostitution?

Consumption, the commodification of pleasure and prostitution in Western modernity

Many commentators concur on the importance of understanding consumption in understanding contemporary Western society and suggest that it involves, in the paradigm cases of malls and theme parks, the creation of spaces where we can be entertained as we consume (see, for example, Bauman 1983; Campbell 1984; Haug 1986; Williamson 1986; Baudrillard 1988; Campbell 1989; Gardner and Sheppard 1989; Mort 1989; 1996; Jameson 1991; Tomlinson 1990; Featherstone 1991; Cross 1993; Lash and Urry 1994; Donaldson 1996). Colin Campbell identifies the roots of development of the modern form of consumption as locus of identity and key leisure activity in the eighteenth century, among the middle classes. His explanation relies heavily on his concept of 'imaginative hedonism'; the quest for pleasure in dreaming of how consumer goods might enhance one's life, given the particular emphasis he places on pleasure as a defining characteristic of modern consumption (Campbell 1989: 69).

In particular, Campbell asks how pleasurable consumption came to be legitimized, even idealized, among a puritan and ascetic social class. Here he offers a complex theological argument, beginning with the Reformation doctrine of Calvinism, and its central tenet of predestination. However, for another strand of eighteenth-century Protestantism, also Puritan in origin, predestination's claim that one's life on Earth had no relation with or possible influence on whether one ascended to Heaven, and the corollary that Calvinists spent their lives seeking signs that they had been chosen by God, were intolerable, begging the question how 'Infinite Goodness [could] design or delight in the misery of his Creatures' (Crane, cited in Campbell 1989: 111). Predestination was seen to render incomprehensible any concept of God's eternal love; these dissident Protestants preferred to suggest that humans are made in a loving God's image, that this love must be felt as well as expressed in charitable acts and, centrally, that there was pleasure to be derived from charitable acts. Campbell claims that this progressed in some tracts towards an 'altruistic emotional hedonism' – the idea that we should do good for the pleasure it affords.

Furthermore, Campbell also points out that the place of emotions in Calvinism itself is significant in analysing the development of modern consumption – particularly the melancholia which properly characterized those of the devout who sought signs of their elect status (that is to say, 'the misery of [God's] Creatures' referred to above). Displays of feeling that pointed to a doubt that one was saved were seen to indicate that one was in fact a member of the elect. However, the self-mortifying pleasure experienced as a result of these negative emotions began, suggests Campbell, to be an end in itself. Thus he argues that the 'kindliness' of altruistic emotional hedonism eventually met with the 'self-pitying morbidity' of Calvinism in 'a common concern with the pleasures of feeling' (Campbell 1989: 135).

Here, then, Campbell identifies the way in which emotions became legitimized as a source of pleasure during the eighteenth century and therefore formed the foundation for the onset of modern consumption, as characterized by imaginative hedonism. For him, the key changes are socio-cultural, driven by the various forms of Protestantism of the Reformation era. Baudrillard (1988) concurs with this position, suggesting that the basis of modern consumerist society is the replacement of a puritan morality with a hedonistic morality based on pleasure.

Campbell's thesis of a shift in cultural values can, moreover, be seen to work in tandem with the thesis that Bauman (1983) and others present of consumption offsetting the rigours experienced by the modern worker. The commodification of pleasure and the recognition of the right of individuals to enjoy at the very least a specific and sectioned part of their lives, such as the weekend, as a respite from possibly degrading and demeaning work, created a space for the (re)construction of identity (Donaldson 1996). George Orwell in *The Road to Wigan Pier* (1975) noted that this was true even of the working class who found themselves out of work during the Depression of the 1930s. These men and women, he writes, often spent their money in one single extravagance or big night out and then starved for a few days, rather than eking it out during the week:

> Life [on the dole] is still fairly normal, more normal than one really has the right to expect. Families are impoverished, but the family system has not broken up ... in a decade of unparalleled depression, the consumption of all cheap luxuries has increased ... You may have three-halfpence in your pocket and not a prospect in the world ... but in your new clothes you can stand on the street corner, indulging in a private day dream of yourself as Clark Gable or Greta Garbo.
>
> (Orwell, cited in Campbell 1984: 227)

Beatrix Campbell (1984) found a similar phenomenon among the unemployed of the early 1980s, in the same areas of Northern England visited by Orwell. This sectioning off of areas of our lives where pleasure is allowed rein, and a different kind of identity work gets done, has significance for the recognition of prostitution as a consumer industry. However, it also has significance for the regulation of industry as a whole for, as Gramsci (1971: 297) points out, industrialists, and particularly Ford, have been concerned with the sexual conduct of their employees, because 'the new type of man demanded by the rationalisation of production and work cannot be developed until the sexual instinct has been suitably regulated and until it too has been rationalised' (see also Marcuse 1969; Burrell 1984; 1992a). Moreover, despite the fact that our understanding of sexual matters has changed considerably since Gramsci's original comments, as Hawkes (1996) argues, the regulatory constraints and anxieties surrounding sex have shifted in focus rather than lifted. Now it matters not only that we have sex in particular areas of our lives (night, the weekend, at home), but what kind of a consumer of sex one is has also assumed primary significance. Disciplinary control is exercised through the labelling of lifestyle choices rather than via the imposition of socio-cultural mores or workplace regulation (also see Brewis and Grey 1994: 74). In today's disposable society, then, varieties of the sex act not available through 'naturally occurring' relationships may be legitimately (although not necessarily legally) purchased from others – as 'plug-ins' to satisfy specific unassuaged desires within an otherwise stable relationship pattern, or as psychological prostheses for self-identity. Whether the legal framework recognizes it fully or not, and notwithstanding the fact that the encounter with a prostitute might often be made more exciting because it is in other ways illicit (as we pointed out in chapter 7), there is arguably a strong sense among prostitutes' clients that they come *legitimately* to seek pleasure and satisfy needs in their lives through payment for sexual services, to be someone that their everyday relationships do not allow them to be, to be released from diurnal constraints (McKeganey and Barnard 1996: 48–57; O'Connell Davidson 1995a: 6–7; 1996: 190). This is entirely consistent with the historical development of self-identity through consumer consciousness. Clients buy what they need ... face-lift, Armani suit, liposuction, phalloplasty, Porsche, blow-job, a whipping or bondage session ... to enhance their self-esteem in the most appropriate way (Hawkes 1996: 117). The way in which leisure has come to play an important role in modern life, as a deserved respite from work, the positioning of the quest for pleasure as a crucial aspect of this free time, and the transformation of consumption from an activity carried out for sustenance alone into an activity which is seen to afford pleasure are, therefore, all important in the recognition of prostitution as a consumer industry in late Western modernity. As Mancunian masseuse Karen (quoted in *Vice: The Sex Trade*) puts it, her clients are 'coming in basically for a service'.

However, prostitution is also an occupation in which what is produced and simultaneously consumed is the body, or at least its parts. Such occupations, where the worker's person may be seen to actually constitute the service on offer, often threaten to 'consume' them in the process – that is to say, they may pose a threat to self-identity (Roach 1985: 138; Höpfl and Linstead 1993: 86). This, as intimated above, may require the prostitute to engage in the emotional labour necessary to maintain a sense of self-identity distinct from that involved in their business arrangements, given that the body and its sexuality, as O'Connell Davidson points out, are not actually fully commodified, the definition of prostitution as a service industry notwithstanding:

> Prostitutes and clients alike are socialized in a world where particular meanings are attached to human sexuality ... a world in which it is widely held that the only legitimate sex is between men and women who love each other and that 'money can't buy you love'.
>
> (O'Connell Davidson 1995a: 9, 1996: 193–4)

Prostitutes, due to the intensity and intimacy of their physical involvement in their work, do not necessarily find the distancing process easy, and a variety of styles and methods are employed to sustain the mask/s which make earning a living in the sex industry possible. Consequently, our focus here is on the implications of the occupation of prostitute, and the ways in which the body is consumed in this occupation, for individual workers' identities. Moreover, although we discuss the discourses which give shape to sex work in chapters 7 and 9, it is important for our purposes here to note that this commodification of the body as an object for consumption – where the legitimate leisure activity of the client is serviced by the legitimate business activity of the prostitute – has been fully embraced by certain sectors of the sex industry itself. This has produced the 'sex worker' argument wherein prostitutes represent themselves (and are represented by others) as service workers who happen to be selling their sexuality as opposed to other dimensions of their labour power, such as their social skills or their physical strength. Mary, for example, comments that 'I'm a working girl ... I work with my body' (Mary, quoted in O'Neill 1996: 20). O'Connell Davidson (1995a: 1; 1996: 180–1) suggests that this discursive representation of the prostitute is informed by the understanding that they are free to sell their labour to the highest bidder in a mutual exchange, as are other workers under capitalism.[1] It is therefore emphasized by advocates of the sex worker perspective that all prostitutes seek this freedom within their labour process, even those who seem to work in the most dangerous and unpredictable situations. For example, McRae reports how Leila, a streetworker in London's Notting Hill, observes potential clients through their car windows and rejects them if they make her feel uncomfortable, even though this often makes the clients angry (McRae 1992: 242; see also discussion of making the sex contract in McKeganey and Barnard 1996: 31–5). Likewise, Mary, who also has street experience, says that she is careful both to 'suss' her clients out, to try and get inside their heads, but also to keep her distance so that, if a client turns out to be dangerous, she has a chance to get away (Mary, quoted in O'Neill 1996: 20). In understandings of prostitution informed by the sex worker perspective, the line between *sex as leisure activity* (required by clients) and *sex as work* (performed by the prostitute) is easy to draw, but important for individual workers to maintain – primarily because of the ambiguous status of the body as commodity, as described above.[2]

One prevailing conceptualization of prostitution in late Western modernity, then, is that of a consumer service industry. With this in mind, and recalling the fact that it is the body that is sold here, the demands of the client encounter may nonetheless comprise a significant challenge for the prostitute. Some clients may prove rebarbative; worse still, some may turn out to be 'funny', that is to say, violent (Phoenix 1998: 25). Street prostitutes in particular live in the shadow of violence and rape, as is demonstrated by the activities of the Yorkshire Ripper in the early 1980s (Smith 1989) and the more recent murders of seven street-workers in Glasgow (Donegan 1998; Nelson 1998; Rafferty 1998). As London street prostitute Jemma (quoted in *Vice: The Sex Trade*) puts it, 'every single time [you work] your life is in danger'. She herself was abducted and gang-raped by six men who bundled her into a car during a shift. Moreover, escorts are also at risk, and even parlour workers have been threatened and attacked. The situation overall is not helped by the ways in which agents of law enforcement operate as regards prostitution. For instance, in 1991 in Australia, the Supreme Court of Victoria upheld a ruling by Judge Jones in the Victorian County Court that a prostitute, as a result of her work, would be less psychologically damaged by sexual assault than a 'chaste' woman, and used this to justify the imposition of a light sentence for the rape of a prostitute (Scutt 1994). A similar attitude to violence against sex workers is visible in the UK, according to the English Collective of Prostitutes (1997), such that, even at the level of attacks being reported to the police, this is dismissed as 'part of the job'.[3]

With some of the potential rigours of a prostitute's working life established – that it may be terrifying, unpredictable and risky at times – we can now turn to examine the various techniques which prostitutes may (and equally may not) rely on to construct and manage their personal and professional identities, to fulfil the demands of their jobs at least cost to themselves in terms of emotional labour. One of the most important strategies in this regard is the way in which prostitutes label and define different types of sexual encounter. Browne and Minichiello (1995), in a study of male sex workers in Melbourne, identify several categories which parallel reported accounts from females in the industry, but are expressed more systematically. Their respondents differentiate between relational sex, which is reserved for partners and 'being in love' (which female sex workers also display); work sex, which is purely physical and uninvolved, and may involve making the client feel wanted (also a category for female sex workers); and recreational sex, where the worker in their private life needs to be wanted for themselves, although in a relatively impersonal way (for example, anonymous homosexual encounters such as those characteristic of beats or cottages or the bathhouse). Female sex workers do not appear to report this last category as frequently as males, which may be a result of different lifestyles, many of these women being single parents, whereas many male prostitutes only work part-time, having other employment commitments. Nonetheless, this definitional separation of work sex from relational or recreational sex, if it is employed, must be constructed, sustained and reproduced on a daily/nightly basis. In maintaining an appropriate degree of psychological distance from the client encounter, or at least from certain aspects of it, and thus preserving the division between 'work' and the private domain, one technique employed by some prostitutes is the use of drugs.

Maintaining the mask (i): drug use

Drug use appears to play a paradoxical role in prostitution. Soft drugs (caffeine, nicotine, alcohol, valium, amphetamines, marijuana, etc.) are widely used – sometimes to keep the workers awake during long days and nights, often with nothing to do, sometimes to relax them and dull the unpleasantness of the job. Soft drug use may also help sex workers to play the role/s required, to become the product that clients demand and to distance their everyday selves from the work. For instance, Lisa (working name La Toya), a Sydney transsexual prostitute, talks about how her use of soft drugs enables her to keep her work personality separated from her 'real' self:

> I take speed, pills – for the personality change but it keeps you warm as well. Especially on cold nights. It keeps your mouth going. If I was straight I could not do it … When I'm down at work I'm not me, Lisa, any more, I'm La Toya and that's where the drugs come in. You have to put on the attitude that you're that other person. Keep away from reality. When I'm down at work I'm in a totally different world. *At first it was hard, splitting the two apart.*
> (Lisa/La Toya, quoted in Cockington and Marlin, 1995: 94–5; emphasis added)

In contrast, the use of hard drugs seems to be incidental to the pressures that Lisa describes – at least in any causal sense – as most injecting prostitutes take to sex work as a means of funding an already established habit, either their own or that of their partners (European Intervention Projects AIDS Prevention for Prostitutes [EUROPAP] 1994). Nevertheless, all McKeganey and Barnard's (1996) injecting prostitutes suggested that they took a dose before going 'on duty' and that it helped them to cope with the work. These women said, in fact, that they need to do so to numb their awareness of the work they are doing. For example:

> If I've no had a hit, you jus' want it over an' done with. If you've had a hit, you can stand and work nae bother, it doesnae bother you, you know what I mean. But ye see if you're straight, ye start to think about it, then things start flooding back intae your mind and you're sayin' 'I don't want to dae this', you know what I mean.
> (Glasgow streetworker, quoted in McKeganey and Barnard 1996: 91)

However, although Webb and Elms's (1994: 283) Australian drug-dependent respondents also indicated that their drug use made the work more bearable, they also suggested that it compromised their ability to negotiate safe sex with clients. Drug usage in any case is more common among street prostitutes because parlours and brothels usually ban hard drugs; and many will not even tolerate marijuana, pills, even alcohol, especially in the higher class establishments. Inga (quoted in Cockington and Marlin 1995: 172), who admits to having used valium, ecstasy and marijuana in the past, now remains drug-free and clear headed at all times; primarily because she says that she found that 'the straighter I was, the more money I made'. Now working in an upmarket parlour in Melbourne, there is the expectation that she will make conversation with clients, which requires concentration, but also arguably places greater demands on her for the maintenance of the professional mask.

Furthermore, working to finance a habit tends to breed a vicious circle – the more money that is available, the more gets spent on drugs. Consumption here becomes addictive, although users report that they are able to break the habit and reduce their consumption again when they feel it is getting too much, so the addiction may be as much to the consumption as to the substance, depending on their drug of choice. Of course, some users do not make it back from the street, and drug-related murders of prostitutes, usually ones involved in dealing in some way, are not uncommon in all the locations covered by the research reviewed here. Indeed, the seven street prostitutes murdered in Glasgow in the seven years up to and including 1998 were all drug users (Donegan 1998; Nelson 1998; Rafferty 1998).

In this regard, and also recalling that streetworkers in particular face the likelihood of the funny punter *per se*, the need to be aware of personal safety issues, especially in the absence of definite legal recourse or protection, leads some prostitutes to be vehemently anti-drugs:

> Because if you're putting it across to the punters that you're a timorous wee thing, they're gonna treat you like a mug, they will and I think that's the trouble. I don't get much hassle because they can see that I'm straight. I'm *compos mentis* all the time and that and very matter of fact about it, you know, I don't mess about.
>
> (Glasgow streetworker, quoted in McKeganey and Barnard 1996: 33)

Thus the use of drugs by prostitutes is complex – although many may use soft drugs in particular as a way of tolerating the rigours of selling sex for money, they also recognize that this is not without its attendant difficulties. In particular, it may be the case that drug use renders the individual worker less able to take care of themselves in an environment where there is little legal protection of prostitutes. Having judgement unimpaired by substance abuse is critical for the assessment and selection of clients – although this increased effectiveness in terms of being better able to manage encounters is mitigated against by the advantages drug use gives in enabling workers to distance themselves from their labour, as well as in overcoming long periods of inactivity. But how do those who labour as prostitutes make it through their working lives, maintaining an intact sense of self, *without* resorting to the use of drugs? What other distancing strategies are available to them?

Maintaining the mask (ii): bodies, rituals, geography

Prostitutes, as we have seen, may need to erect a psychological barrier between their bodies and those of their clients and one way to do this is by insisting on the use of a condom. In the Australian fieldwork, only one worker, a more mature parlour worker, said she offered unprotected sex, but only to selected clients and at her discretion. A streetworker also offered unsafe sex but only orally, and again at her discretion. All other workers were fastidious, especially the parlour workers, and one streetworker claimed that she always used two condoms. Moreover, although there is some evidence that drug users may offer unprotected sex, and that many clients still demand it, the incidence of HIV positive prostitutes in all three countries in our core context seems generally to be related to the sharing of needles by injectors rather than unsafe sexual activity. Not one case of HIV sero-positivity has been shown to be the result of commercial sex in Australia, and the numbers of the population of sex workers in the country who are HIV positive overall is also relatively small (Harcourt 1994: 205–13; Sharp 1994: 228–35). Moreover, in the Centers for Disease Control and Prevention *HIV/AIDS Surveillance Report* (1994), only 123 of 202, 665 adult and adolescent males diagnosed with AIDS since 1981 suggested that the *sole* risk factor to which they had been exposed was sex with a female prostitute. In the UK, Ward and Day (1997: 141) quote studies from Glasgow (2.5 per cent of female workers found to be HIV positive in 1991), Sheffield (no women found to be infected – 1986–7) and Edinburgh (14 per cent of all prostitutes had the virus in 1988). As they also point out, 'The higher prevalence in Edinburgh reflects the inclusion of male sex workers in the sample and the local epidemic of HIV in injecting drug users.' Their own research, likewise, links HIV infection among sex workers to injecting, or to sex with an infected partner (*not* a client). Ward and Day (1997: 142; see also O'Neill 1997: 16–17) conclude that:

> The various studies in the UK therefore suggest the following general picture in relation to HIV risk: women working as prostitutes report high levels of condom use in commercial sex, but remain at some risk from HIV from injecting drug use and from unprotected sex with non-paying partners. At present [however] these two factors have not led to high levels of HIV infection.[4]

Of course we could argue that the broad insistence by Western prostitutes on clients using condoms is entirely attributable to reducing the likelihood of HIV transmission; but if we take into account Ward and Day's assertion (also made by Maggie O'Neill) that prostitutes very often will not use condoms with their partners (that is, in relational sex), we can perhaps see that the sheath provides more than simply prophylactic reassurance. A Norwegian respondent of Järvinen's (1993: 144, cited in Scambler 1997: 115) backs this up: 'He [the punter] will never be able to reach me, I think to myself. It is like the condom guarantees that he will never touch me.'

Other activities indicated by prostitutes which fall into this category of managing the body include faking penetrative sex ('trick sex' between the well lubricated upper thighs) or faking oral sex using the hand (see, for example, O'Neill 1996: 23). Moreover, workers may follow strict guidelines as to what they are actually willing to do for clients. Self-employed prostitute Desiree, working in the UK's East Midlands, for instance, does not engage in unsafe sex but also will not agree to 'practices which she personally finds too repulsive (like giving enemas), too intimate (like kissing) or too hostile (like ejaculating in her face)' (O'Connell Davidson 1995a: 6; 1996: 186). Hence Desiree has developed a code as to which areas of her body she is prepared to allow her clients access, and which are off limits, so as to protect her sense of herself as a professional prostitute, as selling sex *for money alone* in her working life. Kissing, for example, is rejected because it is too similar to the kind of behaviour in which she would engage with a non-commercial sexual partner, it smacks too much of genuine desire and love for the other person. Trice (1993, cited in Ashforth and Kreiner 1999: 427) argues that this is in fact a common reason given by sex workers for refusing to kiss clients, and it is true that Charlotte (quoted in Salvadori 1997: 118), who works from a flat in London, and Maggie O'Neill's (1996: 23) street-workers offered similar justifications.[5] Scambler, likewise, suggests that, while some prostitutes will perform any service as long as they are paid for it, others' 'own *code of practice*, which typically extends well beyond an insistence on hygiene and condom-use, proscribes sexual (and other) acts outside a pre-defined set of categories' (Scambler 1997: 115). He goes on to cite Gillian, who will not indulge clients wanting to act out baby fantasies because she believes that these men need therapy as opposed to the reinforcement provided by such indulgence (also see Inga, quoted in Cockington and Marlin 1995: 169–187; McKeganey and Barnard 1996: 29–31).

Other strategies for establishing the psychological context of the encounter involve running through preparatory routines (for example, making up and hairstyling in specific ways, or only putting on particular clothes for work which are not worn at other times, or engaging in rituals such as always having a cup of tea before leaving the house for work), through which role-playing becomes automatic. McKeganey and Barnard (1996: 85) see these rituals as entailing 'the detailed preparation of both mind and body' and go on to quote one of their respondents in this regard:

> I keep ma clothes in the wardrobe, they're for ma work and I never wear them apart from that. Anyway I sit there on the sofa and basically I switch off. I have ma cup of tea before I go. I say, 'Right, that's it, that's me'. I go and phone for ma taxi.

These techniques also include the aforementioned sussing out of the client; attracting them, figuring out what they want and are likely to need, and reading their body language to anticipate potential problems, a skill which extends into the encounter (Goodley 1994: 127–8; Browne and Minichiello 1995: 612–13;

McKeganey and Barnard 1996: 34). Workers may also have a range of internal dialogues or techniques for use during the encounter which operate to keep them detached or aroused as the need may arise, to take their minds off unpleasant things, and to help them to leave the work behind when necessary. Charlotte, for example, says that:

> After having sex with punters for a while you get to the stage where you want sex for yourself, a proper private life. That's how I know I can still separate my emotional life and sex work. For example, when I have to do oral, I put on the rubber and close my eyes. But sometimes I open them halfway through and think, 'This is absolutely absurd – I've got some stranger's dick in my mouth.'
>
> (Charlotte, quoted in Salvadori 1997: 122)

In *Vice: The Sex Trade*, streetworker Jemma, masseuse Karen and escort Cat agreed that work sex differs from relational sex and that it is relatively simple to keep the two apart:

> I know how sex feels when you love someone. It is so different from when you just go and lie down with someone and it's a quick sorta like money thing. With customers how can you possibly be intimate?
>
> (Jemma)

> With a client it's not really feelings. You can still enjoy it but there's not actually emotion … at the end of the day you're just having sex and that's it. There's no feelings. Once it's over, it's over, whereas with your boyfriend you'd still be snuggled up, curl up and go to sleep, whereas you wouldn't do that with a client.
>
> (Karen)

> There's absolutely *no* emotion involved at all. Attraction, yeah, but there's no emotion whatsoever.
>
> (Cat)

Phoenix's (1998: 11) MidCity (a pseudonymous UK location) respondents reported, if anything, a more pronounced belief that sex with clients was entirely different from sex in other contexts. Janet suggested that: 'You don't have sex with punters! Fuck no! That's not sex, you don't even think of it as sex. That's money. It's a job.' Jasmine, likewise, told Phoenix that her relations with clients constituted work, not sex, and Ingrid stated that: 'You don't think that's sex with clients. You don't think of that as sex.' Furthermore, Phoenix (1999) suggests that these women tended also to see those prostitutes who have orgasms during sex with clients as lacking in professionalism. Scambler (1997: 115) echoes this in his assertion that intimate relationships between clients and workers, and workers orgasming with clients, are rare and that such accounts are 'normally' regarded

by other prostitutes as 'unprofessional'. This argument, however, has many coun-
terfactuals, as implied in Karen and Cat's comments, and we will discuss this in
more detail below.

The management of geographical place in demarcating public and private
identities in sex work is also relevant here; Desiree, for example, as reported by
O'Connell Davidson (1995a; 1996; O'Connell Davidson and Layder 1994), has
decorated the house from which she works entirely in pink and grey. It is
described as extremely neat and tidy, to the point of seeming sterile and impersonal; indeed, O'Connell Davidson (1995a: 5; 1996: 183) says it has the feel of a
'fashionable private dentist's surgery'. She also notes that Desiree uses separate
linen and towels for her customers from those used in her actual living quarters
(O'Connell Davidson 1995a: 4).

For many of the workers described above, then, their 'real' selves are located
outside of work, removed from encounters with clients (O'Neill 1996: 23) and it
is their distancing practices which allow them to maintain this self-image as
working in prostitution only for the economic rewards which it offers. Moreover,
there are similarities between psychological survival in prostitution and in other
occupations[6] and the function of the distancing practices described above is
reminiscent of that of the humour employed by the male manual workers
studied by Collinson (1988), which consisted of constant references to their own
sexual capacities or to their role as family breadwinner and head of household.
This humour, suggests Collinson, points to a need on the part of these men to
prove themselves to be something more than shopfloor employees, working for
low wages in a tightly controlled and alienating work environment. Indeed, prostitutes also use humour as a method of identity management, for example, Sam
and Mary telling O'Neill that they wind their clients up, 'getting one over' on
them (O'Neill 1996: 22) to seemingly emphasize that they are not simply pieces
of sexual meat, that their intelligence and sarcasm are very much part of who
they are (also see O'Connell Davidson 1995a: 3).

Maintaining the mask (iii): the meaning of work

Prostitutes may also labour to lock their work into a specific and tightly bounded
place in their identities in other ways. An instance of this is the fact that Desiree
does not select or reject clients on the basis of any particular attraction to or
repulsion from them. While allowing her to make a good living from prostitution, this can also be seen as ensuring that she does not feel herself to be 'merely
indulging a personal taste for anonymous sexual encounters involving the
exchange of cash' (O'Connell Davidson 1995a: 9; 1996: 193). Her acceptance of
any kind of client, as long as they will play by her rules (some of which we have
already seen), therefore perhaps also functions as part of her attempt to keep
work and non-work distinct. This management of the symbolic location of
commercial sex as reported by other workers also includes treating clients very
differently from non-commercial sexual partners (for example, using a
pseudonym with and never disclosing personal information to clients). Others

report stealing from clients ('rolling' or 'skanking'), or taking their money and then refusing to service them on the grounds of having begun to menstruate (O'Neill 1996: 23).

Prostitutes may also emphasize the multi-faceted nature of their lives in, it might be argued, a similar effort to compartmentalize their work. Here they appear to be rejecting society's attempts to label their occupation as their 'master status' (Becker 1973) – refusing to accept that prostitution must by definition assume the most significant place in their lives. For example, Maggie O'Neill (1996: 22) reports that Sam and Mary

> talked about the many different roles they play, mothers, their lives in the black community; visiting their own families, working class employed and extended families; and going out with clients 'dressed up to the nines' and then doing 'feminism' by supporting other women working as prostitutes.

She goes on to report the activities of feminist prostitutes at the First European Whores' Congress, held in Frankfurt in 1991 (O'Neill 1996: 22; see also O'Neill 1997: 27), as well as an anecdote from Moira, who argues 'who better to educate the clients but the prostitute?' (Moira, quoted in O'Neill 1996: 21). Here Moira tells of a client who demanded oral sex without a condom. Moira refused him, also stating that the other girls in her area would do the same. In the end the client returned to her – some two hours later – and agreed to her terms. Moira says that she made sure that 'everybody' heard her when, upon his return, she reiterated her insistence on the use of a condom and implies here that her work is not just about satisfying the pent-up sexual desires of lonely or frustrated men, but is also a matter of social responsibility. Here she lends herself legitimacy by characterizing her work as potentially educational, at least in part. The following self-description of Sara Dale as a 'sex therapist' might also be seen as evidence of this attitude on the part of prostitutes. Dale (quoted in McRae 1992: 110) states emphatically that:

> it hurts when [the media] call me 'tart' for it cheapens the work and it hurts my children. But [my family] realize that people are going to call me all sorts of names, that there might well be some kind of vendetta against us – but I *know* that my work is healing, whatever they might say.[7]

Furthermore, prostitutes may also demand that they are granted the same rights as others both in performing the work that they do and in other walks of life – that they should, for instance, enjoy the same degree of police protection as the rest of the population.[8] As Australian prostitute Sara says:

> Whether you're a worker or not, whether it's an older worker or a new one, you have the right to go to the police, just like any other male or female in this world whether you are a prostitute or not. It's not fair the way a lot of

girls get treated like dirt. They get pushed over. They are not there to be used and abused. They are there to do a job.

(Sara, quoted in Webb and Elms 1994: 275)

In a similar vein, Carol Leigh refutes the perception that a prostitute cannot really be raped – the idea, as we have already seen in a particular court judgement, they somehow will be less likely to experience forced sex as traumatic because they sell their bodies for others to use. This follows an account of her work at a massage parlour, which resulted in her rape at knifepoint by two men who had forced their way inside the premises. As she argues, this was traumatic because she feared she was going to be killed or seriously hurt – not because she didn't get paid for sex in this particular instance (Leigh 1994: 247–9).[9]

The client body: typologies

It seems, then, that prostitutes may rely on a variety of distancing techniques – drugs, managing geographical place or their bodies, particular rituals, etc. – to secure their sense of themselves as only offering sex to punters for money. However, different logics with regard to the need to maintain strict boundaries between private and public selves may be applied with different types of client; and again, as with definitions of the sex act, these appear very similar for prostitutes of both sexes. Browne and Minichiello (1995) report that the service provided, and the workers' attitude towards the client, depends at least partly on the categorization of that client into a specific type. For example, 'marrieds' look for something their wives can't give them, tending to expect discretion and very little beyond the act of sex itself. 'Easy trade' are clean, gentlemanly, come quickly or only want non-penetrative sex, pay and go. In contra-distinction, workers would prefer not to service 'undesirables', violent, dirty or obese types, and/or those who try to break safe sex rules. Distancing, therefore, is arguably more necessary with undesirables than it is with marrieds or easy trade clients.

These categories of punter also, for both male and female sex workers, include 'romantics':

It's worse when you get a client who actually falls in love with you, which is really hard. The Golden Rule of the sex industry is don't fall in love with a client … it's just too hard emotionally … They always want you to get out of the industry and it just makes it too hard.

(male prostitute, Melbourne, quoted in Browne and Minichiello 1995: 609)

Oh I hate that, really that is ma hate, when they try and get all lovey dovey. I mean any guy that tries to get lovey dovey with a prostitute is off his head … I mean I've had one guy in a big fight … I stopped having him because it was just a nightmare, he was going 'I love you, I love making love to you …'

you don't fall in love with prostitutes and this guy was, I mean, I broke this guy's heart.

(Glasgow streetworker, quoted in McKeganey and Barnard 1996: 89–90)

'Sugar daddies' may also turn out to be difficult clients, being older than the workers and therefore having little in common with them, and often proving unreliable financially. 'Heaven trade' – clients whom the worker finds irresistibly attractive – can also prove problematic, as here most of all prostitutes may be tempted to cross the divide between work and personal life, or to allow unsafe sex. However, they may also guard against this temptation by remembering that 'It's never going to happen because the clients see you as a worker. That is all you are to them. They don't want to make a boyfriend out of a worker' (male prostitute, Melbourne, quoted in Browne and Minichiello 1995: 611).

It is therefore problematic to claim that every prostitute will necessarily seek to establish a strict boundary between work and non-work with every client – encounters are influenced not least by the category in which the prostitute places individual punters. There is also evidence that some prostitutes generally enjoy their work and derive sexual pleasure from it.[10] Greta is an example; 'she practised prostitution which was not so much "post-Big Bang modernism" than [*sic*] "pre-Crash revelry", the Wall Street Crash of 1929 … For Greta, pleasure and prostitution were not mutually exclusive entities' (McRae 1992: 254–5). Greta apparently likes clients to have a drink and a chat before sex and reacts in disgust to McRae's stories of other prostitutes specializing in sadomasochism, because she cannot see where pleasure for the worker might lie in such activities.[11] Her home, where she entertains clients, is described as

> a domain where it appeared that it was 1927 forevermore … with gramophones, Bix Beiderbecke records, cut-glass bowls, feather-boas, silk curtains and photographs of Lilian Gish, Louise Brooks, Scott and Zelda Fitzgerald, Noel Coward, Josephine Baker, Anna Akhmatova and the definitive Garbos.
>
> (McRae 1992: 255)

Her management of place demonstrates how different Greta is from prostitutes like Desiree, who places a great deal of emphasis on having a sterile and businesslike working environment. It is a quirk of Greta's that McRae himself notes. However, what is also significant about Greta is that she is a post-operative transsexual who sets a great deal of store by her surgically acquired femininity. Indeed, Brewis *et al.* (1997a) suggest that the transsexual is frequently driven by a sensed biological imperative to physically become the other sex. Their activities often therefore reinforce the discursive rigidity of the gender divide – by surgical alteration of their bodies, they seek to become another sex, and thereby another gender. A confirmed and stable gender identity, then, is crucial to the psychological health of many transsexuals and we could argue that Greta enjoys her work for the pleasure it affords *because this fits her image of what a woman should be like*.

Nonetheless, there is also evidence from non-transsexual prostitutes that real desire and real love might be present within the prostitute–client encounter, not least two members of the profession interviewed as part of our Australian field-work. Katrina said that she did the job because she enjoyed it and that most of the clients she met were really pleasant. She enjoyed the sex, she said, enjoyed having orgasms, enjoyed dressing up and 'developing new talents' (those already described in chapter 7), and enjoyed the conversation. Taylor said she'd been 'really lucky' and liked all her regular clients; indeed, she had even dated one of them and felt she was on the point of falling in love with him (that is, he represented heaven trade). Further, high class Melbourne brothel worker Kelly said, in response to a question from interviewer Tottie Goldsmith on the Australian television programme *Sex/Life* as to whether she ever gets bored at work:

> Ohhh ... [laughs] ... I'd be lying if I said yes ... honestly ... I sort of like ... in my bookings ... I sort of like to put my whole effort into it ... but there is [*sic*] days when you think to yourself ... oh God, do I really have to do this?

[*TG*]: Do you ever orgasm when you're having sex with clients?

> Oh yes ... [emphatically]

> How many a day?

> It can depend on the clientele that come in ... if you get someone that you really get into it with you can actually really [nods head emphatically] enjoy it.

Similarly, McKeganey and Barnard were told of the content of a discussion between two working girls on this subject:

> she says to me, 'Do you ever enjoy it when you go wi' a punter?' I says 'No!' And I went 'I hate them,' and she went 'Oh I do.' I says, 'How do you?' an' she says 'Like do you ever come when you're wi' a punter?' 'cos she does all the time. She says, 'How do you turn yerself off?' I says 'Quite fuckin' easy, look the other way and think o' the money, ye know what I mean.'
>
> (Glasgow streetworker, quoted in McKeganey and Barnard 1996: 86)

Finally, and interestingly in the light of the above discussion, Maryann comments that:

> One of the things I realized was that those orgasms [with clients] were mine. They didn't belong to anybody else ... It had nothing to do with who I was with; it wasn't about me being so turned on by this guy instead of that one. It was about me. It really challenged the idea that orgasms are something a man 'gives' you.
>
> (Maryann, in Chapkis 1997: 85)

So Maryann here actually uses her at-work orgasms to *draw the boundary* between self and role, self and other, body and soul, as a means of maintaining her self-integrity and bodily autonomy.

Moreover, when the worker (like some but not all of those sex workers described in the foregoing discussion) wants to maintain a divide between work and private lives, and despite the variety of techniques available, this is always permeable. Maintaining the mask that preserves self-identity is not necessarily an easy matter for sex workers.

Work versus leisure in prostitution

In this regard, Jane states quite explicitly that a prostitute's life becomes part of her work, rather than the other way around, because of the demands of 'being used' by others for money (O'Neill 1996: 20). Mary suggests a similar problem in separating work from non-work – that a prostitute is never, strictly speaking, off duty, because everything is subsumed by the need to make money. She argues that a prostitute may end up working even if they are officially 'off' because of this:

> You give everything of your life into prostitution ... that is all that is around you all the time ... on [the] street the car stops 'are you doing business?' you tell them the price ... and you get in and go ...
>
> (Mary, quoted in O'Neill 1996: 19)

Jane also comments that it is difficult for her and her co-workers to tell others what they do for a living, and that, as a result, prostitution consists of a 'closed circuit' (O'Neill 1996: 21) where other prostitutes become the friends with whom one socializes. O'Connell Davidson (1994c: 17), similarly, says that Desiree 'has very little contact with her family, who do not know what she does for a living, no social life outside her business and requires constant emotional support and reassurance from her receptionists'. Inga (quoted in Cockington and Marlin 1995: 172) adds that prostitutes are her only friends, indeed, that she tends to avoid socializing outside of the industry so as to avoid questions about what she does for a living. Trice (1993, cited in Ashforth and Kreiner 1999: 420) suggests that this is a general tendency among work groups who feel distanced from society – it is certainly true, for example, of Ackroyd and Crowdy's (1990) slaughtermen. Here, however, as we have seen in chapter 4, workers make no apparent effort to disguise or compartmentalize what they do for a living. Indeed, their display of pride in the stigmatized elements of the occupation is an important part of their collective identity work. This tactic is adopted by prostitutes as well – by political activists like Annie Sprinkle or Carol Leigh – but, as we have already suggested, one could suggest that the bourgeois Western consciousness finds it easier to publicly accept the necessity of killing animals for sustenance than it does the open hiring of women's bodies for pleasure.

It is also true that the spillover of work into personal life is perhaps most evident in the prostitute's own sex life. Indeed, the most evocative evidence of the distance that many female prostitutes attempt to put between themselves and the work that they do is their identification as lesbian in their personal lives. Thus sex with men does not intrude into their identities as private individuals – it belongs to their working identities only. An interview with four young prostitutes in the North of England revealed that two of the women had become sexually involved with each other as a direct result of their work. Moreover, all four had entered the sex industry because of a lack of real alternatives for supporting themselves financially – they reported disadvantaged home lives, educational underachievement and a depressed labour market in their home town. Thus, although they had become prostitutes of their own volition, it is questionable as to how far this *was* a free choice (echoing our earlier allusions to consensual versus forced prostitution). Probably as a consequence of the circumstances of their entry into prostitution, the girls found their work disgusting and degrading, and harboured feelings of contempt for their male clients. This contempt had crossed over into the private lives of two of these girls so that they had apparently sought sexual 'solace' in becoming lesbians, even though both had heterosexual 'pasts' (source unknown).

Moreover, Jane extends her comment that prostitution means being used for money into a suggestion that the emotional labour required makes even her non-commercial sexual activities somewhat 'cold': 'you come home from work and your man wants to be kept happy and you've been at work all day pretending and you can't be bothered and sometimes you have to pretend with your man' (Jane, quoted in O'Neill 1996: 20). Jackie, likewise, says that she and her partner Tyrone rarely if ever have sex – the heroin to which he is addicted often extinguishes any desire on his part, and she is also quite literally 'fucked, forty times over … I miss it sometimes, you know, fucking for love, fucking 'cos it's what *I want*' (Jackie, quoted in McRae 1992: 146). Inga reports that her work also places pressure on her relationship with her partner Steve. He is jealous of her male clients, even though for her sex with them is 'just a job', and it is, she says, often difficult for her to have sex with Steve in any case because (a) working as a prostitute means that she transfers her feelings of hatred for her male clients to him; and/or (b) she, like Jackie, is usually so tired that all she wants is a 'cuddle' (Inga, quoted in Cockington and Marlin 1995: 186). Sheena tries to cope with the difference between punters and intimates by 'switching off' the 'wee switch I've got in ma head' (Sheena, quoted in McKeganey and Barnard 1996: 84), and others engage in rituals of separation when returning home after work – changing clothes, bathing/showering, or sitting quietly, all in order to shed the self that has been carefully constructed for work. Yet even so they have difficulty coping with what they have done – and for some even drugs are no help:

It doesnae matter how much you take or what you take, you've still got to wake up in the morning and go 'I done that, I went out and done that'.

Nothing's going to stop you waking up next day and knowing what you done last night.

(Glasgow streetworker, quoted in McKeganey and Barnard 1996: 92)

Conclusion

Our comparative review of data has enabled discussion of the management of identity by UK, US and Australian prostitutes, given that the consumption of their bodies in the process of commercial sex can be seen to place pressure on their sense of themselves both professionally and personally, as well as their occupation also being potentially boring and risky. We have established that, while there is a degree of similarity between the tactics and approaches employed by prostitutes in terms of maintaining the professional mask/s and distancing their work from their personal lives, there are also significant differences depending on individual circumstances and a concomitant need for caution in the study of prostitution, given that workers do not necessarily, in every encounter, or even more generally, want or need to maintain these strict divides. Moreover, it is clear from our analysis that the boundary between work sex and relational sex is not easy to maintain, even for those workers who undertake this labour of demarcation.

The management of identity in prostitution, then, frequently points to a seeming need on the part of the prostitute to maintain boundaries between their commercial and non-commercial lives, and sexual activities especially. This has, like all social constructions, to be accomplished and is done so through a variety of means. Moreover, it cannot be said to be uniform. Control/distancing and enjoyment are two contrasting aspects of everyday life in the sex industry and the patterns and tensions which emerge between them vary according to time, place, mood and the interactants. Prostitutes may need to try to fill their day with some kind of meaningful activity between business encounters, yet when they are within the encounter itself they may also need to empty it of any meaning. On re-entering their 'normal' lives, sex workers also often report needing to ritually shed the events of the working day/night, to rid themselves of the personae they earlier assumed to get them through their shift. On the other hand, some workers do not perceive the psychological divide between work and the private domain to be important or necessary, and the varying ways in which prostitutes understand the work that they do, and in which they seek to represent this to themselves and to others, points to the variety of discourses employed to define themselves and their clients. We will expand on this issue in chapter 9 because it is partly through the more or less powerful operations of these various discourses that individual prostitutes understand and experience their work, and (re-)construct the selves who do it.

9 Context and career in sex work

Introduction

Following from our analysis in chapter 8, in this chapter we suggest that the ways in which individual prostitutes understand themselves, the work that they do and their relationships with clients, and thus construct and manage their identities, are at least partly informed by the discursive context of their labour. Attitudes towards sexuality, work, leisure, etc. may delimit or enable the possibilities that sex workers have for establishing and developing themselves as subjects. Here we discuss the range and variety of discourses which currently shape and organize prostitution in the modern West, extending themes we initially raised in chapter 7, and establish the different ways in which individual sex workers may engage with these discourses to make sense of their life-world, for example, whether they understand themselves as victims of patriarchy or as feminist activists. Here, our focus moves from the identity work which surrounds the client encounter to the prostitute's career more generally, and issues of entrance to and exit from this occupational field are discussed, as well as that of continuing life within the occupation itself. Where in chapter 8 we explored the process of the negotiation and construction of identity within and around the commercial sex transaction, concentrating on the interactional features of identity construction, then, in this chapter we focus on the discourses which shape this process. In chapter 10 we will move on to consider material contextual effects, so as to round out our analysis of the double effect of placing, and to establish the key point that the sex industry, as a result, exhibits much of the variety in organizational structure and job content that other industries display, demanding a variety of skills of the woman who expects to make prostitution a successful career. These may include marketing, accounting, business planning, property management, financial control, promotion, entrepreneurship, knowledge of the law, political skills, education, acting, counselling and human resource management, even without considering those more specific *ars erotica* upon which the profession is founded. Differences in legal and cultural frameworks, policing practices, political pressures and social and cultural institutions (for example, education and health) provide a highly specific local context for the organization of sex work, and ultimately govern whether it becomes recognizable as an industry or not. Labour markets, economic forces and the development of horizontally segmented and vertically stratified markets further produce an array of different possibilities for establishing and cementing professional identities.

Moreover, as we also argued in chapter 8, the movement from the traditional belief that identity turns on what one does or makes towards a locating of identity in the process and artefacts of consumption renders sex work an increasingly important site for the understanding of contemporary self-identity. Here areas traditionally (p)reserved as private, such as the body, are commercially traded and consumed as the boundary with the public sphere is rendered permeable. To what degree this boundary dissolves, and to what degree it is sustained, however leakily, for individual prostitutes is also to some extent dependent on the prevailing discourses which surround these sites of social interaction. We have already discussed the 'sex worker' discourse in terms of its effects on individual workers, arguing that this account of what prostitutes and clients are and do has been mirrored by the sex industry itself, with prostitutes being presented, and some presenting themselves, as business people legitimately servicing a social need and, as such, proud of their skills, knowledge, professionalism and altruism. We now extend and develop this argument in, first, addressing discourses which position prostitutes as more or less feminist in their activities; second, dealing with the discursive continuum between prostitutes as a disease-ridden social menace and prostitutes as educators, counsellors and social workers; and, third, considering the discourses surrounding prostitution as a career. The key points which emerge from all three sections of the discussion are that (a) there is little agreement on these issues; and (b) the competing understandings of prostitution are reflected in and constituted by accounts from prostitutes themselves – that is, as we have already said, they form part of the discursive context of the profession.[1]

Victims or feminists?

Certain commentators have suggested that prostitution is always and already more than sex work; that is to say, the labour of a prostitute is qualitatively different from that of other workers. Even 'conventional' occupations requiring emotional labour (Hochschild 1983) are seen here as much less demanding than prostitution. The prostitute is understood, as we have already implied might be the case in chapter 8, to be far more a part of the 'product' that is consumed, which therefore leads to her 'self' being consumed along with her services. Perhaps the most notable contributor to this position is Pateman (1988), who takes issue with the sex worker perspective on two fronts. First, she contends that 'labour power', the possession of particular skills, capacities and attributes that individuals are free to sell to employers as if they could be separated from the body of that individual, is a 'political fiction' because employers gain 'the right of command over the use of the worker's labour, that is to say, over the self, person and body of the worker during the period set down in the employment contract' (Pateman 1988: 203). Likewise, in prostitution, the punter gains control over the prostitute's 'person and body' as opposed to simply buying her sexual services. However, Pateman's second and perhaps more significant point is that the *prostitute* is involved in the contract with the *punter* in a different way from the way in which '*ordinary*' workers are involved with their *employers*. She argues that, although the employer gains access to their employees' 'persons' during the working day, they are not as interested in this aspect of the contract as they are in the commodities that the worker produces and the resultant profit. Punters, on the other hand, have 'only one interest; the prostitute and her body' (Pateman 1988: 203). In this regard, Pateman (1988: 207) cites McLeod's (1982) work with clients in Birmingham, and their complaints about prostitutes being cold and mercenary, in support of her case that there is more to prostitution than selling sex. For her, prostitution at its core involves the patriarchal affirmation of masculinity. Pateman (1988: 205–6) also sees prostitution as different even from other occupations in which bodies are bought and sold (for example, sport) in the sense that the prostitute is paid for direct sexual use of her body, as opposed to the right of command over how she uses it (as professional sportsmen and women are in terms of their training, diet regimes and coaching). Finally, Pateman (1988: 207) makes the point that sexuality and self are intimately connected, so that 'when a prostitute contracts out use of her body, she is thus selling *herself* in a very real sense'.

There is also evidence that some prostitutes understand their occupation in the way implied by Pateman – that they feel they quite literally sell their selves when they contract with clients. Inga, for example, says 'Personally it's mentally destroyed me. I've had nervous breakdowns. I've had an overdose. I've been that depressed I wouldn't go out anywhere. I didn't want to live any more … I've cut my wrists and stuff like that' (Inga, cited in Cockington and Marlin 1995: 169) and 'It mucks people's brains up totally. It's mucked my brain up totally … *The worst thing is the screwing. The screwing of my mind and body*' (Inga, cited in Cockington and Marlin 1995: 183–4; emphasis added). Lois's account is even more emphatic in this regard in that she, as Phoenix points out, differentiates herself from those prostitutes with particular skills (for example, bondage and domination – B&D – specialists)[2] and those who offer 'time and companionship' (for example, high class brothel workers such as, ironically, Inga):

> It hit me when I was 19 that I was actually a prostitute, I didn't really think about it before – it was just work. But then it hit me. I was actually selling myself. I was just a hole. I was nothing more than a body men paid to fuck.[3]
>
> (Phoenix 1998: 11–12)

Sammy, likewise, says that 'In the end you hate yourself for selling your body. They do what they want to you. Your body's an object and you've got no control over it' (Phoenix 1998: 13). Echoing Sammy and Lois's construction of prostitution as something which men 'do' to women, in which women become no more than a commodity, Fiona Broadfoot, speaking to those attending the John School in Leeds, points out that she was fifteen when she entered prostitution. She was forced to do so by her boyfriend who was a pimp, and was so frightened of him she felt she had no choice other than to acquiesce. Moreover, after a brutal rape by a punter, Fiona's pimp cleaned her up and sent her back to the streets, explaining that if she did not return immediately she probably never would (Mills 1999: 33).[4]

Pateman, then, we have seen, refutes the liberalist sex worker perspective, suggesting that other forms of labour power are not inextricable from self-identity in the same way that sexuality is, that selling other forms of labour power does not involve the direct use of one person's body by another, nor such an overt 'acknowledgement of patriarchal right' (Pateman 1988: 208).[5] This representation of prostitutes, often supported by their own accounts as is visible above, frequently centres on the active steps that prostitutes take to distance themselves (/their selves) from the work that they do, as discussed in chapter 8, and acknowledged by Pateman (1988: 207) who argues 'the integral connection between sexuality and sense of self means that, for self-protection, a prostitute must distance herself from her sexual use'. Moreover, as we also argued in chapter 8, distancing may take many forms and is also is more or less difficult, more or less effective and more or less possible depending on the individual circumstances of the prostitute.

In her own critique of the 'sex worker' perspective, O'Connell Davidson (1995a: 8) argues, in a similar vein to Pateman, that the emotional labour of a prostitute is more intense than that required in even the most demanding of non-sexual service jobs, and that the prostitute therefore usually works very long hours.[6] O'Connell Davidson suggests that this last allows her to earn an income that makes the work 'tolerable'. Moreover, again as stated in chapter 8, in the West at least the prostitute is selling something – their body – which is not conventionally seen as a commodity. Therefore they dishonour themselves in the eyes of society – and O'Connell Davidson (1995a: 9, 1996: 194) suggests that the monetary rewards, even if 'substantial', do not actually buy an 'escape' from this 'stigma'. Both Pateman and O'Connell Davidson therefore make a case for prostitution being different from other forms of wage labour, and seek to undermine the power of the sex worker argument. In contra-distinction, Gherardi turns the sex worker argument on its head, suggesting that 'conventional' service jobs are much more like prostitution in its true sense (the literal selling of sex) than the actual work of a prostitute in reality (which sometimes involves no conventionally defined sexual acts at all):[7]

> Sexual skills … are acquired and incorporated into the organizational role. The organization acquires command over the sexuality of its employees, within certain limits. Women with jobs that require, implicitly or explicitly, an attractive appearance – hostesses, saleswomen, receptionists, secretaries – are duty-bound to be agreeable or seductive, and must be or pretend to be 'sexy' in their dealings with the public.
>
> (Gherardi 1995: 43)

Gherardi suggests that the demands of the mainstream service job are often sexualized – for her, women in particular may well be forced to prostitute themselves in a very real sense in order to satisfy employers or clients.[8] Here she echoes Pateman in her claim that there is no such thing as merely selling one's disembodied labour power, in prostitution or elsewhere. However, Gherardi's argument manages to avoid the naïve generalizations of the sex worker argument, while also sidestepping the trap laid by insisting, as Pateman and, to a lesser extent, O'Connell Davidson do, that prostitution always and already poses more of a risk to the worker's self-identity than (almost) any other occupation.

Moreover, there is not necessarily a clear divide between feminists who see prostitutes as freely labouring in the occupation of their choice and those who see them as instruments or victims of patriarchy – the discursive picture is a good deal more complex than this. Helpfully, Sullivan (1994) gives a lucid summary of pro- and anti-prostitution arguments within feminism, including the stance that marriage and prostitution are both forms of the patriarchal enslavement of women (also see McIntosh 1994). Tabet (1991, cited in Sullivan 1994: 265), for example, argues that there is 'a continuum of forms of sexual service, not a dichotomy between marriage and the other relations implying sexual–economic exchange', although different forms of sexual slavery, as Pateman asserts, achieve the same objective. Agreeing that prostitution is an outgrowth of patriarchy, Shrage (1989), Overall (1992) and Pheterson (1996) nevertheless emphasize that it 'makes sense to defend prostitutes' entitlement to do their work but not to defend prostitution itself as a practice under patriarchy' (Overall, cited in Sullivan 1994: 266). However, Sullivan, echoing Grosz (1994), points out that this stance has its weaknesses – simply that there are no pure positions outside patriarchy and phallocentrism or, so we would argue, free of social or psychological repression. One cannot escape complicity because all struggles are bound up with what they struggle against, and are thus inherently impure (Grosz 1994; see also Foucault 1982). Not all struggles are equal – some challenge the dominant paradigm, some stretch and bend as opposed to subverting it, others are content with the status quo. Again, with Foucault, we would argue that this can only be determined by a close examination of the micropractices which constitute 'prostitution' in specific and located forms, as a field of power/knowledge.

There are also important disagreements between feminists who are sympathetic to prostitutes. Perkins, on the one hand, views sex work as inherently empowering, arguing that 'female prostitution is a social situation in which women have more power over sexual interactions than in any other circumstance involving both sexes interacting' (Perkins 1991: 389). For Perkins, because

> prostitutes can set limits on the work they do, can acquire economic power and a knowledge of 'true' male sexuality, they are a far cry from the common feminist assumption of prostitutes as the most explicit example of female oppression.
>
> (Perkins cited in Sullivan 1994: 267)

Again this construction of prostitution is reflected in accounts from workers themselves. We have already made reference to the 1986 study by Diane Prince (cited by the *Prostitutes' Education Network*) which found that call girls and brothel workers had developed higher self-esteem as a result of entering the sex industry; 97 per cent of call girls liked themselves 'more than before'. An anonymous contributor to *SIN* (South Australia Sex Industry Network) magazine supports this: 'I like being a sex worker because I am a feminist and as a feminist I am working in a profession that is empowering and is a celebration of my woman- hood in a way that no other profession is.' Barbara, in the UK, comes at the issue from the other side, stating that:

> It makes me furious when [prostitute] women are portrayed as walking, downtrodden victims ... Why are girls always portrayed the way they are in the media? We are portrayed as women who stand on street corners, who wear microscopic miniskirts, who are foul-mouthed junkies, who are violent, with severe psychiatric disorders, and who were abused as kids.
>
> (Barbara, quoted in Scambler 1997: 105)

Rachel Collins also attacks the depiction of prostitutes as 'victims with pimps with no power over our own lives'. She states, in contra-distinction, that 'I know I have the intelligence and ability to take up any profession I put my mind to and I have chosen to be a prostitute' (Collins 1998). Moreover, Perkins' work was based on a sample of sex workers in Sydney which demonstrated them to be very similar to other more 'conventionally' employed women in terms of defining themselves as engaged in work that is empowering, or in work which is a form of political activism. However, this study has been criticized for taking as its sample a group of higher-class workers and ignoring the dangers faced by lower- class workers (for an illustration see Inga's account in Cockington and Marlin 1995, and our discussion of employment stratification and mutual support in chapter 10). Sullivan (1994: 267–8) does, nonetheless, recognize the merits of both arguments, suggesting that prostitution is not 'inherently empowering' but that feminists should not therefore 'condemn female prostitutes' or the sex industry for failing to conquer patriarchy. She suggests that feminist accounts of prostitution need to respect what prostitutes do while also focusing on 'gendered structures of power in *all* work and personal relations' (emphasis added). Thus she extends Shrage, Overall and Pheterson's arguments without singling out prostitution as an exemplar of patriarchy, and also avoids the assumption that what exists beyond patriarchy is somehow free from the 'taint' of power.

With the above discussion in mind, it seems reasonable to suggest that it is difficult to represent prostitution as either entirely like, or as entirely unlike, other forms of wage labour. Like the prostitute herself, the category of sex work is a liminal one, existing, as O'Connell Davidson (1995a: 9; 1996: 194) puts it, 'in a space between two worlds, incompletely dominated by the ideology of the free market and yet detached from pre-market values and codes [shame, dishonour etc.]'. Thus the identity work on the part of the prostitute is both like and unlike the strategies employed by the alienated worker to allow them to 'make it through' the rigours of the working day without too many consequences for their sense of themselves as we suggested in chapter 8. However, it is also clear that the ways in which prostitutes seek to manage their identities in line with the work that they do may vary depending on the extent to which they see their work as oppressive and degrading, or on the other hand as empowering and/or as feminism/political activism.

Another possible discursive representation of prostitution is of these workers as sexual educators, counsellors or therapists, which again is supported in some measure by accounts offered by prostitutes themselves. We seek in the next section to compare this positioning of prostitution, as more or less an extension of the fields of social work, health care and education, to the more conventional folk-devil depiction of prostitutes as the disease-ridden scourge of society (Harcourt 1994). At this point it is perhaps incumbent upon us to remind the reader that we deal here with data from our core context specifically, and that data from elsewhere suggest that prostitutes in other locations, as a result of their social and educational position and working conditions, may genuinely be a risk to clients' health as opposed to being able to educate or counsel them (Centers for Disease Control and Prevention 1994; Reuters 1994; see also chapter 8, note 4).

Social problem or sexual educators?

> I really like that I am very skilled and professional at what I do and that clients acknowledge this and are grateful for it ... I like being a sex worker because the sex worker community brought the safe sex message into the general heterosexual community. I am a sex educator and proud of it. I show my clients how to have sex as safely as possible, no matter what type of sex they engage in.
>
> (Anonymous contributor to *SLN* magazine)

> In April 1992 the King's Cross police were reported in the press alleging that ... 'of the 50 hard-core regulars who work the streets around the station ... three out of four have the virus [HIV]' ... When we asked for the source of such 'information' they told us it came from a police survey. A copy of it revealed that it asked no question about either HIV or AIDS ... The police have never apologized for or corrected their scaremongering disinformation.
>
> (English Collective of Prostitutes [ECP] 1997: 96)

Historically, prostitutes have been depicted as among the major sources and disseminators of sexually transmitted diseases. For example, in 1864, at the beginning of its efforts to implement legislation controlling prostitution, the Buenos Aires Municipality suggested that 'as it exists today prostitution enervates, sterilizes and even destroys ... all classes of society' (Buenos Aires Municipality, cited in Guy 1995: 48). Hershatter (1997: 226–41), similarly, discusses representations of prostitutes as 'a deadly conduit of disease' (p. 226) in late nineteenth- and twentieth-century Shanghai. Indeed, legislation concerning venereal disease more generally at this point in history focused on 'inspecting prostitutes, denying them liberty if they were thought to be infected' (Ward and Day 1997: 142–3). Moreover, the ECP quote above and current practices such as compulsory health checks for registered prostitutes in Germany, Austria and Greece (Ward and Day 1997: 143; EUROPAP 1994; European Network for HIV/STD Prevention in Prostitution) imply that this depiction is still pervasive, although, in the West at least, there is certainly little substance to it. Our review of the research in fact suggests that workers in the sex industry in this part of the world tend to see safe sex with clients as *de rigueur*, as our discussion in chapter 8 demonstrates; and Western prostitutes have also often played an active role in getting the safe sex message across to the wider community, not just to clients, but by campaigning publicly for safe sex practices. Support for sex industry workers through the health care framework has also increased dramatically, and the community works hard to educate its members (Van Beek 1994; McKeganey and Barnard 1996; O'Neill 1997: 16–17).[9]

Furthermore, sex workers are compared to social workers by Webb and Elms (1994: 175), who argue that education and counselling are a significant part of the services that both groups must provide, and that they need many similar skills. Our earlier references to what is provided by prostitutes above and beyond sex – as evoked by workers themselves, such as Sara Dale's insistence that her work is 'healing' and Moira's pride in educating a client regarding the use of condoms – are also relevant here, as is Sarah's comment that 'Prostitution is giving yourself and your attention to someone for a period of time ... You're offering more than just a body: you're offering an experience which usually they remember quite well' (Sarah, quoted in Scambler 1997: 114). Bella Lamou, a self-identified sex healer, who has also worked as a hostess, call girl, glamour model and acted in pornographic films, says in a similar vein that Western civilization has 'taken [its] toll on our sexuality', and that we are now fearful of using its full potential. She points to sex workers' capacity to heal 'single, shy, lonely people' and says that this ought to be respected by society. Bella also writes that she doesn't 'suck' or 'fuck' but instead works with the body 'integrated with the mind and, most importantly, inner self' (*Consenting Adults* 1997/8). Rachel Collins (1997), likewise, states that prostitutes are needed by society for 'lots of reasons; not just the despunking of men'. These include, she says, teaching men about their own bodies and those of women, and providing physical contact and comfort. Rachel also specifically reports that she gets great satisfaction from serving disadvantaged social groups:

> His helper brought him up to the flat I was working in and helped me to communicate with him using a letter board and a pointer stick attached to his head. He used to shake violently on the bed when he was unstrapped from his wheelchair but after he had come all his muscles would relax and he was content and happy cuddling into my bosom ... imagine what it is like for a man or a woman who not only can't get sex but also can't even have a

wank because their arms and hands don't work properly. What a frustrating nightmare!!

(discussing a former client of hers who was paraplegic – Collins n.d.)

Inga feels the same way:

I've seen guys with no arms or legs which a lot of girls would go 'Ugh' about. OK maybe I'm getting paid for it. But to me I get more enjoyment – if you don't mind me swearing – fucking a guy with no arms or legs. Not enjoyment. What's the word? Satisfaction. I get more satisfaction … We have to be there for people like that. And people definitely don't respect us for that. Obviously I'm only fucking him because he is paying me. But I don't look at him any different.

(Inga, quoted in Cockington and Marlin 1995: 175)

Gemma, a 20-year-old Greek/Italian with very striking good looks and one of the most requested girls in her parlour, was interviewed during our Australian fieldwork and expressed similar views – that she was always happy to service disabled clients because she felt these were worthwhile encounters which had real social value. Indeed, Margot Alvarez, Director of the Red Thread in Amsterdam, now works exclusively with the institutionalized disabled (Chapkis 1997: 203). Here again, then, discourses surrounding the industry vary – and some workers define their work as educational or socially valuable in other ways, which informs and underpins how they manage and construct their personal and professional identities.

Moreover, as with the discourse that constructs these workers as a diseased menace to society, prostitutes are also frequently seen as engaging in their chosen occupation solely as a means of economic survival. This discourse connects and overlaps with that which positions these workers as patriarchal instruments. There is, to be sure, little doubt that money is a major motivator for some sex workers, but we now address this representation of prostitution as wholly instrumental in the light of an alternative conceptualization – of the prostitute as career professional.

Scraping a living or career professionals?

We have already established that prostitutes are often cast as victims of patriarchy, by feminist commentators such as Pateman (1988) and workers themselves. This representation concentrates on the ways in which men exploit women's bodies and the subjective consequences of selling one's body for money. It is also true that some sex workers see prostitution as one of their only options in making a 'reasonable' living (McKeganey and Barnard 1996). As Maggie O'Neill (1997: 5) puts it, 'For most women and young women working as prostitutes, economic need is the bottom line where entry into prostitution is concerned.' O'Connell Davidson's (1995a: 7) 'dull economic compulsion' and

Chapkis's (1997: 51–3) discussion of the blurring of the divide between 'forced' and 'free choice' prostitution on economic grounds, as noted in our Introduction, are also relevant here. Moreover, Fiona Broadfoot tells her John School 'students' that prostitutes may fake desire for punters but in reality are only interested in their money (Mills 1999: 33). Finally, it is worth noting Phoenix's (1999) assertion that the 'start-up' costs of prostitution, even without the purchase of a premises from which to work, may be such as to impose further debt on a woman who has decided to sell sex to overcome existing financial pressures. In Gail's case, this included the purchase of condoms and tissues, renting a flat, taxis home from work in an unsafe district and child-minding. Such costs, and the vicious circle they may generate, are also implied in our discussion of the assemblage in chapter 7.

However, these accounts are nuanced by the claim that the entry into prostitution, while certainly fuelled in many instances by economic necessity, is less a case of there being no other option than a proactive choice to resist poverty and dependence on others. As the English Collective of Prostitutes (1997: 99) have it, 'for many the choice is between prostitution, destitution, low-waged jobs or other forms of exploitation'. They focus in particular on single mothers in this regard, pointing to the introduction of the Child Support Agency in the UK, the deduction of fathers' maintenance payments from mothers' benefits and the consequent dependence of these women on men with whom they no longer share a relationship or a home, who may be violent towards them or unable to afford the payments set by the Agency. Consequently, the ECP identify the entry into prostitution as a choice requiring not inconsiderable courage, as an assertive and autonomous attempt to support oneself and one's child in the face of unappealing alternatives such as benefit dependency, dependency on an absent partner or a badly paid and insecure job:

> I think that part of the motivation for the prostitution laws is precisely to undermine those of us who are prostitutes and those of us who solve our financial problems in other ways that are supposed to demoralise us. We retain our dignity, at least we keep more of our dignity than they like. And the powers that be are bloody angry that we are able to survive as well doing things that they said we should not do.
>
> (Selma James, cited in English Collective of Prostitutes 1997: 99–100)

Phoenix also points out that many of her respondents defined themselves as survivors in the face of unpromising odds, and that they were often adamant in their support for prostitutes who are 'standing out on the streets, doing it for themselves, taking their money home' (Lois, quoted in Phoenix 1998: 22). Moreover, McLeod asserts that accounts like these can be understood as 'resistance to the experience of relative poverty or the threat of it' (McLeod 1982: 26). However, Phoenix (1999) suggests that this 'resistance' is perhaps better understood as a negotiation and organization of risk which positions prostitution as the *least risky* among a field of options. In relation to the economic issues surrounding entry into the profession in particular, prostitution seemed to the group of women that Phoenix researched to present a preferable alternative to the unsatisfactory options listed above, in the sense that it was understood to be policed in a more upfront and less insidious way than the payment of benefits (for example, raids to ascertain whether or not one is co-habiting) and to be a means of making the largest sum of money that one's physical capacities would allow (and certainly more than in other jobs available to them). What we see in Phoenix's analysis is that the women involved in her research did have choices – but what Phoenix refuses is the translation of economic motivations into politicized forms of action, as is visible in McLeod's analysis in particular.

Further, other sex workers see prostitution as a positive career move and say it is an occupation which they enjoy. They may define themselves as entrepreneurs with freedom of choice of where and when they work and the kind of services they offer to their client base; they may be proud of their skills, ethics and professionalism, including their sense of confidentiality towards their clients which many, as visible both in the literature and our Australian field research, take considerable pains to preserve. We might also recall here the study by Prince (1986) in which sex workers had developed higher self-esteem since entering the industry. For some sex workers, then, prostitution offers an opportunity for self-development and liberation rather than forced labour:

> Many intelligent, self-confident women ... have *chosen* to work in this industry ... By depicting sex workers as either too emotionally crippled or too stupid to escape a fate which apparently any decent woman would find unspeakably degrading they [certain feminists] help perpetuate the sorts of patronizing stereotypes a true women's liberation movement should strive to eradicate.
>
> (Karen, law student and nude dancer in New York, 1994, cited in Strossen 1995: 179; emphasis added)

Moreover, it is not unusual for sex workers, as we have already seen, to claim their labour for feminism in the face of radical critique, and they may also connect this with an emphasis on the growthful dimensions of prostitution. American sex worker Nancy Hartley claims that the industry

> provides a surprisingly flexible and supportive arena for me to grow in as a performer, both sexually and non-sexually ... an intelligent, sexual woman could choose a job in the sex industry and not be a victim, but instead emerge even stronger and more self-confident, with a feeling, even, of self-actualization.
>
> (Nancy Hartley, cited in Tanenbaum 1994: 18)

For others this reported sense of growth and liberation blends with a sense of being in business, being an entrepreneur:

I'm a business woman. I try an' do ma best. They're payin' me for it and this is ma business. This is how I earn ma livin'. I don't jus' take the money and go 'och, fuck 'em'. They're getting what they paid for, that's the way I work. But only what they pay for an' no more. So I do ma' best.

(Glasgow streetworker, quoted in McKeganey and Barnard 1996: 88)

About two years ago I thought to myself that the proper way to work is without an old man [partner/pimp] altogether. So I said to myself, if I work from now on, it will be on my own terms – for myself and by myself. You gotta be serious about this business, otherwise you won't have anything to show for it.

(Ingrid, quoted in Phoenix 1998: 16)

It's a business to me, it's my career. So I put the effort in. It's the same as any job. If I want to do well then I'm going to put the effort in and I'm going to hit the top with it.

(Gina, massage parlour worker, quoted in *Vice: The Sex Trade*)

Overall, a review of data from our core context therefore suggests two significant dimensions on which the experiences of sex workers vary related to their 'career' in prostitution – the business career and the moral career. With regard to the first, it is true to say that even the street is not necessarily the dead end which it is commonly assumed to be. Street prostitute populations often have a considerable shifting element of casuals and, in small areas like Australia's Port Kembla,[10] the whole population may turn over in a few months, especially during the summer which tends to attract visiting workers. The phenomenon of pimping is also relatively rare here, as it is in Glasgow and certain parts of London and women may therefore move into and out of the industry at this level fairly easily.[11] For instance, Jackie McAuliffe, a transsexual prostitute who played a leading role in BBC TV's docusoap *Paddington Green*, entered prostitution in 1995 in North London's Seven Sisters area, later moving to West London's Bayswater. She worked solely to finance the cosmetic surgery on breasts, nose and chin she felt was needed to complete her transformation from man to woman. Jackie left the industry in late 1998, having successfully achieved her aim. She also found that, even when she was working in Seven Sisters (a 'low rent' area both literally and metaphorically), there were no pimps controlling the girls on the street (Flett 1999).

Other workers move on/up within the sex industry itself. Sam and Mary have previously worked on the street and in saunas, but presently work either at home or as outworkers in hotels or on trips with clients, by virtue of having developed a group of regular punters (O'Neill 1996: 22). Still others try parlour work, or set up on their own. A worker interviewed in Australia was taking a course on running your own business for one half day a week; another saved her earnings from prostitution to set up an electrolysis business and serviced clients from within and outside the sex industry. Prostitutes may also save for a deposit on a house to work from, or end up operating more than one establishment (Barlow 1994: 134–5). Such women may also act as a mentor to their staff in more than simple work terms – Barlow herself helps her colleagues with domestic arrangements, support and counselling. However, few prostitutes who are not self-employed and working from their own premises seem to continue in the profession after the age of thirty-five; this is because, when in competition with other girls, older women may find their services in much less demand.[12] One way to prolong their business life is to specialize in services such as B&D (for example, Mandy and Simone, quoted in McRae 1992; Blain 1994: 119–20; Martine, quoted in Perkins 1994: 171; Julia, quoted in Cockington and Marlin 1995: 189–211), Tantric sex tuition (for example, Jahnet de Light, *Consenting Adults* 1997/8) or sex therapy (for example, Sara Dale, quoted in McRae 1992: 97–11; Bella Lamou, *Consenting Adults* 1997/8). Barlow (1994: 137), however, argues that although 'the more organised women have a financial plan, with the help of a good accountant many leave the industry with nothing to show for it'. This aside, we would still argue that prostitution for some entrants into the profession is simply that – a chosen profession promising particular kinds of self-development, skills acquisition and/or career progression. For others, it is a short-term income generating strategy as opposed to a long-term career choice. In any event, what we have tried to demonstrate is that prostitutes are not necessarily *forced* to undertake this work in the absence of any other options – their decision to enter may be a good deal more proactive than that. Nor, once in, do they always find it difficult to exit from or progress within the profession, even if they enter at street level.

The 'moral career', on the other hand, refers to the way in which women become involved in the industry, how they manage the process of having their first client, how they become accommodated to the fact that they are a sex worker and how and whether they come to satisfactory terms with their actions. Moira tells the following story:

> my boyfriend's friend sat watching telly and said 'Look at them dirty prosti-
> tutes' ... and I said 'Just remember I am a prostitute and this is my settee
> paid for by prostitution and my TV and my carpet' and everybody looked at
> me horrified ... I was so horrified *in the beginning* ... the first punter just
> wanted to look ... I had these durex and I wasn't even sure how to put it on
> properly ... I had real horrible nightmares that night ... and I just counted
> my money, that was my comfort.
>
> (Moira, quoted in O'Neill 1997: 7)

Despite initially feeling 'horrified', Moira now appears to have come to terms with her occupation, in part because it affords her financial sustenance and she is also able to justify her activities to others on these grounds. In a similar vein, Jackie McAuliffe was depicted in one episode of *Paddington Green* as consoling herself for not having reached her night's target by saying that she had at least earned more during her short shift than many do all day. Other prostitutes offer similar accounts of the work that they do, and often emphasize the fact that their occupation is not only relatively highly paid, but also affords a degree of flexibility which others do not permit:

> It suits me down to the ground to do two hours work and get the same money that most people get for doing 40 hours ... it's easy money ... I wouldn't go back to scrabbling around on £50 a week again.
>
> (Gillian, quoted in Scambler 1997: 114)

> I choose when I work. I choose my clients. I say 'No' if I'm busy ... I don't feel that I'm trapped in any kind of vicious circle, or being pressurized by any men at all.
>
> (Sarah, quoted in Scambler 1997: 114)

> I like being a sex worker because I get paid what my time, experience and skill is worth. I like that at over $130 an hour I am one of the very few women who earn more than men. I like that I can work when I want to – day, evening, 2 hrs a day or 12 hrs a day, it is entirely up to me. This means that I can fit my work around my busy schedule instead of, like most jobs, having to fit my life around my working week.
>
> (Anonymous contributor to *SIN* magazine)

The construction of prostitution as a short-term stop-gap is also relevant as a device for moral rationalization (Ashforth and Kreiner 1999: 430). We have already seen that women may move into and out of the industry relatively unencumbered, and this is supported by accounts from workers such as Sarah (quoted above), who saw one client per week through an escort agency to support her postgraduate studies, and Marie-Anne Mancio, who took a job as a hostess and sold sex to clients out of hours during the final year of her PhD (Valentine 1998: 25). Marie-Anne (a) is emphatic that she has no reservations about calling herself a 'whore'; (b) suggests that the women she worked with included other students, single mothers and a dancer who wanted to attend classes during the day and work at night (and thus that they all desired the same kind of flexible working pattern as she did); and (c) points out the irony of telling such women that they should depend on state benefit because prostitution is exploitative, when in their situation they earned a great deal of money (£500 a client) and, moreover, kept all of this income. Still other prostitutes take a more politicized position, such as Carol Leigh (1994), whose stance is discussed in detail in chapter 8. As analysis there suggests, Leigh focuses on the fact that prostitution afforded her an opportunity to live out her feminist and radical political beliefs, given the challenge that it presented to conventional sexual mores.

Overall, then, it is clear that some prostitutes, even though staying in the industry long-term, never fully come to terms with it and tensions remain in their working and private lives, whereas others, like Moira, adapt more easily

(Barlow 1994: 134; Blain 1994: 113–4; Cockington and Marlin 1995: 170–1; Kerkham 1997: 108–9; see also chapter 8). Some may decide that prostitution is what they want to do even before they try it, with great single-minded determination (Goodley 1994; Leigh 1994: 246). Nonetheless, how the worker views their occupation in this regard – as a career, as a stop-gap, as a means of developing self, as the only choice in particular socio-economic circumstances, as a feminist protest, as a flexible and well-remunerated alternative to the 9 to 5 etc. – makes a significant difference to their self-construction and to the degree of self-reflexivity they demonstrate in their everyday activities.

Conclusion

In chapter 8, we suggested that prostitutes engage in differing types of identity management, which vary according to the way in which an individual prostitute understands herself, the work that she does, and her relationship with her clients. Our argument in this chapter has extended analysis of the double effect of placing on sex work in its assertion that the particular kind of self-identity which a prostitute develops and seeks to maintain is informed by the discourses available to her – that is to say, these discourses form part of the context of sex work. Discourses reviewed here include those which position the prostitute somewhere on the continuum between 'sex worker' and 'victim of patriarchy'; those which construct the social role of the sex worker – diseased and dangerous or educator/social worker/counsellor; and those which construct her business and moral career. Our overall objective in this and the previous chapter has been to emphasize the complex and fragmented character of the profession, to suggest that uni-dimensional interpretations of prostitution as always degrading or, on the other hand, always empowering (although this is less likely given the current moral climate) are unhelpful when seeking to explore and understand the labour process of the modern Western prostitute. Moreover, the ways in which individual prostitutes understand themselves are equally complex and tend to involve protracted identity work in order for an individual worker to retain a temporarily coherent and therefore functional sense of herself; to be able to continue in her profession; or possibly to make the effort needed to leave the industry for more 'conventional' employment, and perhaps thereafter to be able to edit her personal history in order to think of and present herself as a subject 'untainted' by prostitution. In this regard, our analysis seeks to depict prostitution simultaneously as an occupation which has features in common with many other occupations (especially, we have suggested, those service jobs which involve direct contact with clients); as an occupation in which the tensions characteristic of other forms of employment may be writ large (such as the editing of personal biographies following exit from the occupational field); and as an occupation which has its own distinctive and discrete features (including the selling of a commodified sexuality).

In chapter 10, we further develop our analysis by suggesting that it is not only discursive context which shapes and helps to explain variations of experience in prostitution – here we move to focus on the significance of the materialities of prostitutes' locations in order to address the second dimension of the double effect of placing on sex work.

10 Material variations in sex work

Introduction

Having examined the discursive positioning of prostitution in detail in chapters 7, 8 and 9, this chapter moves to consider the second and more concrete aspect of the double effect of placing on the sex industry. Here we emphasize the importance of spatially located materialities as giving shape to sex work, and conclude that this placing of the individual prostitute as regards legislative climate (more or less tolerant of prostitution as a means of earning a living), market segment (specialized forms of sex work as opposed to generalist services), labour market (such that those who work on the streets are worse off in many ways than those who operate in brothels, hotels or in their own or clients' homes) and co-worker support networks (varying from highly organized political campaigns to individualism in which workers compete as opposed to co-operating with each other) gives rise to a highly localized experience of sex work in any one area. Here then we suggest that theories and frameworks generated by research undertaken in particular locations, or focusing on individual sex workers, are localized in themselves; they inevitably reflect the local and intimate knowledges characteristic of specific sites within the industry, which are developed by workers as a way of making sense of and coping with the material exigencies of those locations. Our analysis also suggests that these aspects of place bear extended consideration in terms of their relationships with each other, and reiterates our theme that the sex industry is fragmented and complex. Further, we identify several aspects of sex work contexts which arguably transect our four key dimensions, including gender relations and race and ethnicity.

Our argument draws in particular upon the arguments made in chapter 7 which, following Deleuze and Guattari's (1984; 1987) discussion of the Body without Organs, outlined some of the ways in which identity may be symbolically inscribed upon the prostitute's body. Here, we examine institutional inscriptions which have significant material as well as symbolic effects on the practice of prostitution. Our discussion is informed by perspectives from (a) politics, legal studies and criminology, in terms of the impact of different legislative frameworks both across and within nation–states; (b) economics, in that we see prostitution as an industry segmented by market; and (c) sociology and urban geography, because we locate prostitution within communities exhibiting both employment stratification and a variety of mutual support networks.

Sex and place

The symbolic anthropologist Geertz (1983) argues that the social anthropological study of particular communities tends to surface knowledges which are specific to the conditions in which those communities subsist, and which are concrete and pragmatic, helping members of those communities to live their lives success-fully in the community's milieu, wherever that might be (the Amazon rainforest, the Russian Steppes, the streets of Glasgow, the massage parlours of Melbourne). Social structures and rules of behaviour adapt to these circum-stances, albeit sometimes in subversive and oppositional forms, and concepts such as fact, evidence, justice and legality shift and vary across cultures. Indeed, even the metaphysics of these knowledge-producing communities, though targeted at the transcendental, will have strong local elements in their formula-tion, with the effect that social concepts often taken to have synonymous meanings in different places – such as leadership – appear somewhat incommen-surate on closer examination (Westwood and Chan 1992; Westwood 1997). Accordingly, what it is possible and necessary for human beings to do in carrying on their everyday business varies with cultural context. We can expect, therefore, that a prostitute 'trained' on the streets of King's Cross, London would not immediately be able to operate successfully on the streets of King's Cross, Sydney, nor from a high class parlour in either location, as they would not have the requisite local knowledge – the techniques and the interpretive under-standing of the other social, legal and economic context/s – to do so. Consequently, conclusions drawn from the streets of North London and the streets of New South Wales are unlikely to be identical, or applicable in their entirety to any other location where prostitution takes place and this caution applies to those situations which we might assume are relatively similar (as in the examples of streetworkers in the UK and Australia given above), as well as those (such as comparing self-employed mature First World sex workers with enslaved Third World child prostitutes) which common sense tells us are not. Similarly, and as we have also argued in chapter 7, at the more metaphysical level, the notion of desire which is taken to animate the sex industry will be subject to local variation (Pettman 1996: 195–6). Overall, then, we need to regard local knowl-edge first for what it is – spatially (and temporally) located – before attempting the process of translation into other contexts. Indeed, as Hubbard (1997: 130) points out of his own discipline, geography, there has been 'little attempt' to explore how the spaces within which prostitutes work 'contribute to the social construction of [their] identities'. In this and a later paper (Hubbard 1998), he therefore explores the intersection of place and identity in terms of, for example, the ways in which place maps on to the labelling of prostitutes as Other in the UK. Here we build on analyses such as that provided by Hubbard to offer a cross-cultural analysis within our core context.

Haraway (1991) extends Geertz's analysis, arguing that, in this world of situated knowledge:

> local knowledges have also to be in tension with the productive structurings that force unequal translations and exchanges – material and semiotic – within the webs of knowledge and power. Webs have the power of systematicity, even of centrally structured global systems with deep filaments into time space and consciousness, the dimensions of world history … Gender is a field of structured and structuring difference, where the tones of extreme localization, of the intimately personal and individualized body, vibrate in the same field with global high tension emissions.
>
> (Haraway 1991: 195)

That is to say, local knowledge is in tension with global disseminations of knowledge. Within the global context it occupies an uneasy position, being disempowered by both exchange and symbolic systems and therefore having little pragmatic or communicative value outside of its milieu. Here, on the other hand, it is highly significant, mediating, filtering, and often challenging or subverting knowledge produced and distributed on broader spatial scales. The ways in which we come to understand our bodies form part of this tension – local bodily knowledge is intense and personal, yet global commercial and political forces from Coca-Cola advertisements to International Monetary Fund and World Bank solutions for Third World debt (see, for example, Bauman 1998: 112) constrain and produce the ways in which we use and define our bodies in relation to generalized and abstracted socio-economic systems. This struggle over the body inevitably has consequences for the various understandings of sexuality on which prostitution rests, and local knowledge is one way in which people exercise agency even while their bodies are subject to colonization and commodification.

For Haraway, therefore, embodiment (and even the body itself) is best understood as a 'node' in a set of fields, where what moves through the fields is in tension and resonates, structured by sets of social relations from the global to the most intimate which necessitate unequal translations and exchanges. This she calls a 'geometry of difference' and contrasts it to views of relational difference emphasizing only hierarchical dominance. Here we identify the prostitute's body as such a node, as it is what is traded and negotiated over, and what is signified in various ways: that is to say, it represents the contested terrain of the prostitute's work. Where, as established in chapter 9, most accounts of the prostitute's body tend to see it at one end or the other of a hierarchy of domination and resistance (something which is expropriated and exploited by male punters as both condition and consequence of patriarchy versus a means of earning a living and/or locus of free labour power), we argue in this discussion for a view of this body as spatially mediated through a geometry of *multiple* difference (McDowell 1996: 35). Through a variety of complexities and inflections, each node a 'web of relations of domination and subordination, of solidarity and cooperation' (Massey

1992: 81), place therefore provides a basis for prostitutes to interpret and experience the work that they do.

Finally, Bauman's (1998) discussion of 'global law' as against 'local orders' is also highly relevant to our discussion here. Here Bauman (1998: 105) suggests that, in order for the movements and investments of global capital to be 'flexible', the rules which govern these dynamics need to be made and unmade with relative ease, according to the market itself as the law. Moreover, the situation of those at the lower levels of the economic hierarchy – the suppliers of labour – must be as rigid as possible; that is to say, 'their freedom to choose, to accept or refuse, let alone to impose their own rules on the game, must be cut to the bare bone' (Bauman 1998: 105). It is precisely existence at these levels, and the limited opportunities it provides for alternative employment, that can drive people into and trap them within prostitution and it is this lack of choice against which the English Collective of Prostitutes and its sister organizations worldwide are prominent in campaigning. Local knowledge, which attempts to increase the mastery or sovereignty of the individual over the immediate situation, is therefore also in tension with local orders.

This increasing rigidity at the lower levels of socio-economic activity coupled with increasing flexibility at the higher levels is also reflected in what are becoming key differences between what Bauman calls the first world, which contains the globally mobile, and the second world of the locally tied. But this division is not the established one between the old world, the new world, the developing world and the underclass of the 'fourth world' (Castells 1998: 70–165). It may overlap with these geographical distinctions, but in itself refers to a gap which is opening up between the mobile and the immobile within all societies.[1] This has resulted from the growing flexibility of investment, which has increased the mobility of those who are paid to follow it, and the restriction of choice of those subject to its fluctuations. As Bauman puts it, globalization therefore means that residents of the First World live in *time*. Space is not a significant barrier to them, given that electronic communications enable the geographical world to be spanned instantly and travel across huge distances is possible in a matter of hours. Time, on the other hand, is what these individuals complain they don't have enough of. Residents of the Second World – who may well be physically proximate to those in the First World, living on a council estate only a mile or so from a financial district full of high and frequent flyers – exist in *space* which is 'heavy, resilient, untouchable, which ties down time and keeps it beyond the residents' control' (Bauman 1998: 88). Their problems relate to their confinement in space, their inability to transcend it so as to move where there are more choices, and the difficulties they have in moving across borders, boundaries, state lines and territories. Travel for those in the Second World can be illegal, as well as making them prey to traffickers and debt-bonders and possibly trapping them into an occupation (such as prostitution) or a location from which they find it difficult to escape. After all, it is not difficult to see that the stripping of local knowledge which results from an individual being trafficked to a place which they do not know, and an occupation they were not perhaps prepared for, diminishes their agency and self-identity. Furthermore, Seabrook's comments, cited by Bauman (1998: 79), are also worth considering here – that the poverty which puts people into this kind of situation is not a disease of capitalism, a sign of its ill health, but 'quite the reverse: it is evidence of its robust good health, its spur to even greater accumulation and effort' (Seabrook 1988: 15). In our analysis we therefore remain mindful of the effects of this drive to accumulate, the part it plays in the shaping of prostitution as a social practice and its reliance on the restricted temporal and spatial activity of those at the lower end of the economic scale in order to preserve its own power (Castells 1998: 165).

The context of sex work

As we have already suggested above, there is much evidence from our core context that the codes, conventions, markets, employment strata and networks within prostitution vary from country to country, city to city, and between urban sites and rural conclaves. Epistemological space thus co-exists with, marks and defines physical space. Deleuze and Guattari (1987), as we have seen in chapter 7, identify two types of epistemological space, differentiating between smooth space – private, personal, unregulated – and striated space – public, regulated, inhabited by various constraints on the individual. The prostitute–client encounter, as we also argued earlier, can therefore be seen as necessitating an attempt to create the illusion of smooth space (the worker as lover, as non-commercial sexual partner) in the striated space of a time-bounded, rule-governed, commercial transaction, within which certain areas of the body (for example, the lips or the anus) may be off limits. In this chapter we argue that it is the particular character of the striated epistemological space around the encounter which gives locality its variable impact and which generates specific local knowledges.

Drawing on data from the study of prostitution as well as on general social anthropological concepts, we derive, as suggested above, four dimensions along which local knowledges of sex work vary and through which they are shaped. The first is *social order*, the framework of rules and understandings which maintains more or less stable patterns of relationships and defines the boundaries of the permissible in any one location. As regards prostitution, we take this to be indicated by legislative climate, including the formalities of (de)criminalization of sex work and the informalities of enforcement and tolerance by agencies of the law. The second dimension is *economic performativity*, the patterns of production and consumption which shape the subjectivities of workers and customers, and the types of goods and services offered and demanded. Applying this to sex work, we use the concept of market segmentation. The third dimension is *economic stratification* and, at the level of a particular occupation, types of professional or business hierarchy which we would expect to find in an advanced industrial society. This differs from the concept of career, with its associations of progression and moral positioning (see chapter 9), but is of course partly sustained by such a concept, as Hubbard (1998) notes of the 'moral geography' of sex work. We use the term 'employment stratification' to connote the relevant aspects of prostitution. Our final dimension is *social community and kinship* and here we follow Linstead and Grafton Small (1986, 1990) in arguing that modern professional groups are sustained through organized neo-kinship relations. For sex workers, this emerges as a variety of patterns of mutual support, including that of individualism where such support is effectively absent.

This, then, is our framework for describing the key dimensions of the contexts in which sex work develops – it does not attempt a complete categorization of *all* dimensions of sex work, but focuses on those which can be held to be contextual and for the most part outside the individual motivations of sex workers and clients in the encounter itself. We classify each of the four according to the degree of specificity they exhibit – for example, a highly and formally regulated legislative climate would be highly specified, whereas a context where there may be no formal laws, and which therefore appears to be unregulated (although it may have informal social rules constraining behaviour), we would term poorly specified or unspecified. Moreover, high degrees of specification do not occur across all dimensions simultaneously, and it is the combination of different positionings on each of the dimensions that produces contextual variety in sex work environments. Market segmentation, for example, depends on the ability of the sex worker to define a niche and publicize that niche to potential customers but this is difficult if the relevant legislative climate prohibits the promotion of prostitution.

As already noted, there are also aspects of the contexts in which sex work occurs which may cut across our four dimensions, especially when a more global stance is undertaken. We briefly develop six of these cross-dimensional influences below.

Cultural context

Edward Hall (1959, 1969) argues that different cultures can be distinguished by the extent to which they are integrated with their physical and social environment, and the extent to which that environment plays a part in sense-making and the construction of identity. Individuals in low context cultures tend to communicate through the use of explicit verbal codes, symbols, written instructions, questions and explanations, formal agreements and contracts. Rules and regulations are the norm, and are frequently followed to the letter. Laws and their application would therefore tend to converge, there being less interpretational latitude and greater emphasis on individual responsibility in law-breaking. Those in high context cultures, on the other hand, tend to make sense of situations by gathering clues and information from the physical environment and from what they have learned from their own past experience, that is to say, cues for action are taken from the immediate life-world rather than from the 'rule book'. Rules and regulations may exist, but are generally reinterpreted according to the situation, and informal understandings may have greater social significance than written rules and codes of practice. Law-breaking (in so far as laws exist at all in high context cultures) may also be legitimate if the demands of community are collectively felt to override the strictures of regulation. There are, furthermore, heterogeneous societies where high and low context cultures have mingled and left their mark on each other – Hong Kong would be a good example of a society which is well regulated formally but in which familiarity with unwritten understandings and relationships can be essential for social and economic activity to proceed successfully.

It is also important to note that low context–high context may not always be synonymous with our highly specified–poorly specified/unspecified classification across all our four dimensions. It is possible, for example, that a high context culture may informally prescribe behaviours so as to allow highly specified market segmentation to occur. That is to say, the cultural aspect remains an important consideration to bear in mind when attempting to explain the distribution of features of a particular sex work context across the dimensions.

Legal ideologies

Underpinning the various legislative systems regulating prostitution are differing moral positions or legal ideologies although it is also important to realize that the prevailing ideology is not always or necessarily reflected in the way that legislation is enforced, as discussion in a later section ('Social order in sex work: legislative climate') demonstrates. However, as Wijers (1998: 72) points out, most countries, or states within those countries, seem to adopt the underlying position that prostitution is unacceptable, which is also the basic stance of the 1949 United Nations *Convention on the Suppression of the Traffic in Persons and the Exploitation of the Prostitution of Others*. Some, such as most of the United States, adopt a *prohibitionist* ideology. Here the object of the law is to eradicate prostitution, so that most or all of its aspects are criminalized. In practice, however, punitive measures are targeted at the prostitute, not those who employ or use her services. As a result the prostitute is marginalized, cut off from legitimate support and placed at the mercy of pimps, procurers, corrupt police officers, brothel keepers and organized crime, which we discuss below.

Others, like Germany, opt for *regulationism*. Prostitution is recognized as existing and in the interests of public order is legalized by various forms of regulation – taxation, registration, licensing, regular testing for a 'health certificate'. However, as implied in discussion of this approach in chapter 9, just as a legal sector is produced, so is an illegal sector. Because of the stigma still attached to prostitution and the rather degrading approach taken to regulatory procedures, many women do not register as they fear the social consequences of being a 'registered prostitute'; for example, those whose migrant status is in question cannot register. A criminal sector is thus created and marked out by the very regulatory practices intended to eradicate it.

A third category includes countries such as the UK, Belgium and the Netherlands which take an *abolitionist* attitude. Here prostitution is regarded as evil, as a threat to family values, and thus it is felt that the State should take no part in regulating or legalizing it. Prostitutes are cast either as victims or as suffering from a sickness, and accordingly 'need' to be 'helped' through the punishment of others involved or counselling and therapy (Lerum 1999). No distinction is made between forced and consensual prostitution in these contexts, such that working girls are effectively denied agency in and responsibility for their own situation.

The final position, which seems at the present time to be approached only by New South Wales, is one of *equitarianism* in which prostitutes are assumed to have the same rights to autonomy and protection against exploitation as any other set of workers. Decriminalization of the act of selling sex is accompanied here by the decriminalization of the business of prostitution, and policy is developed on this basis, recognizing prostitutes' right to self-determination. The problems associated with prostitution – violence, trafficking, forced labour, exploitation, drug abuse – are then attacked directly through existing laws, rather than indirectly through prostitution laws.

Gender relations

Although 'social relations involving sexual labour are not inherently tied to gendered roles or bodies' (Kempadoo 1998a: 5; see also Karim 1995a), the ways in which being male or female are differentially defined in different cultural contexts do have significant material consequences. Across our four core dimensions, social and legal regulation of the kind of jobs that women may do; the age of consent; marriage and divorce; suffrage; property ownership; provision of education and training; fiscal regulation; maternity provision; childcare; parental welfare; patterns of sex discrimination and equal opportunities (and so on) will affect what is available to women in or out of employment, above and beyond the regulation of the actual sale of sex. The overall position of women in society, and the classification of certain types or groups of women as acceptable or otherwise – such as mistresses – will also affect how prostitution is treated. This will in turn impact on the types of service that are developed and are allowed to develop, and the sort of products on offer within particular sexual markets, with corresponding implications for skills, career development and labour market stratification. It is also true to say that male prostitution constitutes a different discourse to that of female prostitution, as initially argued in the Introduction to this book, despite the increasing blurring of boundaries with the development of bisexual and transgender prostitution. Following Marlowe (1997), we therefore acknowledge that male prostitution is a separate position within the overall discourse, yet one that is capable of being analysed through the same categories as female prostitution.

Race and ethnicity

Race relations between different ethnic groups have often had a sexual dimension to them, whether the fabled exoticism of Far Eastern women for Western men (Troung 1990; Bishop and Robinson 1998), or European women's attraction to black Caribbean men (de Albuquerque 1999). Yet the growth of multi-culturalism in our core context,[2] along with patterns of migration in South East Asia, have acted to make the exotic both more accessible and more familiar, and have allowed a greater degree of cultural diversity to emerge within both consumer and labour markets more generally in these societies. Indeed, historical attitudes towards and legislation on immigration, the process of issuing work permits and the degree of integration of immigrant groups into the host society across various social contexts will have a varying impact on demand for and the sort of work available to women from different ethnic groups, as intimated in the Introduction. These factors will also impose an additional cultural layer on top of that of the host culture which may inhibit or facilitate the growth of the sex industry (see McClintock 1992). Recent patterns of migration into the Netherlands, for example, have led to a situation where 30–60 per cent of sex workers are estimated to be from Third World countries, particularly Latin America (Brussa 1989, 1991). Moreover, the ways in which cultural integration is promoted or segregation sustained will depend considerably on legislation; cultural attitudes will primarily affect the ways in which racialized markets develop and employment hierarchies emerge; and ethnic community values will be the source of either support or disapproval for the workers involved.

Migration and trafficking

So far we have attempted to carve out dimensions which can be used to map any indigenous sex work context, even a multi-cultural one. However, the mobility of sex workers across national boundaries has produced considerable variegation in the ethnicity of sex work populations in certain parts of the world and has also resulted in racism and ethnic persecution within the industry, at least where immigration is resented and/or met with active hostility. Given difficulties in determining actual numbers of working prostitutes,[3] there is also debate over whether this mobility has intensified over the past two decades, in line with the increased global movement of labour more generally (Kempadoo 1998a: 14–15). Nevertheless, women certainly do migrate for work, and many of these migrants either choose to enter or find themselves in the sex industry. Filipina workers are well represented in Japan; Russian workers can be found in Europe but also in Macau, the Middle East and China, where Vietnamese are also found; Afghans and Bangladeshis work in Pakistan; Mexican women can be found in Japan, as can Thais, who are also prominent in Australia. Suriname hosts Brazilians and Guyanese; Curaçao entertains Dominicans and Colombians; the Côte d'Ivoire welcomes Ghanaians; Nigerians work in Senegal, Ethiopians in the Middle East and a wide variety of Eastern and Southern Europeans in Germany and Austria. In some cases women move only temporarily and seasonally, going into debt for transport and visa provision for a short time (Kempadoo 1998b); in others they may be debt-bonded for considerable periods and subject to prolonged abuse. Where there is a well developed sex tourism industry, as in

Thailand where estimates place its value at $5 billion, airlines, hotel chains and local business and military elites form networks with police, pimps and crime bosses to ensure the maintenance of the industry and a regular flow of labour (Petras and Wongchaisuwan 1993). Moreover, although there are considerable debates about the definition of trafficking, as well as arguably widespread myth-making around the phenomenon and its extent which makes it more difficult to recognize those workers who do move freely and autonomously (Murray 1998; Watanabe 1998; Wijers 1998), there is no doubt that the phenomenon is common, large scale and affects the character of the labour market in the desti-nation location.

Organized crime

In Castells's (1998) summary of the evidence for the existence of a 'global crim-inal economy', trade in drugs, weapons, nuclear material and body parts, along with money laundering, are the major activities of worldwide criminal networks and strategic alliances. However, his list of such activities also includes the trade in illegal immigrants – including the trafficking of women and children. For example, Castells (1998: 177) argues that the Hong Kong Triads and Japan's Yakuza (we might also add the People's Liberation Army of China) control the trafficking of women and children in Asia, which he says is believed to have grown into a multimillion dollar business. It is of course difficult to draw an accurate line between illegal immigration and trafficking, but there is a clear overlap, as there likely is between trafficking and the movement of drugs. Wijers (1998: 74–76) also notes, as Castells (1998: 179) observes of drug trafficking, that the integrity of the networks necessary to sustain the traffic is maintained by often extraordinary levels of violence. Further, trafficking is difficult to identify, and hence difficult to combat. This is because trafficked women (a) have little confidence in the police system, which itself often abuses them; (b) live in constant fear of reprisal for themselves or their families at home, or of deporta-tion, if they report what has happened to them; (c) can expose little of the criminal network as they only know part of it, and are thus of limited value to the law but very vulnerable to the network itself; (d) learn survival strategies based on attaining the grace and favour of certain key individuals within the network, rather than fighting openly; and (e) may not be regarded by local enforcement agencies as having the rights of a normal citizen because they are working as prostitutes – indeed, they may even be seen as expendable. The crim-inal networks who operate trafficking and the sex industry in certain areas therefore exert a powerful influence on sex work locations embedded in such networks, and these of course are not limited to the more obvious cases in Asia. Crime is global, and similar, if fewer, cases can be found all over the world (Brockett and Murray 1994).

Having established what might cut across our four dimensions, we now discuss some key variations in legislative climate, market segmentation, employ-ment stratification and mutual support through an examination of the available data. We then identify some of the inter-relationships which can be discerned.

Social order in sex work: legislative climate

One major variable in the organization of sex work in striated space is the legislation relating to prostitution which operates in any one country, or in a specific locale within that country (for example, a state in the USA or Australia). Prostitution itself (that is, the act of selling sex for money) is not a criminal activity in many countries, but the law varies widely as to its perspective on the ancillary activities associated with prostitution,[4] and police and judiciaries also vary as to the latitude or inflexibility they exercise in interpreting and enforcing that law. This can and does produce marked variations in the ways in which prostitutes live out and understand their profession, ranging from a desired, high earnings occupation for the young and ambitious to the last resort of the desperate and destitute. That is to say, the specific nest of legal constraints, interpretations and enforcement practices, along with the moral tone adopted by communities, generates certain locally significant characteristics of and variations in the experience and interpretation of prostitution, as we will now discuss.

At what we designate as the highly specified end of the scale, there are legislative environments in which prostitution is criminalized. Adelaide, South Australia, where Roxy Blain's (1994) career as a prostitute began,[5] is one example. Here selling sex is strictly illegal, although escort work may be tolerated and campaigning sex workers periodically run their own radio programme. As Blain points out, parlours therefore had to have respectable fronts as dating agencies or massage parlours; and this often required workers themselves to adopt particular personae, through the attainment of certification of expertise in massage therapy, for example. Care in answering the door was also required, as the police often sent plain clothes investigators to pose as clients (the so-called 'sting' operation). In order to circumvent the legislation and its associated enforcement activities, Blain and colleagues had to go to some lengths in order to offer sex. Clients might be asked to undress before any description of services above and beyond massage was offered, as police were apparently not supposed to remove their underpants whilst working, even though plain clothes officers were technically out of uniform! Alternatively, Blain also used the following approach:

> Halfway through a service I would say something like 'I wouldn't normally do this, but you're so cute would you mind if I hop into bed with you?' – to which the client would respond with 'yes'. Thus we avoided arrest by propositioning every client with sex *which was offered free of charge to those who had paid to use the premises*.
>
> (Blain 1994: 116; emphasis added)

Blain mentions the frequency of police raids in which, from time to time, possession of condoms was taken as *prima facie* evidence that prostitution is taking place at a particular address.[6] Indeed, police harassment frequently necessitated parlours closing down and re-opening elsewhere under another name, affording relief if only on a temporary basis. Working in South Australia, then, requires a measured and careful response on the part of prostitutes in order that they stay on the 'right side' of the law.

Prostitution in the USA is also illegal, except in certain counties in Nevada, as is visiting prostitutes. Police often carry out 'sting' operations against workers, especially those on the street. In fact, data from the *Prostitutes' Education Network* suggest that US police activities aimed at reducing prostitution tend to be targeted at the streetworker sector. Furthermore, a particular form of discrimination operates such that arrests for activities associated with prostitution are made up of 70 per cent female workers, 20 per cent male workers, and 10 per cent customers, as already implied in our discussion of the ways in which legislation in prohibitionist countries tends to work.[7] *Network* statistics also show that a disproportionate number of sex workers arrested are women of colour, and that a large proportion of these women are sent to jail. Moreover, these activities are costly. A figure of nearly $2,000 per arrest is cited, with 100,000 individuals being arrested on charges related to prostitution in America in 1994. US cities are also shown to spend an average of $7.5 million on prostitution control every year, with New York spending $23 million.

However, as we have already suggested, criminalization of prostitution is relatively rare, in 'developed' countries especially. Indeed, fifty signed the 1949 United Nations resolution referred to above, which decriminalized the act of prostitution but retained the illegal status of the ancillaries of advertising, promoting and living off the earnings of prostitution. Moreover, examination of countries where prostitution is not itself illegal but ancillaries are reveals substantial variations – one sub-category being locations where this legislation is stringently enforced, such as the UK. As O'Connell Davidson (1995a: 3; 1996: 182) points out, to the list of illegal ancillaries mentioned in the 1949 resolution, UK law adds the organization of prostitution, and we have already seen that kerb crawling became an offence in England and Wales as recently as 1985. In the enforcing of this legislation, furthermore, condoms may be used as evidence of the crimes of soliciting or loitering, and streetworker arrests are frequent. Leila had three convictions after only seven months' street work (McRae 1992: 241), the English Collective of Prostitutes (1997: 85) cite an instance of a woman being arrested forty-eight times in fifty-two days and Phoenix's (1999) MidCity respondents describe regular police 'purges' where officers will swoop on the local red light area and round up all the girls working that night.

For a UK prostitute to engage in her trade without breaking the law, then, demands that they (a) advertise without being specific about the nature of their services or stating prices; (b) do not employ others to sell sex (although taking on staff to act as maids or receptionists is permissible); (c) operate from their own property; and (d) live alone. Desiree, O'Connell Davidson's self-employed prostitute, has in fact achieved all of the above, entering prostitution to meet mortgage payments on a flat (although her earnings have now allowed her to purchase a house), and also having to ensure that her marketing (as a masseuse in a national tabloid and via contact magazines) is ambiguous enough to sidestep legal censure but at the same time attractive to potential punters. Indeed, as O'Connell Davidson (1995a: 2) puts it, marketing 'this form of prostitution does not and cannot centre on extending "product" awareness, but rests fundamentally on attracting the custom of men with existing knowledge (if not experience) of the service'. Therefore, in the UK as elsewhere, euphemisms such as 'French' for oral sex, 'Greek' for anal sex, and 'Spanish'[8] for sex between the breasts have developed to enable sex workers to subvert legal constraints to some degree by reaching those customers who can read the code (Smith 1999). Desiree's receptionists also have to be careful so as not to explicitly reveal the nature of her services to those who ring to enquire – actual services are only discussed when the enquirer becomes a customer, arriving at the premises and asking to avail himself of Desiree's wares (O'Connell Davidson 1994c: 6; 1995a: 3). The receptionists also need to be fully conversant with the aforementioned argot of the sex industry, which is exacerbated by the fact that Desiree specializes in B&D, the language of which represents a code within the code of UK prostitution (O'Connell Davidson 1994c: 6). By way of contrast, Karen, who owns, runs and works in two massage parlours in Manchester, and works in a third in Shrewsbury (McCoy 1998: 72, 114), actually does break the UK law because she employs other girls as prostitutes. However, Karen and her employees avoid any legal problems by using an approach that we have seen above in discussion of Blain's time in Adelaide. As she says, 'They're paying for a massage, that's it. *And then we just throw in a bit extra for free.* We're not charging for that; we're charging for the massage' (Karen, quoted in *Vice: The Sex Trade*; emphasis added).

The wider moral climate of the UK, as well as the enforcement practices of its various agencies, is also visible in evidence from Birmingham's Balsall Heath. Here, a group of local residents began an active campaign against prostitutes working in their locale in June 1994. Actions taken varied from picketing with placards through street patrols to violent attacks on prostitutes and their homes. The police also extended a certain legitimacy to this campaign by registering seventy pickets as official participants in the Home Office's Street Watch campaign, giving them identity cards and incident sheets, and consequent authority to patrol the Balsall Heath area. The effect was substantial – in fact estimates suggest that up to 450 prostitutes have been forced to leave the area as a result of the community campaign, which continues (Hubbard 1998; Mills 1998; Mitchell 1998).

Other locations where prostitution is partly decriminalized form a second sub-category, given that the strategies employed by law enforcement agencies here point to a more overtly selective, *de facto* form of regulation. Here we return to Blain's (1994) autobiography, and her move to Perth, Western Australia (where she set up following a move from New South Wales – see p. 255). In this state, again, prostitution itself is decriminalized but employing others (that is, organizing prostitution) is not. Moreover, Blain found that prostitution in any case was actually controlled by the police. She was contacted by the Vice Squad after placing her first advertisement, and told she had to register with them in order to be able to work and, although she later discovered that this was not a legal requirement, other prostitutes told her that it was enforced via harassment of and violence against local workers. Thus if Blain did not register, the Vice Squad would, so it was claimed, come to her home and take her away for questioning in marked cars. This would usually lead to complaints from her neighbours and eventual eviction. The police might also send thugs round to pose as clients and to beat prostitutes up; and if the women then rang the police they would only be given assistance if they were registered. Moreover, Blain's account very carefully skirts the issue of protection money being paid, but recent exposés of police activity, especially in New South Wales, have suggested that this is a widespread practice in Australia. Perth police also gave the personal details of everyone registered as a prostitute to the Special Tax Audit of the Australian Tax Office (Western Australia) which specialized in the sex industry. The august officers of this group, with little apparent regard for human rights, insisted that they could only assess whether a girl was paying the correct amount of tax (that is, proportionate to an accurate assessment of her yearly income) by seeing her in her working clothes, so as to calculate her likely earnings! Special Tax Audit staff therefore regularly visited working girls to interview them in their lingerie. The police also allowed a number of so-called containment parlours to operate, under close supervision – even though this contravened the existing law on organizing prostitution. The workers in these parlours were tightly controlled by the madams, who determined shifts, hours, services offered, clothing and so on. They also, by various forms of creative accounting, took 70–75 per cent of the girls' total earnings, including elements for tax. The problem here was, as Blain puts it, that the madams were tightly networked and had a stranglehold over the industry, maintained by police support so that if you fell foul of one you were unlikely to work in that town again. Furthermore, madams took so much of the girls' money that the weaker ones were more likely to take the risk of unprotected sex, as extra money for this was always on offer from clients. Thus the safe sex message was being undermined by those very groups who were supposed to be spreading it.

New South Wales could be argued, on the other hand, to represent a third sub-category within those locations where prostitution is decriminalized but ancillaries are not, as here the tendency of policy is towards the decriminalization of ancillaries and the decriminalization of the prostitution business (Wijers 1998: 74). Here prostitution itself, soliciting and parlours are all within the law, albeit given certain constraints related to (a) the area where street work takes place – it is illegal within sight of a school, hospital, church or ground floor residential dwelling – and (b) keeping an orderly house, public nuisance, neighbourhood residents' annoyance, and so on (the Disorderly Houses Act). Parlours, furthermore, are not allowed to advertise sex as well as spa and massage. However, the police appear to take a relatively relaxed view of the regulations that do exist, and the decriminalization process coupled with better standards of community policing has helped to maintain more supportive relationships between sex workers and the public (Lazarus 1994). A sex worker's posting to the *World Sex Guide* suggests that 1979's decriminalization has also reduced the involvement of organized crime in prostitution, as well as pimping, trafficking and police corruption. Perhaps unsurprisingly then, Blain (1994), moving to New South Wales to escape the stress of working in Adelaide, noticed that her attitude to prostitution changed when operating in a system which offered some relief from the constant threat of police raids. Not only did she begin to enjoy prostitution, she began to think of it as a possible career, rather than something to be done intensively for a couple of years before getting out. The change of place, in this case, also caused Blain to reorient herself towards time, structuring her week differently and establishing a work pace which she felt she could maintain comfortably and without pressure until she reached the age of thirty-five, when she would retire. Furthermore, it enabled her to consider specializing, which she did for five years, in the B&D sector. New South Wales, then, provided Blain with an environment in which she could actually begin to enjoy, not to say reconsider, her occupation.

Similarly, the approach taken in the Netherlands and Germany might also be understood as one of fairly liberal pragmatism regarding both legislation and its enforcement – despite the fact that the underlying ideology remains, at the present time, one of Lutheran disapproval, as noted above. In the Netherlands, a signatory to the 1949 UN resolution, prostitution is not illegal but, until very recently, all forms of exploitation of prostitution – such as organizing or pimping – were. However, the official state policy (as distinct from ideology) over the last two decades has been one of pragmatism and tolerance, with the result that the sex industry has been able to flourish quite openly in various ways, such as the proliferation of window girls in Amsterdam (EUROPAP 1994; Van Doorninck 1999). Moreover, the current feeling is that this *laissez-faire* stance will not continue to work so well as the industry increases in size. This has produced a bill which, although it failed in 1993 on moral grounds (perhaps illustrating the residual strength of the abolitionist ideology), was passed by the Dutch Parliament in February 1999, and ratified by Senate in October of the same year. When this law comes into effect (expected to be during the summer of 2000),

> the Dutch penal code will no longer treat organizing prostitution of an adult female or male person as a crime when it's done [with] the consent of the prostitute. If she [or he] regards prostitution as the best option to earn a living, she [or he] shall have the same rights that any other worker has. Any form of forced prostitution, pimping and trafficking will remain in the penal code with the maximum penalty up to six years' imprisonment. So a sharp distinction will be made between the exploitation of voluntary prostitution, which will be licensed, and the exploitation of forced prostitution, including minors, which will be punished more severely.
>
> (Van Doorninck 1999)

That is to say, the organizing of voluntary prostitution has been legalized, and brothel owners who abide by strictures concerning the location of their premises as well as the condition of the building and its management will be granted licences to operate. The benefits of this change in the law, Van Doorninck (1999) suggests, are that it will provide a regulated and more professional sex industry where workers have rights and duties as in any other occupation, as well as making entry into prostitution more of a considered choice and allowing State monitoring of employment conditions.

In Germany, registration schemes operate across most of the country and workers within the confines of such schemes are required to have regular health checks. Pimping and the general promotion of prostitution are against the law, and legislation also allows for the introduction of prohibited zones where prostitution cannot take place, on the basis of protecting the local youth, for example. Furthermore, these zones may be temporal as well as geographical. However, although the German Civil Code (GCC) categorizes prostitution as *sittenwidrig* (which roughly translates as immoral), and therefore does not regard it as a legitimate business activity, EUROPAP (1994) describe the general approach to prostitution in Germany as being one of 'toleration and control'. Moreover, the German Minister for Women and the Family Christine Bergmann aims during 2000 to make legislative provision for the recognition of prostitution as a profession 'to a large extent' – that is, to remove the moral stigma which the GCC attaches to this occupation, and to extend social security rights to sex workers. This should also address the anomalous situation of the present moment where, because the contract between prostitute and punter is seen as morally unacceptable, the worker cannot sue for outstanding monies due if the client refuses to pay her, whereas a dissatisfied client is legally at liberty to claim a refund from the prostitute. Under Bergmann's proposals 'it should also be possible [for the prostitute] to sue for non-payment for services'. Moreover, she is considering whether to decriminalize the promotion of prostitution (*Tagesspiegel Online* 1999).[9]

Nonetheless, even in apparently tolerant environments such as these, where indeed in some cases legislative changes are planned which on the face of it will improve the lot of sex workers, those involved in prostitution may still have to live more or less by their wits. In Germany, for example, EUROPAP (1994) argue that certain legal rulings deriving from the existing anti-promotion legislation

> go so far as to construe all forms of good working conditions in brothels, or brothel[-]like businesses, such as good sanitary equipment, internal social arrangements, and even the supplying of condoms, as a promotion of prostitution ... The result of this is that all measures which would lead to improved working conditions for sex-workers are waived by the owners of brothels or brothel-like businesses. This is a counter-productive practice as far as health promotion and infection prevention measures are concerned.

EUROPAP go on to suggest that the existence of prohibition zones makes bribery of officials a daily activity in the relevant areas, and that those who 'do not, or cannot' work (often drug users or migrant prostitutes) within the zones must labour in areas where they are more vulnerable to attack as well as to financial exploitation by those renting rooms and/or pimps.

As far as the Netherlands is concerned, as EUROPAP (1994) point out, one current problem is that:

> The semi-legal status accorded to brothels gives owners the freedom to do business without enabling local authorities to impose punishment for operating infractions, such as the mental or physical mistreatment of employees or the lack of hygienic working conditions.

That is to say, although what they do for a living is strictly speaking illegal, brothel owners are arguably more free in certain respects than those running fully legal businesses. In a similar critique of Dutch legislation and enforcement practices, Venicz (1997) notes that women from outside the EC are explicitly excluded from working legally as prostitutes. She goes on to argue that:

> When prostitution is considered as work it is not strange that illegal prostitutes are excluded. Basically this happens in all legal parts of the economy. The strange part is that it is defended with a discourse that claims to do it for their own good.
>
> (Venicz 1997: 20)

For instance, she cites the round-up of a group of Dominican prostitutes in Amsterdam. These women were said by a police press officer to be existing in 'inhuman' living conditions but, as Venicz somewhat acerbically states, 'In other words, the women on the accompanying photo [which appeared in a national newspaper] that walk handcuffed to a police bus were actually rescued from this situation' (Venicz 1997: 5). That is to say, she questions how arresting someone and physically restraining them could constitute a humanitarian act, the more general point being a challenge to the claim by the Dutch authorities that their enforcement activities involving illegal prostitutes are for the benefit of the workers themselves. In fact, Venicz argues that not all migrant sex workers in the Netherlands are exploited (and therefore in need of 'protection') – indeed, she suggests that they may have chosen to enter prostitution as opposed to being prostituted by others. However, she also states that enforcement protocol means this group are more vulnerable to police harassment and raids, and often depend on 'smuggling' operations (which she differentiates from trafficking) to allow them access to the country itself. Venicz's conclusion is that the official approach to these prostitutes overall is informed by a wider anti-immigration stance in the Netherlands.

Van Doorninck (1999), in a related set of comments, argues that illegal immigrants working in the Dutch sex industry may go underground as a result of the new law, given that legal brothels will be unable to employ them. A related problem which may also surface is that those brothel owners who cannot or will not abide by the licensing regulations would, likewise, have to operate illegally in order to stay in business. Might this legislative change then mean, asks Van Doorninck, that the most vulnerable workers (illegal immigrants) end up being employed by the most exploitative brothel owners?

Finally, at the poorly specified or unspecified end of the scale, there is what we have termed the unregulated context, which might more correctly be referred to as the *effectively* unregulated context. Most countries have some form of legislation against prostitution, whether grounded in the hypocrisy of colonial legislation, in the historical tradition of the Napoleonic Code (as in Egypt), in religious strictures (as in Muslim law), or sometimes in combinations and layers of different influences. We have already noted that these legal ideologies may be important, although often they are not clear. Indeed, in circumstances of social and political upheaval, economic turbulence or protracted instability, the rule of law itself may be in question. At best, its interpretation and application might be at variance with the law as drafted. This is why, when referring to certain parts of Latin America, India and Africa, the *World Sex Guide*, often so informative about many other regions across the world, is less so – many of the details about the African countries, for example, carry the injunction that the legal situation there is 'unknown' (except for Morocco, where prostitution is 'probably illegal' and Nigeria, where it is illegal but 'tolerated'). The same is true of information about Latin America – in Chile prostitution 'appears to be legal', in Paraguay the situation is unknown, as it is in Ecuador and Colombia, whereas reports vary concerning Venezuela (although the conclusion is that prostitution is tolerated there). In India, prostitution is described as 'technically illegal' but 'widely tolerated'. The point to be made here is that the *Guide* is not intended as a legal document, but instead functions as a practical 'handbook' for consumers, workers and researchers as to the conditions applying 'on the ground' to the industry in each location – and it is here where the confusion is felt most keenly. Furthermore, as we have already seen, despite the apparent freedoms generated by a seeming absence of government interest in the activities of those working in the sex industry, prostitutes in such regions, due to their disadvantaged status in broader socio-economic terms, are less likely to take precautions to ensure their own health or that of their clients (Centers for Disease Control and Prevention 1994; Reuters 1994). It is also worth adding that the result of the relaxed attitude to regulation in Australia's Tasmania (which is somewhat in contrast to the state's repressive stance on homosexuality) is high levels of violence against workers and an industry predominantly controlled by organized crime.

In summary, it appears that particular legislative climates produce particular forms of local knowledge which workers draw upon so as to enable them to work on the right side of more or less punitive legislation, or to avoid specific forms of enforcement activity. A high degree of skill and ingenuity is demanded in those places towards the more highly specified end of the scale in this regard. These legal constraints, and their interpretation and enactment, therefore give a very different shape to the industry in different contexts, even as far as affecting the prostitute's sense of time and structure in client encounters, and as regards their career.

Economic performativity in sex work: market segmentation

Place-specific legislation is only one determinant of meaning and experience for prostitutes. The degree to which the market for prostitution is segmented in particular locations (consumption), and whether the prostitute decides to specialize or not within this market (production), also plays a part. At the highly specified end of the scale, there are workers such as Blain (1994: 118–20) during the New South Wales period of her career, when she was employed by a B&D house – a sub-division of a larger brothel. Here straight sex was not provided and clients who wanted it were sent elsewhere. Instead the girls serviced

> Men who wanted to be forced to eat dog food and be locked in a backyard for days; men who wanted to be treated like the Christmas tree fairy and told to fly away – even men who wanted to be given enemas and to be bound in plastic wrap when they released them.
>
> (Blain 1994: 120)

Other B&D specialists include London-based prostitutes Simone Maillard and Mandy Kavanagh (McRae 1992) and Martine (Perkins 1994: 171), working in Sydney, whose specific expertise is apparent in her anecdote about one client being saved from jumping out of the window during a particularly intense session by the fact that his penis was tied to the ceiling (see chapter 11). In another market segment, Layla, based like Mandy and Simone in London, caters specifically for 'adult babies'. Services within her main speciality include breast feeding, and she also offers extras such as spanking or toys (for example, vibrators). Again, however, Layla does not sell penetrative sex. Indeed she suggests that it is 'Absolutely wonderful being able to provide a service without having to lay down and open your legs' (Layla, quoted in *Vice: The Sex Trade*). We have also seen references to other specialisms within prostitution, such as sex therapy and Tantric sex teaching, in chapter 9. In these highly specialized market niches, prostitutes may not offer penetrative intercourse, and will in any case have high levels of expertise – albeit perhaps concomitantly low levels of skill variety.[10] More common perhaps are those who do both specialist and generalist work, such as Desiree, another B&D specialist who, as we know, also offers straight sex (O'Connell Davidson 1994b; 1994c; 1995a; 1996). Others elect to charge more for particular acts, such as those few workers at London's Maison Demi-Monde offering anal sex or allowing customers to give them enemas. The usual charge for such services is double what at February 1998 was a half-hourly rate of £60, but the girls involved also exercise their discretion (*Maison Demi-Monde*). Here

of which she was able to keep for herself. Moreover, while she says she was no different from a street prostitute in that she sold sex for money, she always insisted on safe sex. She also points to the fact that her hotel visits actually felt safe because she was with men who had paid by credit card at the club where she was officially employed (Valentine 1998: 25). Similarly, outworkers interviewed by tabloid journalists Levine and McMullen (1998) gave prices varying between £250 and £300 an hour, and up to £2,000 for the night.

The next stratum, those who work in lower-end brothels or parlours, or perhaps in saunas, includes Charlotte, employed in a 'working flat' in London's Soho. Charlotte charges £60 for oral and penetrative sex but is herself charged overheads of between £200 and £250 a day (which covers, for example, wages for the flat maids and for those who distribute her advertising cards around the local area). Workers like her, as a consequence, do not earn as much as those who are self-employed, the high-class brothel prostitutes or the higher paid outworkers, as well as labouring in less luxurious surroundings. However, Charlotte does work in a fairly safe environment, given that the maids answer the phone, let punters in and out and take their money – thus they provide a 'buffer' between worker and client. She is also, despite earning less than certain other sex workers, still in a financial position to refuse any offers of unsafe sex (Salvadori 1997). In one of her two establishments in Manchester, Karen's price is slightly lower – £40 for massage and sex – but, because she manages the parlour, she does at least keep all of her profits (*Vice: The Sex Trade*).

At the poorly specified or unspecified end of the scale, penetrative sex from a streetworker in Desiree's area of the East Midlands cost £20–25, as opposed to £70 for her services, at the time of O'Connell Davidson's research (O'Connell Davidson 1995a: 4; 1996: 182). Similarly, Jemma, on the street in the East End of London, offers 'French and sex' for £20; and Maggie O'Neill's (1996) respondents talk of street sex being offered for as little as £15. A street prostitute also often gets into a stranger's car or provides services somewhere equally unfamiliar, secluded and therefore unsafe. Street prostitutes, then, to a greater extent than others, are at risk of violent attack or rape, as we have already seen – although it is important to note that, despite the higher incidence of violence at street level, in the sex industry as a whole violence is not endemic, nor is it more prevalent here than in other sectors of society. As an illustration of this, Strossen (1995: 190) cites FBI reports which claim that 'the home is the centre of violence in twentieth-century America' as well as pointing out that one in every six violent crimes happen at work (of all types), including 8 per cent of all rapes, 16 per cent of all assaults and 4 per cent of all homicides. Lamplugh (1996) makes a similar point about work in the UK – that workers are often subject to violence and she is not talking about the sex industry. Nonetheless, these data do not undermine the fact that the street prostitute is worse off in this regard than many of his or her counterparts elsewhere in the sex industry and that they are also more vulnerable to police harassment, as was established above. In terms of susceptibility to HIV/STD transmission, moreover, Moira (cited in O'Neill 1996: 24) suggests that it may take as little as £5 or £10 for a client to be able to persuade a streetworker in her area, particularly a younger girl, to have sex without a condom. There is also the fact that streetworkers are more likely to be drug users, and that, as we have already suggested, hard drug use is reported to dull the prostitute's ability to negotiate safe sex, or to make her generally less able to adjudge potential punters in what is already a very insecure locale. Many of the women who held the lowest opinion of the clients in McKeganey and Barnard's (1996) research were, in fact, the ones who were working to earn money for drugs, and who presumably felt they had little choice regarding what they did and who they worked for.

Also in contra-distinction to higher end workers, many street prostitutes are pimped. Although, as noted in chapter 9, pimping is geographically specific (Phoenix 1999), pimps controlling a particular area may make it difficult for a newcomer to sell sex there without coming under their 'wing'. Alternatively workers may choose to enter into one particular pimping relationship to escape another one and/or because of the threat of violence from clients:

> The street's a dangerous place. If you're gonna be smart you have to have a man to protect ya and make sure no one kidnaps you or drives off with you. So what if you have to give him some money?
>
> (Anna, quoted in Phoenix 1998: 16)

However, the 'opportunity costs' incurred in such relationships are very obvious. Anna killed her pimp because he beat her, took her earnings and made her engage in bestiality – and many of Phoenix's women feared being murdered by their pimps. Leila (quoted in McRae 1992) had also been regularly beaten by her former boyfriend/current pimp when she failed to earn enough money. Moreover, in pimping relationships, workers lack autonomy and must hand over at least some of their earnings to their pimp. Susan (quoted in O'Neill 1996: 21–2) is emphatic on the rigours associated with this sort of relationship – in this case a 17 year old working for a group of crack dealers to whom her partner owed money. This girl was forced not only to work to settle her partner's debt, but also to pay for a hired car to get the money from Brighton to Nottingham where the dealers operated, and for their hotel bills. Moreover, Phoenix (1999) cites the case of Lois who was given £2.50 a day by her pimp, which left her with the choice of buying cigarettes *or* food *or* condoms, as well as pointing to women who worked six days a week for their pimps, being permitted to work the seventh to earn money for themselves. She also suggests that nineteen of the twenty-one women in her respondent group had been pimped, had often had several pimps during their careers, were often 'corralled' by these men such that they could not see family, friends or even other workers and were on occasion traded between pimps as if they truly were commodities.

Nonetheless, street work is not always as desperate as the above data suggest. We have already seen evidence of entry and exit at street level, and of career progression within prostitution from the street upwards. Based on these data, and following Oliver Williamson (1985), this progression may entail movement from the high risk market of the streets – where low-trust relationships exist between workers, clients and pimps, where the clientele are casual and there is less likelihood of developing regulars, where prices and services may be negotiable to the detriment of the worker, where the workers very often lack autonomy as well as being unlikely to have high levels of expertise (meaning that they are also replaceable) and where the contract between worker and client is often broken, sometimes violently – to the high-trust hierarchy of the self-owned premises – where pimps are not involved and workers and clients may have high-trust relationships, where workers have discretion, a regular clientele, high security, high autonomy and high levels of expertise and skill, and where there is much less likelihood of the contract being broken (see, for example, discussion of Desiree's techniques for ensuring payment in O'Connell Davidson 1994b and chapter 11).

Furthermore, street prostitutes may exercise great care to maximize their chances of working safely. We have already seen that McRae's (1992: 242) Leila checks potential clients out through their car windows and that Mary (quoted in O'Neill 1996: 20) always maintains a certain distance between herself and her clients. As she says, therefore, 'I always have my head clear to work … I've got to be alert.' Others refuse to have sex without a condom, and will turn punters away if they demand such services – Moira, another of O'Neill's interviewees, practises this approach, as we have seen. Jackie McAuliffe has also been depicted asking a client to let his friend out of the car before she got in with him, to ensure that she was not outnumbered (*Paddington Green*). Indeed, Jemma, in many other respects a 'stereotypical' streetworker (disadvantaged childhood, has a child in care, works for a pimp, hates what she does for a living and detests her clients), refuses to get into clients' cars at all and services them in a back street – which often means that she, like Leila, loses potential punters who do not want to get out of their cars (*Vice: The Sex Trade*). In sum, then, although employment stratification within prostitution means that streetworkers are, by and large, less well remunerated, less safe and less autonomous, experiences even in this stratum of sex work are differentiated.

Social community and kinship in sex work: mutual support

As implied above in the discussion of legislative climates and working conditions, it may well pay off for sex workers to support each other, providing safety in numbers as well as psychological and emotional succour. Nonetheless, as we might expect from the analysis so far, the degree to which this mutual support exists, and the extent to which it is organized, varies from locale to locale. At one end of the scale lie examples of highly organized relations between sex workers such as prostitutes' rights groups, including Sex Workers' Alliance of Vancouver in Canada; COYOTE (Call Off Your Old Tired Ethics), North American Task Force on Prostitution and PONY (Prostitutes of New York) in the US; SWEAT (Sex Worker Education Agency and Taskforce) in South Africa, SWEETLY (Sex Workers! Encourage, Empower, Trust and Love Yourselves) in Japan; and the

English Collective of Prostitutes, Prostitution Pride and the Network of Sex Work Projects in the UK. Similar alliances exist across the world and numbers are growing. Many groups have Internet sites and, as implied in chapter 8, actively campaign for prostitution to be recognized as a legitimate form of labour, no different from any other, and therefore as deserving of equal rights and legal protection. Events such as the aforementioned First European Whores' Congress, where prostitutes met to discuss their work, echo these developments (O'Neill 1996: 22; 1997: 27). Such activities are also evident in the appearance of important collections of writings by women working in the sex industry, with discussions ranging from the emotional labour of sex work to the case for legalization and regulation (Delacoste and Alexander 1987; Chapkis 1997).

The collectives discussed above operate almost as (old-style) trade unions in their provision of counselling, advice and solidarity, as well as a vision of a better future for those working in prostitution. Maggie O'Neill (1997: 26) suggests that: 'The European and international prostitutes' rights movement has to date had most impact in Germany, the Netherlands and North America, generating interagency support, backing and campaigning and lobbying for social change.' Furthermore, these groups are self-organized and tend only to involve sex workers (and former sex workers). However, as we implied earlier on, prostitutes may gain similar levels of support from research and policy groups, social care programmes or outreach projects, where agencies external to the sex industry often play a role. In the Netherlands, for example, the Mr A. de Graaf Foundation (1997: 1) describes itself as involved in 'research, policy, advice, documentation and public information' concerning Dutch prostitution. WHIP (Women's Health in Prostitution), POW! (Prostitute Outreach Workers) and Soliciting for Change are all UK outreach projects focusing on health, welfare, drug use, vocational and educational guidance, counselling, violence and legislative reform, with an ethos of self-help, peer education and empowerment for working women (O'Neill 1997: 25–6 – also see McKeganey and Barnard 1996). A further instance of the kind of support provided in this sector of the taxonomy is the production of the manual *Hustling for Health* by the European Network for HIV/STD Prevention in Prostitution.[14] This, in line with the Network's concern 'with the prevention of HIV and other communicable diseases, and with sexual health more generally', as well as with the provision of 'appropriate, accessible and acceptable services for sex workers across the continent', presents the 'collective experience [of its members] in the form of a practical manual, with ideas and guidance for those who would like to start and develop sex workers' health projects' (European Network for HIV/STD Prevention in Prostitution). Finally, external agency support for those in the sex industry also includes the Glasgow police campaign to encourage street prostitutes only to pick up punters in the city centre where CCTV is in operation (Nelson 1998), following the aforementioned murders of working girls, which have taken place over a period of seven years without a single conviction being secured.

However, groups and projects like those described above are predominantly to be found in the West where, as established in chapter 8, supportive family networks are frequently not available to prostitutes due to the stigma which attaches to the profession in the relevant countries. This is not necessarily true of the East. Hershatter's (1997) historical data suggest that a substantial number of Chinese women were sold or pawned ('loaned' as prostitutes for a finite period of time) by their families, usually for economic reasons and with the women's full consent. Indeed, she contrasts the 'filial piety' justification for entering prostitution, to which these women had recourse, with that used by others who claimed they had been abducted (Hershatter 1997: 194, 199). Moreover, modern migrant prostitutes such as those in the Netherlands, who originate in the main in the Dominican Republic, Colombia, Ghana, Nigeria, Thailand and Eastern Europe, often say they are working for 'their families back home', given that prostitution is the best paid occupation available to them as illegal workers (Venicz 1997: 7). Here family support, albeit at such distances, may be significant in sustaining the prostitute's sense of self and enabling a passage into and out of the occupation without stigma, perhaps even with honour. In a similar vein, 'the idea that Thai prostitutes are young girls dutifully sacrificing themselves for their rural families' (Cook 1998: 264) has become a common justification for prostitution among the Thai middle classes. Indeed, as already implied in the Introduction, this image of dutiful daughters and cultural continuity redeeming an otherwise shameful occupation has widespread empirical support, and it is also true that poverty and landlessness in rural areas place enormous demands on families to find whatever means of support they can (Pongpaichit 1982; Hantrakul 1988; Van Esterik 1992; 1995; Karim 1995a). Nonetheless, it is also important to point out that this situation is subject to widespread exception. Many parents take advantage of their daughters and squander their earnings (thus destroying the redemptive qualities of the act); many daughters feel compelled to follow their sisters to the cities; many are pushed by their village communities as well as pulled by the opportunities of the city, regardless of their wishes.[15]

In contrast, at this more informal level it tends to be friendship within the profession, as opposed to other forms of social networks, that provides support for Western prostitutes. Sam and Mary, two of O'Neill's respondents, talk as we have already seen of 'supporting other women working as prostitutes' (O'Neill 1996: 22), and others refer to the practice of working in 'doubles', and sharing the money, for extra safety (p. 24). Moira (quoted in O'Neill 1996: 17) also recounts how she threatened to break a man's windscreen after he and his friend snatched back the money they had just paid over to a friend of hers. Our fieldwork in Australia suggests that workers in this context have similar ways of looking out for each other, including one worker telling another when she is leaving her 'beat' to service a punter, so that the woman who remains behind can raise the alarm if necessary.

By way of contrast, and again as discussed above, other women are 'protected' by their pimps, who may also be their sexual partners. However, the problems that pimping creates for prostitutes are clear in the data, and have already been discussed. There is also evidence of pimping dividing prostitutes – Mary (quoted in O'Neill 1996: 24) points out that working for a pimp may mean that women compete for his love and attention by struggling each to pay him more than the other women under his jurisdiction. Phoenix's respondent Katrina suggested, in a similar vein, that:

> You want your ponce to look good, man. You want them to dress good, get nice cars and wicked gold. You give them your money so they can look good … If I were some stupid crackhead or something, I couldn't be earning the money I earn to make my man look good.
>
> (quoted in Phoenix 1998: 16)

Katrina says she looks on all of this as good advertising – that is to say, her pimp's appearance and accoutrements symbolize her talents as a sex worker. However, we might also surmise that her desire to supply her pimp to the best of her ability also has to do with her loyalty to him as a sexual partner, especially in her reference to 'my man', and that this is connected with some form of competition with other women working in her area. Such individualism, where prostitutes do not support each other, is also evident in Fran's (quoted in O'Neill 1996: 24–5) claim that younger entrants into prostitution are causing a problem where she works, because they are willing to charge a client less for sex than the informally agreed street rate, and no longer share information about difficult clients, which makes street work more dangerous as well as harder to come by. Moira's (quoted in O'Neill 1996: 24) point about younger workers being willing to take relatively small bribes for unsafe sex is also relevant here.

Place, then, not only influences how vulnerable the sex worker is to legal harassment and censure, the strategies they develop to avoid such attention, the type of work they actually undertake (and therefore, in part at least, their attitudes to clients and the occupation in general), their income, autonomy and safety, but also the level of support they can expect from those inside and outside the profession.

Having established four main dimensions of place within sex work, within each of which a particular continuum of experience can be observed, we offer a summary of the data in Table 10.1.

Modelling 'model' relationships

We can now reflect on the relationships between the dimensions which emerge from our discussion. These interpretations remain to be tested empirically, but if the common problem of access to sufficient respondents (as discussed in chapter 7) can be overcome then it would certainly be possible to use our hypotheses to guide future research. We should also remind readers that our four columns (legislative climate, market segmentation, employment stratification and mutual support) are not co-occurrent, such that one geographical place might be located high on one dimension yet low on another. Thus Table 10.1 should be read vertically as opposed to horizontally.

Table 10.1 Characteristics of sex work environments

Degree of specification	Legislative climate	Market segmentation	Employment stratification	Mutual support
Highly specified	Criminalization – enforced	Specialist-skill variety possibly low but expertise high	Self-employed/ employ others	Political campaigns/ lobbying, sex workers' rights groups
	Criminalization – tolerated			
	Decriminalization of act, criminalization of ancillaries – enforced	Specialist- and occasional generalist-skill variety high, expertise moderately high	High end parlour/brothel worker	Research and policy groups, social care programmes and outreach projects – external agency involvement
Moderately specified or hetero-geneous	Decriminalization of act, criminalization of ancillaries – selective tolerance/ *de facto* regulation	Certain acts command a high price and/ or others excluded	Outworker/ visiting escort	Family networks – not Western
	Decriminalization of act, regulation of ancillaries (eg, legalization)		Lower end parlour/ brothel worker	Informal support networks
	Decriminalization of act and ancillaries, relaxed regulation		Street, drug free, not pimped, possibly seasonal, part time or casual	
Poorly specified or unspecified	Unregulated	Undifferentiated	Street, drug user, pimped, sole occupation but may be erratic	Individualism

The most straightforward relationship here could be visually represented by a falling or rising straight line graph, and we would expect such a relationship to exist between legislative climate and market segmentation and market segmentation and employment stratification respectively.[16] Where prostitution is criminalized and such criminalization enforced (highly specified legislative climate), we suggest that this would make the circulation of information needed for a segmented market to develop and communicate its needs impossible without attracting the attentions of the law. This would produce a falling graph. In contra-distinction, when market segmentation and employment stratification are plotted against each other, we would expect a rising graph, as each tends to require the other to be high in order to maximize returns.

More interesting are the potential relationships between legislative climate and mutual support, and market segmentation and mutual support. Each of these should, we anticipate, produce a backwards bending graph. Where, for example, cultural context is high, legislative climate poorly specified and regulation practically low, such as in parts of Africa, prostitutes are usually completely individualized – whether for reasons of poverty, drug addiction or other afflictions, they would tend to be so close to desperation as to make co-operation with others of no interest whatsoever. Where cultural context is low, and legal regulation restrictive, prostitutes also may be forced to keep such a low profile that, again, mutual support and collective action become difficult. It is therefore in the middle ranges, where prostitution itself is decriminalized but attitudes to ancillaries vary, and where the cultural context may be mixed or without a pronounced tendency in either direction, that mutual support and political campaigning should emerge most strongly. Moreover, where the market is not segmented, this usually reflects the need for prostitutes to do whatever they can, to compete strongly enough to be able to make a living, so that mutual support in these circumstances is likely to be patchy at best. At the other end of this scale, high market segmentation, especially when it entails little mobility between segments, means that prostitutes specialize within their niche and generally either work alone or with a few colleagues. Where the market is diverse but movement between the segments is noticeable, communication and co-ordination are more likely and a higher level of support is to be expected.

Finally, the relationship between mutual support and employment stratification is of particular significance because it would appear to conform to a normal curve, split into three sectors. That is to say, we would expect peer support to be low where employment stratification is both high and low, as employment stratification is related to market segmentation, although the conditions when employment stratification is low would conform to the unregulated free market, while when employment stratification is high the conditions of economic hierarchy would prevail. In the central area of the curve, where mutual support is high, we would expect clan conditions to be predominant, as some professional identity develops with the growth of stratification and individual aspirations are shared. These inferences suggest that it would be desirable to carry out research which enables identification and comparison across categories in prostitution. This might surface with greater clarity some of the common features and shaping forces of the industry.

Conclusion

We have sought in the foregoing chapters to demonstrate that the construction of self-identity for the prostitute is an embedded process, which may also be in tension with knowledge circulating at a more global level, but in any case is shaped by the materialities and institutions surrounding the profession, the social

11 The temporal organization of sex work

Introduction

In the previous four chapters we have dealt extensively with the importance of place in prostitution. However, time is also highly significant in analysing this profession. Our main interest in this chapter is therefore in the ways in which workers and punters experience time in and around the encounter; and we argue that time is typically experienced and constructed very differently by each party. That is to say, time spent with a prostitute is leisure time for the client but is also time in which he seeks, as we have noted, to buy whatever is not forthcoming via naturally occurring relationships, time which is spent seeking to bolster and enhance self-identity which may be challenged in other situations, at home and at work. Time for the prostitute, on the other hand, is work time, which must be carefully managed in order to maximize income and to ensure safety for the participants, in B&D sessions in particular, but which may also threaten self-esteem.[1] The prostitute is therefore engaged in identity work before, during and after the encounter, given that sex work can be boring, unpredictable, risky and potentially degrading. Moreover, prostitutes need to be able to manage time within the encounter so as to satisfy clients' demands efficiently and thus must create a convincing simulation of a 'real', mutually desiring sexual encounter. The socially degraded status of prostitution in our core context also means that sex workers may need to use time both inside and outwith the client encounter to attempt to reshape definitions of the profession – in political campaigning, for example.

These differences in clients' time and prostitutes' time might to some extent be attributed to the fact that most prostitution, as we know, takes place between a male client and a female prostitute – that is to say, these differences are *gendered*. Nonetheless, because time itself is also gendered, the characteristics of time as experienced in the encounter may, paradoxically, be the reverse of the participants' gender, such that the differences identified above are neither rigid nor invariable. Female workers may live out interactions with clients as (masculine) time which needs to be controlled and rationalized or as (feminine) time during which emotion runs high and a sense of connection is felt. Clients, similarly, may look for (feminine) affection and intimacy, or alternatively seek to script and dictate the encounter (a masculine orientation to time) – to avoid arrest or being ripped off, or to ensure that their specific requirements are met. Time here is not pure, but complex, contaminated, even reversible and the ways in which the interactants experience and interpret time emphasize the complexity of identity work, as already discussed in chapters 8 and 9 specifically.

Time and the labour process

Recently time has received renewed attention in the social and organizational sciences. Giddens (1984; 1991) places time and space at the centre of his sociology, particularly in relation to identity. Harvey (1990), Lash and Urry (1994) and Nowotny (1994) see changing social conditions arising from accelerated changes in our experiencing of time and space as characterizing postmodernity, a point also made by Baudrillard (1987) and Virilio (1986). Sociological approaches frequently consider specific organized forms of time structuring, as well as its institutionalization (see Clark 1978; Hassard 1990; 1991; 1996), as summarized in collections such as Young and Schuller (1988). Moreover, the processes and effects of the intensification of the monitoring of time by management have been extensively explored by Donaldson (1991; 1996) and more focally by Sewell and Wilkinson (1992). Such treatments of time usually also defer to E.P. Thompson's (1967) classic study and mention the empirical work of Roy (1955), but then range widely – for example, the functionalism of Goodman (1973) and Butler (1995), the more phenomenological theorizing of Clark (1985; 1990), the resurgent but reflective Marxist empiricism of Donaldson (1991; 1996) and the postmodern analyses of Burrell (1992a; 1992b; 1997), Cooper and Law (1995) and Holmer-Nadesan (1997). Useful reviews in this regard include Blyton *et al.* (1989) and Das (1992). More recently, gender and postmodernism have been brought together in the work of Game (1991) and Grosz (1995) – and Collinson and Collinson (1997) use this type of analysis to examine the gendered nature of work time, which is also discussed in its structural context by Hantrais and Letablier (1997).

This resurgence of interest in time, the labour process and gender leads us inevitably to consider the significance of time as the final dimension of our study of the contours of prostitution – perhaps the most conspicuously gendered form of labour. Nonetheless, as we have established, prostitution differs from other industries because what is being sold here – the prostitute's sexuality – is usually associated with the non-commercial private sphere and its values of intimacy, love and affect (O'Connell Davidson 1995a: 8–9; 1996: 193–4). Still, from the client's perspective, it is also important to acknowledge the modern commodification of pleasure and the recognition since the mid-nineteenth century of the right of individuals to periods of leisure as a deserved release from work, also discussed in chapter 8. Prostitution, therefore, can be considered to be both a consumer industry *and* a service industry, scarcely different in its sale of sexual services from the provision of fast food or of cinematic entertainment.[2] Given its gendered character, its liminal status and the obvious significance of time for those involved in the industry, then, we now turn to examine in more detail the interplay between time and the social practice of prostitution.

Time and sex work

It may seem banal to remark upon the importance of time in prostitution, given that prostitutes are usually hired by the hour, or fragments or multiples thereof. However, as we shall demonstrate, time plays a deeper, indeed often paradoxical role in shaping the social and psychological character of prostitution. We have already seen that, though organized, prostitution is simultaneously highly de-centralized and ranges in the degrees of both formalization and specialization with which it is conducted. Moreover, it is intensely proximal as a profession but also displays clear distal effects (Cooper and Law 1995). The prostitute attempts to regulate the experience for the client to achieve appropriate outcomes (evening out or 'flattening' experience across time) and employs both interac-tional strategies and technologies to do this which consist mainly of non-verbal social negotiation between bodies. She then has to react and adapt to the effect of these strategies on the client's body, sometimes increasing urgency, sometimes reducing it (see chapter 5's discussion of the infliction of pain by the dominatrix prostitute, as explained by Sellers, 1992: 43–4, for example).

Prostitution is also affected by the passage of natural time – the busiest periods in the industry are at night – but also by cyclical time, given that human sexual activity is known to increase in spring and summer (Donaldson 1996: 27). Further, the menstrual cycle may affect both working days and working moods as a result of PMS and menstrual symptomatology, and the encounter itself involves the acceleration and control of body rhythms such as the heartbeat. This type of work is also influenced by the prostitute's life-cycle – as we have established, there are usually a limited number of years in which she can enjoy being in great demand – and by the life-cycles of others (for example, the fact that many prostitutes are single parents working to support their children). Moreover, again as we already know, prostitution is bounded by institutions and regulations which emerge and change over time and are frequently the subject of political lobbying and pressure, which means that at least some members of the profession have to remain oriented to history, to past campaigns, and to the speed of social change.

Finally, the acceleration of technological innovation can be seen to have affected the time within which contemporary prostitution takes place. While prostitution has arguably always been a 24/7 industry (Brewis *et al.* 1997b), inno-vations such as the mobile phone or the pager now mean that the prostitute is potentially always within easy reach of her clients (Ecstavasia 1994). This, on the one hand, may be seen to allow the maximization of earnings, as well as making working within legislative boundaries (for example, those which make soliciting or advertising illegal) easier. Perhaps this technology may also render street work in particular safer, as it provides a straightforward way to call for help. However, it also means that the divisions between work and leisure, permeable at the best of times, could become harder to draw for individual workers. Once equipped with a mobile phone and/or a pager, a prostitute's working day/night may conceivably be endless, because they are always 'available'. A rather amusing instance of this is Layla's mobile phone conversation with a potential customer in her local drug store – she carefully details her services and prices while a curious security guard looks on (*Vice: The Sex Trade*).

Another important technological innovation, the Internet, can also be seen to have impacted on time within prostitution. Given that the Net allows for 'virtual sex', for intimate contact without physical proximity, there are several interesting ramifications for the nature of the prostitute–client encounter. Not least of these is the requirement for the prostitute to create the appropriate ambience for the interaction, to give punters 'a good time', or to facilitate their giving themselves a good time, without necessarily ever meeting them (Higgins *et al.* 1999). The Net also permits this virtual commercial sex to take place in real time across different time zones – and suggests interesting lines of enquiry in terms of the degree of embodiment, or the construction of the virtual Body without Organs, experienced by both punter and prostitute in the encounter itself (Deleuze and Guattari 1987; Ecstavasia 1994).[3]

As we have already suggested, though, the obvious connection between prostitution and time is the sale of the prostitute's time (among other things) in the client encounter. This interaction is bounded by time constraints, and a rhythm has to be created which moves the interaction to a conclusion at the appropriate point. Between encounters and across the day, however, time may move at a different rate. Additionally, the fact that most encounters are between male clients and female workers raises the question of whether men's time and women's time are commensurable, and also relates to how the division between work and leisure is achieved in the light of the relative investments of self-identity in the interaction – especially with regard to the motivations of the male client. However, with Bergson (1913, 1950), Game (1991: chapter 5), and Lash and Urry (1994: 239) we see time, body and space as intertwined and inextricable, such that time cannot be pulled out of this intertext leaving some essence intact. That is to say, people are temporal. In this regard, then, the time of the prostitute–client encounter is also one which defines a new type of space. Using Deleuze and Guattari's (1987) conceptualization, this space is smooth (personal, private, intimate), but simultaneously is also striated (public, commercialized, regulated). In smooth space time *flows*, but in striated space it *ticks*, and the artifice of the successful sex worker is in making this ticking clock-time seem to flow. The issues that this raises for both client and worker are discussed in detail in our substantive analysis, which follows.

Clients' time: men's time?

The encounter between client and worker, as suggested above, represents free time or leisure time for the client, but is working time for the prostitute. We will explore this intersection first by looking at the meaning of 'male' time, and some of the reasons why men may choose to spend their leisure time buying sex.

As Donaldson (1991: 21–2) sees it, traditional patriarchal masculinity involves self-sacrifice; the man becomes a 'real man' by sacrificing himself for his family's well-being through an arduous working day. However, this feeling of self-sacrifice can become inverted, so that the family comes to be seen as a millstone. As the son of a carpet-layer reported: 'He would come home in the evening and be all tied up in self-hatred and hatred towards us, who he saw as the reason he had to go through all this shit' (Weissman 1977: 198, cited in Donaldson 1991: 22). 'Real men', then, men with families, cannot just walk away from work when bad things happen; they have to remain and endure the 'constant humiliation … and the upfront aggravation' of work (Donaldson 1991: 25; see also Collinson 1988). Ehrenreich (1983: 2–3) therefore recognizes that the power that patriarchal capitalism produces is accompanied by a certain level of entrapment for men, and Barrett (1980: 216) agrees, suggesting that the role of breadwinner is not necessarily intrinsically desirable. Consequently, men often see the workplace as some kind of bizarre or, as Donaldson puts it, 'unreal' game. By way of contrast, at home they are different people because this is a place where a man can be himself, where he does not need to be aggressive, where he can be vulnerable, revealing his feelings and his pain in a way which he can't to his colleagues or even to his male friends, and where he can receive support. Sex, another feature of private relationships, may likewise provide a resource for the sustenance and repair of male identity. Where labour and, increasingly, management (Collinson and Collinson 1997) have been degraded by capital, private love-making represents an area of men's lives which at least is not the direct target of workplace discipline, even though it may be affected by work-related stress and fatigue.[4] As Donaldson (1991: 26) notes:

> In lovemaking masculinity is asserted and powerfully reflected back … even when, perhaps, men may wish it wasn't … In sex male workers have increasingly sought solace, release, and the assertion of power. Sex is often the only way a man's emotional control is shaken, where he can contact and express his deeper feelings.

Sex therefore represents an emotional escape from work for many men, which is also necessary to accommodate the need to return to work (Lippert 1977: 212; Orbach and Eichenbaum 1984: 23; Donaldson 1991: 26). If it is men's individuality, self-assurance, competence and confidence which win them love in the first place, these are, arguably, also what is most under threat in the modern workplace. Consequently, sex becomes an important reassurance for an individual man that he still has the (desir)ability to win or retain love, a significant bolster to self-worth.

However, this self-worth is also fragile; in particular, it can be diminished by the female partner having an affair, such that a man's whole psychological world is threatened by female unfaithfulness. Relations between men and women are therefore more than a simple matter of 'property rights'. Nonetheless, a man's own sexual behaviour is irrelevant in this regard. He may psychologically invest a great deal in one relationship but, ironically, the insecurity experienced in acknowledging the vulnerability this entails may cause its divergence into one or more shallow relationships. It is in this psychologically fragile space that the encounter with the prostitute may be located, such that the client seeks a mock intimacy with the worker in order to shore up a simulacrum of the 'secret self' which relationships with a steady partner may have rendered vulnerable or diffi-cult to express. Some prostitutes therefore feel the need to fake orgasm for the client's benefit. As London prostitute Charlotte says, 'The men really want to believe that you fancy them. They love it when you make a lot of noise. They really kid themselves that you're enjoying it' (Salvadori 1997: 120). Streetworker Jemma (quoted in *Vice: The Sex Trade*) makes a similar comment: 'Some of them say "Oh I want you to enjoy it" and you say "Alright". Then … you pretend.' Moreover, Barbara (1994: 18, cited in Bishop and Robinson 1998: 234) writes that clients like these are especially demanding: 'The worst ones are the ones who don't turn you on and think that all women have to have about six orgasms before they will penetrate them.' Attributing the need to fake multiple orgasms to the impression given by pornographic films (where the woman has ample time to recover between takes – that is, even simulation is physically tiring), she goes on:

> you have to do this dramatic, over-the-top fake. And they manage to really believe it. They really do … But I don't fake all the time. Sometimes I do get turned on. But if you were to have a real orgasm, they wouldn't believe you.

As Bishop and Robinson comment, the experience of real pleasure (as discussed in earlier chapters) therefore does not obviate the need to fake – in other words, simulation is always some part of the prostitute's experience. So the sex worker's own pleasure becomes commodified as well as that of the client – at least for some sex workers and some clients, as Bishop and Robinson also give examples of clients who were not impressed with the dramatic efforts of some of the sex workers they visited.[5]

Thus the time of the encounter for the client is not necessarily just leisure time, where he can relax without encumbrance. It may be a variety of things, but imported into it will be the pressures and circumstances of the workplace and the dynamics and tensions of the home. Moreover, no matter how swift and shallow the encounter, the client's sense of masculinity and his attempt to locate himself within an acceptable understanding of what it means to be a man are also likely to be at issue. Some men will need a degree of intimacy from the encounter, some men will need to feel powerful, some will need to feel wanted, attractive, sexually gifted. Others may seek sexual add-ons, to satisfy specific unmet needs within relationships with which they are otherwise content, or to be released from their everyday limitations through the relaxation of constraints – where being short, fat, bald, old, ugly or poorly endowed will not matter (McKeganey and Barnard 1996: 48–57; O'Connell Davidson 1995a: 6–7, 1996:

190). Clients therefore seek to buy whatever is not present in their personal relationships from the sex worker.[6] As a result, the prostitute must enable clients to
achieve this self-esteem, to fit in with whatever 'time of their life' they are experiencing – indeed, to give a client 'the time of their life' is literally what the
successful sex worker must do – while also remaining in control of the time of
the encounter. In this regard, then, let us look at some of the ways in which time
can be managed by the skilled and aware practitioner.

Workers' time: making money, playing safe

It seems from a review of the available data that prostitutes tend to attempt to
manage time very carefully in their encounters with clients. O'Connell Davidson
(1995a: 5–6; 1996: 185) reports that Desiree can manage an encounter with an
inexperienced client so that he is with her for only fifteen minutes – and, given
that she charges £70 for penetrative sex, it is clear that her control of time is
crucial in maximizing the money that she makes. As we have already implied,
moreover, even with the more experienced and therefore more demanding
clients, Desiree's sexual knowledge is such that she can ensure a rapid
turnaround. For example, she exercises her pelvic floor muscles regularly so as to
enable her to 'milk' the man who penetrates her, so bringing him to orgasm
much faster. Indeed, as Ecstavasia notes from advice given by an escort, the prostitute needs to know exactly how long the encounter has been running, its
immediate past and incipient future, without letting this intrude on the
encounter, because time is money:

> So you get in the elevator and you go on up. Before you knock on the client's
> door, be sure to check your watch, because it's important to know what time
> you arrived – and nobody likes a clock-watcher. Incidentally, it's helpful to
> wear a watch that's easy to read in a dim light with just a glance.
>
> (Ecstavasia 1994: 187–8)

Also indicative of Desiree's time management skills is her method for dealing
with time wasters (whom she calls 'pilchards') who simply derive pleasure from
seeing her – a 'real, live prostitute' – in the flesh, and then disappear to mastur-
bate without paying her anything. To combat such problems, Desiree has
instructed her receptionists only to give her address out when a man books a
definite appointment; and every client is charged an appointment fee of £20 on
arrival, whether he is actually 'serviced' or not. If a client proves recalcitrant in
this regard, perhaps claiming that he has called in on the off-chance or does not
have any money, Desiree emphasizes the appointment system and may even
remove personal effects from him, telling him that she will return them when he
comes back with the £20 (O'Connell Davidson 1994c: 11). However, as
O'Connell Davidson (1995a: 6; 1996: 186) also points out, particular types of
client – especially those wanting her services as a dominatrix – 'exact more for
their money' from Desiree, because her emotional labour here is far more

intense. Physical time in a domination encounter is arguably less the issue than the actual work performed – and the domination client is therefore not as profitable in any sense, because Desiree has to work harder (and, it is implied, longer) with him.

In contra-distinction, accounts from street prostitutes suggest that sex bought in this locale can perhaps be seen more legitimately as a simple commercial transaction, to be completed as speedily and efficiently as possible. For Maggie O'Neill's (1996: 23) respondents, the average time spent with a street client is seven minutes and Jemma (quoted in *Vice: The Sex Trade*) backs this up, suggesting that ten minutes is her maximum. Järvinen (1993: 144, cited in Scambler 1997: 115), similarly, quotes a Norwegian prostitute describing a 'good' customer as a 'fast' customer. These encounters, then, represent the literal 'turning' of a 'trick' whereas Desiree's higher priced services must of necessity be handled with more care and discretion. Indeed, higher-class establishments usually have the expectation that the worker will make good conversation, which requires concentration and, of course, takes time (Cockington and Marlin 1995). Here the street prostitute, who is usually relatively badly off as compared to workers higher up the sex work 'hierarchy', scores a rare victory over the woman who works from her own premises, from a parlour/brothel, or as an outworker – their clients are less likely to be highly demanding or discriminating regarding the quality of service delivery (O'Connell Davidson 1995a: 4, 1996: 193).[7]

Careful time management, however, has other ramifications beyond the maximization of income; as some clients discover, it can have an important impact on safety during the encounter, especially in B&D sessions:

> People go crazy in sessions sometimes, but because we're usually dominant in the arrangement we can control the situation ... One guy tried to jump out of a top storey window once, but his dick was tied to the ceiling. Had his dick not been tethered he would have killed himself. We had to jump on him and hold him down, and he cried for about 15 minutes. They get pretty close to breaking sometimes, but as a mistress you have to learn people's breaking point.
>
> (dominatrix Martine, King's Cross, Sydney, quoted in Perkins 1994: 171)

Time management is clearly significant in the assessment of where and when the B&D client's 'breaking point' – when pleasure tips over into excruciating pain – is likely to occur, and demands qualitatively different skills to those employed by the streetworker, or even the high class prostitute who entertains her clients with more than just sex. In fact, during this kind of encounter, when the client moves into the simulation of smooth space, the likelihood that the repressed body will surge through and rupture the understanding between him and the prostitute is increased. The negotiated masks of both prostitute and client are therefore always threatened by the presence behind them of real, passionate bodies (Game 1997; see also discussion of Bodies without Organs in chapter 7).

However, despite the mutual benefits that might arise, there is a clear tension as regards the control of time when the perspective of the prostitute and of her client are considered side by side. While the sex worker tends to seek to orchestrate the encounter for the reasons we have outlined above, clients (both potential and actual) often want to feel in control themselves – and a key concern for those using street prostitutes in particular is the danger of being arrested by an undercover police operation, reflecting institutional striations of the encounter. Clients, in a short space of time, want to discount the possibility of having picked up a police officer, which affects the opening up of the interaction:

> stop your car somewhere close to the girl, wait for her to come to you and get in. DO NOT negotiate with her until she is in the car and you are driving away ... NEVER solicit sex from a girl standing outside of your car: if she wants to talk about sex before she gets in your car, just drive away (even if she is not a cop, it is too risky to find out) ... after she is in your car, drive away, but if she TELLS you where to go, be very suspicious ... you can ask her to 'prove' that she is not a cop by lifting her shirt and letting you squeeze a tit ... some girls will ask you to unzip and pull it out: the hope is that if the girl is a cop, anything she says or does after she lets you feel her tits is entrapment, and would probably be thrown out of court[.]
>
> (Punter giving advice to others on the *World Sex Guide*)

Another requirement for the client may be a guarantee that what he pays for will give him whatever it is that he seeks – as O'Connell Davidson (1996) suggests in her description of the very detailed instructions issued by some of Desiree's B&D clients. This of course entails the punter being in control even when it appears that he has ceded it to his dominatrix. A further instance of such attempts at quality assurance is George McCoy's *McCoy's British Massage Parlour Guide* (1998), which he has compiled and regularly updates himself by means of visits to some 500 UK establishments. As George (quoted in *Vice: The Sex Trade*) says, there is what he perceives to be a 'ready market' for a 'detailed guide' to what is 'decent' and what is 'the pits', although he does acknowledge that his publication is careful not to mention precisely what is offered by each parlour or the relevant charges, because of UK legislation concerning the advertising of sexual services. It is also worth recalling evidence that streetworkers' clients in particular may seek to haggle over price, also implying a desire to control what happens during the encounter in the sense of not wanting to be ripped off.

In sum, then, the capacity to control time and thereby script the prostitute–client encounter may be something which both participants strive to achieve. Their respective abilities to achieve dominance are also undoubtedly mitigated by their levels of experience, as O'Connell Davidson (1995a, 1996) asserts. Clients seek to emerge from the encounter with their masculinity intact, not to say bolstered. The prostitute, on the other hand, faces different challenges to her sense of self within the interaction. Thus she has an equal investment in the management of time both within and outside of the encounter, which goes beyond simply maximizing income and ensuring client safety.

Workers' time: slow time, identity time, political time

Despite its racy image, prostitution can be a dull and tedious occupation. As Scambler (1997: 114) puts it, there is 'a great deal of waiting around' involved. In this sense, managing time as a prostitute can be compared to structuring the day in occupations where boredom is a problem and psychological survival a paramount concern (Roy 1960; Willis 1977; Burawoy 1979; Collinson 1988). O'Connell Davidson suggests, for example, that Desiree

> has days when only one or two men turn up ... A great deal of her time is spent sitting or pacing around in a state of restless boredom. She can chat to the receptionist, drink cups of coffee, endlessly reapply her make-up, but she must keep herself psychically prepared for work and cannot settle to anything else, as a punter might knock on the door at any moment.
>
> (O'Connell Davidson 1995a: 3)

This tedious downtime is generated by the regularity with which Desiree's punters fail to turn up for appointments – and is exacerbated by sheer unpredictability. Because Desiree is never sure whether or not a particular client will make an appearance (unless they are regulars, whose custom she particularly tries to cultivate), she must remain on guard for their possible arrival. She also frequently makes appointments with several men for the same time of day, in the assumption that only one (or even none) will show up at the given time – and in the event that more than one makes an appearance, Desiree relies on her receptionist to give them coffee and a video to watch. Hence her boredom is not precisely equivalent to the boredom experienced by the unskilled manual worker. Desiree can never switch off entirely and simply daydream; her occupation falls into that most stressful category of boring, yet demanding of full attention at all times.

We can also see how difficult downtime might be in an article by Salvadori (1997) which describes Charlotte's professional life in a London flat. The text of the article is accompanied by several photographs of Charlotte hanging over the stair rail looking bored; slumped in a chair; re-doing her makeup; having a manicure; talking to friends on the phone; making out her advertising cards, and so on. The use of such images for dramatic effect notwithstanding, they all point to Charlotte having to fill time between clients during her twelve hour shifts by a variety of means. As she herself says:

> the majority of [flat] maids are easy to get along with. They need to be, since we spend twelve hours cooped up together. You sit, you chat, you drink coffee and smoke. We chat about men, families, life in general.
>
> (Charlotte, quoted in Salvadori 1997: 118)

Likewise, Connie has it that 'whoring is boring, but lucrative' (Taylor 1991: 17, quoted in Scambler 1997: 114).

Moreover, and by the same token, time spent with clients may hang heavily, especially if the client is one that the prostitute dislikes or fears. We can see this particularly clearly in the account of the relationship between dominatrix prostitute Mandy Kavanagh and Alistair, one of her regular clients:

> time never flew when Mandy was with Alistair. Instead, the minutes between three and four dragged, as if they made up a day rather than an hour ... the hours preceding and following his every visit left their own trail of slime down her day. She had learnt the long way that this slippery feel of dirt did not become easier to bear with repetition.
>
> (McRae 1992: 13–14)

We have already offered sustained discussion of the particular feminist position that identifies prostitution as much more than just sex work because selling one's sexuality is potentially traumatic, demanding and degrading in a way that even the most appallingly routine and deskilled of conventional occupations could never be (see chapter 9). The distancing that this position sees as a fundamental requirement of prostitutes' working lives, again discussed in detail in earlier chapters, is also evident in data regarding the use of time in sex work. For example, on further examination, it is possible to conclude that the strategy of keeping the encounter as short as possible is not just about maximizing earnings, but also prevents the client encounter coming to resemble relational or recreational sex, neither of which are usually time bounded/striated. Jemma's comment that her ten minutes is 'all they're getting ... once I get my money I just wanna go' is particularly revealing in this regard. She goes on to say that 'I can't take much more [than ten minutes] ... Even when they [clients] touch me I'm just like "Just back off!" ... They make me cringe' (Jemma, quoted in *Vice: The Sex Trade*). Escort Cat, likewise, describes a hotel visit as follows: 'As soon as I arrive at the hotel, it'll be right, get in, sort the situation out, weigh things up and get out as soon as possible ... it is purely going to work.' She also says that: 'The sooner you're faking your orgasm, the sooner it's all over. It does come down to the fact that it's just a job and it's the money' (Cat, quoted in *Vice: The Sex Trade*).[8] In a similar vein, O'Neill recounts an anecdote told to her by Mary which again reveals a desire on the part of the prostitute to terminate the client encounter quickly:

> One time I remember doing a double with Sam and I was mouthing 'fucking hurry up' ... she was in hysterics ... and then I went into my 'YES ... YESS ... YESSS' and when he came I shouted 'EUREKA' ... she nearly pissed herself with laughter.
>
> (Mary, quoted in O'Neill 1996: 23)

Here again we see Mary faking her orgasm to encourage the client to reach his own climax. Her success, nonetheless, also reveals the possibly tenuous nature of the prostitute's control over the length of an encounter. That her partner Sam began to laugh when Mary 'went into' her act demonstrates how easy it is for the prostitute to make a mess of role – that is, to reveal to the client that all they are really doing is having work sex as opposed to anything more involved or intimate and, as a result, 'discrediting or contradicting the definition of the situation that is being maintained' (Goffman 1971: 231–2). Inga also indicates how hard she works to maintain the façade – and how subtle she has to be in this endeavour. She is always, for example, surreptitious in looking at her watch during an encounter to see how long she has been with a client:

> People ask if I have to pretend to enjoy having sex. You'll probably think this is terrible, but he's laying there and I'm laying there and I don't let him see me checking my watch. Because it's high class it would be the wrong thing to do. You know when your time's up. Then you get buzzed and you check your watch. But when you're actually with a guy, you don't constantly look at your watch. You do it sneaky.
>
> (Inga, quoted in Cockington and Marlin 1995: 179)

The distancing discussed above, moreover, often starts and ends, as we have seen in chapter 8, with time spent on 'psyching up' and 'psyching down' rituals. These function as 'markers of separation' between private life and work (McKeganey and Barnard 1996). Further, what is also clear from foregoing discussion is that there are some things, and some clients, that many prostitutes will not entertain – money cannot buy everything, even from a prostitute (or at least, not every prostitute). What is on sale, therefore, is more than time, and more than the body may be at stake – hence not everything has its price. Finally, and again as already established, prostitutes may seek not only to manage time as part of maximizing their income while preserving their sense of self, as well as ensuring safety and enjoyment for their clients – they also use time outside and inside their working lives to attempt to change those perceptions of their labour which create and perpetuate their liminal status.

Conclusion

From our review, it seems reasonable to suggest that clients' time often differs from prostitutes' time. Clients seek sexual satisfaction from their encounters with prostitutes, as arguably mediated by the understanding that they have the 'right' to pursue pleasure in their free time. However, as we have also suggested, there may well be more to the encounter for the client than a simple consumerist fix, such as is experienced in the purchase of a McDonald's burger or in watching a film at the local multiplex; they often seek, through their interactions with prostitutes, a bolstering of their masculinity, a confirmation that they are 'real men' in every important respect. Where work and home life present challenges for the man concerned to preserve his sense of himself as masculine, the encounter with the prostitute can provide an opportunity to consolidate his identity via a simulation of affection and sexual desire. The client, then, may seek (a convincing simulation of) smooth, intimate, affective space, wherein the way that time is managed is governed only by mutual desire and enjoyment (Deleuze and Guattari 1987). Prostitutes, on the other hand, are engaged in work when they encounter clients. Consequently, their experience and interpretation of time tends to be differently structured to the clients' – by the desire to maximize income, and/or to avoid boredom and/or to avoid cost to self-esteem. Moreover, time spent on identity work, intended to protect self from the rigours of selling sex for money, may also extend into a politicized *Weltanschauung* within which the sex worker seeks at both macro and micro levels to use time within and outside the client encounter so as to challenge prevailing perceptions of prostitution as degrading and demeaning. At the same time, the prostitute is always and already engaged in managing the client's experience so that they have little inkling of her lack of involvement, and therefore leave the encounter satisfied in the ways mentioned above. The prostitute, then, largely experiences the encounter as striated space (Deleuze and Guattari 1987) where time ticks so as to mark off what has been sold and what has been earned but must work to convince her punter that they are experiencing smooth space, within which time flows.

Thus, the prostitute–client encounter is perhaps most fruitfully understood as an empty space which both participants attempt to inscribe in some way, and within which the incommensurabilities between the different selves at play produce, whether implicitly or explicitly, a struggle to be able to control time within the interaction. The ability to do so, as we have argued, depends on the relative experience of each interactant, but may also vary with factors discussed in chapter 10 such as the legislative climate within which the encounter takes place (how far is prostitution tolerated in specific locations?), the market sector within which the prostitute operates (is the individual client dependent on this one worker for specific services?; what do clients expect for their money?), the geographical space of the encounter (streetworkers arguably being less able to dictate the precise timing of an encounter than their counterparts in brothels, hotels, self-owned premises etc., except to the extent of working to keep it short) and the mutual support upon which the prostitute can draw (are there others on hand to help her out if she gets into difficulties with a rebarbative client?).

It is also interesting to consider whether these differences in clients' and prostitutes' time stem from gender differences. As Grosz (1995: 100) puts it:

> It is not clear that men and women conceive of space or time in the same way, whether their experiences are naturally presented within dominant mathematics or physics models, and what the space-time framework appropriate to women, or to the two sexes, may be.

Nonetheless, commentators such as Knights and Odih (1995) follow a well-established feminist tradition which argues that men and women experience time differently, due to the fact that women can carry and give birth to children and men cannot, and that women also experience the unique biological processes (menstruation and the menopause) associated with this capacity (also see Martin 1989: especially 198; O'Brien, cited in Shilling 1993: 61). Women, by virtue of their role in reproduction, are seen here to be fundamentally more connected with others, as well as more sensitized to the past, the future and the passing of time, as opposed to simply being aware of the here and now. This tradition, which connects with and reinforces arguments about the gendered division of labour within capitalism, suggests that women's time is therefore relational, cyclical and processual, whereas men's is monadic, linear and segmented. Women's time is as a consequence less suited to organizational environments, being more difficult to measure and control. In contra-distinction, Collinson and Collinson (1997: 385), 'while acknowledging (socially constructed) gender differences in relation to time and space ... question the use of categorical or essentialist statements regarding the very nature of time'. They suggest that to differentiate between 'men's' and 'women's' time is to privilege gender above other differences such as race, nationality, class and age, and therefore to homogenize male and female experience to an unacceptable degree. They also criticize this argument for its essentialism, stating that it locks our experience of time into our bodily configurations, and disallows the possibility, as demonstrated not least by their own empirical work, that experience can produce and mediate our attitude to and experience of time in ways unconnected with our biological sex.

The above established, and with respect to clients' time and prostitutes' time within the encounter, clients (who, we will recall, are male more often than not) could be seen to be moving into a more feminine time – relational, emotional, intimate, connected to others. This is based on our conjecture that the client's pursuit of the encounter is driven by more than simple sexual hedonism; that they may seek love and sexual affection outwith their everyday relationships to shore up their sense of themselves as a lovable, worthy, 'real man'. Further, prostitutes (female more often than not) could be seen to be moving, at the same time, into a more masculine time – linear, sequential (client after client), controlled and technical – to maximize income, ensure safety and protect self. This echoes Collinson and Collinson's claim that our experience of and attitude towards time is more social than it is biological, as well as suggesting that client and prostitute move in this regard into times which connect with and consolidate their socially constructed gender identities, but belie their biologies. Nonetheless, the permeability and reversibility of prostitute and client time is considerable; the differences are not, therefore, necessarily rigid and invariable. There is, for instance, considerable evidence, as cited in earlier chapters, that prostitutes very often find their work sexually stimulating, and may even go further, finding punters attractive or falling in love with them. Workers may therefore experience their encounters with clients as intimate, emotional, connected (feminine) time, and in this regard would presumably experience much less difficulty in the simulation of smooth space referred to above. Equally, male clients may approach the encounter determined to striate, segment, control and script the interaction in a rational and mechanistic (masculine) way – for fear of being arrested, to try to negotiate over price or to ensure that they get exactly what it is they are looking for from the prostitute. Moreover, Cixous, amongst others, posits that the discursive dualism of gender (man/woman) inevitably privileges the man above the woman as the active subject of sex, the initiator of sexual activity, the penetrator; while the woman becomes the passive object of sex, the recipient. As she argues: 'Thought has always worked by opposition ... by dual, *hierarchized* oppositions. Superior/Inferior ... the hierarchization subjects the entire conceptual organization to man ... woman is always on the side of passivity' (Cixous 1988: 287–8). Therefore, the male client may desire to take control of the encounter in a way that satisfies his need to consolidate the dominant side of his masculinity, as expressed in a certain distance from the prostitute, perceived in this instance as little more than a receptacle for his desires.

As our examples and counter-examples suggest, then, the experience and interpretation of time in the encounter is neither predictable nor pure – indeed, it may even be reversible. Consequently, the ways in which interactants in prostitution experience and relate to time can be seen to emphasize the social construction of self-identity, that our identity work is complex, varied and may pay attention to particular aspects of our identities at one moment in time, and to others in different settings and on different occasions. Prostitution, as our discussion here and in this part of the book more generally suggests, can be seen to provide a fragile analytical space in which this identity work is writ large, where particular but not necessarily predictable struggles are waged by interactants to consolidate and build on a coherent sense of self. This self is always at risk and at play, but understanding its construction demands that attention be paid to the significance of both place and time.

Conclusion

One of the central themes of this book has been, to add to a popular aphorism, that in the midst of life we are in death, *and vice versa*. That is to say, although the prevailing construction of the relationship between life and death is that they are in opposition, here we move even beyond the Freudian dialectic of *eros* and *thanatos* to argue, with Bataille, for a *contiguity* of life and death. Moreover, it is precisely this inextricability of life and death which we have been at pains to identify in our analysis of sex, work and sex work. Although conventional analyses, as we have pointed out, tend not to recognize the darkness, the ever-present abject, and the promise of death in sexuality and in organization, our objective has been to foreground both the light *and dark* sides of these phenomena. Thus we have addressed three key questions in our discussion.

The first part of our conundrum is the question of the relevance of sexuality to the study of work. This we would address by suggesting that sexuality is a crucial conceptual tool by which to unpick the processes involved in modern organizations – as we have said several times, organizing for us is a sexual process, and we have expanded on this in part I of the book in particular. However, at this point we wish to go further and suggest that we must acknowledge sexuality – in all its facets, in particular the co-habitation of desire and death – in order to fully comprehend human behaviour in modern organizations. Accepting that Bataille's *erotism* is what makes us human – that is to say, taking up the position that our key problematic as human beings is to select *acceptable* ways in which waste, to squander, to dispose of the accursed share in laughter, art, poetry, music, dance, orgy or sacrifice (or else face 'unacceptable' outbreaks of excess such as war) – means we also have to accept that humans are erotic beings. In other words, they will habitually struggle with and frequently break free from cultural constraints, in more or less dramatic ways depending on the strength of the taboo that exists in the first instance. Sexual harassment, for example, which involves unwanted sexual approaches from one individual to another, is constructed as problematic because of the prevailing discursive conceptualization of sexuality as necessarily mutual and equal, contained and containable. But it is deemed to be much more problematic in the work organization than it is in, say, a bar, primarily because of the equally widespread belief that sex is an unwelcome intruder into the organization. Indeed, harassment is almost universally associated with the organization and thus to make unwanted sexual advances to a work colleague tends to be seen as a good deal worse than approaching someone who does not reciprocate one's interest in a social situation (see discussion in chapter 3). This example also shows that our 'breaking free' is just as likely to take place in the organization as it is to take place elsewhere precisely because organizing is a human activity.

Two other key issues here are: (a) that conventional organizational analysis does not acknowledge that sex takes place in work organizations – indeed, it depicts sex as highly problematic at work where it mentions it at all; and (b) that the arguments provided by re-eroticization theorists point to the sexualization of working environments and/or contend that work needs to become more eroticized, or at least that its existing eroticization be fully recognized. However, in neither of these schools of thought are the connections between death and desire discussed, such that the picture which emerges even in re-eroticization theory is a somewhat idealized portrayal of sex at work, a portrayal which does not embrace the shattering intensity of the dissolution of self, the teetering on the brink of death, the collapsing of *eros* and *thanatos* and the dread of loss of being which is what is entailed in our reading of desire. That is to say, existing portrayals of the sexuality of organization display a kitsch sexuality – in their opposition to mainstream descriptions of work as sterile, rational, logical and cerebral they simply create a different but equally oppressive form of homogeneity, as Bataille would predict.

What we are arguing for here, instead, is what we have referred to as a *heterotics* of organization, a development and analysis of what happens *in between* the poles of sex as organizational rupture, sex as break with the rational effort to generate utility, and managerial appropriations of the erotic such as the corporate culture programmes to which we referred in chapter 6. We suggest that this heterotics will embrace the fact that, in organizations, we are constantly being sexual, being human, wasting and squandering excesses of energy in erotic ways, and that this paradoxically creative and productive labour is constantly shifting, as well as giving organizations the sexual flavour that we have already outlined. There needs, then, to be further development of the project of acknowledging the sexuality of organization – but this development needs to encompass the dark side of desire, its inhabitation by death, the joy *and terror* of the erotic, just as much as it does the lighter side. We have begun such a development here – in chapters 1 through 6 especially – and would urge its forward movement in future analyses of sex and work.

The second part of our conundrum, which is directly related to the first, is the question of the re-eroticized organization – can we (re-)structure organizations in ways that better embody the flow of desire? Perhaps paradoxically, what we have argued is that the fully and completely eroticized organization, at least in the way that we have understood the erotic, is an impossibility, a contradiction in terms. Although sexuality is inseparable from organization – because organizing, as already noted, is a human activity – that is not to say that the political project of re-eroticization can be progressed. This is because sex and work, quite unlike sex and death, *are* in effective opposition – indeed, the latter represents a concerted effort to push out or abnegate those elements of the former that it cannot subdue and channel. Work disavows the erotic, or at least attempts to, because the erotic is abject; it reminds us of our impending death, it leads us to the abyss of self-loss and permits us to gaze in. This, as we already know, is terrifying as much as it is fascinating. As Bataille argues, following a thread from Hegel, Marx and Durkheim, work dehumanizes us while ideologically offering itself as the way to attain a fuller humanity – to achieve that which desire lacks, to pursue the Body without Organs of capital. This construction of humanity turns on individuality, is separate from and indeed 'superior' to 'abject nature', and in its singularity marks us out from the 'lower order' existence of animals, plants and other organisms – thus it is also a humanity that represses, and alienates us from, the real nature of desire. As long as we cling to this notion of humanity, as long as we labour (pointlessly) to put off death, we cannot experience the full dread, or the full ecstasy, of life (-and-death) as Bataille constructs it. So we cannot eroticize our organizations because to do so would mean abandoning their core purpose, that of productive acquisition. As we have already suggested, re-eroticization would mean moving beyond the organization per se, leaving behind its purposeful endeavours in favour of collectives devoted to uselessness and waste (which could then hardly be said to be organizations at all).

In short, therefore, we cannot offer to develop or extend re-eroticization theory because to do so would be to ignore the ways in which we have sought to construct organization, economy and work, desire, abjection, sexuality, the erotic and eroticization throughout this book. We could of course simply list ways in which we would like to see existing organizations change – change and loss being necessary consequences of the aleatory flow of desire – but this would not accord with any notion of eroticization, and as such could form no real part of our discussion here. Our re-reading of desire has allowed us to move beyond conventional understandings of organizations, to expand on the notion that work is always and already sexualized, in positive *and* negative ways, and for this reason the analysis can have no performatives. Nor, indeed, should we want it to.

Furthermore, this book has also taken seriously Gherardi's argument that all work is a form of sex work, in that our sexuality is ineluctably engaged in performing our everyday organizational lives. In the second part of the book we therefore explored whether the examination of sex work itself could illuminate more conventional modes of organizing, and to what extent conventional organizational features could be found operating in this arena of the abject. Our analysis here suggests that even to begin by asking the question 'What has sex work got to do with organization theory?' is to speak from a position which already constructs sex work in a particular way – as not normal work, as different, as not formally organized, as not legitimate, perhaps even as immoral. Indeed, how sex work is viewed depends a great deal on how other concepts – sexuality, masculinity and femininity, and desire for example – are defined and discursively constructed. What we found in our exploration was that not only is sex work complex – far more complex than most treatments acknowledge – but it also blurs many of the conventional boundaries which frame it.

Consequently, although sex work may well be primarily a dyadic interaction, the nature of that interaction and its significance for participants is affected by local communities, language, legislation and global movements of capital, among other things. It may not always be organized in terms of large formal organizations, but it displays degrees of formalization and specialization, and develops market features. It may also be connected to global syndicates of organized crime, who themselves, as Castells points out, have already mastered many of the cutting edge techniques of 'virtual organization'. There may be few career step-ladders, but many prostitutes have a clear sense of an emerging 'career' which has both economic and moral aspects.

Questions of identity, and how identity is formed and sustained through consumption, which are central problems for contemporary social theory, are also right at the heart of sex work, where clients come to seek some form of support for an identity under threat, or perhaps even impossible, in everyday life – a rehearsal room where they will be helped to carry off a performance that isn't working on stage. Moreover, sex workers do not sell their bodies – they sell both far more and far less than that – because sex work is always incompletely commodified and it is the nature of that partiality that workers must negotiate, with others and with themselves. Sex workers therefore struggle with peculiarly intense demands of emotional labour and often (but not always) need to be especially inventive in adapting their identity skills towards preserving some distance between themselves and their work. They may even come to operationalize multi-dimensional understandings of the nature of working time. The work itself is, of course, not the person but an event – and it may be an event which is always unpleasant, or always enjoyable, or a mixture of both, occasionally ecstatic and sometimes fatal. Death and the erotic often come close in a literal sense – violence is always a presence, always a possibility, always an influence on the structure of the work. Further, although they are not formally organized as such, the structures that emerge, even across locations, do display some regularities and these may be identified in terms of the contextual features which provide the source and the setting for sex work.

Indeed, what we see in looking at sex work is an abject, excluded means of earning a living, morally censured, often illegal, permeated by crime and violence, and yet one which is a mirror of the society which seeks to expunge it and is, regardless of ideology or legislation, sustained by that society. When looking at sex work, we constantly see, not a foreign object, not something alien and Other, but ourselves – refracted and sometimes distorted, to be sure – but another side of ourselves, not opposed, but connected. The further we explore the complexities of sex work, the clearer the few significant differences from normal organizing emerge, but the similarities and the inseparability of sex work from other forms of work, and other manifestations of sexuality, are unavoidable.

For us, all of the above makes the question 'What has sex work got to do with organization theory?' an impossible one to ask, let alone to answer. Sexuality and organizing are intertwined, although they lead in different directions, and they are in tension. 'Normal' sexuality is irrevocably implicated in the sexuality of sex work, as the one creates the other in the process of its own construction. The denial of certain forms of sexuality is a form of self-denial, and this abject part of the social self is always present, even if it is not in focus. If we seek to understand sexuality, as we have argued following Bataille, we need to look at both its lighter and darker sides and, if we seek to understand the nature of its presence in organizations, we need again to keep both of these dimensions in focus. In seeking to gain some understanding of sex work, which is commonly understood as representative of the darker and dirtier side of sexuality, we have discovered once more that both elements are present – that sex work can be rewarding and redemptive as well as degrading and deathly. However, and more importantly, we have discovered the chiaroscuro of sex work, the nuances of light and shade which go to make up the textural complexity of the phenomenon.

Reading this back into organizational sexuality, we must re-emphasize the importance of the shading across the erotic field that lies between continuity and integrity, life and death, the one and the Other. Despite the fact that we have argued strongly against the tendency of current theories of sexuality in organizations to ignore the necrotic at the expense of the erotic, it is not a question of restoring the one over the other but of recognizing their co-presence, their co-determination, their co-constitution. Simply put, this means allowing the contradictions and messiness of the experiential real, however discursively mediated, to emerge through our abstractions. In doing so, we need to remain mindful that, in bringing bodies and minds, ideas and feelings, together in analysing organization in all its fluctuation and changeability, we are not simply keeping both good and evil in focus, but working in a space beyond either.

Notes

Introduction: reading sex into organization, reading organization into sex

1 It is, however, only fair to note that Burrell's (1997) more recent work distances itself from his earlier arguments, and attempts to introduce some darker and more 'demonic' considerations, including death and putrefaction, into the theorizing of organization.

2 Bishop and Robinson (1998: 219–20) suggest that much of the argument for the 'natural' properties of prostitution in fact implicitly naturalizes the historical situation of patriarchy and male domination of which prostitution may be regarded as a symptom. The fact that this condition has been widely disseminated globally is not evidence in support of its status as natural human behaviour, but an unfortunate social development.

3 Throughout the book we use discourse in its Foucauldian sense to indicate a linked field of talk, text, practice, institution and action (Foucault 1972, 1979, 1980, 1986a, 1990).

4 Any digressions we make from our three main source countries are related to this core context in the sense that they throw a particular argument into relief or extend that argument.

1 Violence, masculinity and management

1 This is not to say that women are not affected by these things, our argument being that 'masculinities' and 'femininities' are not the sole preserve of those biologically designated 'male' or 'female'. However, we would contend that those labelled male in Western society acquire particular historical baggage regarding the significance of violence in thought and action. For a fuller discussion see Linstead (forthcoming).

2 We do not wish to import an air of structural finality to our argument here, and are aware of Foucault's critique (1967, 1973, 1977, 1979) of the way that the category of the 'normal' has been epistemically constructed in psychiatry, health, criminology and sexuality. However, we believe the term can still have a modest utility here.

3 Examples of this last include the medieval Japanese torture of captives to 'atone' for their being captured and hence dishonoured, a 'better death' giving them a better future in the beyond, and on their return to earth in another life; and the Christian Brothers' argument that their abuse of young boys had been ordered by God so as to cleanse the children involved (Davies, K. 1994: 174).

4 Allan is a successful manager in his mid-forties. The extracts used in this chapter are taken from a series of wide-ranging discussions which were not explicitly focused on the issue of violence, inside or outside organizations. The interviewer (Steve Linstead)

also had the opportunity for other such discussions with Allan's parents. The purpose of these discussions was loose, exploring the background of a reflective manager who, in the process of recollecting his own strengths and weaknesses, came to relate them to experiences he had with his father and grandfather. It is important to note that in this chapter we deliberately refrain from making any direct causal inferences from his father's behaviour to specific behaviours of Allan's. However, sufficient parallels emerged from these reflections relating Allan's experiences of his father to his father's experiences of his grandfather to suggest the basis of an emerging framework, which we also illustrate from other sources. We are grateful to all those people who shared their often difficult experiences with us.

5   The process of turning a part, or potential part, of the *subject* into the *object* is to *reject* (literally to throw or cast *back*). That which is thrown or cast *down* or *away*, but retains a recognizable connection with the subject, as a failed or mutated variety of it, a literal *ab*omination, becomes the *abject* (literally thrown *from* the subject). The cast-away is a useful model for the social abject. The remaining subject, having thus torn part of itself away in the abject, remains incomplete, lacking, hollowed out, or *deject* (literally thrown *down* – by having the abject cast down from it, the subject is *downcast*). The existence of the abject continually questions the adequacy of the subject.

6   Also see Brown (1997) for a summary of other characteristics of narcissism.

7   There is no room here to discuss the character of Hallie (Vera Miles) in detail, although her importance in the story cannot be overstated. Simon (1996: 110–12) addresses some aspects of her significance and also the fact that she is symbolically present throughout as the common denominator 'steak' over which the three confront each other, and to which each archetypal character is a response. For Valance, she is the rejecting mother – he could never win her, and could if anything only take her, which he hints at darkly; for Doniphin, she is the appreciative audience for his performance of an unwritten code that is never spoken and ultimately, as he discovers, was never really shared or understood; for Stoddard, she is the rejuvenation of the masculinity that had become arid and abstracted through the law. Yet despite these roles, she is a strong character in her own right, and has the last word in questioning the whole edifice of masculinity through the image of the cactus rose which she places on Doniphin's coffin.

8   Simon (1996: 108–9) discusses in some depth the fact that the three types of narcissism as presented in the story *all* ultimately fail. Even putatively successful Stoddard has a childless and, it would appear, passionless marriage to Hallie; their relationship possesses an asexual quality which is represented by the juxtaposition in image and dialogue of the cultivated ('real' to Stoddard) rose and the wild cactus rose. As Simon notes, romantic passion perhaps needs to feed off narcissism for both men and women and, where subjugated to the demands of social honour, it fades away.

9   We also discuss Canetti's sting in chapter 5.

10 Duff (1996) did address this issue in his later novel *What Becomes of the Broken-Hearted?* which deals mainly with the rehabilitation of Jake, but also with the consequences of the series of tragedies for the others involved. The book is disappointing in that its central difficulty is that of backtracking over Grace's suicide and the incestuous rape which precipitated it, seeking to cast doubt that it was in fact Jake who did the deed. Jake at least convinced himself of this – but Duff employs no obvious irony, of which he is otherwise a master, to suggest that Jake can only survive through continued self-deception and that his self-discovery will remain partial because his abjection was so profound. On the contrary, Duff seems to be trying to justify the Hollywood screenplay that he wrote which would allow rape but not incest, in which he placed the blame for Grace's rape on a family friend. Her death, then, was just a tragic mistake, and not an inevitable consequence of Jake's behaviour, and Jake therefore becomes, despite his culpability, a victim of injustice.

2 Power, gender and industrial relations

1   Burrell (1997: 230–3) incorrectly attributes the authorship of the document to Heather Höpfl.
2   Asiana, Korean Air, Singapore, Malaysian and Thai all had major campaigns running at the time of the strike.
3   It is perhaps worth mentioning here that the contribution of crew hired from Taiwan's China Airlines was decisive in breaking the strike, so much so that the Taiwanese workers took out an apologetic advert in the local press. Cathay's own Manila-based crew acted as both strike breakers and hosts for Hong Kong-based crew who wished temporarily to relocate in order to keep working. The 'reserve army' was an even more significant threat if Cathay was considered as a South East Asian airline, and not just a Hong Kong or South China airline.

3 Sexual harassment

1   We are aware that women can and do harass men, as the Barry Levinson film *Disclosure* (1994) suggests. Indeed, although the film's reading of organizational gender relations and harassment is problematic in key respects, it is true to say that the negative effects on 'harassee' Tom Sanders' personal and professional life echo what is often reported as characteristic of the experience of harassment (Brewis 1998). Same sex harassment also occurs. In US case Doe v. City of Belleville, Ill. (1997), for example, 16-year-old twin boys complained of male co-workers calling them names such as 'fag' and 'queer' and issuing sexually loaded threats. In a similar vein, Oncale v. Sundowner Offshore Services (1998), which reached the Supreme Court, consisted of an oil rig worker being sexually humiliated by his male colleagues, often in the presence of other staff. The harassment included forcing a bar of soap into the plaintiff's anus whilst he was in the shower. His supervisor also threatened to rape him. Nonetheless, the available evidence suggests that it is most commonly men who harass, and that their targets are usually women. Indeed, if we understand harassment to be violence of a sort, then we already know from discussion in chapter 1 that men are responsible for the bulk of violent behaviours, both symbolic and actual. We discuss the gender relations seen to be characteristic of harassment in further detail later in the chapter.
2   The estimates which are common in writings on sexual harassment of how much such behaviours cost an organization in terms of absenteeism, lost productivity, wastage, low morale, labour turnover and so on, quite apart from the legal expenses or payouts which may result from a claim of harassment being brought, exemplify this aspect of its discursive construction. As we will see later in the chapter, harassment, because it is understood to be a sexualized abuse of power, is deemed bad enough on its own, discursively speaking. However, such estimates, the first of which were arguably US Merit Systems Protection Board (1981, 1988) figures for the annual costs of sexual harassment for the American federal workforce ($188.7 million in 1981, and $267.3 million when the research was repeated in 1987), continue to appear. Indeed, Knapp and Kustis suggest that it is crucial to publicize the financial aspects of harassment given that 'Problems viewed as inconsequential to the organization are often perceived differently once their direct impact on the bottom line is more fully understood' (Knapp and Kustis 1996: 202). There is also a related theme in this œuvre that addressing harassment helps to 'aid the recruitment and retention of women' (see, for example, *IRS Employment Trends* 1992a: 5), as well as allusions to the adverse publicity that can result from cases of harassment becoming public (see, for example, *IRS Employment Trends* 1992b: 5).
3   As Jameson notes, being in possession of a past, present and future is crucial to identity. Indeed, those with personality 'disorders' such as schizophrenia (and animals –

see also chapter 4, note 2), do 'not know personal identity in our sense, since our feeling of identity depends on our sense of the persistence of the "I" or the "me" over time' (Jameson 1983: 119, cited in McNay 1992: 134).

4   Linda Davies worked in three merchant/investment banks in the City for a period of seven years.

5   Also see MacKinnon (1979); Renick (1980); Gutek and Morasch (1982); Schneider (1982); Somers (1982); Crocker (1983); Schover *et al.* (1983); Weeks *et al.* (1986); Stockdale (J. 1991); Yount (1991); Frazier and Cohen (1992); and Stockdale (M. 1996).

6   Similar divisions are arguably present within associated discourses such as that which surrounds rape, or the sexual abuse of children. As Simon (1996: 133) has it, moreover, 'dominant cultural scenarios ... insist upon nonhierarchic motives' – that is to say, 'good' sex is widely understood to turn on the equality of sexual partners.

7   Also see our discussion of the formation of self in Bataille, and Deleuze and Guattari, in chapter 6.

8   However, it is important to note Paetzold and O'Leary-Kelly's (1996: 97–102) analysis of Harris v. Forklift Systems, Inc. (1993) in this regard. The Supreme Court's decision in this case enforced the legal requirement for a working environment to be judged hostile both subjectively (by the plaintiff) and objectively – but suggested the use of the reasonable person standard as opposed to the reasonable woman standard in undertaking the latter. As Paetzold and O'Leary-Kelly (1996: 101) point out, 'because *Harris* may have rejected the "reasonable woman" standard, it signals that a generic, all-purpose standard [that is, reasonable person] provides an appropriate filter through which to view the plaintiff's response to harassing conduct'. In a similar vein, Mayer and York (1994) suggest that the Harris decision effectively means that the reasonable woman standard is no longer the appropriate measure in hostile environment cases, and therefore that research is needed to identify exactly what reasonable *people* would designate as a hostile environment.

9   Again, rape discourse makes similar claims. Lees (1996: chapter 5), for example, cites the fact that the complainant's sexual character and history – the men she has slept with, the make-up she wears, details of her menstruation, her childcare arrangements, her marital status and so on – are commonly admitted as evidence in UK rape trials in an attempt to suggest that she has in some way asked to be raped. The defendant's criminal record, on the other hand, can only be admitted at the judge's discretion or, if he has no such record, used as proof of his good character in mounting a defence. Self-blame in instances of rape is also extensively documented. For example, Koss (cited in Brooks and Perot 1991) found that 43 per cent of the women she surveyed, all of whom had undergone experiences which conformed to the American legal definition of rape, refused to describe themselves as victims of rape on the basis that they thought they had in some way provoked their attacker's behaviour.

10 Strossen notes the Robinson v. Jacksonville Shipyards (1991) case in this regard, commenting that the American Civil Liberties Union, of which body she is president, filed in order to challenge the court ruling that the behaviour in this instance amounted to sexual harassment. The issue was that of whether the display of the sexually explicit material at the heart of the case represented free speech, as protected in the First Amendment, given that the original judge required that such displays be prohibited in this organization.

11 This emphasis on the special place of sex in the human condition (Foucault 1979) is also evident in the discursive construction of rape – for example, Brownmiller's claim that the roots of the institution of marriage are in men's ability to deny women jurisdiction over their sex lives, such that women historically were forced to seek the protection of one man to assuage 'fear of an open season of rape' (Brownmiller

1975: 16). However, Brownmiller sees this protection as costly, arguing that married women subsequently signed the sexual autonomy they had been looking to protect over to their husbands.

12　It is probably worth pointing out that, as stated earlier in the chapter, harassment cases tend to be presented to courts as instances of sex discrimination. In the appropriate circumstances, then, the law in the USA and the UK sees proven instances of *quid pro quo* loss (or gain) and/or emotional distress arising from harassment as sex discrimination, given their detrimental economic, career-related and/or psychological effects on the recipient's working life. Outside the courts, as we have also seen, commentators may separate economic and career-related consequences from psychological consequences, dubbing only the former discriminatory.

13　*West* also states that 'The [US] courts recognize that a hostile work environment will detract from employees' job performance, discourage employees from remaining in their position, and keep employees from advancing in their career' such that 'actual psychological injury' caused by abusive work environments need not be proven. This is because these courts operate by the principle that 'To maintain such a requirement [proving psychological injury] would force employees to submit to discriminatory behavior until they were completely broken by it.'

14　'Anor' is legal shorthand for 'another'.

15　The definition of sexual harassment provided within the Commission's Code of Practice, which is included in the Recommendation (issued 27 November 1991) entitled *On the Protection of the Dignity of Women and Men at Work*, states that harassment is simply a matter of unwanted sexual conduct that affects the dignity of working women and men; that such conduct can be physical, verbal (oral or written) or nonverbal (cartoons, posters, and so on); and that it should be up to the individual affected to decide what they personally find offensive (European Commission 1991: 8 – also see IDS Employment Law Handbook 1993; Rubenstein and De Vries 1993; *IDS Brief* 1995).

16　Chapter 8 also discusses this issue in the context of demand for the services of prostitutes.

17　See chapter 7 for a fuller expurgation of Hollway's identification of this and other key discourses which underpin sexual attitudes and behaviour in Western modernity.

18　An alternative of course is for such men to avail themselves of a prostitute, as discussed in chapters 7 and 8. Chapter 7, moreover, also makes it clear that men's use of female prostitutes appears to be the most prevalent form of market demand by far in this industry.

4　Working with sex offenders

1　It is also worth noting the interest taken in prostitution by wider society, which again speaks of its abject status. The recent proliferation of UK television programmes on the subject, like *Vice: The Sex Trade*, *Paddington Green* and *Under The Sun*, is an example. Bataille gives considerable attention to forms of spectating such as watching these programmes in his work, in particular concerning the onlookers at a sacrifice, which event he says represents:

> the revelation of continuity through the death of a discontinuous being to those who watch it as a solemn rite. A violent death disrupts the *creature's* continuity: what remains, what the tense onlookers experience in the succeeding silence, is the continuity of *all existence* with which the victim is now one.
>
> (Bataille, cited in Boldt-Irons 1995: 95; emphasis added)

The brush with death and the consequent horror and fascination experienced by those who watch the sacrifice are Bataille's key point here. We could therefore suggest that, to a lesser degree, the same combination of opposing sensations is what explains the apparent demand for programmes about jobs which are located in the space of the abject, such as prostitution. In fact, the apparent equivalent of watching these programmes in Bataille is reading literature, and novels more specifically. This he suggests 'has received sacrifice as a legacy: at the start, this longing to lose, to lose ourselves and to look death in the face, found in the ritual of sacrifice a satisfaction it still gets from the reading of novels' (Bataille 1997: 260). We can therefore conclude with Bataille that, although reading novels or watching programmes dealing with the abject is not as horrifying and fascinating as spectating at a sacrifice, such activities are 'closer to us, and what [they lose] in the way of excess is gained in the way of verisimilitude' (Bataille 1997: 261).

2   Ackroyd and Crowdy (1990: 9) emphasize that this work 'is so centrally concerned with blood, entrails and death, that it is impossible to deny these even to the superficially informed, and the idea that the work is necessary does little to reconcile the squeamish'. However, social distaste for this occupation is perhaps less in degree than that which attaches to prostitution. Abattoir work is at least 'necessary' because it generates some form of utility, as Ackroyd and Crowdy (1990: 11) point out, although it involves causing death, it creates 'a valued product' at the same time. Prostitution, on the other hand, consists of 'a sudden and frantic squandering of energy resources' (Bataille 1991: 35). It has little, discursively speaking, to do with more 'useful' forms of sexual activity, such as procreative sex and/or the 'good' sex that we spoke of at length in chapter 3, except for its 'safety valve' role in the 'discharging' of male sexual libido (for development, see discussion of Hollway's three discourses in chapter 7). As Ashforth and Kreiner (1999: 430) suggest, morally tainted jobs may be seen as more 'evil' than 'necessary', whereas the reverse is true of work which is physically tainted.

Second, abattoir work involves the killing of animals and, if we follow Bataille, we see that human efforts to disavow the 'abject nature' from which we emerge turn on a distancing of ourselves from animals, voracious, instinctive and unrestrained as they are seen to be, lacking in

> an elementary operation of the intellect, which distinguishes between action and result, present and future, and which, subordinating the present to the result, tends to substitute the anticipation of something else for that which is given in the moment, without waiting.
>
> (Bataille 1997: 245)

Therefore the death of an animal does not have the same power to shock and terrify as the death of a human being, as Bataille's (1985: 69) reference to sacrificing animals as 'a cowardly gesture' also makes clear.

3   This slang term is peculiarly apposite here!

4   Although Arluke and Hafferty (1996: 222) suggest that justifications, unlike other forms of motive work, do not 'morally elevate the [socially distasteful] behavior', we would, as our use of Knights and Willmott's and Ashforth and Kreiner's work suggests, contend instead that the particular form of justification employed by Ackroyd and Crowdy's slaughtermen in fact does bestow honour on their occupation.

5   Knights and Willmott (1989: 548) describe this type of identity work as follows:

> Insofar as subordination erodes the very dignity associated with the experience of being an independent subject with individual rights and responsibilities, employees are forced back on a defensive and often private sense of their own worth. A common response to subordination, therefore,

is to develop a mental (role) distance from those conditions of domination which contradict their sense of their own independence and self-worth ... By assuming an indifference to much of what happens at work other than the pay packet, workers discount the indignity of their subordination at the same time as privileging the meaning and significance of their private lives where they experience a greater measure of choice and independence.

This captures very well the labour of demarcation in which many prostitutes engage, speaking of the ways in which they acknowledge the widespread degradation and derogation of their profession but deal with this in a subjective sense by minimizing the importance of prostitution in their lives.

6   This version of Megan's Law, otherwise known as the Jacob Wetterling Crimes Against Children Law, came into existence following the death of 7-year-old Megan Kanka who was bound, gagged, raped and strangled by her neighbour Jesse Timmendequas. Timmendequas had two prior convictions for sex offences. Intending that this should not happen to another family, Megan's mother Maureen campaigned for legislation to be passed 'providing for police registration and community notification when sex offenders are released into a particular neighborhood'. The resulting federal law required every state to have passed its own Megan's Law by September 1997 or lose federal aid. Individual states were also empowered to choose how they wished to make such information public, and to decide how to classify offenders according to the risk that they pose. In New Jersey, where the Kankas live, the relevant state law sets out that only the police should be told about low-risk offenders, whereas schools and daycare centres need to know about medium-risk offenders and anyone who may come into contact with a high-risk offender must be informed that they are resident locally (*Court TV Online: Verdicts*).

7   On 14 March, 2000, McKilligan, originally convicted for rape and murder, successfully appealed against the rape charge, though not contesting the murder conviction. His own defence admitted that the killing was sexually motivated and that McKilligan got sexual pleasure from his acts. The consequence of this is that if McKilligan is eventually released, he will not appear on any sexual offenders register. At the time of writing, public feeling is so strong on this issue that the Newcastle newspaper *The Journal* is leading an appeal, which is being supported by McKilligan's mother, to the Home Secretary for a change in the law.

8   For an overview of the legislative situation regarding prostitution in a range of countries worldwide, see chapter 10.

9   In support of this claim, it is significant that male-on-male rape has only been a criminal act in the UK since 1994. Moreover, services for survivors such as rape crisis centres or helplines are in short supply compared to the provision for women, and under-reporting is also assumed to be rife because of lack of understanding of or sympathy for victims' experiences (*BBC News: Health*). From an American perspective, Scarce (1997) agrees that male rape is hugely under-reported and under-recognized – indeed, his own research suggests that we often refuse to believe that men can be raped at all.

10   'Cottaging' is the UK term for sexual liaisons between men in public toilets (cottages), whereas one would 'walk/work the beat' if one sought the same activity outdoors, such as in a park. 'Flashing' means to expose one's genitals to others in a public place.

11   However, as John also pointed out, the 'pure' right to silence was effectively removed in UK legal proceedings by the Criminal Justice and Public Order Act (1994), given that refusing to answer questions at police interview can now be interpreted adversely by a court as an inadequate defence.

12   Here John suggests that those who are directly responsible, as he sees it, for actions that may restore a sex offender's liberty are perhaps those who should carry the heav-

iest burden for re-offending. In a related comment, Judge Perleman suggests that he sees the corroboration warning which the judge, prior to the 1994 Criminal Justice and Public Order Act, was required to make in UK rape trials as an 'anachronism' and an 'insult'. This warning consists of the judge telling the jury that they cannot rely on the complainant's testimony unless it has been corroborated by another witness. Judge Perleman says that 'I do it [give the warning] because I have to do it, and I take a deep breath, but I don't like to do it' (Judge Perleman, quoted in Lees 1996: 112). As his comments imply, some of those involved in the legal system clearly do feel uncomfortable about the responsibility that they perceive themselves to have in the processing of sexual offences in particular, which therefore suggests that, in John's words, these individuals may well 'lose sleep' when re-offending occurs.

13 It is also worth noting Lees's (1996) emphasis on the high number of acquittals in such cases, which she argues has much more to do with the sexism embedded in the UK legal system than the fact that most defendants are innocent.

14 At the time of the interviews Peter was engaged in clinical trials, such that his case load was 'much lighter than ... would be the case if you were in the Health Service'.

5 Sadomasochism and organization

1 If Foucault's interest in S/M is well documented, Bataille, in a similar vein, appears to have had masochistic tendencies, in his love for his violent and abusive father in particular. In 'Dream', he writes 'I'm something like three years old my legs naked on my father's knees and my penis bloody like the sun. This for playing with a hoop. My father slaps me and I see the sun' (Bataille 1985: 4). Bataille was also fascinated by Sade, and sought in particular to reclaim the 'divine Marquis' from the surrealist interpretation that he could not have meant what he says. Bataille argues that this 'made it impossible for us to hear [Sade]' (Dean 1992: 172), suggesting instead that Sade is very much to be taken seriously, that 'the brilliant and suffocating value he wants to give human existence *is* [conceivable] outside of fiction' (Bataille 1997: 93; emphasis added). Moreover, Bataille understood Sade's writing as 'compelled by a death-wish, an impossible desire to be "released" through self-destruction' (Dean 1992: 188), which of course resonates powerfully with his own theorizing.

2 For further discussion of the normalizing heterosexism which characterizes prevailing discourse on sex and sexuality, see chapter 3.

3 Hart, speaking specifically of lesbian S/M, also points out that the misrepresentation of S/M practice as homogeneous collapses 'this richly varied experience into an oppositional construct and thus reinstate[s] a spurious binary divide between "vanilla" and s/m lesbians, which are hardly distinct categories'. What she implies here is threefold:

1 S/M is not necessarily a lifestyle, but rather a kind of sex that may be enjoyed at times, whereas at others 'vanilla' (non-sadomasochistic) sex is found to be more pleasurable;

2 vanilla sex sometimes, if not frequently, contains elements of S/M;

3 S/M sometimes, if not frequently, contains elements of vanilla sex.

There also appears to be considerable debate around the boundaries of S/M, in the USA in particular. As the *Deviants' Dictionary* puts it:

> Today as it is normally used, the term 'sadomasochism' usually suggests mutual consensual activity for the purposes of sexual arousal which involves some sort of pain, restraint or domination ... Some people, however, do attempt to maintain the distinction between interests in pain and in other

activities like dom-sub, clothing fetishes, bondage for its own sake and so on, and reserve the term sadomasochism for pain games.

Our use of the terms 'S/M' and 'S/M practitioner' should therefore be understood against this backdrop.

4   A manual of S/M sex for the gay man, originally published by Olympia Press in 1972 but now available, according to Internet site *Welcome to the World of Larry Townsend*, in three different versions – *The Original Leatherman's Handbook* (the original as reissued by L.T. Publications), *The Leatherman's Handbook: Silver Jubilee Edition* (the amended original, having been updated to reflect behavioural changes and to add health warnings not required in the early 1970s) and *The Leatherman's Handbook II* (a sequel to the original book, which focuses mainly on safe S/M and picks up where its predecessor left off).

5   Again, chapter 3 establishes that the modern discourse of sex and sexuality tends to construct 'good' sex as taking place between those who have an equal say in what transpires.

6   Such extreme examples of S/M might, however, also be read as problematically macho – as discussion in the 'Sadomasochism and ritual' section establishes.

7   Nonetheless, in contrast to Jardine and Hart's arguments, S/M has attracted sustained criticism from feminists who suggest that it represents 'an eroticization of power relations … derived from patriarchal models such as master/slave, Nazi/Jew' (Ramazanoğlu 1989: 168) or that 'like male/female or butch/femme roles, the roles of sadist and masochist are based on the division into powerful and powerless people' (Nichols *et al.*, cited in Harriss 1988: 11). These critics argue that seeking pleasure in sexual acts in which one partner explicitly and overtly dominates the other is actually to caricature (and therefore trivialize) oppressive social relationships such as dominant man–passive woman, and to be complicit in the perpetuation of such relationships through a failure to problematize them. However, as we have already suggested in chapter 3, such an understanding of sex is problematic in itself, given that it assumes the existence of 'a certain sphere of sexuality … were it not the object of mechanisms of prohibition brought to bear by the economic or ideological requirements of power' (Foucault 1979: 98). Moreover, the ironicization of power relationships in S/M, which we will discuss in more detail in a later section of this chapter, also means that the criticisms levelled here misunderstand the fluidity of power in this form of sex, as well as failing to acknowledge the importance of mutuality, dialogue and trust in such relationships.

8   See chapter 6 and especially chapter 7 for a detailed discussion of the Body without Organs.

9   Hart also notes that these preparations are decidedly erotic in themselves, because they indicate that desire is present before the sex begins, as well as critiquing the heterosexist 'myth' that sex must be spontaneous. Such an emphasis on spontaneity, she claims, has made it difficult for women in particular to ask for what they want, or to show their partners how they prefer to make love. S/M, of course, 'violates this mystification of sexuality' (Hart 1998: 152).

10 According to Bataille, and as we have seen in earlier discussion, animals are generally considered to be much closer to 'abject nature' than we humans are. Taking on the role of an animal, then, helps (as Sellers points out) to facilitate the loss of self, propelling the Bottom towards the 'natural given', towards the void.

11 However, it is worth noting Hart's objection to representations of S/M as cerebral more than it is physical. She argues that 'the tendency to disavow s/m's physicality is due, in large part, to a history in psychological/psychoanalytic studies of denying that the masochist actually desires to feel pain' (Hart 1998: 134). In other words, what is being reproduced here is a failure to understand that 'people *feel* sensations differ-

ently' (Hart 1998: 135). Here Hart fundamentally blurs, indeed eradicates, the boundaries between pain and pleasure, especially when she emphatically states that 'there is no such phenomenon as pain per se' (Hart 1998: 135).

12 The implications of the subject position/s of 'real man' are also discussed in chapters 1 and 3.

13 And the reality, given the numerous stories of Sade's sadistic exploits, including his flagellation and locking up of beggar Rose Keller, for which he was later imprisoned.

14 However, there is arguably a difference between commercial and non-commercial S/M in this regard. The transaction between client and professional dominatrix is likely to be less fraught with such difficulties than that between non-commercial partners, given that the dominatrix may expect little more than the requisite payment from an S/M encounter. The casual description offered by one woman in this profession of what she inflicts upon her clients certainly seems to suggest her detachment from their (and her) pleasure:

> Some guys want needles through the skin of their cocks and balls. Some like to see their own blood. One guy likes to be blindfolded; I put 20 needles in him and make him remember their position. If he forgets, I call him a 'useless pig'.
>
> (dominatrix, quoted in Weinberg *et al.* 1984: 382)

We discuss the commercial sex contract and its implications for prostitute and client in more detail in part II of the book.

15 One could, of course, suggest that the intimacy which characterizes S/M is instrumental, in the sense that the trust on which each scene relies is geared towards 'successful' sex, and thus that there is not so much difference between this intimacy and that which prevails in most organizations. However, we would contend that the pleasure of S/M exists mainly in the process, the unfolding of the encounter, the actual relationship between Top and Bottom – and therefore that intimacy and trust in this regard are ends in themselves.

16 Willmott also suggests that what he refers to as corporate culturism promises, by way of contrast, to bring irrationality, affect, passion and emotion 'back in' to organizations. However, as analyses like his, Burrell's (1992a) and Kerfoot's (1999) make clear, the rhetoric of such initiatives is much more powerful than the reality, not to mention their explicit objective of enhancing the bottom line.

6 Re-eroticizing the organization

1 It is, as we have intimated, true that Freud also established that the restrictions of civilized modern society result in conflicts and neuroses, given the trade off between an entirely instinctive existence, one in which the human being is in thrall to his or her passions, and a more repressed existence in which the reality principle dominates the pleasure principle. However, he also, and simultaneously, tends to remain on the side of reason and the repression of the passions, and remarks on the way in which what he understands as civilization makes the world serviceable to us, ensuring beauty, cleanliness, security and order. Freud appears to conclude, therefore, that his civilization is a heavy but necessary burden for the modern individual to carry – whereas other commentators, as we will see later in the chapter, suggest that it is both heavy and unnecessary.

2 There are interesting similarities between Reich and Marcuse's claims regarding the disappearance of 'the perversions', and their references to prostitution in particular, and O'Connell Davidson's (1995a: 9) argument that destigmatizing prostitution as a

302 *Sex, Work and Sex Work*

profession would probably extinguish all demand for prostitutes' services, which we outline in chapter 7.

3   Marcuse also suggests that sexuality may actually be encouraged at work as a way of fully exploiting labour power and productive potential. His concept of repressive desublimation refers to the ways in which

> without ceasing to be an instrument of labour, the body is allowed to exhibit its sexual features in the everyday work world and in work relations ... The sexy office and sales girls, the handsome, virile junior executive and floor worker are highly marketable commodities, and the possession of suitable mistresses ... facilitates the career of even the less exalted ranks in the business community ... Sex is integrated into work and public relations and is thus made susceptible to (controlled) satisfaction ... But no matter how controlled ... it is also gratifying to the controlled individuals ... Pleasure, thus adjusted, generates submission.
>
> (Marcuse 1968: 70–1, cited in Pringle 1989: 163)

Here he foreshadows Burrell's argument about managerialist appropriations of the erotic.

4   This project can be identified as radical feminist for the most part – see, for example, the work of Griffin (1980) and Daly (1984a, 1984b).

5   See Brewis (1996: 268–9, 271–2, 322–3) for a discussion of this kind.

6   Nonetheless, as we have seen in chapter 3, the discourse of rape and the discourse of sexual harassment, both of which make exactly this connection between the discursive 'sexualization' of women and their being targets of male sexual aggression, have problematic effects of their own. This bears out Foucault's recommendation that *all* discourses be examined for their likely implications. As he explains:

> My point is not that everything is bad, but that everything is dangerous which is not exactly the same as bad. If everything is dangerous, then we always have something to do. So my position leads not to apathy but to a hyper- and pessimistic activism.
>
> (Foucault 1986b: 343)

7   Kojève (1980: 6) argues that 'Desire is human only if the one desires, not the body, but the desire of the other'. He goes on to say that:

> to desire a Desire is to want to substitute oneself for the value desired by this Desire ... to desire the Desire of another is in the final analysis to desire that the value that I am or that I 'represent' be the value desired by the other: I want him to 'recognize' my value as his value. I want him to recognize me as autonomous value. In other words, all human, anthropogenetic Desire – the Desire that generates Self-Consciousness, the human reality – is, finally, a function of the desire for 'recognition'.
>
> (Kojève 1980: 7)

This echoes Hegel's observation that self-consciousness has a primary end, 'to become aware of itself as an individual in the other self-consciousness, or to make this other into itself' (Hegel 1977: 217). The auguries of Lacan are clear enough.

8   Although Bataille sees waste or squandering as inevitable, he also advises that we can make choices as to how to waste the excess energy available to us, that 'It is only a matter of an acceptable loss, preferable to another that is regarded as unacceptable: a question of *acceptability* not utility' (Bataille 1991: 31).

9 It is therefore unfortunate that the mechanical metaphor (along with their fondness for mathematical imagery) has created interpretative difficulties for many readers who do not find the physical flux which Deleuze and Guattari intend to convey to be adequately represented by the rigidity of the machinic image.

10 The concepts of desiring-machines, organ-machines and energy-machines might, we argue, be echoed in Foucault's understanding of sex as nothing more and nothing less than 'bodies, organs, somatic localization functions, anatomo-physiological systems, sensations and pleasures' (Foucault, cited in Dews 1984: 93), 'anatomical elements, biological functions, conducts, sensations and pleasures' (Foucault 1979: 154). Indeed, read through Bataille, what appears to be an enduring contradiction in Foucault's work may cease to exist. It is well documented that his anti-essentialism, his refusal that there is any such thing as a transcendental 'humanness', at times seems to waver. His position in *Madness and Civilization* (1967), for example, that there is a 'zero point' at which the human condition becomes colonized by knowledge and that madness exists prior to this point is an instance of this (as well as being another echo of Deleuze and Guattari, and their concept of delirium – that is to say, pure flow without form – in particular). Although this reading of madness is one that Foucault (1980: 118–19) later explicitly disowned, there are other traces of what is usually seen as essentialism in his œuvre. One example is the suggestion that we should seek to reclaim 'bodies and pleasures' from the modern discourse of sexuality:

> It is the agency of sex that we must break away from, if we aim – through a tactical reversal of the various mechanisms of sexuality – to counter the grips of power, with the claims of bodies, pleasures, and knowledges in their multiplicity and their possibility of resistance.
>
> (Foucault 1979: 157)

Here there appears to be a valorization of physical pleasure as lying beyond the reach of power/knowledge. Foucault's celebration of sadomasochism, discussed in more detail in chapter 5, also seemingly contains examples of this essentialism, as when he talks of S/M as plunging the body into a kind of 'anarchy' where it 'opens itself … tightens … throbs … beats … gapes' (Foucault, cited in Miller 1993: 274). However, what exactly is Foucault implying here? Is it, as MacCannell and MacCannell (1993: 229) argue, 'less a classical "liberal" posture than a demand for liberation from all restrictions on pleasure and power', and therefore some form of totally unrestricted utopia where we can get back to being 'who we really are'? Apparently not. If we look to Bataille, we can argue that 'madness' as 'zero point', 'bodies and pleasures' and the body 'throbbing', 'beating' and 'gaping' are not references to a *human* essence, but rather to what precedes the development of the singular, monadic self, the point at which we have not become separated from the circuit of energy which ties all living matter together – Bataille's general economy and Deleuze and Guattari's economy of flows. Indeed, Miller (1993: 273) suggests that Foucault's stance on sexuality in particular implies that 'the human organism is an intrinsically formless flux of impulses and energies, impossible though it may be to articulate this intuition within the "games of truth" played by modern science.'

11 This happens through processes which Baudrillard would call seductive, the more obvious of which would be advertising and performance incentives, but which extend ever more subtly throughout capitalist culture.

12 As well as arguably leading to certain misinterpretations and criticisms of Foucault's work – see note 10 above.

7 Discourse and desire in sex work

1   This study, which found that prostitutes tended to develop higher self-esteem as a result of entering the industry, is cited by the *Prostitutes' Education Network*.

2   Where sexuality has come increasingly into focus in the West, it has done so under the experimental gaze of science, and great attention has been paid to the physiognomy of sexuality by the *scientia sexualis*. In contrast, Foucault (1979) observes that Eastern discourses *throughout* history have emphasized the importance of sexuality to human life. For example, many Eastern discourses recommend special forms of love-play – specific positions, delaying of orgasm, chanting during sex and other *ars erotica*. In Buddhism, moreover, celibacy is invoked as part of the discipline which enables one to achieve the spiritual enlightenment of *nirvana* (Watts 1975).

3   Indeed prostitutes themselves are often very aware of the effects of the have/hold discourse in this regard, and their consequent positioning as fallen women. They may also seek to refute such constructions. Caroline (quoted in *Vice: The Sex Trade*), for example, points out that she is not a 'nymphomaniac', that she is not 'gagging for sex', but instead works as a prostitute because she is 'trying to keep going' in an economic sense.

4   This, as we have already seen, is a Freudian assumption – that the lack of the object of desire is a necessary condition for the maintenance of the desire itself.

5   Also see discussion of Reich and Marcuse's stance on 'the perversions' in chapter 6.

6   Sydney's 'Wall' area is a notable exception to this rule.

7   In fact, the experiences of *Sex and the City*'s main protagonist Carrie and at least one of her three close female friends (Charlotte) suggest that affairs even in the postmodern urban space of New York might, for these women, be characterized by certain longings for the more traditional heterosexual relationship of marriage, and its associations of home, hearth and stability.

8   At the time of writing this magazine is temporarily off-line and has no web address.

9   Escort is effectively synonymous with sex in this locale; clients wanting sex will be quoted for escort work.

10 We expand on self-validation as regards punters' reasons for visiting prostitutes in chapter 11, and on the problems in assuming that prostitutes never want to be intimate with their clients, or show affection for them, in chapter 8.

11 'Beats' in Australia include all public places where men meet to have casual, often anonymous sex, such as parks, toilets, beaches, car parks or isolated roads (Phillip Keen, beats outreach worker, cited in Joseph 1997: 83). 'Beat' in the UK, as we have seen in chapter 4, has a similar meaning, but excludes public toilets – known as 'cottages' in this context – and may include the 'street area where [female] prostitutes work' (Day 1994: 187). In the US, the equivalent of a cottage is a 'tearoom' (see, for example, Humphreys 1970).

12 O'Connell Davidson (1997) argues that men who use prostitutes may become child abusers, not because of any clinical problem they have such as paedophilia or hebephilia (the love of young people, deemed pathological when displayed by a much older individual), but because they are already prostitute users with no or low levels of discrimination as to who they exploit. Apart from the fact that there are a range of psychiatric disorders beyond those mentioned which might contribute to child abuse, and notwithstanding that her arguments are true of *some* abusers, O'Connell Davidson is able to make this statement because the only reasons for prostitute use which she employs as the basis of her argument are negative ones couched in terms of exploitation. These may well apply to the particular population of abusers which she considers, but she argues that these reasons have a much wider application. These attributions of potential paedophilia to prostitute users by O'Connell Davidson are more relevant to her purpose of attacking prostitute users than addressing the problem of paedophilia. The Wood Commission findings (Gunn 1997) indicate that

there is no typical paedophile, most cases are committed by family members or close relatives and friends, and are repeated over time within the relationship. Offenders are usually recidivists and build up from minor to major abuse, tending to convince themselves that their victims enjoy the attention. They are also commonly found in positions which give them authority or influence over, and access to, young people. The Commission identifies more than a dozen categories of offender, of which the characteristics of the parapaedophile (the non-discriminatory abuser who may abuse any age or sex) and possibly the sadistic offender could well apply to some of O'Connell Davidson's group of prostitute users – but only some.

13 The danger of publicly making the kind of moves which O'Connell Davidson advocates and branding all prostitute users as potential paedophiles can literally be fatal. In 1996, former Australian Supreme Court judge David Yeldham was named under Parliamentary privilege by Senator Franca Arena as having been questioned by the Wood Commission into police corruption in connection with paedophilia. Yeldham was a grandfather who happened also to be a closet bisexual. He occasionally visited male prostitutes and picked up adult men in public toilets for sex. He was questioned in relation to two occasions on which he had been stopped by the police in toilets in Sydney but not charged. The Commission was concerned that, as a former judge, Yeldham may have received special treatment from the police, and accordingly questioned him. There was no evidence of paedophilia, although he admitted to his sexual proclivities and behaviour. Arena insisted that the Commission itself was shielding Yeldham, and she named him before the Commission published its report. The content of the interviews with Yeldham was made public. On 8 November 1996, with no charges against him nor likely to be laid, his family life and public reputation in ruins, David Yeldham took his own life by gassing himself in the family car. Despite the fact that his bisexuality and use of male prostitutes, and his deceit of his family for so long, were sufficiently stigmatic in themselves, the accusation of paedophilia was one which he could never properly refute once made, and for which he probably felt he had been tried and found guilty despite his denials. In its report, the Commission regrets that the revelation alone so affected its investigation that they were unable either to make a case or clear Mr Yeldham (Balogh 1997).

14 Moreover, even if, in the examples we use here, the escort was really a maid, or on active service, the client's BwO would still not be attainable because his BwO relies on a fetishized version of the 'real' maid or woman soldier. The fetish, as we saw in chapter 5, is not in and of itself considered to be erotic in conventional terms, but possesses an erotic charge for particular individuals. It calls up memories of a previous experience or image which the fetishist found erotic, or of an individual to whom they were/are powerfully attracted.

15 Chapters 10 and 11 also deal with the significance of smooth and striated space in prostitution.

8 Consumption and the management of identity in sex work

1 See our discussion of Chapkis's (1997) work in the Introduction for an alternative purchase on this argument. We develop this issue in particular in chapters 9 and 10, and identify the ways in which varying degrees of this freedom are apparent in different places within the sex industry.

2 Other discursive representations of the prostitute–client relationship place less emphasis on prostitution as a consumer industry, constructing it instead as a political activity, a strategy for economic survival, an exemplar of patriarchal society and so on, as we will see in chapter 9. Consequently, while a prostitute who defines themselves as a sex worker will understand themselves to be labouring during the client encounter, and may impose strict demarcations between their work and their free

time as a result, the boundaries between professional activity and leisure may be more blurred if other discursive representations are employed. A degree of such blurring is evident in the following passage, written by Carol Leigh (alias Scarlot Harlot), a prostitute who takes a highly politicized view of her work, describing herself as a 'rebel' and a 'famous slut':

> I'm not saying I loved the tricks or the work. It can be fun, especially if you like things like skydiving or hang gliding. But what I liked was getting this insider's view, this secret story to tell. The silence of prostitutes became overbearingly loud.
>
> (Leigh 1994: 246)

Her access to the 'secret story' seems to have been a way for Leigh, as she herself puts it, to live out her radical political persuasion, her feminism and her curiosity about sex, and to respond to judgments made of her for having had sex before marriage. There is, consequently, much more to prostitution for Leigh than simply earning a living – and we might suggest that, as a result, she does not necessarily understand herself as working when she is selling sex to punters.

3 For further discussion of the law and its enforcement as regards prostitution in our core context, see chapter 10.

4 Nonetheless, it is worth stating that the relationship between unsafe sex and HIV transmission in prostitution is complex and variable both within localities and, perhaps more significantly, globally (Ward and Day 1997: 143). Figures for Zaire in 1994, for example, suggested an HIV infection rate among prostitutes of some 40 per cent which researchers attributed to extreme economic recession, ignorance about HIV and AIDS and cultural reluctance to speak out about sex (Reuters 1994). Even more worryingly, the Centers for Disease Control and Prevention (1994: 7, 11, 17) *HIV/AIDS Surveillance Report* estimates that the rate of HIV sero-positivity is running as high as 80 per cent among prostitutes in sub-Saharan Africa.

5 However, this is not necessarily the practice or rationale adopted across the board. Instead, in line with the general emphasis on safe sex as a means of protecting against HIV infection, kissing is often avoided because research has been inconclusive as to whether saliva can spread the virus and, although the intimacy argument certainly has some credibility in the prohibition of kissing by prostitutes, the safe sex argument is much more widespread. Moreover, the intimacy argument has to some extent been mythologized, but it is unclear whether this is by researchers or by some of the workers themselves. Nonetheless, it is clear from our examples that other prostitutes as well as Desiree manage the physical terrain of their bodies as part of the labour of demarcation between work and private lives.

It is also worth noting that some workers may use acts that others refuse to perform as a marketing tool – Karen, for example, tells all telephone enquirers that the girls who work for her do kiss clients (*Vice: The Sex Trade*).

6 Also see discussion of downtime in chapter 11.

7 We discuss this self-representation of prostitutes as educators or counsellors in more detail in chapter 9.

8 Another part of this 'likening' strategy may be an emphasis that prostitutes do exactly what other women do, except that a prostitute at least charges, explicitly and upfront. Leigh (1994: 243), for example, suggests that women who have sex with men to avoid being accused of frigidity, or to keep a relationship going, are 'cheaper' than prostitutes. Sam (quoted in O'Neill 1997: 12), in a similar vein, asks 'how many women prostitute themselves in relationships they don't want to be in but stay in a marriage for financial gain?'. In an Internet article fellow sex worker Rachel Collins, likewise, suggests that she was 'what was commonly called a slag' before she started to charge

for sex, and now gets much more respect from her punters than she did from the men she 'gave it to for free' (Collins 1997). Caroline and Cat (both quoted in *Vice: The Sex Trade*) make related points – Caroline saying that sex with clients is 'only the same' as what one does with a partner or with someone met during a night out, and Cat that 'eight times out of ten' women will sleep with a man who has bought them 'drinks all night' in a bar. Both of them, however, state that the key difference is the fact that, as Caroline puts it, 'they [punters] hand over the money'. Indeed, McIntosh (1994: 6) agrees with the working girls quoted above that all heterosexual sex could be understood to be exploitative to some degree, and therefore that prostitutes can be seen as more honest because at least they demand money for sexual services.

9 An adjunct to Leigh's position is the suggestion that, among the London prostitutes Day (1994: 172–3 – emphasis added) talked to at least:

> work [as a prostitute] involves a broad 'inclusive' definition of rape which is documented … by reference to the 'broken contract'. *This refers equally to physical assaults, cheques that bounce, and the duplicity involved when a client deliberately removes a condom.* In contrast, prostitutes' personal relationships involve a more 'exclusive' view which is similar to other common ideas about rape … a naturalistic understanding of sexual violence which is seen in the use or threat of force that will be visible in the body of a victim.

10 By way of an aside, it is interesting to note Rival *et al.*'s (1998: 318, n11) suggestion that evangelical missionaries, while translating part of the Bible for Huaorani Indians, could not find Huaorani words for 'adultery' or 'prostitute'. They therefore invented the neologisms *'nano tohue nono'* and *'èè quète ante nè tohuenga'*, which, when literally rendered, become 'someone who's having fun' and 'someone who's repeatedly having fun' respectively.

11 Mandy Kavanagh, on the other hand, freely admits to deriving pleasure in her work *only* from beating or torturing her B&D client Alistair, because she loathes him and feels him to be so utterly beyond redemption (McRae 1992: 15).

9 Context and career in sex work

1 Instantiating what Giddens (1976) calls the 'double hermeneutic'.

2 B&D is also used to mean bondage and discipline, in which case it tends to refer to 'bondage and role-playing or humiliation *but little or no pain*' (*Deviants' Dictionary*; emphasis added). Bondage and domination (for which an alternative is D/S – domination and submission), on the other hand, may include all of these activities *as well as* the infliction of pain. To add to the semantic confusion, discipline used alone could encompass both the imposition of rules and the infliction of painful punishment. See also chapter 5 note 3.

3 However, elsewhere in the same paper (Phoenix 1998: 10), Lois is quoted as suggesting that what she does is like any other job – one of the 'paradoxical stories of prostitution' on which Phoenix's argument is based.

4 The John School has been set up as a joint venture between the Centre for Violence, Abuse and Gender at Leeds Metropolitan University, the police and the Probation Service. The idea is American in origin, and involves those arrested for kerb crawling (men soliciting commercial sex from women – so-called due to the common practice of driving slowly at kerb side in red light areas to select a prostitute) being confronted with testimony from prostitutes, residents of red light areas and police in an effort to persuade them not to re-offend by revealing the 'dark side' of the industry. The 'alternative' is a court appearance, and being identified in media reports of the case. The success rate in the USA is, if statistics are to be trusted, impressive: of 1,400 attending

a Los Angeles scheme, only four have re-offended, compared to an average of 60 per cent recidivism among those who are processed through the legal system. Indeed, although the Leeds scheme is in its infancy, of the forty men attending thus far, none has as yet re-offended. However, there is opposition to this approach. The English Collective of Prostitutes feel that any crack down on kerb crawling directly impacts on prostitutes' livelihoods, may force them to work in unfamiliar and possibly unsafe areas, and also to work longer hours to compensate for there being fewer punters (Cari Mitchell, quoted in Mills 1999: 35). They also point out that legislation prohibiting kerb crawling, introduced in England and Wales in 1985, 'has equalized women down by taking away some of the rights men had which women were fighting to get: instead of prostitute women not being arrested for soliciting men, men are being arrested for soliciting women' (English Collective of Prostitutes 1997: 90). In a similar vein, *Hustling for Health* suggests that legislation against kerb crawling 'shorten[s] the time for negotiating a service between sex workers and clients on the streets. This could seriously decrease sex workers' ability to insist upon condom use and safety measures.' (European Network for HIV/STD Prevention in Prostitution). Moreover, co-author of *Hustling* and EUROPAP UK National Co-ordinator Hilary Kinnell writes, in a letter to UK newspaper *The Observer*, that 'Many of those involved in sex work projects have grave concerns' about the John School, which include the possibility that 'trying to inculcate guilt and shame in clients might increase rather than decrease levels of violence and hostility towards sex workers' (Kinnell 1999: 30).

5   Pateman excepts surrogate motherhood from this argument; her position being that the contract between surrogate mother and prospective parents puts the surrogate's self at more profound risk than even prostitution would, because the surrogate promises to sell the right to the 'unique physiological, emotional and creative capacity of her body, that is to say, of herself as a woman' (Pateman 1988: 215).

6   O'Connell Davidson (1995a: 6; 1996: 187–8) does, however, differentiate her position from Pateman's by critiquing in particular Pateman's assumption that sexual pleasure for the male client is irrelevant to what she (Pateman) sees as his overall objective of securing patriarchal masculine identity. O'Connell Davidson suggests that such pleasure is actually a significant, if not the only, reason why men visit prostitutes.

7   Pateman offers a very narrow definition of prostitution as consisting only of the sale of penetrative sex, fellatio and hand relief. Other activities such as B&D she says are not prostitution, but 'part of the wider sex industry' (Pateman 1988: 199). Pateman also suggests that prostitution in its truest sense involves the sale of sex by a woman to a man, because of her insistence that the sale of sexual services has its roots in patriarchy. Admittedly, as we have argued, this form of transaction does prevail in the sex industry worldwide. However, Pateman's argument does not adequately account for men selling sex (see Docherty's story in McRae 1992; Goodley 1994; Prestage 1994; Browne and Minichiello 1995; Davies and Feldman 1997), or transgender prostitution (Pheterson 1996: 23; Joseph 1997), or even child prostitution (O'Connell Davidson and Sanchez 1996; O'Connell Davidson 1997; Levy 1998; Montgomery 1998), although she somewhat reluctantly acknowledges at least the first of these forms of prostitution. Hers is also a very restricted reading of what constitutes prostitution, not to mention its neglect of the fact that prostitutes may move between market segments within the industry during their careers, or may offer different types of service to different punters. For example, Blain (1994) has sold straight sex and B&D during her time as a prostitute, and Desiree (O'Connell Davidson 1994b, 1995a, 1996) offers both as part of her repertoire of services. Indeed, O'Connell Davidson argues that the reason why Pateman explicitly excludes B&D from her definition of prostitution is because the masochist client sits uneasily in an analysis which understands prostitution to consist solely of the patriarchal domination of women by men.

8   Jo Brewis in fact recalls being told, while working behind a bar, to flirt with the male customers to 'keep them happy'. She was also encouraged to wear make-up and short, tight clothes.

9   However, as suggested in chapter 8, note 4, the industry is not perfect in this regard, and the likelihood of HIV or STD transmission as a result of commercial sex fluctuates even within our core context, usually related to the prostitute's position within this highly stratified market (also see chapter 10). Indeed, EUROPAP (1994) have found that the ability to practise safe sex on the part of individual prostitutes is diminished by a range of factors: demand by clients for unprotected sex; urgent need for money; alcohol abuse; homelessness; ignorance; lack of resources; and younger age. On a related issue, this report also points out that European healthcare institutions are often unsympathetic to prostitutes' needs, that healthcare workers may lack knowledge about their specific circumstances and that opening times are not sufficiently flexible for prostitutes to be able to access the services provided. Similar points are made in *Hustling for Health* (European Network for HIV/STD Prevention in Prostitution).

What is also interesting is that, in countries which operate 'registered sex worker' schemes, evidence suggests that many prostitutes choose not to participate, often because registration requires submission to some form of compulsory health check, or perhaps payment of taxes, or indeed because the woman is working illegally. For example, EUROPAP (1994) data suggest that the ratio of registered to unregistered workers in Athens is 400 to 5,000. In Germany the same ratio is estimated at 50,000 to 150,000. Historical data from other countries outside our core context – such as Argentina (Guy 1995) and China (Hershatter 1997) – further consolidates evidence that prostitutes often resist regulatory attempts to make them register, to limit their activities to certain geographical areas and to require them to submit to health checks. Ironically, then, the efforts of national administrations in this regard may be counterproductive.

10 This is one of three centres of street prostitution in New South Wales, the others being Sydney's King's Cross and Newcastle.

11 There is in fact a growing body of work which examines and attempts to model the factors affecting the ability of the prostitute, particularly the streetworker, to leave the industry. Mansson and Hedin's (1999) research provides a basis in Sweden for the supply of support services, advice and counselling for those women who, because of financial hardship, drug addiction, exploitative relationships, coercion and low self-esteem, find it difficult to break the cycle of prostitution and establish an identity for themselves outside of the occupation. Mansson and Hedin's work is particularly helpful in identifying the problems that those women who accept a negative view of themselves (this often having been established through abusive relationships early in life) have in maintaining a positive self-identity, even many years after leaving prostitution, when because of the moral strictures of bourgeois society they have to hide or reinvent their personal history. However, this group of women do not and should not be taken to stand for all prostitutes in terms of their ability to leave the industry, and survive outside of it, as and when they choose to.

12 Exceptions to this include certain streetworkers quoted by McKeganey and Barnard (1996), several of Phoenix's (1998, 1999) respondents and Caroline, who started on the streets in Wolverhampton at the age of 58 after being made redundant from her job at a local factory (*Vice: The Sex Trade*).

10 Material variations in sex work

1   Castells (1998: 164–5; emphasis added) makes a similar observation that the fourth world is

made up of multiple holes of social exclusion throughout the planet. The Fourth World comprises large areas of the globe such as much of Sub-Saharan Africa, and impoverished rural areas of Latin America. *But it is also present in literally every country, and every city, in this new geography of social exclusion...* [it] is inseparable from the rise of informational, global capitalism.

2   This has been particularly noticeable in Australia, has also occurred in the UK, and has affected some parts of the USA.

3   This is because they often do not identify themselves, or may work in more than one place, only at certain times of year, or in a clandestine fashion, especially if they are illegal immigrants. Numbers are not easy to determine even in a more 'open' environment such as New South Wales, due to the casualization of the work. In the Wollongong/Port Kembla area of the Illawarra, for example, estimates based on our 1997 field studies identified approximately sixty to eighty women working intermittently on the street. Between two and twelve would actually appear on any one evening, depending on the weather. Twelve brothels were open on a long-term basis, compared to the previous year when police had identified as many as seventeen. Each brothel employed between four and twelve women, with some variability. Numbers of independent operators also varied, mostly from four to ten. The overall population engaged in the sex trade at this time in this small area therefore totalled anything from 110 to over 230. Moreover, this degree of variance is small compared to the divergence in estimates for India (from 100,000 to 600,000), or Thailand, where numbers involved in child prostitution have been estimated as being low as 2,500 and as high as 800,000 (Kempadoo 1998a: 15).

4   Among these ancillaries, we include legislatively defined activities such as benefiting from immoral earnings, materially or financially; organizing prostitution (brothel keeping, running a house of ill repute); procuring; permitting premises to be used for immoral purposes (letting); advertising sexual services; soliciting and loitering; consorting with prostitutes; living with prostitutes; unlawful presence on a premises; lodging or entertaining to the annoyance of neighbours (keeping a disorderly house); kerb crawling; causing a public nuisance; indecent exposure; and operating outside a permitted area/toleration zone.

5   Blain deals in general with the differing effects of prostitution laws across several Australian states. Also see Neave (1994) for an overview of Australian legislation in this regard.

6   The possession of condoms might also be taken as proof of engagement in prostitution in the USA and, as we will see, in the UK as well (O'Connell Davidson 1995a: 2).

7   EUROPAP (1994) and Phoenix (1999) suggest that police activities also focus on the street in the UK, and EUROPAP add that prostitutes are again much more likely to be prosecuted than their clients in this context – this last despite the difference in legal ideology between the USA and the UK. Both sources also note that prostitutes convicted of loitering or soliciting in the UK are not sent to prison, but fined instead, a legislative change which came about as a result of the Criminal Justice Act (1982). Phoenix extends this argument by suggesting that this has in fact been counterproductive, given the economic motivations which often accompany entry into prostitution (see chapter 9) and the fact that many women are therefore unable to pay the fine imposed. Indeed the numbers of prostitutes going to prison have in fact risen because of those arrested *defaulting* on these fines – and EUROPAP point out that, despite the introduction of means-testing in the setting of fines in 1991, women are still being imprisoned on this basis. Further, Phoenix cites a court clerk as saying that fining translates into a 'revolving door policy' given that it brings women in front of the court, points out to them that loitering and soliciting are 'wrong', but then

imposes monetary penalties such that the woman has no choice but to return to prostitution – and thereby risk being arrested again – in order to fulfil her obligations (also see Hubbard 1998: 65).

8 The *World Sex Guide* refers to this activity as 'Russian'.

9 We are indebted to Andreas Hoecht for alerting us to this article and for translating the original German into English.

10 This last does, however, depend on the individual's career history. For example, Jahnet de Light, the Tantric sex teacher referred to in chapter 9, has worked as a sauna girl and a dominatrix. Bella Lamou, also quoted earlier, worked as a hostess, call girl, actress in pornographic films and glamour model before taking up her current profession as sex therapist (both sources *Consenting Adults* 1997/8) and Roxy Blain (1994), as noted several times, has moved in and out of the straight sex sector of the industry. That is to say, these women, all specialists or former specialists of one kind or another, have also arguably developed a range of skills by virtue of their involvement in different sectors of the sex industry.

11 Desiree's standard rate is cited as £70 per hour for penetrative sex but, as O'Connell Davidson points out, the majority of her clients in this category stay only half an hour, including massage, showering and dressing, given that Desiree is so skilled in inducing orgasm. If they want 'another go', they are either charged double, whether the hour has elapsed or not, or refused if Desiree has other clients waiting. This equates to charging for the act itself, as streetworkers do.

12 See Freedman (1997) for a discussion of the ways in which outworkers gain access to hotels.

13 These various freedoms may of course be diminished if the woman concerned works through an escort agency. The agency could, for example, charge her a per client fee, such as McRae's (1992: 176) citation of £50 for a mid-range agency in Surrey in the early 1990s.

14 This collective came about following the 1996 merger of TAMPEP (Transnational AIDS/STD Prevention Among Migrant Prostitutes in Europe Project) and EUROPAP.

15 The debate here has, as Montgomery (1998) argues, become simplistic and politicized. Those commentators who adopt an anthropological approach, such as the contributors to Karim (1995b), find that the situation is more complex than it might appear – even in the case of child prostitution (for an alternative view see O'Connell Davidson 1995b, 1997; and O'Connell Davidson and Sanchez Taylor 1996). Montgomery argues for a greater respect to be given to the voices of those involved in the sex industry, and for attention to be paid to the ways in which they understand what they are doing.

16 For each pair of variables, we have assumed that the former is plotted on the vertical axis and the latter on the horizontal axis.

17 However, prostitutes are not passively determined by the epistemological or geographical place in which they work and we would not wish to suggest that place plays *the* definitive role in shaping the meanings they attach to their work or the experience that they have of it, although some may need help to be able to break free of their environment and reintegrate into other occupations (also see chapter 9, note 11). Cross-dimensional influences – degrees of cultural context, gender relations, racial and ethnic characteristics of populations, migration and trafficking and the influence of organized crime – will also have an effect on the overall shape and texture of the picture. The analysis here merely aims to suggest that social landscapes vary across certain common dimensions, which allow some comparison. It is through these discursive frames, or equally in opposition to or subversion of them, that individual prostitutes locate their sense of themselves and their interpretation of the occupation through which they support themselves. It is also within these constraints that they

characteristically conduct their present activities and construct their future possibilities both inside and outside the occupation.

11 The temporal organization of sex work

1   Nonetheless, as we have pointed out in note 2, chapter 8, this construction of the client encounter as work may vary with the way in which the individual prostitute understands her profession.

2   Of course, the cinematic and fast food industries (a) are fully legal and (b) generate outputs which are normally consumed in public. The provision of sexual services, on the other hand, enjoys a more complex legal status across our core context, as we have seen in chapter 10 – and such services are also consumed in private (or at least in places that provide some semblance of privacy, such as a car or a secluded back street). Nonetheless, legislative issues and the ways in which these different services are consumed are less relevant to our argument here than the fact that cinema, fast food and prostitution can all be seen to represent consumer industries which provide workers with some respite from the rigours of working life. Furthermore, although cinema in general is not a consumer activity which attracts particular moral censure, visits to cinemas specializing in pornographic films may necessarily be undertaken rather more discreetly; which argument also consolidates our point about the incomplete commodification of sexuality.

3   As an adjunct to our discussion in chapter 10, it is also true to say that the Internet has opened up enormous and relatively low cost possibilities for prostitutes in terms of advertising their services to a global market (Waldman 1998).

4   However, as we have established in part I, sexuality may be instrumentally channelled in various complex ways in *organizational* life.

5   Moreover, men who use prostitutes' services are not necessarily unaware that the worker is not enjoying the sex that takes place. Indeed, male clients may relish the thrill of paying someone to do what they want, when they want, how they want. This ties in with our discussion later in this chapter concerning men scripting their encounters with prostitutes so as to reinforce the dominant side of their masculinity. Indeed, the key issue in this later analysis is that time in prostitution is reversible and permeable for both interactants. Thus some men, on certain occasions, may approach prostitutes looking for a simulation of smooth space; in other times and in other places, they may seek to segment and striate the way that time unfolds within the encounter.

6   It is worth noting that the argument that we present here and in chapter 8 differs in important ways from Pateman's suggestion, as discussed at length in chapter 9, that men use prostitutes primarily to reinforce their patriarchal masculinity. Our position here is that what men seek from prostitutes may often be a somewhat complex validation of their sense of self-worth as men, not the simple exercising of right of ownership over a woman's body as achieved through penetrative intercourse, which Pateman claims is the case. O'Connell Davidson, moreover, differentiates between affirming masculinity and stepping outside of its manifold demands, suggesting that visits to prostitutes represent an instance of the latter. However, we would suggest that this stance again is problematic given that it does not explain the particular need that the client is seeking to fulfil in paying for sex and seems to construct all such needs as transgressive of masculine identity. We argue, on the contrary, that the needs which men pursue through their exchanges with prostitutes are very often importantly and inextricably linked to the contradictions and complexities of being a man, in the sense that being a man may be difficult to do in what we have designated as naturally occurring relationships. Our discussion in chapter 7 is also relevant in this regard.

7   Jemma's experience suggests that her clients are mainly concerned with the price that she charges, as opposed to the quality of her services, and will often haggle even over her £20 fee.

8   Cat, of course, is not a streetworker, although she certainly shares Jemma's desire to get the encounter over with as soon as possible. She also displays a similar attitude to clients – an example being her comment that 'All men are bastards' (Cat, quoted in *Vice: The Sex Trade*). However, the fact that Cat refers to faking her orgasm as part of the job points again to what is demanded of workers at this higher end of the industry – she cannot get away with the straightforward 'trick-turning' approach employed by Jemma and other street prostitutes.

Bibliography

Abdoolcarim, Zoher (1993) 'Lessons for staying in better shape', *Asian Business* June, 41–3.

Ackroyd, Stephen and Crowdy, Philip A. (1990) 'Can culture be managed? Working with "raw" material: the case of the English slaughtermen', *Personnel Review* 19, 5: 3–13.

Adorno, Theodor (1999) *Aesthetic Theory*, London: Athlone Press.

Aggleton, Peter (ed.) (1999) *Men Who Sell Sex*, London: UCL Press.

Albrow, Martin (1992) '"Sine ire et studio" or do organizations have feelings?', *Organization Studies* 13, 3: 313–30.

alt.culture: an a–z of the 90s. Online. Available HTTP: <http://www.altculture.com/> (accessed 21 September 1999).

Alvesson, Mats and Billing, Yvonne Due (1997) *Understanding Gender and Organizations*, London: Sage.

Alvesson, Mats and Willmott, Hugh (1992) 'On the idea of emancipation in management and organization studies', *Academy of Management Review* 17, 3: 432–64.

Anechiarico, Barry (1998) 'A closer look at sex offender character pathology and relapse prevention: an integrative approach', *International Journal of Offender Therapy and Comparative Criminology* 42, 1: 16–26.

Anthony, Peter (1989) 'The paradox of the management of culture or "he who leads is lost" ', *Personnel Review* 19, 4: 3–8.

—— (1994) *Managing Culture*, London: Open University Press.

Arluke, Arnold and Hafferty, Frederic (1996) 'From apprehension to fascination with "dog lab": the use of absolutions by medical students', *Journal of Contemporary Ethnography* 25, 2: 201–225.

Ashforth, Blake E. (1994) 'Petty tyranny in organizations', *Human Relations* 47, 7: 755–78.

—— and Kreiner, Glen E. (1999) '"How can you do it?": dirty work and the challenge of constructing a positive identity', *Academy of Management Review* 24, 3: 413–34.

Bailey, Frederick George (1977) *Morality and Expediency: The Folklore of Academic Politics*, Oxford: Blackwell.

Baker, Douglas D., Terpstra, David E. and Cutler, Bob D. (1990) 'Perceptions of sexual harassment: a re-examination of gender differences', *Journal of Psychology* 124, 4: 409–16.

Baker, Elsworth F. (1982) 'Sexual theories of Wilhelm Reich', *Journal of Orgonomy* 20, 2. Online. Available HTTP: <http://www.acoreich.org/article_008.html> (accessed 21 September 1999).

—— (n.d.) 'Medical orgonomy', *Journal of Orgonomy* 11, 2. Online. Available HTTP: <http://www.acoreich.org/article_005.html> (accessed 21 September 1999).

Balogh, Stefanie (1997) 'Arena fallout compromised Yeldham enquiry', *The Australian* 27 August: 4.

Banks, Olive (1981) *Faces of Feminism: A Study of Feminism as a Social Movement*, Oxford: Martin Robertson.

Barak, Azy, Fisher, William A. and Houston, Sandra (1992) 'Individual difference correlates of the experience of sexual harassment among female university students', *Journal of Applied Social Psychology* 22, 1: 17–37.

Barbara (1994) 'It's a pleasure doing business with you', *Social Text* 11, 3: 13–22.

Barbaree, Howard E., Marshall, William L. and McCormick, Jennifer (1998) 'The development of deviant sexual behaviour among adolescents and its implications for prevention and treatment', *Irish Journal of Psychology* 19, 1: 1–31.

Bargaining Report (1992) 'Sexual and racial harassment at work', 114, February: 13–15.

Barlow, Carol (1994) 'A brothel owner's view', in R. Perkins, G. Prestage, R. Sharp and F. Lovejoy (eds) *Sex Work and Sex Workers in Australia*, Sydney: UNSW Press, 132–9.

Barrett, Michèle (1980) *Women's Oppression Today: Problems in Marxist Feminist Analysis*, London: Verso Editions/New Left Books.

Bartky, Sandra L. (1988) 'Foucault, femininity and the modernization of patriarchal power', in I. Diamond and L. Quinby (eds) *Feminism and Foucault: Reflections on Resistance*, Boston: Northeastern University Press, 61–86.

Bataille, Georges (1970–1979) *Georges Bataille, Œuvres Complètes 5*, Paris: Gallimard.

—— (1982) *The Story of the Eye*, London: Penguin.

—— (1985) *Visions of Excess: Selected Writings, 1927–1939*, A. Stoekl (ed.), Minneapolis: University of Minnesota Press.

—— (1986) *Erotism: Death and Sensuality*, San Francisco: City Lights Books.

—— (1991) *The Accursed Share, Volume 1: An Essay on General Economy*, New York: Zone Books.

—— (1997) *The Bataille Reader*, F. Botting and S. Wilson (eds), Oxford: Blackwell.

Baudrillard, Jean (1983a) *Simulations*, New York: Semiotext(e).

—— (1983b) *In the Shadow of the Silent Majorities*, Paris: Semiotext(e).

—— (1983c) 'The ecstasy of communication', in H. Foster (ed.) *Postmodern Culture*, London: Pluto Press, 126–34.

—— (1987) *The Ecstasy of Communication*, New York: Semiotext(e).

—— (1988) *Selected Writings*, M. Poster (ed.), Cambridge: Polity Press.

—— (1990) *Seduction*, Basingstoke: Macmillan Education.

—— (1993a) *Symbolic Exchange and Death*, London: Sage.

—— (1993b) *The Transparency of Evil: Essays on Extreme Phenomena*, London: Verso.

Bauman, Zygmunt (1983) 'Industrialism, consumerism and power', *Theory, Culture and Society* 1, 3: 32–43.

—— (1987) *Legislators and Interpreters: On Modernity, Postmodernity and the Intellectuals*, Cambridge: Polity Press.

—— (1993) *Postmodern Ethics*, Oxford: Blackwell.

—— (1998) *Globalization: The Human Consequences*, Cambridge: Polity Press.

BBC News: Health (1999) 'Male rape "must be tackled"', 9 March. Online. Available HTTP: <http://news.bbc.co.uk/> (accessed 7 September 1999).

Becker, Howard, S. (1973) *Outsiders: Studies in the Sociology of Deviance*, New York: Free Press.

Bedarf, Abril R. (1995) 'Examining sex offender community notification laws', *California Law Review* 83, 3: 885–939.

Bell, D. Wallace (1979) *Industrial Participation*, London: Pitman.

Benjamin, Jessica (1995) 'Sameness and difference: toward an "over-inclusive" theory of gender development', in A. Elliott and S. Frosh (eds) *Psychoanalysis in Context: Paths between Theory and Modern Culture*, London: Routledge, 106–22.

Benson, Donna J. and Thomson, Gregg E. (1982) 'Sexual harassment on a university campus: the congruence of authority relations, sexual interest and gender stratification', *Social Problems* 2, 9: 236–51.

Bergson, Henri (1913) *Creative Evolution*, London: Macmillan.

—— (1950) *Time and Free Will*, London: Allen and Unwin.

Berliner, Lucy, Schram, Donna, Miller, Lisa L. and Milloy, Cheryl Darling (1995) 'A sentencing alternative for sex offenders: a study of decision-making and recidivism', *Journal of Interpersonal Violence* 10, 4: 487–502.

Bhabha, Homi (1988) 'The commitment to theory,' *New Formations* 5, 5–23.

—— (1994) *The Location of Culture*, London: Routledge.

Billig, Michael (1997) 'Freud and Dora: repressing an oppressed identity', *Theory, Culture and Society* 14, 3: 29–55.

Bishop, Ryan and Robinson, Lilian S. (1998) *Night Market: Sexual Cultures and the Thai Economic Miracle*, London: Routledge.

Blain, Roxy (1994) 'A female sex worker's view', in R. Perkins, G. Prestage, R. Sharp and F. Lovejoy (eds) *Sex Work and Sex Workers in Australia*, Sydney: UNSW Press, 113–25.

Bland, Linda and Mort, Frank (1997) 'Thinking sex historically', in L. Segal (ed.) *New Sexual Agendas*, London: Routledge, 17–31.

Blumenthal, Stephen, Gudjonsson, Gisli H. and Burns, Jan (1999) 'Cognitive distortions and blame attribution in sex offenders against adults and children', *Child Abuse and Neglect* 23, 2: 129–43.

Blyton, Paul, Hassard, John, Hill, Stephen and Starkey, Ken (eds) (1989) *Time, Work and Organization*, London: Routledge.

Boldt-Irons, Leslie Anne (1995) 'Sacrifice and violence in Bataille's erotic fiction: reflections from/upon the *mise en abîme*', in C.B. Gill (ed.) *Bataille: Writing the Sacred*, London and New York: Routledge, 91–104.

Bologh, Roslyn Wallach (1990) *Love or Greatness: Max Weber and Masculine Thinking – A Feminist Inquiry*, London: Unwin Hyman.

Bond, Michael Harris (ed.) (1986) *The Psychology of the Chinese People*, Hong Kong and Oxford: Oxford University Press.

Bordo, Susan (1986) 'The Cartesian masculinisation of thought', *Signs: Journal of Women in Culture and Society* 11, 3: 439–56.

Boyatzis, Richard (1974) 'The effect of alcohol consumption on the aggressive behaviour of men', *Quarterly Journal of Studies on Alcohol* 35: 959–72.

Brandenburg, Judith B. (1982) 'Sexual harassment in the university: guidelines for establishing a grievance procedure', *Signs: Journal of Women in Culture and Society* 8, 2: 320–36.

Brannon, James M. and Troyer, Rik (1995) 'Adolescent sex offenders: investigating adult commitment-rates four years later', *International Journal of Offender Therapy and Comparative Criminology* 39, 4: 317–26.

Bremer, Barbara A., Moore, Cathleen T. and Bildersee, Ellen F. (1991) 'Do you have to call it "sexual harassment" to feel harassed?', *College Student Journal* 25, 3: 258–68.

Brewer, Marilynn B. and Berk, Richard A. (1982) 'Beyond nine to five: introduction', *Journal of Social Issues*, 38: 4, 1–4.

Brewis, Joanna (1996) 'Sex, work and sex at work: a Foucauldian analysis', unpublished PhD Thesis, UMIST.

—— (1998) 'What is wrong with this picture? Sex and gender relations in *Disclosure*', in J. Hassard and R. Holliday (eds) *Organization/Representation: Work and Organizations in Popular Culture*, London: Sage, 83–99.

—— and Grey, Christopher (1994) 'Re-eroticizing the organization: an exegesis and critique', *Gender, Work and Organization* 1, 2: 67–82.

—— Hampton, Mark P. and Linstead, Stephen (1997a) 'Unpacking Priscilla: subjectivity and identity in the organization of gendered appearance', *Human Relations*, 50, 10: 1275–1304.

—— Linstead, Stephen and Sinclair, John (1997b) 'Any time, any place, anywhere: 24/7 and the organization of sex work', paper presented to the After Dark? The Organization of Night-Time Work and Leisure in 24/7 Cultures Conference, Bolton, March.

Bristow, Joseph (1997) *Sexuality*, London: Routledge.

Brittan, Arthur (1989) *Masculinity and Power*, Oxford: Blackwell.

Brockett, Lynda and Murray, Alison (1994) 'Thai sex workers in Sydney', in R. Perkins, G. Prestage, R. Sharp and F. Lovejoy (eds) *Sex Work and Sex Workers in Australia*, Sydney: UNSW Press, 190–202.

Brooks, Libby (1998) 'The happy hooker', *The Guardian* 7 January: 4.

—— (1999) 'You expect to be beaten up. You know society hates you. And you're terrified of yourself', *Guardian Unlimited Archive*, 21 June. Online. Available HTTP: <http://www.guardian.co.uk > (accessed 27 August 1999).

Brooks, Linda and Perot, Annette R. (1991) 'Reporting sexual harassment: exploring a predictive model', *Psychology of Women Quarterly* 15, 1: 31–47.

Brown, Andrew D. (1997) 'Narcissism, identity and legitimacy', *Academy of Management Review*, 22, 3: 643–86.

Browne, Jan and Minichiello, Victor (1995) 'The social meanings behind male sex work: implications for sexual interactions', *British Journal of Sociology* 46, 4: 598–622.

Brownmiller, Susan (1975) *Against Our Will: Men, Women and Rape*, London: Secker and Warburg.

Brussa, Licia (1989) 'Migrant prostitutes in the Netherlands', in G. Phetersen (ed.) *Vindication of the Rights of Whores*, Seattle: Seal Press, 227–40.

—— (1991) *Survey on Prostitution, Migration, and Trafficking in Women: History and Current Situation*, Council of Europe: EG/Prost.

Buchbinder, David (1994) *Masculinities and Identities*, Melbourne: Melbourne University Press.

Burawoy, Michael (1979) *Manufacturing Consent: Changes in the Labour Process under Monopoly Capitalism*, Chicago: University of Chicago Press.

Burke, Kenneth (1969) *A Grammar of Motives*, Berkeley, CA: University of California Press.

Burrell, Gibson (1984) 'Sex and organizational analysis', *Organization Studies* 5, 2: 97–118.

—— (1992a) 'The organization of pleasure', in M. Alvesson and H. Willmott (eds) *Critical Management Studies*, London: Sage, 66–88.

—— (1992b) 'Back to the future', in M. Reed and M. Hughes (eds) *Rethinking Organizations*, London: Sage, 165–83.

—— (1997) *Pandemonium: Towards a Retro-Organization Theory*, London: Sage.

—— and Hearn, Jeff (1989) 'The sexuality of organization', in J. Hearn, D.L. Sheppard, P. Tancred-Sheriff and G. Burrell (eds) *The Sexuality of Organization*, London: Sage, 1–28.

—— and Morgan, Gareth (1979) *Sociological Paradigms and Organizational Analysis*, Aldershot: Gower.

Butler, Judith P. (1990) *Gender Trouble: Feminism and the Subversion of Identity*, New York and London: Routledge.

—— (1993) *Bodies That Matter: On the Discursive Limits of 'Sex'*, New York and London: Routledge.

—— (1997) *The Psychic Life of Power: Theories in Subjection*, Stanford, CA: Stanford University Press.

—— (1999 [1987]) *Subjects of Desire: Hegelian Reflections in Twentieth-Century France*, New York: Columbia University Press.

Butler, Richard (1995) 'Time in organizations: its experience, explanations and effects', *Organization Studies* 16, 6: 925–50.

Cain, Maureen (1993) 'Foucault, feminism and feeling: what Foucault can and cannot contribute to feminist epistemology', in C. Ramazanoğlu (ed.) *Up Against Foucault: Explorations of Some Tensions Between Foucault and Feminism*, London: Routledge, 73–96.

Campbell, Beatrix (1984) *Wigan Pier Revisited: Poverty and Politics in the Eighties*, London: Virago.

Campbell, Colin (1989) *The Romantic Ethic and the Spirit of Modern Consumerism*, Oxford: Blackwell.

Canetti, Elias (1987) *Crowds and Power*, London: Penguin.

Carpentier, James and Cazamian, Pierre (1977) *Night Work: Its Effects on the Health and Welfare of the Worker*, Geneva: International Labour Office.

Castells, Manuel (1998) *End of Millennium*, Oxford: Blackwell.

Castoriadis, Carlos (1987) *The Imaginary Institution of Society*, Cambridge: Polity Press.

Centers for Disease Control and Prevention (1994) *HIV/AIDS Surveillance Report*, 5, 4, Atlanta: US Department of Health and Human Services.

Chapkis, Wendy (ed.) (1997) *Live Sex Acts: Women Performing Erotic Labour*, New York: Routledge.

Chasseguet-Smirgel, Janine (1985) *The Ego Ideal: A Psychoanalytic Essay on the Malady of the Ideal*, New York: Norton.

—— (1986) *Sexuality And Mind: The Role of the Father and the Mother in the Psyche*, New York: New York University Press.

Chia, Robert (1994) 'The concept of decision: a deconstructive analysis', *Journal of Management Studies* 31, 6: 781–806.

—— (1995) 'From modern to postmodern organizational analysis', *Organization Studies* 16, 4: 579–604.

—— (1996) *Organizational Analysis: A Deconstructive Approach*, Berlin: Walter de Gruyter.

Cixous, Hélène (1988) 'Sorties', in D. Lodge (ed.) *Modern Criticism and Theory*, London: Longman, 286–93.

Clark, Peter (1978) 'Temporal innovations and time structuring in large organizations', in J.T. Fraser *et al.* (eds) *The Study of Time*, vol. 3, New York: Springer Verlag.

—— (1985) 'A review of the theories of time and structure for organizational sociology', in S. Bacharach and S. Mitchell (eds) *Research in the Sociology of Organizations*, vol. 4, Greenwich, CT: JAI Press, 35–70.

—— (1990) 'Chronological codes and organizational analysis', in J. Hassard and D. Pym (eds) *The Theory and Philosophy of Organizations*, London: Routledge, 137–63.

Cobb, Sidney and Rose, Robert M. (1973) 'Hypertension, peptic ulcer and diabetes in air traffic controllers', *Journal of the American Medical Association* 224, 4: 489–92.

Cockburn, Cynthia (1991) *In the Way of Women: Men's Resistance to Sex Equality in Organizations*, Basingstoke: Macmillan.

Cockington, James and Marlin, Linda (1995) *Sex Inc: True Tales from the Australian Sex Industry*, Sydney: Ironbark Pan Macmillan.

Collins, Eliza G.C. and Blodgett, Timothy B. (1981) 'Sexual harassment … some see it … some won't', *Harvard Business Review* 59, 2: 76–95.

Collins, Rachel (1997) 'The happy hooker', *Head* issue 7. Online. Available HTTP: <http://www.users.dircon.co.uk/~rachelc/rachel.html> (accessed 5 February 1999).

—— (1998) 'Thought for the day – the Rachel diaries'. Online. Available HTTP: <http://www.users.dircon.co.uk/~rachelc/rachel.html> (accessed 5 February 1999).

—— (n.d.) 'Rachel trying to be creative'. Online. Available HTTP: <http://www.users.dircon.co.uk/~rachelc/rachel.html> (5 February 1999).

Collinson, David L. (1988) ' "Engineering humour": masculinity, joking and conflict in shopfloor relations', *Organization Studies* 9, 2: 181–99.

—— (1992) *Managing the Shopfloor: Subjectivity, Masculinity and Workplace Culture*, Berlin: Walter de Gruyter.

—— and Collinson, Margaret (1989) 'Sexuality in the workplace: the domination of men's sexuality', in J. Hearn, D.L. Sheppard, P. Tancred-Sheriff and G. Burrell (eds) *The Sexuality of Organization*, London: Sage, 91–109.

—— and Collinson, Margaret (1997) ' "Delayering managers': time-space surveillance and its gendered effects', *Organization* 4, 3: 375–407.

—— and Hearn, Jeff (1996) (eds) *Men as Managers, Managers as Men: Critical Perspectives on Men, Masculinities and Management*, London: Sage.

Connell, Robert W. (1997) 'Sexual revolution', in L. Segal (ed.) *New Sexual Agendas*, London: Routledge, 60–76.

Consenting Adults (1997/8) 'Sex work: female sex workers' show 'n' tell', issue 2, Winter. Online. Available HTTP: <http://www.sfc.org.uk/adults/issue02/02sexwrk.htm> (accessed 5 February 1999).

Cook, Nerida (1998) 'Dutiful daughters, estranged sisters: women in Thailand', in K. Sen and M. Stivens (eds) *Gender and Power in Affluent Asia*, London: Routledge, 250–90.

Cooper, Robert (1983) 'The other: a model of human structuring', in G. Morgan (ed.) *Beyond Method*, London: Sage, 202–18.

—— (1989) 'Modernism, postmodernism and organizational analysis 3: the contribution of Jacques Derrida', *Organization Studies* 10, 4: 479–502.

—— and Law, John (1995) 'Organization: distal and proximal views', *Research in the Sociology of Organizations* 13: 237–74.

Court TV Online: Verdicts 'New Jersey v. Timmendequas (5/97)'. Online. Available HTTP: <http://www.courttv.com/verdicts/kanka.html> (accessed 27 August 1999).

Cramb, Auslan (1999) 'Mob forces paedophile out of home', *Electronic Telegraph*, 17 May, issue 1452. Online. Available HTTP: <http://www.telegraph.co.uk/> (accessed 6 September 1999).

Crocker, Phyllis L. (1983) 'An analysis of university definitions of sexual harassment', *Signs: Journal of Women in Culture and Society* 8, 4, 696–707.

Cross, Gary (1993) *Time and Money: The Making of Consumer Culture*, London and New York: Routledge.

Daly, Mary (1984a) *Gyn/Ecology: The Metaethics of Radical Feminism*, London: The Women's Press.

—— (1984b) *Pure Lust: Elemental Feminist Philosophy*, London: The Women's Press.

Das, T.K. (1992) 'Time in management and organization studies', *Time and Society* 2, 2: 267–74.

Daudi, Philippe (1983) 'The discourse of power or the power of discourse', *Alternatives* IX: 317–25.

David, Natacha (1998) 'Sexual harassment at the workplace: stop it!'. Online. Available HTTP: <http://www.icftu.org/english/equality/ecamsexharr.html> (accessed 21 April 1999).

Davies, Kate (1994) *When Innocence Trembles: The Christian Brothers Tragedy – A Survivor's Story*, Sydney: Angus and Robertson.

Davies, Linda (1994) 'Merchants of menace', *The Sunday Times* (Style and Travel section) 1 May: 6.

Davies, Peter and Feldman, Rayah (1997) 'Prostitute men now', in G. Scambler and A. Scambler (eds) *Rethinking Prostitution: Purchasing Sex in the 1990s*, London: Routledge, 29–53.

Day, Sophie (1994) 'What counts as rape? Physical assault and broken contracts: contrasting views of rape amongst London sex workers', in P. Harvey and P. Gow (eds) *Sex and Violence: Issues in Representation and Experience*, London and New York: Routledge, 172–89.

de Albuquerque, Klaus (1999) 'Sex, beach boys and female tourists in the Caribbean', in B.M. Dank and R. Refinetti (eds) *Sex Work and Sex Workers (Sexuality and Culture* vol. 2), London: Transaction Publishers, 87–111.

Dean, Carolyn J. (1992) *The Self and its Pleasures: Bataille, Lacan and the History of the Decentered Subject*, Ithaca, NY and London: Cornell University Press.

de Beauvoir, Simone (1989) 'Must we burn Sade?', in D.A.F. Sade (Marquis de) *The One Hundred and Twenty Days of Sodom*, London: Arrow, 3–64.

de Certeau, Michel (1984) *The Practice of Everyday Life*, Berkeley, CA: University of California Press.

Delacoste, Frédérique and Alexander, Priscilla (eds) (1987) *Sex Work: Writings by Women in the Sex Industry*, Pittsburgh and San Francisco: Cleis Press.

Deleuze, Gilles (1971) *Masochism: An Interpretation of Coldness and Cruelty*, New York: George Braziller.

—— and Guattari, Félix (1984) *Anti-Oedipus: Capitalism and Schizophrenia*, London: Athlone Books.

—— and Guattari, Félix (1987) *A Thousand Plateaus: Capitalism and Schizophrenia*, Minneapolis: University of Minnesota.

Derrida, Jacques (1978) *Writing And Difference*, London: Routledge.

—— (1991) *Cinders*, Paris: Gallimard.

Deviants' Dictionary. Online. Available HTTP: <http://public.diversity.org.uk/deviant/index.html> (accessed 17 September 1999).

Dews, Peter (1984) 'Power and subjectivity in Foucault', *New Left Review* 144: 72–95.

Disclosure (1994) Constant c Productions, Warner Brothers and Baltimore Pictures, 128 minutes, director: Barry Levinson.

Doezema, Jo (1998) 'Forced to choose: beyond the voluntary v. forced prostitution dichotomy', in K. Kempadoo and J. Doezema (eds) *Global Sex Workers: Rights, Resistance and Redefinition*, London: Routledge, 34–50.

Dollimore, Jonathan (1991) *Sexual Dissidence: Augustine to Wilde, Freud to Foucault*, Oxford: Clarendon Press.

—— (1998) *Death, Desire and Loss in Western Culture*, New York: Routledge.

Donaldson, Mike (1991) *Time of Our Lives: Labour and Love in the Working Class*, Sydney: Allen and Unwin.

—— (1996) *Taking Our Time: Remaking the Temporal Order*, Perth: University of Western Australia Press.

Donegan, Lawrence (1998) 'Seventh killing of prostitute raises fears in red light area', *The Guardian* 3 March: 7.

Doren, Dennis M. (1998) 'Recidivism base rates, predictions of sex offender recidivism and the "sexual predator" commitment laws', *Behavioral Sciences and the Law* 16, 1: 97–114.

Duff, Alan (1994) *Once Were Warriors*, St. Lucia: University of Queensland Press.

—— (1996) *What Becomes of the Broken-Hearted?*, Sydney: Random House.

Duncombe, Jean and Marsden, Dennis (1996) 'Whose orgasm is this anyway? "Sex work" in long-term heterosexual couple relationships', in J. Weeks and J. Holland (eds) *Sexual Cultures: Communities, Values and Intimacy*, British Sociological Association Explorations in Sociology, 48, London: Macmillan, 220–38.

Dworkin, Andrea (1981) *Pornography: Men Possessing Women*, London: The Women's Press.

Dziech, Billie Wright and Weiner, Linda (1990) *The Lecherous Professor: Sexual Harassment on Campus*, Urbana, IL: University of Illinois Press.

Easlea, Brian (1981) *Science and Sexual Oppression: Patriarchy's Confrontation with Women and Nature*, London: Weidenfeld and Nicolson.

Ecstavasia, Audrey (1994) 'Fucking (with theory) for money: towards an introduction of escort prostitution', in E. Amiran and J. Unsworth (eds) *Essays in Postmodern Culture*, Oxford: Oxford University Press, 174–98.

Edwards, Susan S.M. (1989) *Policing 'Domestic' Violence: Women, the Law and the State*, London: Sage.

Ehrenreich, Barbara (1983) *The Hearts of Men*, London: Pluto Press.

Ehrenreich, Nancy S. (1990) 'Pluralist myths and powerless men: the ideology of reasonableness in sexual harassment law', *The Yale Law Journal* 99, 6: 1177–1234.

Elias, Norbert (1978) *The Civilizing Process: The History of Manners*, Oxford: Blackwell.

Elliott, Anthony (1994) *Psychoanalytic Theory: An Introduction*, Oxford, Blackwell.

Elliott, Richard, Eccles, S. and Hodgson, M. (1993) 'Re-coding gender representations: women, cleaning products, and advertising's "New Man"', *International Journal of Research in Marketing* 10: 311–24.

Ellis, Shmuel, Barak, Azy and Pinto, Adaya (1991) 'Moderating effects of personal cognitions on experience and perceived sexual harassment of women at the workplace', *Journal of Applied Social Psychology* 21, 6: 1320–37.

English Collective of Prostitutes (1997) 'Campaigning for legal change', in G. Scambler and A. Scambler (eds) *Rethinking Prostitution: Purchasing Sex in the 1990s*, London: Routledge, 83–102.

Enloe, Cynthia (1990) *Bananas, Bases and Beaches: Making Feminist Sense of International Politics*, London: Pandora.

—— (1993) *The Morning After: Sexual Politics at the End of the Cold War*, Berkeley, CA: University of California Press.

Equal Opportunities Review (1998) *Discrimination Case Law Digest*, 38, Winter.

EUROPAP, European Intervention Projects AIDS Prevention for Prostitutes (1994) *Final Report EUROPAP 1994*. Online. Available HTTP: <http://allserv.rug.ac.be/~rmak/europap/rapfin.html> (accessed 11 March 1999).

European Commission [Commission of the European Communities] (1991) *Commission Recommendation of 27.XI.1991 on the Protection of the Dignity of Women and Men at Work*, C(91) 2625, Brussels.

European Network for HIV/STD Prevention in Prostitution (EUROPAP/TAMPEP) *Hustling for Health*. Online. Available HTTP: <http://www.med.ic.ac.uk/df/dfhm/europap/hustling> (accessed 20 September 1999).

Evason, Eileen (1982) *Hidden Violence: Battered Women in Northern Ireland*, Belfast: Farset Co-operative Press.

Fain, Terri C. and Anderton, Douglas L. (1987) 'Sexual harassment: organizational context and diffuse status', *Sex Roles* 17, 5–6: 291–311.

Fairclough, Norman (1992) 'Discourse and text: linguistic and intertextual analysis within discourse analysis', *Discourse and Society* 3, 2: 193–217.

Faley, Robert H. (1982) 'Sexual harassment: critical review of legal cases with general principles and preventive measures', *Personnel Psychology* 35, 3: 583–600.

Featherstone, Mike (1991) *Consumer Culture and Postmodernism*, London: Sage.

Feyerabend, Paul (1978) *Against Method: Outline of an Anarchistic Theory of Knowledge*, London: Verso.

Fitzgerald, Louise F. and Ormerod, Alayne J. (1991) 'Perceptions of sexual harassment: the influence of gender and academic conduct', *Psychology of Women Quarterly* 15, 2: 281–94.

Fitzgerald, Louise F., Weitzman, Lauren M., Gold, Yael and Ormerod, Mimi (1988) 'Academic harassment: sex and denial in scholarly garb', *Psychology of Women Quarterly* 12, 3: 329–40.

Fleck, Ludwik (1979) *Genesis and Development of a Scientific Fact*, T.J. Trenn and R.K. Merton (eds), Chicago: University of Chicago Press.

Flett, Kathryn (1999) 'One woman's liberation', *The Observer* (Review section) 31 January: 3.

Foucault, Michel (1967) *Madness and Civilization: A History of Insanity in the Age of Reason*, London: Tavistock Publications.

—— (1972) *The Archaeology of Knowledge and the Discourse on Language*, New York: Pantheon Books.

—— (1973) *The Birth of the Clinic: An Archaeology of Medical Perception*, London: Tavistock Publications.

—— (1977) *Discipline And Punish: The Birth of the Prison*, London: Allen Lane.

—— (1979) *The History of Sexuality, Vol. 1: An Introduction*, London: Allen Lane.

—— (1980) *Power/Knowledge: Selected Interviews and Other Writings 1972–1977*, C. Gordon (ed.), Brighton: Harvester Press.

—— (1982) 'The subject and power', in H.L. Dreyfus and P. Rabinow *Michel Foucault: Beyond Structuralism and Hermeneutics*, Brighton: Harvester Press, 202–26.

—— (1985) 'Sexuality and solitude', in M. Blonski (ed.) *On Signs*, Oxford: Blackwell, 365–72.

—— (1986a) *The History of Sexuality, Vol. 2: The Use of Pleasure*, Harmondsworth: Viking/Penguin.

—— (1986b) *The Foucault Reader*, P. Rabinow (ed.), Harmondsworth: Penguin.

—— (1988) *Michel Foucault, Politics, Philosophy, Culture: Interviews and Other Writings 1977–1984*, L.D. Kritzman (ed.), New York: Routledge.

—— (1990) *The History of Sexuality, Vol. 3: The Care of the Self*, Harmondsworth: Penguin.

Frazier, Patricia A. and Cohen, Beth B. (1992) 'Research on the sexual victimization of women: implications for counselor training', *Counseling Psychologist* 20, 1: 141–58.

Freedland, Jonathon (1994) 'A life dedicated to violent death ends as it was lived – in blood', *The Guardian* 29 November: 13.

Freedman, Cheryl (1997) 'Room service', *Caterer and Hotelkeeper* 4–10 September: 66–8.

Freud, Sigmund (1963a) *Civilization and its Discontents*, London: Hogarth Press.

—— (1963b [1912]) 'The most prevalent form of degradation in erotic life', in *Sexuality and the Psychology of Love*, New York: Collier Books.

—— (1977) 'Fragment of an analysis of a case of hysteria', in *Case Histories*, vol. 1, Harmondsworth: Penguin.

Freund, Kurt and Kuban, Michael (1994) 'The basis of the abused abuser theory of pedophilia – a further elaboration on an earlier study', *Archives of Sexual Behavior* 23, 5: 553–63.

Frosh, Stephen (1997) 'Psychoanalytic challenges: a contribution to the new sexual agenda', in L. Segal (ed.) *New Sexual Agendas*, London: Routledge, 32–42.

Fukuyama, Francis (1992) *The End of History and the Last Man*, London: Hamish Hamilton.

Gambetta, Diego (1988) 'Can we trust?', in D. Gambetta (ed.) *Trust: Making and Breaking Cooperative Relations*, Oxford: Blackwell, 213–37.

Game, Ann (1991) *Undoing the Social: Towards a Deconstructive Sociology*, Milton Keynes: Open University Press.

—— (1997) 'Time unhinged', *Time and Society* 6, 2: 115–30.

Gane, Mike (1991a) *Baudrillard: Critical and Fatal Theory*, London: Routledge.

—— (1991b) *Baudrillard's Bestiary: Baudrillard and Culture*, London: Routledge.

Gardner, Carl and Sheppard, Julie (1989) *Consuming Passion: The Rise of Retail Culture*, London: Unwin Hyman.

Geertz, Clifford (1983) *Local Knowledges*, New York: Basic Books.

Gherardi, Silvia (1995) *Gender, Symbolism and Organizational Cultures*, London: Sage.

Gibbs, John J. (1986) 'Alcohol consumption, cognition and context: examining tavern violence', in A. Campbell and J.J. Gibbs (eds) *Violent Transactions: The Limits of Personality*, New York: Blackwell, 133–51.

Giddens, Anthony (1976) *New Rules of Sociological Method: A Positive Critique of Interpretative Sociology*, London: Hutchinson.

—— (1984) *The Constitution of Society*, Cambridge: Polity Press.

—— (1991) *Modernity and Self-Identity: Self and Society in the Late Modern Age*, Cambridge: Polity Press.

—— (1992) *The Transformation of Intimacy: Sexuality, Love and Eroticism in Modern Societies*, Cambridge: Polity Press.

Gillan, Audrey (1999) 'Dutch make oldest profession just a job', *The Guardian* 30 October: 20.

Gittings, Danny and Wilson, Karl (1993) 'Who really gained from the dispute?', *South China Sunday Morning Post* 31 January: 9.

Goffman, Erving (1961) *Asylums: Essays on the Social Situation of Mental Patients and Other Inmates*, New York: Anchor Books.

—— (1971) *The Presentation of Self in Everyday Life*, Harmondsworth: Penguin.

Golding, David (1980) 'Establishing blissful clarity in organizational life: managers', *Sociological Review* 28, 4: 763–82.

—— (1991) 'Some everyday rituals in management control', *Journal of Management Studies* 28, 6: 569–83.

—— (1996a) 'Producing clarity – depoliticizing control', in S. Linstead, R. Grafton Small and P. Jeffcutt (eds) *Understanding Management*, London: Sage, 51–65.

—— (1996b) 'Management rituals: maintaining simplicity in the chain of command', in S. Linstead, R. Grafton Small and P. Jeffcutt (eds) *Understanding Management*, London: Sage, 78–93.

Goodley, Steven (1994) 'A male sex worker's view', in R. Perkins, G. Prestage, R. Sharp and F. Lovejoy (eds) *Sex Work and Sex Workers in Australia*, Sydney: UNSW Press, 126–31.

Goodman, Richard A. (1973) 'Environmental knowledge and organizational time horizon: some functions and dysfunctions', *Human Relations* 26, 2: 215–26.

Gorer, Geoffrey (1953) *The Life and Ideas of the Marquis de Sade*, London: Peter Owen.

Gowler, Dan and Legge, Karen (1981) 'Negation, abomination and synthesis in rhetoric', in C. Antaki (ed.) *The Psychology of Ordinary Explanations of Human Behaviour*, London: Academic Press, 243–69.

—— (1983) 'The meaning of management and the management of meaning: a view from social anthropology', in M.J. Earl (ed.) *Perspectives on Management: A Multi-Disciplinary Analysis*, Oxford: Oxford University Press, 197–233.

Grafton Small, Robert and Linstead, Stephen A. (1989) 'Advertisements as artefacts', *International Journal of Advertising* 8, 3: 205–18.

Gramsci, Antonio (1971) *Selections from the Prison Notebooks*, London: Lawrence and Wishart.

Grauerholz, Elizabeth (1989) 'Sexual harassment of women professors by students: exploring the dynamics of power, authority, and gender in a university setting', *Sex Roles* 21, 11–12: 789–801.

—— (1996) 'Sexual harassment in the academy: the case of women professors', in M.S. Stockdale (ed.) *Sexual Harassment in the Workplace: Perspectives, Frontiers, and Response Strategies*, Thousand Oaks, CA: Sage, 29–50.

Greenberg, Jay and Mitchell, Stephen (1983) *Object Relations In Psychoanalytic Theory*, Cambridge, MA: Harvard University Press.

Griffin, Susan (1980) *Woman and Nature: The Roaring Inside Her*, New York, Cambridge: Harper and Row.

Grosz, Elizabeth (1994) *Volatile Bodies: Towards a Corporeal Feminism*, St. Leonards: Allen and Unwin.

—— (1995) *Space, Time and Perversion*, Sydney: Allen and Unwin.

Gunn, Michelle (1997) 'Diaspora destroys the raincoat image', *The Australian* 27 August 27: 5.

Gutek, Barbara, A. (1985) *Sex and the Workplace*, San Francisco: Jossey-Bass.

—— (1996) 'Sexual harassment at work: when an organization fails to respond', in M.S. Stockdale (ed.) *Sexual Harassment in the Workplace: Perspectives, Frontiers, and Response Strategies*, Thousand Oaks, CA: Sage, 272–90.

—— and Cohen, Aaron Groff (1992) 'Sex ratios, sex role spillover and sex at work: a comparison of men's and women's experiences', in A. J. Mills and P. Tancred (eds) *Gendering Organizational Analysis*, London: Sage, 133–50.

——, Cohen, Aaron Groff and Konrad, Alison M. (1990) 'Predicting social–sexual behavior at work: a contact hypothesis', *Academy of Management Journal* 33, 3: 560–77.

—— and Koss, Mary P. (1993) 'Changed women and changed organizations: consequences of and coping with sexual harassment', *Journal of Vocational Behavior* 22: 30–48.

—— and Morasch, Bruce (1982) 'Sex-ratios, sex-role spillover and sexual harassment of women at work', *Journal of Social Issues* 38, 4: 55–74.

Guy, Donna J. (1995) *Sex and Danger in Buenos Aires: Prostitution, Family and Nation in Argentina*, Lincoln: University of Nebraska Press.

Habermas, Jürgen (1979) *Communication and the Evolution of Society*, Boston: Beacon Press.

Hall, Edward (1959) *The Silent Language*, Garden City, NY: Doubleday.

—— (1969) *The Hidden Dimension: Man's Use of Space in Public and Private*, London: Bodley Head.

Hall, Lesley (1997) 'Heroes or villains? Reconsidering British *fin de siècle* sexology', in L. Segal (ed.) *New Sexual Agendas*, London: Routledge, 3–16.

Hall, Marny (1989) 'Private experiences in the public domain: lesbians in organizations', in J. Hearn, D.L. Sheppard, P. Tancred-Sheriff and G. Burrell (eds) *The Sexuality of Organization*, London: Sage, 125–38.

Halperin, David M. (1997) 'Forgetting Foucault: acts, identities and the *History of Sexuality*', keynote address to the 1st International Conference of the International Association for the Study of Sexuality, Culture and Society, University of Amsterdam, Amsterdam, The Netherlands, July–August.

Hanson, R. Karl (1998) 'What do we know about sex offender risk assessment?', *Psychology, Public Policy and Law* 4, 1–2: 50–72.

Hantrais, Linda and Letablier, Marie-Therese (1997) 'The gender of paid and unpaid work: a European problem', *Time and Society*, 6, 2: 131–150.

Hantrakul, Sukanya (1988) 'Prostitution in Thailand', in D. Chandler (ed.) *Development and Displacement: Women in South-East Asia*, Clayton, Victoria: Centre of Southeast Asian Studies, Monash University.

Haraway, Donna (1990) 'A manifesto for cyborgs: science, technology and socialist feminism in the 1980s', in L.J. Nicholson (ed.) *Feminism/Postmodernism*, New York: Routledge, 192–223.

—— (1991) *Simians, Cyborgs and Women: The Reinvention of Nature*, London: Free Association Books.

Harcourt, Christine (1994) 'Prostitution and public health in the era of AIDS', in R. Perkins, G. Prestage, R. Sharp and F. Lovejoy (eds) *Sex Work and Sex Workers in Australia*, Sydney: UNSW Press, 203–4.

Harriss, Kathryn (1988) 'What is this big fuss about sadomasochism? Lesbian sexuality and the Women's Liberation Movement', *Women's Studies Occasional Papers*, University of Kent at Canterbury, January.

Hart, Lynda (1998) *Between the Body and the Flesh: Performing Sadomasochism*, New York: Columbia University Press.

Harvey, David (1990) *The Condition of Postmodernity: An Enquiry into the Origins of Cultural Change*, Oxford: Blackwell.

Hassard, John (1990) *The Sociology of Time*, London: Macmillan.

—— (1991) 'Aspects of time in organizations', *Human Relations* 44, 1: 105–25.

—— (1996) 'Images of time in work and organizations', in S.R. Clegg, C. Hardy and W. Nord (eds) *Handbook of Organization Studies*, London: Sage, 581–98.

Haug, Wolfgang F. (1986) *Critique of Commodity Aesthetics: Appearance, Sexuality and Advertising in Capitalist Society*, Cambridge: Polity Press.

Hawkes, Gail (1996) *A Sociology of Sex and Sexuality*, London: Open University Press.

Hearn, Jeff (1987) *The Gender of Oppression*, Brighton: Harvester Press.

—— (1993) 'Emotive subjects: organizational men, organizational masculinities and the (de)construction of "emotions"', in S. Fineman (ed.) *Emotion in Organizations*, London: Sage, 142–66.

—— (1994) 'The organization(s) of violence: men, gender relations, organizations, and violences', *Human Relations* 47, 6: 731–54.

—— and Parkin, Wendy (1995) *'Sex' at 'Work': The Power and Paradox of Organisation Sexuality*, Hemel Hempstead: Prentice Hall/Harvester Wheatsheaf.

——, Sheppard, D.L., Tancred-Sheriff, P. and Burrell, G. (eds) (1989) *The Sexuality of Organization*, London: Sage.

Hegel, Georg Wilhem Friedrich (1977) *The Phenomenology of Spirit*, Oxford: Oxford University Press.

Heidegger, Martin (1967) *Being and Time*, Oxford: Blackwell.

Hershatter, Gail (1997) *Dangerous Pleasures: Prostitution and Modernity in Twentieth-Century Shanghai*, Berkeley and Los Angeles: University of California Press.

Higgins, Rosie, Rushaija, Estella and Medhurst, Angela (1999) 'Technowhores', in Cutting Edge: The Women's Research Group (eds) *Desire by Design: Body Territories and New Technologies*, London: I.B. Tauris, 111–22.

Hines, Ruth (1992) 'Accounting: filling the negative space', *Accounting, Organizations and Society* 17, 3–4: 314–41.

Hirschman, Albert O. (1977) *The Passions and the Interests: Political Arguments For Capitalism Before Its Triumph*, Princeton, NJ: Princeton University Press.

Hochschild, Arlie Russell (1983) *The Managed Heart: The Commercialization of Human Feeling*, Berkeley, CA: University of California Press.

Hoffman, Frances L. (1986) 'Sexual harassment in academia: feminist theory and institutional practice', *Harvard Educational Review* 56, 2: 105–21.

Hofstede, Geert and Bond, Michael (1988) 'Confucius and economic growth: trends in culture's consequences', *Organizational Dynamics* 16, 4: 4–21.

Hollway, Wendy (1989) *Subjectivity and Method in Psychology: Gender, Meaning and Science*, London: Sage.

—— (1996) 'Recognition and heterosexual desire', in D. Richardson (ed.) *Theorising Heterosexuality: Telling It Straight*, Buckingham: Open University Press, 91–108.

Holmer-Nadesan, Majia (1997) '*Essai*: dislocating (instrumental) organizational time', *Organization Studies* 18, 3: 481–510.

Homel, Ross and Tomsen, Steve (1993) 'Hot spots for violence: the environment of pubs and clubs', in H. Strang and S. Gerrull (eds) *Homicide: Patterns, Prevention and Control*, Canberra: Australian Institute of Criminology, 53–66.

Höpfl, Heather J. (1993) 'British carriers', in D. Gowler, K. Legge and C. Clegg (eds.) *Cases in Organizational Behaviour*, London: Paul Chapman, 117–25.

—— and Linstead, Stephen A. (1991) 'Nice jumper, Jim!', paper presented to the European Group for Occupational Psychology Conference, University of Rouen, Rouen, France, March.

—— and Linstead, Stephen A. (1993) 'Passion and performance: suffering and the carrying of organizational roles', in S. Fineman (ed.) *Emotion in Organizations*, London: Sage, 76–93.

Hopkins, Nick (1999) 'Student convicted of boy's murder', *Guardian Unlimited Archive*, 24 July. Online. Available HTTP: <http://www.guardian.co.uk> (accessed 27 August 1999).

Horrocks, Roger (1994) *Masculinity In Crisis*, London: Macmillan.

Hubbard, Phil (1997) 'Red-light districts and Toleration Zones: geographies of female street prostitution in England and Wales', *Area* 29, 2: 129–40.

—— (1998) 'Sexuality, immorality and the city: red-light districts and the marginalisation of female prostitutes', *Gender, Place and Culture* 5, 1: 55–72.

Hughes, Everett (1958) *Men and Their Work*, Glencoe, IL: Free Press.

Humphreys, Laud (1970) *Tearoom Trade: Impersonal Sex in Public Places*, New York: Aldine.

Hutcheon, Linda (1988) *A Poetics of Postmodernism: History, Theory, Fiction*, London: Routledge.

IDS Brief (1995) 'Sex discrimination: sexual harassment – single incident', 534, February: 4–5.

IDS Employment Law Handbook (1993) *Sex Discrimination*, Series 2, No. 2, London: Incomes Data Services.

Illouz, Eva (1998) 'The lost innocence of love: romance as a postmodern condition', *Theory, Culture and Society* 15, 3–4: 161–86.

Irigaray, Luce (1985a) *Speculum of the Other Woman*, Ithaca, NY: Cornell University Press.

—— (1985b) *This Sex Which Is Not One*, Ithaca, NY: Cornell University Press.

IRS Employment Trends (1992a) 'Sexual harassment at the workplace 2: developing policies and procedures', 514: 4–11.

—— (1992b) 'Sexual harassment at the workplace 3: implementing policies, the union role and legal aspects', 515: 8–12.

Jaggar, Alison M. (1983) *Feminist Politics and Human Nature*, Brighton: Harvester Press.

Jameson, Frederic (1983) 'Postmodernism and consumer society', in H. Foster (ed.) *Postmodern Culture*, London: Pluto Press, 111–25.

—— (1991) *Postmodernism, or the Cultural Logic of Late Capitalism*, London: Verso.

Jardine, Alice A. (1985) *Gynesis: Configurations of Women and Modernity*, Ithaca, NY: Cornell University Press.

Järvinen, Margaretha (1993) *Of Vice and Women: Shades of Prostitution*, Scandinavian Studies in Criminology, vol. 13, Oslo: Scandinavian University Press, Scandinavian Research Council for Criminology.

Jensen, Inger W. and Gutek, Barbara A. (1982) 'Attributes and assignment of responsibility', *Journal of Social Issues* 38, 4: 121–36.

Joseph, Sue (1997) *She's My Wife, He's Just Sex*, Sydney: Australian Centre for Independent Journalism, UTS.

Kaite, Berkeley (1988) 'The pornographic body double: transgression is the law', in A. Kroker and M. Kroker (eds) *Body Invaders: Sexuality and the Postmodern Condition*, London: Macmillan, 150–68.

—— (1995) *Pornography and Difference*, Bloomington: Indiana University Press.

Karen (1994) 'Letter to the editor', *Ms* May/June: 4.

Karim, Wazir Jahan (1995a) 'Introduction: genderising anthropology in Southeast Asia', in W.J. Karim (ed.), *'Male' and 'Female' in Developing Southeast Asia*, Oxford: Berg, 11–35.

—— (ed.) (1995b) *'Male' and 'Female' in Developing Southeast Asia*, Oxford: Berg.

Kempadoo, Kamala (1998a) 'Introduction: globalizing sex workers' rights', in K. Kempadoo and J. Doezema (eds) *Global Sex Workers: Rights, Resistance and Redefinitions*, London: Routledge, 1–28.

—— (1998b) 'The migrant tightrope: experiences from the Caribbean', in K. Kempadoo and J. Doezema (eds) *Global Sex Workers*, London: Routledge, 124–38.

Kerfoot, Deborah (1999) 'The organization of intimacy: managerialism, masculinity and the masculine subject', in S. Whitehead and R. Moodley (eds) *Transforming Managers: Gendering Change in the Public Sector*, London: UCL Press, 184–199.

—— and Knights, David (1993) 'Management, masculinity and manipulation: from paternalism to corporate strategy in financial services', *Journal of Management Studies* 30, 4: 659–77.

—— and Knights, David (1996) 'The best is yet to come: searching for embodiment in managerial work', in D.L. Collinson and J. Hearn (eds) *Men as Managers, Managers as Men: Critical Perspectives on Men, Masculinities and Management*, London: Sage, 78–98.

—— and Whitehead, Stephen (1996) '"And so say all of us"?: The problematics of masculinity and managerial work', *Occasional Papers in Organizational Analysis* 5, Department of Business and Management, University of Portsmouth Business School, 43–63.

Kerkham, Gordon (1997) 'A real-life story: Fiona', *Cleo* April: 108–9.

Kernberg, Otto (1975) *Borderline Conditions and Pathological Narcissism*, New York: Jason Aronson.

Keynes, John Maynard (1936) *The General Theory of Employment, Interest and Money*, London: Macmillan.

Kinnell, Hilary (1999) 'Letter to the editor: curb sex', *The Observer* 21 March: 30.

Kirkbride, Paul, Tang, Sara F.Y. and Westwood, Robert I. (1991) 'Chinese conflict preferences and negotiating behaviour', *Organization Studies* 12, 3: 365–86.

Klein, Melanie (1975) *Love, Guilt and Reparation, and Other Works, 1921–1945*, London: Hogarth Press.

Knapp, Deborah Erdos and Kustis, Gary A. (1996) 'The real "Disclosure": sexual harassment and the bottom line', in M.S. Stockdale (ed.) *Sexual Harassment in the Workplace: Perspectives, Frontiers, and Response Strategies*, Thousand Oaks, CA: Sage, 199–213.

Knights, David (1995) 'Refocusing the case study: the politics of IT research and researching politics in IT management', *Technology Studies* 2, 2: 230–54.

—— and Morgan, Glenn (1991) 'Selling oneself: subjectivity and the labour process in selling life insurance', in C. Smith, D. Knights and H. Willmott (eds) *White Collar Work: The Non-Manual Labour Process*, Basingstoke: Macmillan, 217–40.

—— and Odih, Pamela (1995) 'It's about time! The significance of gendered time for financial services consumption', *Time and Society* 4, 2: 205–31.

—— and Vurdubakis, Theo (1994) 'Foucault, power, resistance and all that', in J.M. Jermier, D. Knights and W.R. Nord (eds) *Resistance and Power in Organizations*, London and New York: Routledge, 167–98.

—— and Willmott, Hugh C. (1989) 'Power and subjectivity at work: from degradation to subjugation in social relations', *Sociology* 23, 4: 535–58.

Koen, Clifford M. (1989) 'Sexual harassment: criteria for defining hostile environment', *Employee Responsibilities and Rights Journal* 2, 4: 289–301.

Kohut, Heinz (1977) *The Restoration of the Self*, New York: International Universities Press.

Kojève, Alexander (1980) *Introduction to the Reading of Hegel: Lectures on "The Phenomenology of Spirit"*, A. Bloom (ed.), Ithaca, NY: Cornell University Press.

Konrad, Alison M. and Gutek, Barbara A. (1986) 'Impact of work experiences on attitudes towards sexual harassment', *Administrative Science Quarterly* 31, 3: 422–38.

Krafft-Ebing, Richard von (1965 [1885]) *Psychopathia Sexualis*, New York: Stein and Day.

Kristeva, Julia (1982) *Powers Of Horror: An Essay On Abjection*, New York: Columbia University Press.

Kritzman, Lawrence D. (1988) 'Introduction: Foucault and the politics of experience', in M. Foucault *Michel Foucault, Politics, Philosophy, Culture: Interviews and Other Writings 1977–1984*, L.D. Kritzman (ed.), New York: Routledge, ix–xxv.

Lacan, Jacques (1977) *Ecrits: A Selection*, London: Tavistock Publications.

Lala, Marie-Christine (1995) 'The hatred of poetry in Georges Bataille's writing and thought', in C.B. Gill (ed.) *Bataille: Writing the Sacred*, London and New York, 105–16.

Lamplugh, Diana (1996) 'Gender and personal safety at work', *Occasional Papers in Organizational Analysis* 5, Department of Business and Management, University of Portsmouth Business School: 64–79.

Laqueur, Thomas (1990) *Making Sex: Body and Gender from the Greeks to Freud*, Cambridge, MA: Harvard University Press.

Lasch, Christopher (1991 [1979]) *The Culture of Narcissism*, New York: Norton.

Lash, Scott (1990) *The Sociology of Postmodernism*, London, Routledge.

—— and Urry, John (1994) *Economies of Signs and Space*, London: Sage.

Laurence, Charles (1997) 'The murder that led to Megan's Law', *Electronic Telegraph*, 1 February, issue 617. Online. Available HTTP: <http://www.telegraph.co.uk/> (accessed 27 August 1999).

Lazarus, Mike (1994) 'On a street beat with the police', in R. Perkins, G. Prestage, R. Sharp and F. Lovejoy (eds) *Sex Work and Sex Workers in Australia*, Sydney: UNSW Press, 100–10.

Lecercle, Jean-Jacques (1990) *The Violence Of Language*, London: Routledge.

Lees, Sue (1996) *Carnal Knowledge: Rape on Trial*, London: Hamish Hamilton.

Leigh, Carol (1994) 'Thanks ma', in R. Sappington and T. Stallings (eds), *Uncontrollable Bodies: Testimonies of Identity and Culture*, Seattle: Bay Press, 242–61.

Lerum, Kari (1999) 'Twelve step feminism makes sex workers sick: how the State and the recovery movement turn radical women into "useless citizens"', in B.M. Dank and R. Refinetti (eds) *Sex Work and Sex Workers* (*Sexuality and Culture* vol. 2), London: Transaction Publishers, 7–36.

Levin, David Michael (1988) *The Opening Of Vision: Nihilism And The Postmodern Situation*, London: Routledge.

Levine, Ray and McMullen, Paul (1998) 'Posh vice: high-fliers give up top careers to be hookers', *News of the World* 6 November: 43–5.

Lévi-Strauss, Claude (1989 [1955]) *Tristes Tropiques*, London: Pan Books.

Levy, Allan (1998) 'Punish the perverts', *The Guardian*, 15 December: 37.

Linstead, Stephen A. (1993) 'Deconstruction in the study of organizations', in J. Hassard and M. Parker (eds) *Postmodernism and Organizations*, London: Sage, 49–70.

—— (1994) 'Objectivity, reflexivity and fiction: humanity, inhumanity and the science of the social', *Human Relations* 47, 11: 1321–46.

—— (1997) 'Resistance and return: power, command and change management', *Studies in Cultures, Organizations and Societies* 3, 1: 67–89.

—— (forthcoming) *The Underside of Organization*, London: Sage.

—— and Grafton Small, Robert (1986) 'The everyday professional: skill in the symbolic management of occupational kinship', in A. Strati (ed.) 'The symbolics of skill', *Quaderno*, 5/6, University of Trento, Italy: 53–67.

—— and Grafton Small, Robert (1990) 'Organizational bricolage', in B. Turner (ed.) *Organizational Symbolism*, Berlin and New York: Walter de Gruyter, 291–309.

—— and Grafton Small, Robert (1992) 'On reading organizational culture', *Organization Studies*, 13, 3: 331–55.

Lippert, John (1977) 'Sexuality and consumption', in J. Snodgrass (ed.) *For Men Against Sexism: A Book of Readings*, Albion, CA: Times Change Press, 207–12.

Lott, Bernice, Reilly, Mary E. and Howard, Dale R. (1982) 'Sexual assault and harassment: a campus case study', *Signs: Journal of Women in Culture and Society*, 8, 2, 296–320.

Lotringer, Sylvère (1988) *Overexposed: Treating Sexual Perversion in America*, New York: Pantheon Books.

Lunsing, Wim (1997) 'Are we all prostitutes? Taking sex in fieldwork seriously', paper presented to the 1st International Conference of the International Association for the

Study of Sexuality, Culture and Society, University of Amsterdam, Amsterdam, The Netherlands, July–August.

—— (1999) 'Life on Mars: love and sex in fieldwork on sexuality and gender in urban Japan', in F. Markowitz and M. Ashkenazi (eds) *Sex, Sexuality and the Anthropologist*, Champaign, IL: University of Illinois Press, 175–96.

Lyotard, Jean-François (1974) *Economie Libidinale*, Paris: Minuit.

MacCannell, Dean and MacCannell, Juliet Flower (1993) 'Violence, power and pleasure: a revisionist reading of Foucault from the victim's perspective', in C. Ramazanoğlu (ed.) *Up Against Foucault: Explorations of Some Tensions Between Foucault and Feminism*, London: Routledge, 203–38.

McClintock, Anne (1992) 'Screwing the system: sexwork, race and the law', *Boundary 2*, 19: 70–95.

McCoy, George (1998) *McCoy's British Massage Parlour Guide No. 4 '98–'99 Edition*, Stafford: McCoy's Guides.

McDowell, Linda (1996) 'Spatialising feminism: geographic perspectives', in N. Duncan (ed.) *Body Space*, London: Routledge, 28–44.

Macey, David (1995) 'On the subject of Lacan', in A. Elliott and S. Frosh (eds) *Psychoanalysis in Context: Paths Between Theory and Modern Culture*, London: Routledge, 72–86.

McGee, Christine (1993) 'Cathay's broken smiles', *South China Morning Post Saturday Review* 30 January: 1.

McIntosh, Mary (1994) 'The feminist debate on prostitution', paper presented to the British Sociological Association Annual Conference, University of Central Lancashire, Preston, March.

McKeganey, Neil (1999) Statement as part of 'Managing the Sex Industry' panel presentation, Annual Conference of the British Academy of Management, Manchester Metropolitan University, Manchester, September.

—— and Barnard, Marina (1996) *Sex Work on the Streets: Prostitutes and their Clients*, Buckingham: Open University Press.

MacKinnon, Catherine (1979) *Sexual Harassment of Working Women: A Case of Sex Discrimination*, New Haven, CT: Yale University Press.

McLeod, Eileen (1982) *Women Working: Prostitution Now*, London: Croom Helm.

McNay, Lois (1992) *Foucault and Feminism: Power, Gender and the Self*, Cambridge: Polity Press.

McNeil, Maureen (1987) 'Being reasonable feminists', in M. McNeil (ed.) *Gender and Expertise*, London: Free Association Books, 13–57.

McRae, Donald (1992) *Nothing Personal: The Business of Sex*, Edinburgh: Mainstream Publishing.

Maison Demi-Monde Online. Available HTTP: <http://www.users.dircon.co.uk/~rachelc> (5 February 1999).

Malovich, Natalie J. and Stake, Jayne E. (1990) 'Sexual harassment on campus: individual differences in attitudes and beliefs', *Psychology of Women Quarterly* 14, 1: 63–81.

The Man Who Shot Liberty Valance (1962) Paramount Pictures Corporation and John Ford Productions, 120 minutes, director: John Ford.

Mangham, Iain (1996) 'Beyond Goffman', in P. Jeffcutt, R. Grafton Small and S. Linstead (eds) *Organization and Theatre*, special issue of *Studies In Cultures, Organizations and Societies* 2, 1: 31–41.

Mansson, Sven-Axel and Hedin, Ulla-Carin (1999) 'Breaking the Matthew effect: on women leaving prostitution', *International Journal of Social Welfare* 8: 67–77.

Marcuse, Herbert (1968) *One Dimensional Man*, London: Sphere Books.

—— (1969) *Eros and Civilization: A Philosophical Inquiry into Freud*, London: Allen Lane.

Marlowe, Julian (1997) 'It's different for boys', in J. Nagle (ed.) *Whores and Other Feminists*, London: Routledge, 141–4.

Marques, Janice K. (1999) 'How to answer the question "does sex offender treatment work?"', *Journal of Interpersonal Violence* 14, 4: 437–51.

Marshall, Judi (1984) *Women Managers: Travellers in a Male World*, Chichester: John Wiley.

—— (1995) *Women Managers Moving On: Exploring Career and Life Choices*, London: Routledge.

Martin, Charles (1994) 'Satisfaction not guaranteed', *South China Sunday Morning Post Magazine* 27 February: 19.

Martin, Emily (1989) *The Woman in the Body: A Cultural Analysis of Reproduction*, Milton Keynes: Open University Press.

Massey, Doreen (1992) 'Politics and space/time', *New Left Review* 196: 65–84.

Matlock, Jann (1995) 'Delirious disguises, perverse masquerades, and the ghostly female fetishist', *Grand Street* (53) 14, 1: 156–71.

Mayer, Don and York, Kenneth, M. (1994) 'In search of the reasonable person standard after Harris v. Forklift Systems: use of surveys to determine contemporary community standards', *Academy of Management Conference Best Paper Proceedings 1994*, 254–8.

Maypole, Donald. E. (1986) 'Sexual harassment of social workers at work: injustice within?', *Social Work* 31, 1: 29–34.

—— and Skaine, Rosemarie (1983) 'Sexual harassment in the workplace', *Social Work* 28, 5: 385–90.

Miller, James (1993) *The Passion of Michel Foucault*, New York: Simon and Schuster.

Mills, Albert J. (1994) 'No sex please, we're British Airways', paper presented to the 12th Standing Conference on Organizational Symbolism, University of Calgary, Calgary, July.

—— and Murgatroyd, Stephen J. (1991) *Organizational Rules: A Framework for Understanding Organizational Action*, Buckingham: Open University Press.

—— and Tancred, Peta (1992) (eds) *Gendering Organizational Analysis*, London: Sage.

Mills, Heather (1998) 'From vice town to vigilante hell', *The Observer* 6 December: 7.

—— (1999) 'In Leeds, kerb-crawlers have a choice …', *The Observer Magazine*, 7 March: 32–5.

Miner, Michael H. and Dwyer, S. Margretta (1997) 'The psychosocial development of sex offenders: differences between exhibitionists, child molesters, and incest offenders', *International Journal of Offender Therapy and Comparative Criminology* 41, 1: 36–44.

Miner, Michael H., West, Mary Ann and Day, David M. (1995) 'Sexual preference for child and aggressive stimuli – comparison of rapists and child molesters using auditory and visual stimuli', *Behaviour Research and Therapy* 33, 5: 515–51.

Minson, J. (1986) 'Strategies for socialists? Foucault's conception of power', in M. Gane (ed.) *Towards a Critique of Foucault*, London: Routledge and Kegan Paul, 106–48.

Mr A. de Graaf Foundation (1997) *Between the Lines: Newsletter of the Mr. A. de Graaf Foundation – Institute for Prostitution Issues: Research, Policy, Advice, Documentation and Public Information*, June.

Mitchell, Cari (1998) 'Street dread', *The Guardian* (Society section), 11 February: 2.

Montgomery, Heather (1998) 'Children, prostitution and identity: a case study from a tourist resort in Thailand', in K. Kempadoo and J. Doezema (eds) *Global Sex Workers: Rights, Resistance and Redefinitions*, London: Routledge, 139–50.

Moodley, Roy (1999) 'Masculine/managerial masks and the "other" subject', in S. White-head and R. Moodley (eds) *Transforming Managers: Gendering Change in the Public Sector*, London: UCL Press, 214–33.

Moore, Suzanne (1988) 'Getting a bit of the other: the pimps of postmodernism', in R. Chapman and J. Rutherford (eds) *Male Order: Unwrapping Masculinity*, London: Lawrence and Wishart, 165–92.

—— (1994) 'Make way for the third sex', *The Guardian* (Women section) 13 October, 5.

Mort, Frank (1989) 'The politics of consumption', in S. Hall and M. Jacques (eds) *New Times: The Changing Face of Politics in the 1990s*, London: Lawrence and Wishart, 160–72.

—— (1996) *Cultures of Consumption*, London: Routledge.

Moser, Charles and Levitt, Eugene E. (1987) 'An exploratory-descriptive study of a sado-masochistically oriented sample', *The Journal of Sex Research* 23, 3: 322–37.

Murray, Alison (1998) 'Debt-bondage and trafficking: don't believe the hype', in K. Kempadoo and J. Doezema (eds) *Global Sex Workers: Rights, Resistance and Redefinitions*, London: Routledge, 51–64.

Neave, Marcia (1994) 'Prostitution laws in Australia: past history and current trends', in R. Perkins, G. Prestage, R. Sharp and F. Lovejoy (eds) *Sex Work and Sex Workers in Australia*, Sydney: UNSW Press, 67–99.

Nelson, Dean (1998) 'Solicit only in video zone, prostitutes will be told', *The Observer*, 18 January: 8.

Nicholson, Geoff (1995) 'Footsucker', *Grand Street* (53) 14, 1: 181–90.

Nicolson, Paula (1996) *Gender, Power and Organization: A Psychological Perspective*, London: Routledge.

Nott, Sasha (1993) 'Chic campaign on the perfumed picket line', *South China Sunday Morning Post*, 17 January: 2.

Nowotny, Helga (1994) *Time: The Modern and Postmodern Experience*, Cambridge: Polity Press.

O'Connell Davidson, Julia (1994a) 'The sources and limits of resistance in a privatized utility', in J.M. Jermier, D. Knights and W.R. Nord (eds) *Resistance and Power in Organizations*, London and New York: Routledge, 69–101.

—— (1994b) 'On power, prostitution and pilchards: the self-employed prostitute and her clients', paper presented to the 12th Annual International Labour Process Conference, Aston University, Birmingham, March.

—— (1994c) 'Prostitution and the contours of control', paper presented to the British Sociological Association Annual Conference, University of Central Lancashire, Preston, March.

—— (1995a) 'The anatomy of "free choice" prostitution', *Gender, Work and Organization* 2, 1: 1–10.

—— (1995b) 'British sex tourists in Thailand', in M. Maynard and J. Purvis (eds), *(Hetero)Sexual Politics*, London: Taylor and Francis.

—— (1996) 'Prostitution and the contours of control', in J. Weeks and J. Holland (eds) *Sexual Cultures: Communities, Values and Intimacy*, British Sociological Association Explorations in Sociology, 48, London: Macmillan, 180–98.

—— (1997) 'The sex exploiter', working paper for World Congress Against Commercial Sexual Exploitation of Children, Bangkok: ECPAT (End Child Prostitution in Asian Tourism). Online. Available HTTP: <http://www.usis.usemb.se/children/csec/2166.htm> (accessed 5 November 1997).

—— and Layder, Derek (1994) *Methods, Sex and Madness*, London: Routledge.

—— and Sanchez Taylor, Jacqueline (1996) 'Child prostitution and tourism: beyond the stereotypes', in J. Pilcher and S. Wagg (eds) *Thatcher's Children*, London: Falmer Press.

O'Neill, John (1986) 'The disciplinary society: from Weber to Foucault', *British Journal of Sociology*, 37, 1: 42–60.

O'Neill, Maggie (1996) 'The aestheticization of the whore in contemporary society: desire, the body, self and society', paper presented to the Body and Organization Workshop, Keele University, Keele, September.

—— (1997) 'Prostitute women now', in G. Scambler and A. Scambler (eds) *Rethinking Prostitution: Purchasing Sex in the 1990s*, London: Routledge, 3–28.

Orbach, Susie and Eichenbaum, Luise (1984) *What Do Women Want?*, Glasgow: Collins.

Orwell, George (1975) *The Road to Wigan Pier*, Harmondsworth: Penguin.

Overall, Christine (1992) 'What's wrong with prostitution? Evaluating sex work', *Signs: Journal of Women in Culture and Society* 17, 4: 705–24.

Paddington Green (1998/1999) Lion TV production for BBC Television, series 1: 11 programmes (330 minutes), producer: Bridget Sneyd.

Paetzold, Ramona L. and O'Leary-Kelly, Anne M. (1996) 'The implications of U.S. Supreme Court and Circuit Court decisions for hostile environment sexual harassment cases', in M.S. Stockdale (ed.) *Sexual Harassment in the Workplace: Perspectives, Frontiers, and Response Strategies*, Thousand Oaks, CA: Sage, 85–104.

Pateman, Carole (1988) *The Sexual Contract*, Cambridge: Polity Press.

Pefanis, Julian (1991) *Heterology and the Postmodern*, Durham, NC: Duke University Press.

Perkins, Roberta (1991) *Working Girls: Prostitutes, Their Life and Social Control*, Canberra: Australian Institute of Criminology.

—— (1994) 'Female prostitution', in R. Perkins, G. Prestage, R. Sharp and F. Lovejoy (eds) *Sex Work and Sex Workers in Australia*, Sydney: UNSW Press, 143–73.

Peters, Thomas J. and Waterman, Robert H., Jr. (1982) *In Search of Excellence: Lessons from America's Best-Run Companies*, New York: Harper and Row.

Petras, James and Wongchaisuwan, Tienchai (1993) 'Thailand: free markets, AIDS and child prostitution', *Z Magazine* September: 35–8.

Pettman, Jan Jindy (1996) *Worlding Women: A Feminist International Politics*, London: Routledge.

Phelps, Timothy M. and Winternitz, Helen (1992) *Capitol Games: Clarence Thomas, Anita Hill and the Story of a Supreme Court Nomination*, New York: Hyperion.

Pheterson, Gail (1996) *The Prostitution Prism*, Amsterdam: University of Amsterdam Press.

Phillips, Derek L. (1973) *Abandoning Method*, San Francisco: Jossey-Bass.

Phoenix, Joanna (1998) 'Paradoxical stories of prostitution', paper presented to the British Sociological Association Annual Conference, University of Edinburgh, Edinburgh, April.

—— (1999) 'Gender, crime and organisation', paper presented to the Gender in Employment Research Group Seminar Series, University of Portsmouth Business School, Portsmouth, March.

Pile, Steve (1996) *The Body and the City: Psychoanalysis, Space and Subjectivity*, London: Routledge.

Plato (1994) *The Symposium*, R. Wakefield (trans.), Oxford: Oxford University Press.

Polk, Kenneth (1994) *When Men Kill: Scenarios Of Masculine Violence*, Cambridge: Cambridge University Press.

Pongpaichit, Pasuk (1982) *From Peasant Girls to Bangkok Masseuses*, Geneva: ILO.

Poster, Mark (1986) 'Foucault and the tyranny of Greece', in D.C. Hoy (ed.) *Foucault: A Critical Reader*, Oxford: Blackwell, 1986, 205–20.

Prentky, Robert A., Lee, Austin F.S., Knight, Raymond A. and Cerce, David D. (1997) 'Recidivism rates among child molesters and rapists: a methodological analysis', *Law and Human Behavior* 21, 6: 635–59.

Prestage, Garrett (1994) 'Male and transsexual prostitution', in R. Perkins, G. Prestage, R. Sharp and F. Lovejoy (eds) *Sex Work and Sex Workers in Australia*, Sydney: UNSW Press, 174–90.

Pretty Woman (1990) Silver Screen Partners IV and Touchstone Pictures, 119 minutes, director: Garry Marshall.

Prince, Diana (1986) 'A psychological profile of prostitutes in California and Nevada', unpublished Phd dissertation, San Diego: United States International University.

Pringle, Rosemary (1989) 'Bureaucracy, rationality and sexuality: the case of secretaries', in J. Hearn, D.L. Sheppard, P. Tancred-Sheriff and G. Burrell (eds) *The Sexuality of Organization*, London: Sage, 158–77.

Prostitutes' Education Network. Online. Available HTTP: <http://www.bayswan.org/penet.html> (accessed 7 September 1996).

Quinsey, Vernon L., Khanna, Arunima and Malcolm, P. Bruce (1998) 'A retrospective evaluation of the regional treatment sex offender treatment program', *Journal of Interpersonal Violence* 13, 5: 621–44.

Rafaeli, Anat and Sutton, Robert I. (1989) 'The expression of emotion in organizational life', in L.L. Cummings and B.M. Staw (eds) *Research in Organizational Behaviour*, vol. 11, San Francisco: Jossey-Bass, 1–42.

Rafferty, Jean (1998) 'Double jeopardy', *The Guardian Weekend* 14 March: 14–23.

Ramazanoğlu, Caroline (1989) *Feminism and the Contradictions of Oppression*, London: Routledge.

—— and Holland, Janet (1993) 'Women's sexuality and men's appropriation of desire', in C. Ramazanoğlu (ed.) *Up Against Foucault: Explorations of Some Tensions Between Foucault and Feminism*, London: Routledge, 239–64.

Redding, Gordon (1990) *The Spirit of Chinese Capitalism*, Berlin: Walter De Gruyter.

—— and Wong, Gilbert Y. (1986) 'The psychology of Chinese organizational behaviour', in M.H. Bond (ed.) *The Psychology of the Chinese People*, Hong Kong and Oxford: Oxford University Press, 267–95.

Reich, Wilhelm (1969) *The Sexual Revolution: Towards a Self-Governing Character Structure*, London: Vision Press.

—— (1972) *The Invasion of Compulsory Sex-Morality*, London: Souvenir Press.

Reilly, Timothy, Carpenter, Sandra, Dull, Valerie and Bartlett, Kim (1982) 'The factorial survey: an approach to defining sexual harassment on campus', *Journal of Social Issues* 38, 4: 99–110.

Rella, Franco (1994) *The Myth of the Other: Lacan, Deleuze, Foucault, Bataille*, Washington, DC: Maisonneuve Press.

Renick, James C. (1980) 'Sexual harassment at work: why it happens and what to do about it', *Personnel Journal* 59, 8: 658–62.

Reuters (1994) 'Prostitution boom boosts AIDS risk in Zaire', press release, 19 December. Online. Available HTTP: <http://www.worldsexguide.org/zaire_bits.txt.html> (accessed 8 October 1999).

Richardson, Michael (1994) *Georges Bataille*, London: Sage.

Richman, Michèle (1982) *Reading Georges Bataille: Beyond The Gift*, Baltimore: Johns Hopkins University Press.

Ritzer, George (1996) *The McDonaldization of Society*, Newbury Park, CA: Pine Forge Press.

Rival, Laura, Slater, Don and Miller, Daniel (1998) 'Sex and sociality: comparative ethnographies of sexual objectification', *Theory, Culture and Society* 15, 3–4: 295–322.

Roach, Joseph R. (1985) *The Player's Passion: Studies in the Science of Acting*, Newark: University of Delaware Press.

Roberts, Nickie (1992) *Whores in History: Prostitution in Western Society*, London: Harper-Collins.

Robinson, Lilian S. (1993) 'In the penile colony: touring Thailand's sex industry', *Nation* 1 November: 492–7.

Robinson, Paul (1970) *The Sexual Radicals: Wilhelm Reich, Geza Roheim, Herbert Marcuse*, London: Temple Smith.

Roiphe, Katie (1994) *The Morning After: Sex, Fear and Feminism*, London: Hamish Hamilton.

Ross, Cynthia S. and England, Robert E. (1987) 'State governments' sexual harassment policy initiatives', *Public Administration Review* 47, 43: 259–62.

Rothman, Stanley, Lichter, S. Robert and Lichter, Linda S. (1992) *Elites in Conflict: Social Change in America Today*, Greenwich, CT: Greenwood/Praeger.

Roy, Donald, F. (1955) 'Efficiency and "the fix": informal group relations in a piece-work machine shop', *American Journal of Sociology* 1, 60: 255–66.

—— (1960) 'Banana time: job satisfaction and informal interaction', *Human Organization* 18: 158–68.

Roys, Deloris T. (1997) 'Empirical and theoretical considerations of empathy in sex offenders', *International Journal of Offender Therapy and Comparative Criminology* 41, 1: 53–64.

Rubenstein, Michael (1991) 'Devising a sexual harassment policy', *Personnel Management* February: 34–7.

—— and De Vries, Ineke M. (1993) *How to Combat Sexual Harassment at Work: A Guide to Implementing the European Commission Code of Practice*, Luxembourg: Office for Official Publications of the European Communities.

Rubin, Herbert J. and Rubin, Irene S. (1995) *Qualitative Interviewing: The Art of Hearing Data*, Thousand Oaks, CA: Sage.

Ryan, Michael (1982) *Marxism and Deconstruction*, Baltimore: Johns Hopkins University Press.

Saal, Frank, E. (1990) 'Sexual harassment in organizations', in K.R. Murphy and F.E. Saal (eds) *Psychology in Organizations: Integrating Science and Practice*, Hillsdale, NJ: Lawrence Erlbaum, 217–39.

—— (1996) 'Men's misperceptions of women's interpersonal behaviors and sexual harassment', in M.S. Stockdale (ed.) *Sexual Harassment in the Workplace: Perspectives, Frontiers, and Response Strategies*, Thousand Oaks, CA: Sage, 67–84.

——, Johnson, Catherine B. and Weber, Nancy (1989) 'Friendly or sexy? It may depend on whom you ask', *Psychology of Women Quarterly* 13, 3: 263–75.

Sade (Marquis de), Donatien Alphonse François (1964) *Justine, or the Misfortunes of Virtue*, London: Neville Spearman/Holland.

—— (1968) *Juliette, or the Benefits of Vice*, New York: Grove Press.

Salaman, Graeme (1979) *Work Organizations: Resistance and Control*, London: Longman.

Salvadori, Holly (1997) 'UK report: my life in a London brothel', *Marie Claire* October: 116–22.

Sanger, Jack (1996) *The Compleat Observer? A Field Research Guide to Observation*, (*Qualitative Studies Series* no. 2), London: Falmer Press.

Sawicki, Jana (1994) 'Foucault, feminism, and questions of identity', in G. Gutting (ed.) *The Cambridge Companion to Foucault*, Cambridge: Cambridge University Press, 286–313.

Scambler, Graham (1997) 'Conspicuous and inconspicuous sex work: the neglect of the ordinary and mundane', in G. Scambler and A. Scambler (eds) *Rethinking Prostitution: Purchasing Sex in the 1990s*, London: Routledge, 105–20.

—— and Scambler, Annette (eds) (1997) *Rethinking Prostitution: Purchasing Sex in the 1990s*, London: Routledge.

Scarce, Michael (1997) *Male On Male Rape: The Hidden Toll of Stigma and Shame*, New York: Plenum.

Schneider, Beth E. (1982) 'Consciousness about sexual harassment among heterosexual and lesbian women workers', *Journal of Social Issues* 38, 4: 75–98.

—— (1987) 'Graduate women, sexual harassment and university policy', *Journal of Higher Education* 58, 1: 46–65.

Schover, Leslie R., Levenson, Hanna and Pope, Kenneth S. (1983) 'Sexual relationships in psychology training: a brief comment on ethical guidelines and coping strategies', *Psychology of Women Quarterly* 7, 3: 282–85.

Schwartz, Howard S. (1990) *Narcissistic Process And Corporate Decay*, New York: New York University Press.

—— (1994) 'Psychological regression in the politically correct university', paper presented to the 12th Standing Conference on Organizational Symbolism, University of Calgary, Calgary, July.

Scutt, Jocelynne (1994) 'Judicial vision – rape, prostitution and the chaste woman', *Women's Studies International Forum* 17: 345–56.

Seabrook, Jeremy (1988) *The Race for Riches: The Human Cost of Wealth*, Basingstoke: Marshall Pickering.

Seem, Mark (1984) 'Introduction', in G. Deleuze and F. Guattari *Anti-Oedipus: Capitalism and Schizophrenia*, London: Athlone Books, xv–xxiv.

Seidler, Victor J. (1989) *Rediscovering Masculinity: Reason, Language and Sexuality*, London: Routledge.

—— (1997) *Man Enough: Embodying Masculinity*, London: Sage.

Sellers, Terence (1992) *The Correct Sadist: The Memoirs of Angel Stern*, Brighton, Temple Press (now illegal in the UK).

Sewell, Graham and Wilkinson, Barry (1992) 'Empowerment or emasculation: shopfloor surveillance in a Total Quality organization', in P. Blyton and P. Turnbull (eds) *Reassessing Human Resources*, London: Sage, 97–115.

Sex and the City (1998 [UK 1999]) Darren Star Productions/Home Box Office, series 1: 10 programmes (300 minutes), director: various, executive producer: Darren Star.

Sex/Life (1997) Melbourne, Australia, Channel 9.

Sex Offenders Act 1997, Chapter 51. Online. Available HTTP: <http://www.legislation. hmso.gov.uk/acts/acts1997/1997051.htm> (accessed 27 August 1999).

Sharp, Rachel (1994) 'Female sex work and injecting drug use: what more do we need to know?', in R. Perkins, G. Prestage, R. Sharp and F. Lovejoy (eds) *Sex Work and Sex Workers in Australia*, Sydney: UNSW Press, 225–36.

Sheridan, Alan (1980) *Michel Foucault: The Will to Truth*, London: Tavistock Publications.

Shilling, Chris (1993) *The Body and Social Theory*, London: Sage.

Shrage, Laurie (1989) 'Should feminists oppose prostitution?', *Ethics* 99: 347–61.

Sievers, Burkard (1995) *Work, Death and Life Itself*, Berlin: Walter de Gruyter.

Silverman, David (1993) *Interpreting Qualitative Data: Methods for Analysing Talk, Text and Interaction*, London: Sage.

—— and Jones, Jill (1976) *Organizational Work: The Language of Grading/The Grading of Language*, London: Collier Macmillan.

Silverman, Kaja (1988) 'Masochism and male subjectivity', *Camera Obscura* 17: 31–66.

Sim, Stuart (1999) *Derrida and the End of History*, London: Icon.

Simon, William (1996) *Postmodern Sexualities*, London and New York: Routledge.

Simons, Jon (1995) *Foucault and the Political*, London: Routledge.

Simmons, Melanie (1999) 'Theorizing prostitution: the question of agency', in B.M. Dank and R. Refinetti (eds) *Sex Work and Sex Workers* (*Sexuality and Culture* vol. 2), London: Transaction Publishers, 125–48.

Smith, Joan (1989) *Misogynies*, London: Faber and Faber.

Smith, Karen (1999) 'The use of metaphor in the language of prostitution', paper presented to the 2nd International Conference of the International Association for the Study of Sexuality, Culture and Society, Manchester Metropolitan University, Manchester, July.

Smith, Michael Lee (1992) 'Is it sexual harassment?', *Supervisory Management* 37, 4: 5–6.

Somers, Amy (1982) 'Sexual harassment in academe: legal issues and definitions', *Journal of Social Issues* 38, 4: 23–32.

Soper, Kate (1993) 'Productive contradictions', in C. Ramazanoğlu (ed.) *Up Against Foucault: Explorations of Some Tensions Between Foucault and Feminism*, London: Routledge, 29–50.

Spaccarelli, Steve, Bowden, Blake, Coatsworth, J. Douglas and Kim, Soni (1997) 'Psychosocial correlates of male sexual aggression in a chronic delinquent sample', *Criminal Justice and Behavior* 24, 1: 71–95.

The Standard (1993) 'Getting Cathay's message across: PR trouble-shooters keep airline's image in the air', 7 February: 4.

Stivens, Maila (1998) 'Theorising gender, power and modernity in affluent Asia', in K. Sen and M. Stivens (eds) *Gender and Power in Affluent Asia*, London: Routledge, 1–34.

Stockdale, Janet E. (1991) 'Sexual harassment at work', in J. Firth-Cozens and M.A. West (eds) *Women at Work: Psychological and Organizational Perspectives*, Milton Keynes: Open University Press, 53–65.

Stockdale, Margaret S. (1996) 'What we know and what we need to learn about sexual harassment', in M.S. Stockdale (ed.) *Sexual Harassment in the Workplace: Perspectives, Frontiers, and Response Strategies*, Thousand Oaks, CA: Sage, 3–25.

Stokes, Paul (1999) 'Rules left student free to kill boy, 11', *Electronic Telegraph*, 24 July, issue 1520. Online. Available HTTP: <http://www.telegraph.co.uk/> (accessed 6 September 1999).

Stoltenberg, John (1990) *Refusing to Be a Man*, London: Collins.

Stone, Allucquère R. (1995) *The War of Desire and Technology at the Close of the Mechanical Age*, Boston, MA: MIT Press.

Stringer, Donna M., Remick, Helen, Salisbury, Jan and Ginorio, Angela B. (1990) 'The power and reasons behind sexual harassment: an employer's guide to solutions', *Public Personnel Management* 19, 1: 43–52.

Strossen, Nadine (1993) 'Freedoms in conflict', *Index on Censorship* 1: 7–9.

—— (1995) *Defending Pornography*, London: Abacus.

Sullivan, Barbara (1994) 'Feminism and female prostitution', in R. Perkins, G. Prestage, R. Sharp and F. Lovejoy (eds) *Sex Work and Sex Workers in Australia*, Sydney: UNSW Press, 253–68.

Sutherland, Valerie and Cooper, Cary L. (1987) *Man and Accidents Offshore*, London: Lloyd's.

Tabet, P. (1991) ' "I'm the meat, I'm the knife": sexual services, migration and repression in some African societies', *Feminist Issues* Spring: 3–21.

Tagesspiegel Online (1999) 'Prostitution als Beruf: Frauenministerin Christine Bergmann (SDP) kündigt Gesetzentwurf für Anfang 2000 an [Prostitution as a profession: Minister for Women (Labour) Christine Bergmann announces new draft legislation for the start of 2000]', 7 August. Online. Available HTTP: <http://www.tagesspiegel.de> (accessed 4 October 1999).

Tanenbaum, Leora (1994) 'The politics of porn: forced arguments', *In These Times*, 7 March, 17–20.

Tangri, Sandra S., Burt, Martha R. and Johnson, Leanor B. (1982) 'Sexual harassment at work: three explanatory models', *Journal of Social Issues* 38, 4: 33–54.

Tasto, Donald L., Colligan, Michael J., Skjei, E. and Polly, S. (1978) *Health Consequences of Shiftwork*, Washington, DC: NIOSH.

Taubman, Stan (1986) 'Beyond the bravado: sex roles and the exploitive male', *Social Work* 31, 1: 12–17.

Taylor, Allegra (1991) *Prostitution: What's Love Got To Do With It?*, London: Macdonald.

Terpstra, David E. and Baker, Douglas D. (1987) 'A hierarchy of sexual harassment', *Journal of Psychology* 121, 6: 599–605.

Thompson, Bill (1994) *Sadomasochism: Painful Perversion or Pleasurable Play?*, London: Cassell.

Thompson, Edward Palmer (1967) 'Time, work-discipline and industrial capitalism', *Past and Present* 28: 56–97.

Tomlinson, Alan (1990) 'Introduction: consumer culture and the aura of the commodity', in A. Tomlinson (ed.) *Consumption, Identity and Style: Marketing, Meanings and the Packaging of Pleasure*, London and New York: Routledge, 1–38.

Tompkins, Jane (1992) *West of Everything: The Inner Life of Westerns*, New York: Oxford University Press.

Trice, Harrison Miller (1993) *Occupational Subcultures in the Workplace*, Ithaca, NY: ILR Press.

Troung, Than-Dam (1990) *Sex, Money and Morality: The Political Economy of Prostitution and Tourism in South-East Asia*, London: Zed Books.

Turner, Bryan S. (1992) *Max Weber: From History to Modernity*, London: Routledge.

Under the Sun (1998) 'What sort of gentleman are you after?', Scores Associates/BBC Bristol, 1 programme (45 minutes), 7 January, director: Jane Treays.

US Merit Systems Protection Board (1981) *Sexual Harassment in the Federal Workplace: Is It a Problem?*, Washington, DC: Office of Merit Systems Review and Studies/Government Printing Office.

—— (1988) *Sexual Harassment in the Federal Government: An Update*, Washington, DC: Office of Merit Systems Review and Studies/Government Printing Office.

Valentine, Andrew (1998) 'This woman has a PhD and a respectable job as a lecturer. Yet she sees nothing wrong in selling her body for sex. What does her lack of shame tell us about morality today?', *Daily Mail* 6 May: 24–5.

Van Beek, Ingrid (1994) 'A health service for sex workers', in R. Perkins, G. Prestage, R. Sharp and F. Lovejoy (eds) *Sex Work and Sex Workers in Australia*, Sydney: UNSW Press, 279–91.

Van Doorninck, Marieke (1999) Statement as part of 'Managing the Sex Industry' panel presentation, Annual Conference of the British Academy of Management, Manchester Metropolitan University, Manchester, September.

Van Esterik, Penny (1992) 'Thai prostitution and the medical gaze', in P. Van Esterik and J. Van Esterik (eds) *Gender and Development in South-East Asia*, Montreal: Canadian Asian Studies Association.

—— (1995) 'Rewriting gender and development anthropology in South-East Asia', in W. J. Karim (ed.) *'Male' and 'Female' in Developing South-East Asia*, Oxford: Berg, 247–59.

Van Tol, Joan E. (1991) 'Eros gone awry: liability under title VII for workplace sexual favoritism', *International Relations Law Journal* 3, 1: 153–82.

Venicz, Elizabeth (1997) 'A discourse of impotence: Dutch politicians and their efforts to control migrant prostitutes', paper presented to the 1st International Conference of the International Association for the Study of Sexuality, Culture and Society, University of Amsterdam, Amsterdam, The Netherlands, July–August.

Vice: The Sex Trade (1998) London Weekend Television, 3 programmes (180 minutes), director: Jeremy Phillips.

Vinciguerra, Marlisa (1989) 'The aftermath of Meritor: a search for standards in the law of sexual harassment', *Yale Law Journal* 98, 8: 1717–38.

Virilio, P. (1986) *Speed and Politics*, New York: Semiotext(e).

Vittachi, Nury (1993) *Only in Hong Kong*, Hong Kong: South China Morning Post Books.

Wachs, Eleanor F. (1988) *Crime Victims' Stories: New York City's Urban Folklore*, Bloomington: Indiana University Press.

Waldman, Simon (1998) 'Internet stockings', *The Guardian* (Media section) 8 June: 8–9.

Ward, Helen and Day, Sophie (1997) 'Health care and regulation: new perspectives', in G. Scambler and A. Scambler (eds), *Rethinking Prostitution: Purchasing Sex in the 1990s*, London: Routledge, 139–63.

Watanabe, Satoko (1998) 'From Thailand to Japan: migrant sex workers as autonomous subjects', in K. Kempadoo and J. Doezema (eds) *Global Sex Workers: Rights, Resistance and Redefinitions*, London: Routledge, 114–23.

Watson, Tony (1994) *In Search of Management*, London: Routledge.

Watts, Alan (1975) *Psychotherapy East and West*, New York: Vintage Books.

Webb, Louise and Elms, Janice (1994) 'Social workers and sex workers', in R. Perkins, G. Prestage, R. Sharp and F. Lovejoy (eds) *Sex Work and Sex Workers in Australia*, Sydney: UNSW Press, 271–8.

Weber, Max (1968) *Economy and Society: An Outline of Interpretive Sociology*, G. Roth and C. Wittich (eds), New York: Bedminster Press.

—— (1970) 'Bureaucracy', in H.H. Gerth and C. Wright-Mills (eds) *From Max Weber*, London: Routledge and Kegan Paul, 197–244.

—— (1994) 'Bureaucracy', in H. Clark, J. Chandler and J. Barry (eds) *Organisation and Identities: Text and Readings in Organisational Behaviour*, London: Chapman and Hall, 225–31.

Weber-Burdin, Eleanor and Rossi, Peter H. (1982) 'Defining sexual harassment on campus: a replication and extension', *Journal of Social Issues* 38, 4: 111–20.

Weeks, Elaine Lunsford, Boles, Jacqueline M., Garbin, Albeno P. and Blount, John (1986) 'The transformation of sexual harassment from a private trouble into a public issue', *Sociological Inquiry* 56, 4: 432–56.

Weinberg, Martin S., Williams, Colin J. and Moser, Charles (1984) 'The social constituents of sadomasochism', *Social Problems* 31, 4: 379–89.

Weissman, Andy (1977) 'Labor pains', in J. Snodgrass (ed.) *For Men Against Sexism: A Book of Readings*, Albion, CA: Times Change Press, 197–202.

Welcome to the World of Larry Townsend. Online. Available HTTP: <http://www.larry-townsend.com/basic.html> (accessed 11 September 1999).

West Legal Directory 'Sexual harassment'. Online. Available HTTP: <http://www.wld.com/conbus/weal/wsexhara.htm> (accessed 21 April 1999 – now moved to <http://www.lawoffice.com>).

Westley, Frances (1990) 'The eye of the needle: cultural and personal transformation in a traditional organization', *Human Relations* 43, 3: 273–93.

Westwood, Robert I. (1997) 'Harmony and patriarchy: the cultural basis for "paternalistic headship" among the overseas Chinese', *Organization Studies* 18, 3: 445–80.

—— and Chan, Andrew (1992) 'Headship and leadership', in R.I. Westwood (ed.) *Organizational Behaviour: South-East Asian Perspectives*, Hong Kong: Longman: 118–43.

Wijers, Marjan (1998) 'Women, labour and migration: the position of trafficked women and strategies for support', in K. Kempadoo and J. Doezema (eds) *Global Sex Workers: Rights, Resistance and Redefinitions*, London: Routledge, 69–78.

Wilkinson, Brenda (1991) 'Sexual harassment: an organizational challenge', *Equal Opportunities Review* 36, March/April: 9–13.

Williamson, Judith (1986) *Consuming Passions: The Dynamics of Popular Culture*, London: Marion Boyars.

Williamson, Oliver E. (1985) *The Economic Institutions of Capitalism: Firms, Markets and Institutional Contracting*, New York: Free Press.

Willis, Paul E. (1977) *Learning to Labour: How Working Class Kids Get Working Class Jobs*, Aldershot: Gower.

Willmott, Hugh (1993) 'Strength is ignorance, slavery is freedom: managing culture in modern organizations', *Journal of Management Studies* 30, 4: 515–52.

Winick, Bruce J. (1998) 'Sex offender law in the 1990s: a therapeutic jurisprudence analysis', *Psychology, Public Policy and Law* 4, 1–2: 505–70.

Winnicott, Donald (1945) 'Primitive emotional development', collected in D. Winnicott (1958) *Through Paediatrics To Psycho-Analysis*, London: Hogarth Press.

—— (1948) 'Paediatrics and psychiatry', collected in D. Winnicott (1958) *Through Paediatrics To Psycho-Analysis*, London: Hogarth Press.

Wishnietsky, Dan H. (1991) 'Reported and unreported teacher–student sexual harassment', *Journal of Educational Research* 84, 3: 164–9.

Woodhouse, Annie (1989) *Fantastic Women: Sex, Gender and Transvestism*, London: Macmillan.

Words (1992) 'Introduction', in T. Sellers *The Correct Sadist: The Memoirs of Angel Stern*, Brighton: Temple Press, iii–v (now illegal in the UK).

World Sex Guide. Online. Available HTTP: <http://www.worldsexguide.org> (accessed 17 February 1999).

Wright, Will (1975) *Sixguns and Society*, Berkeley, CA: University of California Press.

—— (1994) 'The structure of myth and the structure of the Western film', in J. Storey (ed.) *Cultural Theory and Popular Culture*, London: Harvester Wheatsheaf, 117–32.

Young, Michael and Schuller, Tom (eds) (1988) *The Rhythms of Society*, London: Routledge.

Yount, Kristen R. (1991) 'Ladies, flirts and tomboys: strategies for managing sexual harassment in an underground coal mine', *Journal of Contemporary Ethnography* 19, 4: 396–422.

Zgourides, George, Monto, Martin and Harris, Richard (1997) 'Correlates of adolescent male sexual offense: prior adult sexual contact, sexual attitudes and use of sexually explicit materials', *International Journal of Offender Therapy and Comparative Criminology* 41, 3: 272–83.

Author index

Subject index